Dynamics of Globalization and Development

RECENT ECONOMIC THOUGHT SERIES

Editors:

Warren J. Samuels
Michigan State University
East Lansing, Michigan, USA

William Darity, Jr.
University of North Carolina
Chapel Hill, North Carolina, USA

Other books in the series:

Dynamics of Globalization and Development

Edited by

Satya Dev Gupta
St. Thomas University
Fredericton, New Brunswick
Canada

with

Nanda K. Choudhry
University of Toronto
Toronto, Ontario
Canada

Kluwer Academic Publishers
Boston / Dordrecht / London

Distributors for North America:
Kluwer Academic Publishers
101 Philip Drive
Assinippi Park
Norwell, Massachusetts 02061 USA

Distributors for all other countries:
Kluwer Academic Publishers Group
Distribution Centre
Post Office Box 322
3300 AH Dordrecht, THE NETHERLANDS

Library of Congress Cataloging-in-Publication Data

Dynamics of globalization and development / edited by Satya Dev Gupta
  with Nanda K. Choudhry.
     p.   cm.   -- (Recent economic thought series)
  Includes bibliographical references and index.
  ISBN 0-7923-9977-3
  1. Economic development. 2. Economic policy. 3. International
economic relations. 4. Competition, International. I. Gupta,
Satya Dev. II. Choudhry, Nanda K. III. Series.
HD74.D96   1997
338.9--dc21   97-23308
                                                                   CIP

To Gangadevi

CONTENTS

PREFACE

Globalization is transforming the world at an accelerating pace, expanding and intensifying international linkages in economic, political and social relations. Liberalization of trade and finance, lubricated by revolutionary changes in information technology, has resulted in significant economic growth at the global level. On the other hand, the process of globalization is changing the nature of production relations, threatening the traditional roles of the nation-state, and carrying with it far-reaching implications for sustainable growth, development and the environment.

As the United Nations' *Human Development Report, 1996* indicates, although both developed and developing countries are actively participating in this saga of globalization, nearly ninety countries are worse off economically than they were ten years ago, leading to "global polarization" between haves and have nots. The report further indicates that the gap between the per capita incomes of the industrialized world and the developing countries, far from narrowing, has more than tripled during the last thirty years. A majority of the countries benefiting from globalization have seen a rise in inequality and poverty. This failure of market-driven globalization to distribute its benefits equitably led the United Nations to proclaim 1996 as the International Year for the Eradication of Poverty, and the decade of 1997-2006 as the international decade for the eradication of poverty and the promotion of "people-centered sustainable development".

It is against this backdrop that nearly seventy leading scholars world wide have come together to explore and analyze a variety of challenges facing the "global village". Their research is contained in a set of three volumes. One volume, entitled *Globalization, Growth and Sustainability*, examines the implications of regional and global trade liberalization and complementary macroeconomic policy reforms for growth, equity, and sustainability. Several contributors to this volume point to a set of proactive policies needed to remedy intra-national, international, and inter-generational inequities aggravated by the rapid globalization of the world economy Another volume, *The Political Economy of Globalization* focuses on globalization issues arising from a political economy perspective, including issues such as the erosion of national sovereignty, increasing tensions between the North and the South and between capital and labor, and possible roles for international institutions in ameliorating undesirable outcomes.

Contributors to this anthology debate the role of structural adjustment programs and policies, the implications of financial liberalization for growth and stability, the effects of foreign direct investment and the associated behavior of multinationals in terms of intellectual property rights, the diffusion of technology, growth and development. Many contributors offer innovative insights into the complexities of the process in terms of its micro foundations, and propose efficiency-based multinational policy frameworks. A general thrust of most of the studies in this volume is that the market-driven process of globalization alone will not lead to stable and equitable economic growth. Consequently, several contributors recommend a set of proactive policies to promote greater stability in the system and a more equitable distribution of the benefits of globalization. This anthology will provide valuable insights and important background analysis for scholars working in the field of globalization as well as senior undergraduate and graduate students in a variety of curricula, including economics, finance, development studies, and international studies.

A project of this nature, obviously, can not be carried out without substantial help from others. Nearly two years ago, William Darity Jr. and Warren Samuels, co-editors of the *Recent Economic Thought Series* invited me to edit one volume for the *Series*; I appreciate very much their advice and encouragement as the original concept expanded to a three volume undertaking. My first debt, of course, is to all the scholars who contributed to the project, and I apologize to those who, in spite of their excellent proposals, could not be included. I owe a special gratitude to Nanda Choudhry who has collaborated with me in developing this project and in co-authoring the introductory chapter. I am also thankful to the large number of reviewers whose comments, though invisible, are well reflected in the chapters of this book. In addition, I wish to acknowledge the research grants provided by St. Thomas University, and the encouragement and support of my colleagues including Stan Atherton, Roger Barnsley, Ian Fraser, Tom Good, Jeannette Gaudet, Gary Hughes, John Jennings, Mary Ann Johnson, Santosh Kabadi, Alan Mason, Joan McFarland, Robert Mullaly, Richard Myers, Daniel O'Brien, Andrew Secord and Jim Williams, and the technical assistance of those who have helped me in preparing the camera-ready manuscripts. Zachary Rolnik, Christopher Collins, Yana Lambert and other staff at Kluwer deserve special thanks for their help and understanding in publishing the full three volume set. Finally, I wish to express my deep sense of appreciation to my wife, Sarita, and our children, Hansa and Santosh, who not only went through the usual disruption of family life that such projects entail, but also contributed their labor of love on a number of tasks associated with this volume.

Dev Gupta
April 15, 1997

1

DYNAMICS OF GLOBALIZATION AND DEVELOPMENT: *An Introduction*[1]

Satya Dev Gupta
St. Thomas University, Canada
Nanda K. Choudhry
University of Toronto, Canada

The process of globalization is changing the world—economically, politically, socially and culturally. Its impact is obvious in the everyday life of a typical housold in a developed country. For example, a simple breakfast menu may include items from countries on every continent: bread made from Canadian wheat, cheese from Switzerland, a banana from Costa Rica, juice from New Zealand, and tea from India. If we listed all the countries producing things we use regularly in our daily lives, we would reach 50 without much difficulty! In addition, a person's income and work opportunities may be the result of investment from a number of countries. Economic security in retirement may depend critically on the success of funds invested abroad. Firms, in search of profits, are restructuring their businesses and adapting their behavior in response to global market opportunities. The United Nations' *World Investment Report, 1996* provides an interesting example:

> New York Life insurance clients mail their health insurance claim forms to an address at Kennedy Airport in New York. The claims are sent overnight to Shannon Airport in Ireland, and then by courier to the firm's processing centre in Castleisland, about 60 miles from Shannon. The processing affiliate is linked via transatlantic telecommunications line to the parent company. After processing, the claims are returned by dedicated line to the insurance firm's data processing centre in New Jersey, and checks or responses are printed out and mailed to the clients." (p. 107).

Nation-states are likewise actively participating in the process of globalization, as evidenced by their numerous trade missions, their involvement in regional trade groups, and their continual attempts at the removal of barriers to international trade and investment on a multilateral basis. The role of multilateral institutions as a catalyst to encourage economic integration of the world dates back to the establishment of the General Agreement on Tariffs and Trade (GATT) in 1948.

Global economic integration is proceeding at an accelerating pace in both the developed and the developing countries. The World Bank's *Global Economic Prospects and the Developing Countries 1996* report argues that "[i]ntegration matters because there is an association between growth performance and integration. Fast growth tends to promote a more open economy...integration tends to promote higher growth, through the channels of better resource allocation, greater competition, transfer of technology, and access to foreign savings." The dynamics of globalization therefore necessarily depend on patterns of international trade, investment (both capital and financial), diffusion of technological knowledge, and the nature and behavior of the agents in the process.

Multinational businesses engaged in production, distribution, investment and finance are at centre-stage in the process. While the multinationals have been undergoing a number of dynamic changes in their organizational structure, regional groups such as the European Union (EU) and North American Free Trade Agreement (NAFTA) and the multilateral institutions including the Organization for Economic Cooperation and Development (OECD), the World Bank, the International Monetary Fund (IMF), and the General Agreement on Tariffs and Trade (GATT) and its successor the World Trade Organization (WTO) have played important roles in promoting the market-driven process of globalization.

In many countries, the World Bank and the IMF have been instrumental in promoting structural adjustment programs and macroeconomic policy reforms, which are viewed as complementary to the process of integration. International trade, investment and finance have been progressively liberalized through a wide range of bilateral and regional agreements, and through arrangements established under the aegis of the GATT and the WTO. The WTO, unlike its predecessor GATT, has an international stature commensurate with that of the World Bank or the IMF, and has a much broader scope—in addition to trade in goods, the WTO also covers trade in services (such as banking, insurance, transport, tourism and telecommunications sectors), the provision of labor, trade-related aspects of intellectual property rights (TRIPS), trade-related investment measures (TRIMs) and trade-related environmental issues within a "rule-based system". The agreement reached in February 1997 by 68 countries, under the auspices of the WTO, to liberalize their domestic markets in telecommunications services indicates the potential of this approach.

The removal of the tariffs and non-tariff barriers on merchandise trade has a long history dating back to the end of the Second World War. However, the liberalization of trade in services, investment and finance, which started at the bilateral and the regional levels in the early 1980s, is now being pursued actively at the multilateral level. In tandem with these liberalization programs, the world of business has experienced a shift from vertical integration towards horizontal integration on a global scale—with the internationalization of production, distribution and marketing by multinational enterprises (MNEs) and their foreign affiliates. Worldwide, there are nearly 40,000 MNEs, with some 270,000 foreign affiliates (not counting non-equity linkages), and their sales exceed the value of total world exports.

Multinationals serve as the most important vehicle for foreign direct investment (FDI). The size, direction and composition of FDI affect the size, direction and composition of trade, and *vice versa*. Many view FDI as an important vehicle for obtaining financial resources to supplement domestic savings, firm-specific foreign technology, superior managerial skills, and access to worldwide distribution networks. By organizing and integrating production within a corporate system, MNEs take advantage of intra-firm and international divisions of labor, and smooth trade flows along the lines of comparative and competitive advantage, thus providing better opportunities for dynamic change and economic growth.

Recent growth in foreign direct investment has been phenomenal. Worldwide FDI in 1996 was $315 billion, 40 percent higher than 1995 according to the United Nations' *World Investment Report 1996*. This rate of growth far surpassed the annual growth in exports of goods and non-factor services (18 per cent), world output (2.4 per cent) and gross domestic capital formation (5.3 per cent). The ratio of FDI stock to world GDP and the ratio of FDI stock to gross domestic investment both doubled during the period 1980-94. Foreign affiliates of MNEs accounted for 6 per cent of the world GDP in 1991. However, according to the report: "World FDI inflows have been highly concentrated over the past decade. The ten biggest recipients received 68 per cent of the total in 1995, compared to 70 percent in 1985. The share of the smallest 100 recipients (including all [48] least developed countries) has remained at a mere 1 per cent during the same period". Furthermore, for transnational enterprises (TNCs),"Mergers and Acquisitions (M&As) are their favorite route to their production abroad....About 90 per cent of the parent firms in the world are based in developed countries, while two-fifths of foreign affiliates are located in developing countries...the world's 100 largest TNCs —just 0.3 per cent of the TNC universe—control most international production.", notes the report.

In principle, financial liberalization can also increase the attractiveness of savings through a greater variety of choices, higher returns on investment and flexibility. And it may enable borrowers to have greater access to finance at market-related rates without rationing, and greater freedom for international transactions. Deregulation together with recent technological advances have produced a variety of risk management techniques and instruments, and have contributed to a growing institutionalization and globalization of investment portfolios. In general, portfolio flows move more because of risk diversification by institutional investors and the pursuit of short term capital gains than for purposes of acquiring productive assets. As a result, portfolio flows have fluctuated wildly, destabilizing financial markets in several developed countries, and shaking many fragile economies such as Mexico.

Globalization at the Crossroads?

There is a growing sentiment among scholars and policy makers that the largely unregulated, market-driven process of globalization is at a crossroads. There is increasing evidence that the current process of globalization has resulted in few benefits for a large number of participants. In the words of the World Bank's (1996) report: "A closer look at the changes, however, reveals sharp disparities in integration and unevenness in the distribution of trade and investment flows. Though developing countries in the aggregate kept pace with the world rate of trade integration, the ratio of trade to GDP actually fell in some 44 out of 93 developing countries in the last ten years. There were similar disparities in the distribution of FDIs: two thirds of total FDI went to just eight developing countries; half received little or none." The UNDP's *Human Development Report 1996* expresses similar views; "Economic gains have benefitted greatly a few countries, at the expense of many....The global gap between the rich and poor is widening every day....The World has more economically polarized, both between countries and within countries....If present trends continue, economic disparities between industrial and developing nations will move from inequitable to inhuman."

The erosion of national sovereignty inherent in globalization has rendered nation-states unable to manage many of the economic and social problems associated with it. Social-scientist Rajni Kothari (1995) sees in globalization the "decline of the United Nations, along with that of the nation-state ... at a time when a new phase of world corporate capitalism is ushered in" and when the people of the world need the nation-state to address "the issue of equity between and within nations and re-emphasize the North-South dimension of world order". Former Quebec Premier, Pierre Marc Johnson, believes that North-South tensions have become exacerbated with the increased integration of the industrialized "triad" (North America, Western Europe and Japan), the "jettisoning of some developing countries" in respect of trade and communications, a new and more unequal distribution of wealth, and the "lack of accountability of large multi-national corporations". Petras and Cavaluzzi (1995) argue that the geopolitical context of these trends is "the ideology of hegemonic power in this hemisphere" whose dual outcomes are "the parallel growth of the billionaire class in Latin America and heightened U.S. exploitation".

Nayyar (1997) provides an interesting comparison of the dynamics of late 19th century imperialist expansion and late 20th century globalization, in terms of the game, the players and the rules. The game, he argues, is similar in its underlying patterns, but different in its specific forms. The major differences in the two phases are due to: a change in trade flows from inter-sectoral trade to intra-industry and intra-firm trade, a change in investment flows from the primary sector to the manufacturing and service sectors, a change in capital flows from developing country recipients to developed country recipients, a change in financial flows from productive investment by banks to largely unproductive activities (with better prospects for capital gains) by institutional investors such as mutual funds and pension funds, and a change from relatively unrestricted mobility of labor to stricter immigration laws. The key players, he argues, have also changed from imperial nation states to large multi-national enterprises representing international industrial capital and financial interests. Rather than the "gun-boat diplomacy" of the imperial nations, the rules of the game are now determined by multilateral institutions based on market diplomacy of industrial and finance capital. The system has displayed a striking asymmetry in both periods of globalization; the asymmetry in the present phase, Nayyar argues, has emerged because the "developing countries would provide access to their markets without a corresponding access to technology and would accept capital mobility without a corresponding access to labor mobility."

In this anthology, contributors focus their attention on these and related issues. The first five chapters analyze issues arising from the dynamics of financial liberalization programs and policies. The second set of four chapters examines the behavior of multinational corporations *vis à vis* foreign direct investment, technology, and intellectual property. The last four chapters of this volume offer some innovative perspectives on a range of policy issues surrounding balance of payments deficits, foreign direct investment, the organizational structure of multinational corporations, and policy and program coordination.

Financial Liberalization

Financial liberalization is clearly one of the major elements in the process of global economic integration. It includes deregulation of financial markets, complementary adjustment programs and macroeconomic policy reforms. As part of the process, a large number of bilateral, regional and multilateral agreements have been undertaken since the early 1980s. Contributors to this section examine the implications of structural adjustment programs, foreign aid, macroeconomic policies and deregulation of financial markets on major macro variables such as exchange rates, interest rates, investment and growth.

The poor growth performance of a large number of developing countries in the current phase of globalization has resulted in a renewed interest in inducing structural adjustments in these countries to raise their growth rates through foreign aid . In the first chapter in this section, Kanhaya Gupta and Robert Lensink conduct a detailed examination of the effects of foreign aid on GDP and the level and composition of savings and investment using a four sector simulation model. The model explicitly integrates the roles of the private sector, the banking sector, the government sector and the foreign sector in the presence of foreign aid. By incorporating econometric estimates of the parameters available from previous studies, the Gupta and Lensink model represents "groups of developing countries" instead of representing a specific country. The Gupta-Lensink simulation experiments indicate that the effects of foreign aid depend critically on how it is used by the recipient government. If it is used for consumption purposes or as a substitute for taxes, the aid may have a negative effect on GDP growth, government savings and total savings. On the other hand, if it is used for investment purposes, thus reducing the need for borrowing from the domestic banking sector, it is likely to have a positive effect on investment and GDP growth, although the impact on total savings may still be negative. The latter result can occur because of a decrease in savings in the private sector, and thus presents a dilemma for policy makers.

Often foreign aid to developing countries is offered by donor countries or multilateral institutions such as the IMF and the World Bank conditional on their compliance with some structural adjustment programs (SAPs) including macroeconomic policy reforms. The paper by Manohar Rao and Balwant Singh seeks to identify appropriate macroeconomic policy reforms needed to achieve a sustainable current account deficit for the Indian economy. Working in a financial programming framework, the authors build a 21 equation model consisting of four sectors (private, government, foreign and banking), based on data for 1970-71 to 1993-94. They advocate a depreciation in the exchange rate for the rupee, a decline in foreign exchange reserves, and an increase in the private sector savings via reduced indirect taxes. "Such a policy", they argue, "together with two key elements: (i) a greater allocation of domestic credit to the private sector and (ii) reduced market borrowings, would increase private sector investment considerably thereby resulting in higher output growth." Such a gradualist path", the authors conclude, " would lower the probability of stagflation since the inflation and growth effects of these adjustments would be absorbed smoothly. The resulting monetary stabilization and fiscal adjustment strategy should produce high growth, stable inflation and a sustainable trade balance."

The paper by Paul Deprez and Johan Deprez explores broad issues of monetary-financial integration through a Keynesian prism. Viewed from a Keynesian perspective, attempts to achieve monetary and financial integration through a general process of liberalization often result in sporadic financial crises, failures to meet inflation, debt and deficit targets, and unstable exchange rates. The authors argue that mutually beneficial and sustainable growth requires reform of the monetary structure in order to undermine speculative financial activity, create a stable monetary environment, and facilitate monetary integration. Ideally, they favor a unified monetary system with fixed exchange rates and a strong check on financial speculation. However, in view of the constraints of the real world, they propose, as a second best solution, "a set of policies aimed at insulating financial markets from each other by imposing capital controls, clearing international capital flows through central banks, increasing the domestic requirements of the financial assets held by domestic financial institutions, and generally making it harder for large-scale flight of money towards key currencies and key-currency denominated financial assets."

Maria Sophia Aguirre takes up the issue of monetary integration in the context of the EU, ASEAN and NAFTA. Through an analysis of the volatility of certain financial variables; *viz* inflation, interest rate, exchange rate, foreign reserves, and portfolio investment (both within and between the regional blocs), the author finds that the EU has achieved a greater multi-dimensional integration than either the ASEAN or NAFTA; that the less integrated the bloc, the smaller the degree of intra-regional financial volatility; and that the spillover of volatility from one bloc to another is independent of the degree of integration within each bloc. The Aguirre study shows that intra-regional gains in the rate of growth resulting from economic integration are mainly dependent on the degree of capital flows within each region (as evidenced by the ASEAN experience). The author recommends a more intensive and integrated investment strategy within the EU and NAFTA.

In general, globalization and the consequent relaxation of controls over capital flows from the North to the South are expected to increase capital flows from the industrialized countries to the developing countries. However, the impact of financial liberalization programs on the growth rate of the recipient countries depends critically on whether the capital inflows lead primarily to real capital formation or to what Bhagwati calls directly unproductive profit-seeking (DUP) activities. Ilene Grabel conducts a detailed examination of this issue from a post-Keynesian perspective, and finds that financial liberalization is "growth distorting" as it promotes "new opportunities for DUP activities and thereby misallocates credit toward speculative activities, with destabilizing macroeconomic effects." Based on her analysis and many failed experiments by developing countries with financial liberalization, the author cautions against "speculation-led economic development" characterized by a "preponderance of risky investment practices, shaky financial structures, and ultimately by lower rates of real sector growth than would otherwise prevail." The author concludes her study by expressing an urgent need to establish alternative regulatory regimes which are compatible with broader developmental and social objectives in less developed countries and former socialist countries.

Multinational Enterprises, Investment and Technology

Multinational enterprises, as the conduits for foreign direct investment and technology flows, are often regarded as the *catalysts* in the process of growth and development. Many developing countries (and regional groups) have tried to provide multinational enterprises with greater incentives for capital and technology transfer through policy initiatives such as deregulation of their investment regimes, protection of intellectual property rights, and reforms of their macroeconomic policies. The four contributions in this section examine these strategies from the perspectives of the less developed countries.

The Single European Market (initiated in 1986 and operationalized in 1992) was intended to increase the efficiency of European capital *vis à vis* US and Japanese capital, and to assist the development of EU countries at an intermediate stage of development—in order to create a cohesive economic community as a precondition to successful monetary union. Eleni Paliginis examines the impact of these policies on peripheral countries within the EU such as Spain, Portugal, Ireland

and Greece. She finds that these policies have resulted in a weakening of the structure of domestic capital in these peripheral countries. In particular, she finds that the funds to assist the peripheral countries were quantitatively insufficient and qualitatively inappropriate, and that significant problems have arisen in these countries from a lack of "institutional thickness" (i.e., a strong institutional presence in the form of financial institutions, development agencies, and local authorities) and inadequate linkages between foreign direct investment and domestic capital. In the author's view, "regional development therefore necessitates a careful articulation of endogenous and exogenous opportunities in order to create opportunities within the global economy. In this respect, a selection and assistance of SMEs (small and medium enterprises) which have the potential to develop, either on their own or in co-operation with MNEs, may be a way forward. National or local government assistance could be a way to assist the development of these areas."

Indonesia, which has progressively implemented structural adjustment reforms since the mid-eighties, including far-reaching liberalization of its trade and foreign investment policies, provides an illuminating case study of the impact of increasing global interdependence on developing countries. However, in recent years, there are some signs of retreat and renewal of the debate as to the benefits based on comparative advantage *versus* competitive advantage. William James and Eric Ramstetter conduct a detailed examination of the activities of private domestic and multinational enterprises in Indonesia, with a particular focus on the role of multinational firms in the non-oil manufacturing sector. Based on establishment-level survey data, the authors find that trade liberalization has led to increased exports of those products in which Indonesia has "revealed comparative advantage". However, they argue that its current liberal trading policies will not "lock Indonesia into this pattern of comparative advantage" because increased labor costs as a result of growth will lead to a "gradual shift toward more capital and technology intensive industries".

Michael Bradfield's paper assesses the positive and negative effects on economic development of technology transfer through First World multinationals. While multinational enterprises may promote growth of high-tech products and "value added" exports, he argues that this may result in "dependence, inequality and lost opportunities for real development". To achieve "real development", Bradfield advocates policies that promote "development from below", and an approach to technology that emphasizes "local control" which is neither "xenophobic nor luddite". For recipient countries to maximize potential benefits, "foreign technologies that are imported...should be adapted to a region's needs and incorporated into its technological base".

In their study, David Gould and William Gruben conduct a comprehensive empirical analysis of the role of intellectual property rights in economic growth, based on data from 79 countries. The authors find that protection of intellectual property rights (as measured by patent protection) has a significant positive impact on economic growth, which increases with the degree of openness in the economy. "Although the statistical difference between trade regimes is small, and the results do not capture all market structure subtleties, the findings suggest that the linkage between innovation and intellectual property rights protection may play a weaker role in less competitive, highly protected markets. This is what one would expect if innovation adds less to a firm's market share and profits in less competitive markets."

Micro Foundations

While most of the studies of globalization have focused on macro aspects of the process, the study of the microeconomic structure is equally important for understanding the sectoral and systemic linkages in the process of globalization. The four papers in this section provide some innovative perspectives on the structure and process of globalization based on micro level considerations.

Ravi Batra's paper offers a new approach to understanding one of the overarching themes of this volume, global trade imbalances. His approach seeks an explanation of persistent balance of payments deficits which is more plausible than the traditional "monetary" and "absorption" approaches. He argues, for example, that neither the savings-investment gap nor the budgetary deficit explains the United States' persistent, and growing, bilateral current accounts deficit *vis à vis* Japan; nor does the explanation lie in the relative rate of monetary expansion which has been consistently higher in Japan than in the United States. Batra's approach, which he calls the "price approach" because it deals directly with the question of competitiveness, implies that a country's commercial policies and domestic production structure, if they have the effect of raising its price-level above the level at which its balance of payments would be in equilibrium, tend to curb its expenditures and thus contribute to a payments surplus. He therefore concludes that "countries with high internal price levels such as Japan, Singapore and Hong Kong tend to have surpluses, whereas relatively low price level countries such as the U.S., Canada, Australia and India tend to have deficits".

The study by Robin Rowley and Renuka Jain focuses on the recent revolution in information technology, one of the major forces responsible for the current phase of globalization. Rowley and Jain examine the explanatory power of the existing theories of the firm in the context of these advances, and offer important insights for modeling the behavior of the global firms. In particular, they identify a number of consequences of the microprocessor revolution for large firms, including weaker managerial limits on economies of scale, major changes in the application of information and knowledge, systematic collaboration and inter-firm strategic alliances, and new dynamics of global competition. In order to understand both the behavior of global firms and the process of globalization, they argue that there is a need for "a realistic framework for appraising economic organizations from an adaptive and evolving theoretical perspective that can effectively deal with the spatial relocation of economic activities".

In their paper, Masudul Alam Choudhury and Abdul Fatah Che Hamat challenge the traditional view of the market rooted in a system of exchange, and advocate an alternative vision of markets as a system of social contracts based on knowledge-induced transformation processes and motivational factors. In their view, "endogeniety of various political and economic processes creates a global system of interlinkages among and between policy variables and socioeconomic variables." They explain the theoretical ramifications of such a system in the context of Malaysia. The authors show "how in Malaysia through her singular financial markets based on Islamic instruments, saver-investor preferences are being endogenized in the capital market. Here market prices and material gains are shown to interrelate with non-pricing motivations to create the direction of financial viability and bring about substantial gain." Their model, they argue, makes it possible to marry moral and economic values within the context of globalization. *The Human Development Report 1996* of the UNDP notes that Malaysia is one of a very few countries that has managed to create a "virtuous cycle" through an establishment of strong links between growth and human development in spite of its full participation in the process of globalization.

In the last chapter, Edward English addresses "new economic and other circumstances that are likely to govern the nature of the groupings of countries that will most influence the agenda priorities in international negotiations, especially those that deal with economic and social aspects of international cooperation and the evolution of relevant institutional arrangements, both regional and multilateral."

He discusses a variety of challenges in the areas of competition policies, investment and technology policies, and environmental policies, and proposes multilateral, regional and bilateral channels for developing and administering such policies based on the principles of rational allocation. In the author's view, the WTO is most suited to handling competition policies; the World Bank, investment and technology policies; and a cooperative effort of both these institutions for environmental policies. Regional and sub-regional channels "would be more appropriate for policies where a regional initiative might be valuable, either because the issue is not global in scope or because a regional initiative could be exemplary,...resulting in a code or other scheme open on a conditional MFN basis to all other countries." On the contentious issue of labor standards, the author notes, "action by agreement between countries in the same regional cooperation arrangement seems more likely to command mutual respect of the governments and producers involved."

Conclusion

Liberalization of international investment and international finance has placed multinational businesses and financial intermediaries at centre-stage in the process of globalization. While the world economy has grown dramatically, it has also experienced considerable instability. Moreover, the benefits of growth have been concentrated in relatively few countries while a large number have experienced marginalization. The dynamics of the process has resulted in net transfers of financial resources from the developing countries to the developed world, and in recent years assistance to developing countries has declined in real terms. As Paul Volcker (1996) has observed, "economic performance as we approach the end of the 20th century has not matched—not yet anyway—the rhetoric that has surrounded the triumph of old-fashioned liberalism, open markets, privatization and the priority on price stability". At the same time, nation states have experienced a significant loss in their capacity to maintain and promote the economic security of their citizens.

Contributors to this anthology have analyzed the dynamics of globalization and development from a variety of perspectives and the unique experiences of a number of different countries. They have highlighted important trends, and offered new approaches for analyzing the complex processes of financial liberalization, foreign direct investment and the behavior of multinational enterprises under different market conditions. In their writings, they share an urgent need to recognize and respond to the real economic needs of both the developed and the developing countries. As we enter the 21st century, nation states and multilateral institutions must evolve parameters and policies based on people-centered economic development, and multinational businesses must assume their full share of responsibility. The new millennium is opening on a world which is full of both potential opportunities and potential crises. In the words of Jeffery Sachs (1996): "We have a chance to create an international system based on market principles and the international rule of law. For our security, our prosperity and our children's happiness we must grasp this chance."

Endnote

1. The introductory section of this chapter draws heavily from the material contained in recent reports of various institutions, including the World Bank, the United Nations and the World Trade Organization (including the material posted on their World Wide Web sites). This chapter has also benefited greatly from Tom Good's comments on an earlier draft.

References

Johnson, Pierre Marc. "New Paradigms of Governance in the Globalized Economy." *World Economic Affairs*, Vol.1, No. 1, Summer 1996.

Kothari, Rajni. "Globalisation and the 'New World Order': What Future for the United Nations?" *Economic and Political Weekly*, October 7, 1995

Nayyar, Depak. "Globalization, The Game, the Players and the Rules," in Satya Dev Gupta, ed., *Political Economy of Globalization*, Boston: Kluwer Academic Publishers, 1997.

Petras, James and Cavaluzzi, Todd. "Latin American Liberalisation and US Global Strategy" *Economic and Political Weekly*, January 7, 1995.

Sachs, Jeffrey. "Toward Peace and Prosperity." *World Economic Affairs*, Vol.1, No. 1, Summer 1996.

United Nations (UNCTAD). *World Investment Report 1996: Investment, Trade and International Policy Arrangements.* United Nations Conference on Trade and Development, New York and Geneva, 1996

United Nations. *World Economic and Social Survey: Trends and Policies in the World Economy.* Department for Economic and Social Information and Policy Analysis, New York, 1996.

United Nations (UNDP). *Human Development Report 1996.* United Nations Development Programme, New York: Oxford University press, 1996

Volcker, Paul. "Challenges Facing the International Monetary System." *World Economic Affairs*, Vol.1, No. 1, Summer 1996.

World Bank. *Global Economic Prospects and the Developing Countries 1996* . Washington D.C. : The World Bank, 1996.

2

FOREIGN AID AND GROWTH:
A Simulation Model

Kanhaya Gupta
University of Alberta, Canada
Robert Lensink
University of Groningen, The Netherlands

This chapter uses a four sector simulation model to assess the effects of foreign aid on GDP, savings and investment, as well as the composition of savings and investment. Unlike virtually all other works on the effects of foreign aid on economic growth the model takes into account a number of channels by which foreign aid may affect economic growth. Although foreign aid directly affects the government sector only, it eventually affects all variables in the model via feedback effects between the different sectors.

There is considerable renewed interest in the role of foreign aid in the growth of developing countries, not the least because of the reluctance of the donor countries to provide such aid. While there is voluminous literature on this topic, virtually all of it tends to be based on either single equation models or simple two equation models in which savings and growth are simultaneously determined in the presence of aid (see Riddell, 1988, and White and Luttik, 1994, for exhaustive surveys). However, we argue that this is too limited an approach to ascertain the total effects of foreign aid, because it ignores a number of possible mechanisms through which aid may affect the real economy. In particular, feedback effects between different sectors in an economy are not taken into account.

In this chapter we take a very different approach in two ways. First, we use a model which explicitly integrates the roles of the private sector, the banking sector, the government sector and the foreign sector in the presence of foreign aid. The second major difference between this and the other works is that we do not use real data, time series for a specific country or cross-section for a set of countries, to estimate the model. Instead, we use a simulation approach to examine the implications of the model. In particular, we examine the role of foreign aid when the government is assumed to behave in specific ways as to how it spends aid. This is a crucial point because in the literature on aid and development, while the aggregative aspects are examined on the one hand, the issue of the "fungibility" of aid by the government is examined separately (White and Luttik, 1994). What we do is integrate the two aspects in our model and show the implications of this integration for the aggregative question; i.e., the effects of aid on the real economy.

The rest of the chapter is organized as follows. First, we explain our model in a non-technical manner. Second, we explain how we have determined the coefficients of the model and outlines the simulation strategy, followed by some simulation results in the later section. The last section concludes the chapter.

A Non-technical Explanation of the Model[1]

The main equations of the model we use to assess the effectiveness of foreign aid are specified in the appendix. In this section we give a brief verbal explanation of the main characteristics of the model. The model consists of four sectors: the non-bank private sector, the government sector, the banking sector and the external sector.

The Non-bank private Sector

The non-bank private sector is assumed to be a consolidated sector consisting of households and firms. A special feature of our model is that we use the integrated model of portfolio selection and consumption-savings decision, as proposed by Owen (1981). This implies that the model considers the "direct" effects of changes in the real interest rates on the demand for assets and the "indirect" effects, which operate via changes in consumption-savings and hence wealth, simultaneously.

The non-bank private sector holds five assets: government bonds, physical capital, deposits of the formal banking sector and those of the informal banking sector and an inflation hedge, say foreign currency.[2] The private sector receives credit from the formal and the informal banking sectors. The asset demand equations of the non-bank private sector are derived by using a multivariate adjustment function. We assume that the non-bank private sector is credit constrained, so that credit from both banking sectors is included in the asset demand equations and in the consumption function. Since we assume that the non-bank private sector will absorb whatever supply of credit is provided by the formal and the informal banking sectors, there are no equations for the demand for loans from the formal and the informal banking sector by the private sector.

The Government Sector

The government's expenditure consists of expenditures on consumption, investment and interest payments on outstanding government debt and stock of loans from the formal private banking sector. These expenditures are financed by taxes, by transfers from the central bank, by borrowing from the public (bond issue) and from the private formal banking sector, and by foreign aid. There are a number of distinctive features of our sub-model for the government which deserve highlight-ing. First, in line with the well-known article of Heller (1975), government consumption, investment and taxes are derived by minimizing a loss function subject to the government budget constraint. Second, we explicitly allow for the role of interest payments on government borrowing. It is often the case that this element is ignored both in analytical works and in simulation models. But, as pointed out by Blinder and Solow (1973) long time ago, this omission can have serious consequences. Third, the model allows for the crowding out effect of government borrowing from the banking sector. Given the demand for bonds from the non-bank private sector, the transfers of the central bank to the government and the amount of foreign aid, any residual needs for funds to finance a given budget deficit must come from borrowing from the banking sector. An increase in government's demand for bank credit, *ceteris paribus*, implies a reduction in the credit available for the private sector. The government budget constraint demonstrates an important channel by which aid affects the private sector. An increase in foreign aid, for a given budget deficit, leads to a decline in government's borrowing from the banking sector, and hence leads to an increase in funds available for the credit constrained private sector, which affects private consumption, private investment as well as the other asset demands. It should be noted that foreign aid enters our model via the government sector. This is to say that foreign aid has a direct effect only on the government sector. However, since the government sector is connected to the other sectors, aid eventually affects all variables in the model via a number of channels.

The Banking Sector

This sector consists of three subsectors: the central bank, the formal private banks and the informal credit markets. The formal private banks lend to the non-bank private sector and the government. Moreover, they are assumed to hold reserves at the central bank. Liabilities of the formal private banks consist of bank deposits of the non-bank private sector. The informal banks lends only to the non-bank private sector. Liabilities are in the form of informal deposits held by the non-bank private sector. Also informal banks are assumed to hold reserves at the central bank. The assets of the central bank consist of loans to the government. The liabilities are the reserves of both the formal and the informal banks. Reserves are distributed to the government in the form of a non-interest paying transfer. It should be noted that in contrast to other works in this field, we do not assume that these transfers are only used for unproductive government expenditures, but that they also affect government investment and taxes.

The External sector

The model explicitly takes into account exports and imports of goods. For reasons of convenience, the modelling is as simple as possible. In rates of change, real exports and real imports denoted in foreign prices are specified as functions of the real exchange rate.

Finally, it should be pointed out that the model explcitly considers a demand and a supply-side. It is assumed that firms are operating in a labour surplus economy, so that labour does not constitute a bottleneck in the determination of aggregate supply. Aggregate supply is determined by a Leontief type technology. The goods market is closed by price changes.

The Coefficients and the Simulation Strategy

The model we use is too complex for estimation. Moreover, data for a number of variables are lacking. Therefore, as much as possible, we decided to derive parameter values from available econometric estimates, and to use the adding-up restrictions so that the parameters are consistent with our theoretical model. Since most parameters are based on available econometric estimates for groups of developing countries, they do not pertain to a specific country.

Table 1: Parameters of the asset demand equations and private consumption

F. Deposits	Capital	Bonds	I. Deposits	Cons.
$\alpha_1=0.0227$	$\alpha_{11}=0.0296$	$\alpha_{21}=0.005$	$\alpha_{51}=0.0227$	$\alpha_{41}=0.7$
$\alpha_2=0.01$	$\alpha_{12}=0.2$	$\alpha_{22}=0.107$	$\alpha_{52}=0.02$	$\alpha_{43}=0.255$
$\alpha_3=0.2$	$\alpha_{13}=0.258$	$\alpha_{23}=0.0351$	$\alpha_{53}=0.2$	$\alpha_{44}=0.005$
$\alpha_4=0.0412$	$\alpha_{14}=0.0606$	$\alpha_{24}=0.087$	$\alpha_{54}=0.087$	$\alpha_{45}=0.005$
$\alpha_5=0.0606$	$\alpha_{15}=0.1$	$\alpha_{25}=0.002$	$\alpha_{55}=0.005$	$\alpha_{46}=0.005$
$\alpha_6=0.0087$	$\alpha_{16}=0.02$	$\alpha_{26}=0.0429$	$\alpha_{56}=0$	$\alpha_{47}=0.255$
$\alpha_7=0.0178$	$\alpha_{17}=0.011$	$\alpha_{27}=0.018$	$\alpha_{57}=0.027$	$\alpha_{48}=0.255$
$\alpha_8=0.087$	$\alpha_{18}=0.0005$	$\alpha_{28}=0$	$\alpha_{58}=0.0412$	$\alpha_{49}=0.255$
$\alpha_9=0.2$	$\alpha_{19}=0.258$	$\alpha_{29}=0.0351$	$\alpha_{59}=0.2$	$\varepsilon_{41}=0.015$
$\varepsilon_1=0.5$	$\varepsilon_{11}=0.18$	$\varepsilon_{21}=0.3$	$\varepsilon_{51}=0.5$	

Sources: Morisset (1993), Gupta (1993), Ogawa *et al.* (1994).

Table 1 gives the parameters of the asset demand equations as well as for private consumption. Estimates with respect to the coefficients in the equation of demand for informal deposits and with respect to the coefficients for informal credit in the asset demand and consumption equations are not available. Admittedly rather ad-hoc, we assumed that formal and informal credits affect asset demand and consumption alike. Further, we assume that the composite coefficients have the property of symmetry, *i.e.* $\alpha_c = \alpha_{1,4}$; $\alpha_k = \alpha_{2,4}$ etc.

Table 2 presents the parameters for the government equations, the initial values and the exogenous variables. All initial values refer to the group of Asian Developing Countries (IMF, IFS and World Bank, World Tables). Where figures for the whole group of Asian countries are not available, figures for India are used (IMF, IFS). Note, that all initial values are given as percentages of GDP (y).

Some other assumptions: α in the aggregate supply equation is set at 0.33. η_{10} and η_{11} in the equation for exports and imports are set at 0.60 and -0.85, respectively (based on Marquez, 1990). η_{12} in the exchange rate equation is set at 0. Hence, we simulated with a fixed nominal exchange rate. However, note that the real exchange rate is not constant since inflation is endogenous.

Table 2: Parameters of the Government equations, Initial Values and Exogenous Variables

Govt. Inv.	Govt. Cons.	Taxes	Exog. Variables	Exog. Variables	Start Values	Start Values	Start Values
$\eta_1=0.0$	$\eta_4=0.62$	$\eta_7=0.08$	$i_m=0.05$	$A^*=0.0119$	$f^*=0.75$	$W=3$	$b=0.12$
$\eta_2=0.04$	$\eta_5=0.03$	$\eta_8=0.0$	$i_k=0.05$	$h_f=0.05$	$l_p=0.27$	$k_g=1$	$m=0.4$
$\eta_3=0.19$	$\eta_6=0.0$	$\eta_9=0.19$	$i_b=0.05$	$h_u=0.05$	$l_u=0.08$	$k=2$	$C_g=0.14$
$\beta_2=0.20$	$\beta_4=0.35$	$\beta_6=0.2$	$i_u=0.06$	$\delta=0.05$	$l_g=0.11$	$u=0.085$	$y, y_d=1$
			$p^*=1$	$\pi^*=0$	$imp^{\wedge *}=0.24$	$x=0.22$	$p,e,p^*=1$

The Simulation Results

Our model does not address the problem of actual forecasting. As explained earlier, we use a simulation approach by which effects of aid on macro-economic aggregates are examined under different assumptions with respect to government's use of foreign aid. The simulations should be seen as an analytical contribution to the study of the impact of aid, and not so much as a contribution to quantifying the effects of aid per se. For all simulations, we present figures for total savings as a percentage of income (totsav), private and government savings as a percentage of income (privsav and govsav, respectively), total investment as a percentage of income (totinv), private and government investment as a percentage of income (privinv and govinv, respectively) and GDP (gdp). All variables are presented as deviations from a baseline in which foreign aid is not increased.

Hence,

$$\text{totsav} = (S_{p,1} + S_{g,1})/Y_{d,1} - (S_{p,0} + S_{g,0})/Y_{d,0},$$

privsav = $S_{p,1}/Y_{d,1}$ - $S_{p,0}/Y_{d,0}$,

govsav = $S_{g,1}/Y_{d,1}$ - $S_{g,0}/Y_{d,0}$,

totinv =$(\Delta k_1 + I_{g,1})/Y_{d,1}$ - $(\Delta k_0 + I_{g,0})/Y_{d,0}$,

privinv = $\Delta k_1/Y_{d,1}$ - $\Delta k_0/Y_{d,0}$,

govinv = $I_{g,1}/Y_{d,1}$ - $I_{g,0}/Y_{d,0}$, and

gdp = y_1 - y0;

where S_g denotes government savings (defined as taxes minus government consumption); Y_d denotes disposable income; Δk denotes private investment; I_g denotes government investment; and y denotes production. The subscripts 1 and 0, respectively, stand for after the aid increase and before the aid increase. In all simulations, we examine the effects of a sustained increase in foreign aid by ten times the amount of foreign aid as given in Table 2.

The Base Simulation

We start by running a BASE SIMULATION. In this case all coefficients have the values as presented in Section 2. Figures 1-5 present the results. Our base simulation suggests that an increase in foreign aid negatively affects total savings during the whole simulation period (figure 1). This is in line with most empirical estimates on the effects of aid on domestic savings (see e.g. White and Luttik, 1994). A crucial question now is whether the decline in savings stems from a decline in government savings or in private savings. In that sense our approach has an important advantage in comparison to the traditional estimates of the relation between aid and savings, since our approach enables us to distinguish between private and government savings. Figure 2 suggests that this negative effect is mainly brought about by a decrease in government savings, even though private saving is also affected negatively. However, after 8 simulation periods, it seems, an increase in foreign aid does not affect private savings.

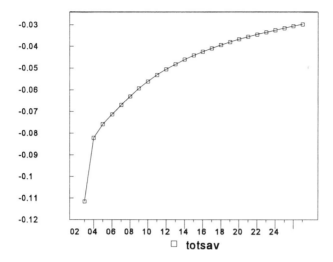

Figure 1: Total Savings

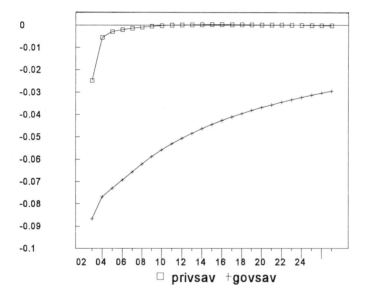

Figure 2: Private and Government Savings

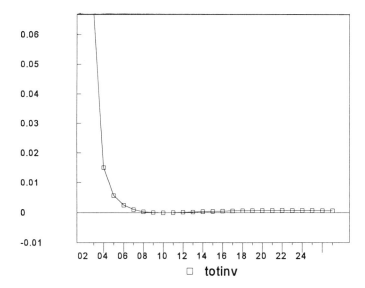

Figure 3: Total Investment

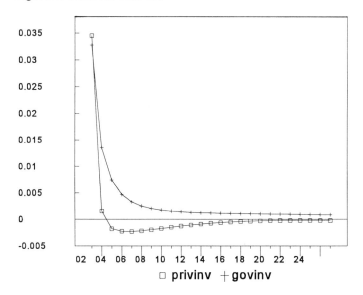

Figure 4: Private and Government Investment

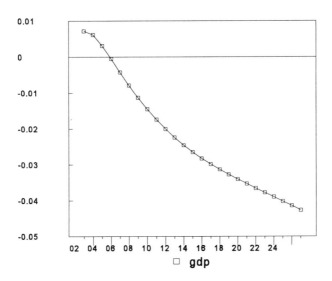

Figure 5: GDP

Although foreign aid has a negative effect on domestic savings, it still may have a positive effect on investment. Before describing our base simulation results with respect to investment, it may be interesting to consider what other studies have concluded in this regard. It appears that there is no consensus about the effects of aid on investment. Some studies conclude that foreign aid does have a positive effect on investment, although there is a partial crowding out due to a negative effect on domestic savings. Other studies (e.g. Boone, 1994) conclude that aid does not have a significant effect on investment, at least for countries with an aid/GNP ratio below 15%. Our simulation results are in line with the estimation results of Boone (1994). Although foreign aid has a strong positive effect in the first simulation periods, thereafter, the effect becomes minor. Regarding the composition of investment, the effects are similar to those of total investment: foreign aid has a strong positive effect on both types of investment only in the first simulation periods. For later years it appears that aid has a minor positive effect on government investment and a minor negative effect on private investment.

Our base simulation is rather negative with respect to the effects of aid on GDP. Although foreign aid seems to have a positive effect on GDP in the first 5 years, the effect on GDP become negative afterwards. This seems to be even more pessimistic than the results of the empirical studies on foreign aid and economic growth, which generally suggest either a small or no positive effect.[3]

The Alternative Simulations

In addition to the BASE SIMULATION we present two alternative simulations with respect to the increase in foreign aid. Since the basic purpose of this chapter is to show how effects of aid depend on government's usage of foreign aid, the alternative simulations relate to changes in the government equations. For the alternative simulations the results are also presented as differences from a baseline in which foreign aid is not increased. Note that the baseline in the alternative simulations differs from the baseline in the base simulation so that it is not possible to compare the magnitudes of the effects in the base simulation and the alternative simulations. The directions of effects are comparable, though.

Our base simulation suggests that an important reason for the negative effect of foreign aid on GDP stems from government behaviour after an increase in foreign aid: foreign aid has a strong negative effect on government savings and only a very minor positive effect on government investment, whereas it has only a minor effect on private savings or private investment. In the first alternative simulation we examine whether an increase in foreign aid still has a negative effect on GDP when the government decides not to use foreign aid for government consumption. This implies that foreign aid only has direct effects on government investment, taxes and government borrowing from the banking sector. Of course, foreign aid may still have an indirect effect on government consumption via effects on other variables, such as production. In the second alternative simulation we examine the extreme case in which the government does not use foreign aid for government consumption and also does not substitute foreign aid for taxes, i.e. foreign aid does not directly affect taxes.

Both alternative simulations are done by changing some parameters in the government equations. The first alternative simulation is carried out by changing the coefficients in the equation for government consumption. If foreign aid does not directly affect government consumption, $ß_4 = 0$. The other coefficients in the equation for government consumption are then recalculated by using the adding-up restrictions for the government. Similarly, coefficients in the equation for government taxes are recalculated in the second simulation. If foreign aid does not directly affect taxes, $ß_6 = 0$. Here also, the other coefficients in the tax equation are recalculated by using the adding-up restrictions for the government sector.

Note that due to the adding-up restrictions, the above presented changes in the coefficients of the equations for taxes and government consumption implicitly imply some changes in the direct effects of foreign aid on government borrowing from the banking sector. We could also have taken into account the changes in the coefficients in the equations for taxes and government consumption by recalculating the coefficients in the equation for government investment, by using the adding-up restrictions. In that case there would not have been a change in the direct effect of aid on government borrowing. We have chosen the first possibility since this is more in line with reality.

Figures 6-10 present simulation results for the first alternative simulation. Figures 11-15 present results for the second alternative simulation.

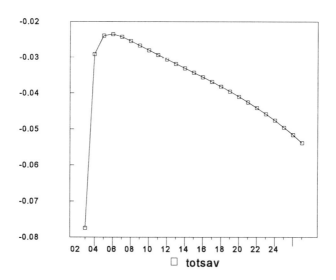

Figure 6: Total Savings

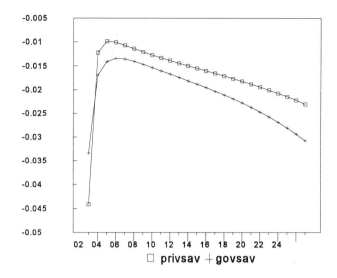

Figure 7: Private and Government Savings

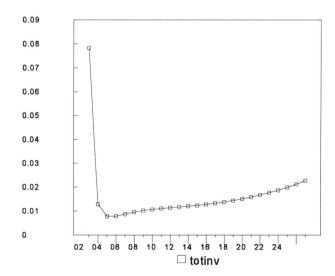

Figure 8: Total Investment

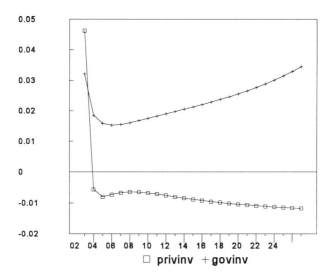

Figure 9: Private and Government Investment

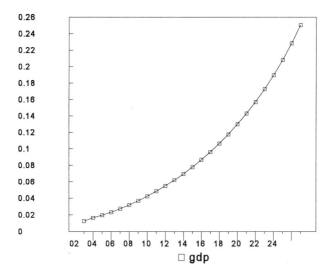

Figure 10: GDP

Figures 6 and 7 show that when the government does not use foreign aid for government consumption purposes, foreign aid negatively affects total savings and government savings. It appears that foreign aid now also has a strong negative effect on private savings. It is difficult to explain the reason behind this negative effect on private savings since in the model all variables affect each other so that the causality is not clear. The explanation may be found by considering the relationship between the government sector and the private sector. If foreign aid is not used for government consumption, the decline in government borrowing from the banking sector becomes more substantial, so that, *ceteris paribus*, more funds become available for the private sector. If this increase in funds has a strong effect on private consumption, a decline in private savings may be the result. In comparison to the base simulation this alternative simulation also suggests that the negative effect on total savings becomes larger during the simulation period.

In the case where the government does not use foreign aid for consumption purposes, foreign aid has a positive effect on total investment during the entire simulation period. The figure even suggests that this positive effect becomes more pronounced at the end of the simulation period (figure 8). This positive effect on total investment stems from a strong positive effect of foreign aid on government investment. The effect on private investment is still negative (figure 9). Figure 10 suggests that, in the case where the government does not use foreign aid for consumption purposes, foreign aid has a positive effect on GDP. So, it appears that the positive effect on government investment more than proportionally counteracts the negative effect on private investment.

In the final simulation we examine effects of aid under the extreme assumption that foreign aid does not have a direct effect on government savings, i.e. on government taxes and/or government consumption. Foreign aid now only affects government investment or government borrowings from the banking sector. It still appears that foreign aid has a negative effect on total savings (figure 11). However, the reason behind the decline in total savings is now totally opposite to the results of our base simulation. Government savings seem to be positively affected by foreign aid, whereas private savings are negatively affected by foreign aid (figure 12). The reason for the decline in private savings may be the same as in the former simulation. The increase in government savings may be the result of an increase in production, which positively affects taxes. This outcome demonstrates another advantage of our approach. Since our model takes into account all kinds of feedback effects between the government sector and the private sector, we are

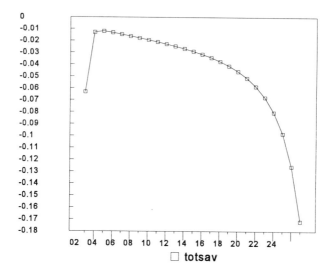

Figure 11: Total Savings

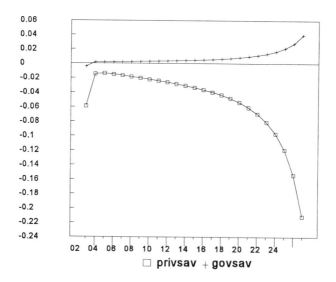

Figure 12: private and government saving

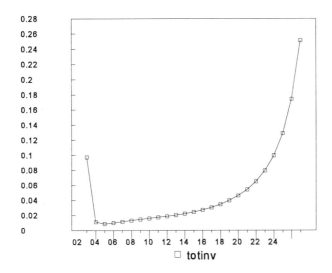

Figure 13: Total Investment

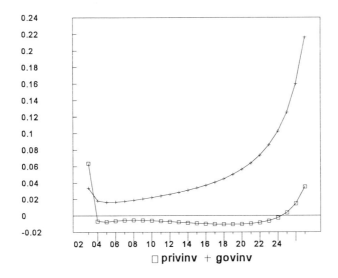

Figure 14: private and government investment

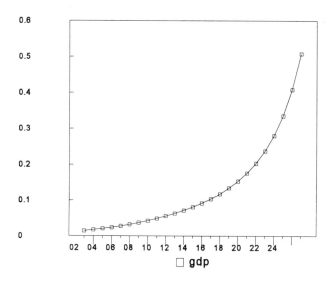

Figure 15: GDP

able to show that the total effects of foreign aid on government savings may be totally different from the direct effects.

With respect to investment the effects are similar to those of the first alternative simulation: foreign aid positively affects total investment and government investment and negatively affects private investment. However, for this case it appears that, in the later simulation years, effects on private investment become positive. The final figure shows that foreign aid also has a positive effect on GDP in this case.

Conclusions

The aim of this chapter is to use a simulation model which can shed light on the effects of foreign aid on some macro-economic aggregates, under different assumptions with respect to government behavior regarding foreign aid. Unlike virtually all other works on the effects of foreign aid on economic growth, our model takes into account a number of channels by which foreign aid may affect economic growth. Although foreign aid directly affects the government sector only, it eventually affects all variables in the model via feedback effects between the different sectors. More specifically, we have assessed the effects of foreign aid on GDP, savings and investment, as well as the composition of savings and investment, by specifying a four sector model. This model includs a portfolio selection model which is integrated with the consumption-savings decision for a credit constrained private sector, an optimizing model for the government in line with the work of Heller (1975), and a banking sector. One important advantage of our approach is that feedback effects between the government sector, the private sector and the banking sector are taken into account, which, to our knowledge, has not been done before.

The simulations presented in this chapter differ with respect to government's behaviour in response to foreign aid. Although the results should not be seen as a contribution to the effects of aid per se, they do point at some important policy issues. Our results for the base simulation, in which aid directly affects government investment, consumption, taxes and borrowings from the banking sector, are in line with many empirical studies on the effects of foreign aid. Foreign aid seems to have a negative effect on total saving, mainly caused by a negative effect on government saving, a minor effect on investment and even a negative effect on GDP. The alternative simulations, however, suggest that the effects of aid become positive in the case where the government gives up using aid for consumption purposes or using aid as a substitute for taxes. If aid is only used for government investment and as a substitute for government borrowings from the banking sector, it positively affects total investment and GDP. The effects on total savings are still negative, though. When government consumption and taxes are not directly affected by foreign aid, it appears that the negative effect on total savings totally occurs from a negative effect on private saving, whereas government savings is positively affected. This may pose a dilemma for the policy makers. If they do not use aid for consumption purposes or as a substitute for taxes, effects on government investment and government savings are favourable. However, it may then be the case that the increase in funds, which become available for the private sector, stimulates private consumption in such a manner that private savings are negatively affected. In the long run, this may have a negative effect on economic growth.

However, we can not say more about the effects of foreign aid on economic growth before more simulations are done. Moreover, effects of foreign aid may have been different if we had also taken into account possible direct effects of aid on the private sector. In this chapter we have abstracted from these effects. This may, however, be an interesting area for further research. Finally, it would be useful to examine the simulations with country-specific parameters, particularly of countries at different stages of development.

Appendix: The Model

In this appendix we present the main equations of the model we have used for the simulations. For a full description of the model see Gupta and Lensink (1996).The list of the notation and the definitions of the variables used is given in table below:

Table 3 - Notations and Definitions used in the Model

(All variables are in real terms, denoted in domestic currency, unless stated otherwise. Δ represents change in the value of a variable, i.e., $x = x-x(-1)$).

Endogenous Variables

Π^e	expected (and actual) rate of domestic inflation
A^*	real foreign aid denoted in foreign prices
b	government bonds
C_p	private consumption
C_g	government consumption
e	exchange rate (an increase represents a depreciation of the home currency)
e^e	expected (and actual) rate of depreciation of the home currency
f^*	real foreign assets denoted in foreign prices
i_{lb}	lending rate of the formal banking sector
i_{lu}	lending rate of the informal banking sector
I_g	government investment
imp	imports
imp*	real imports denoted in foreign prices
IP_g	interest payments of the government
IP_p	interest payments of the formal private banks
IP_u	interest payments of the informal banks
IP_f	interest payments of the foreign sector
k	physical capital of the private sector
k_g	physical capital of the government sector
k_T	total stock of physical capital
L_p	private loans from the formal private banking sector

Table 3: (Continued)

L_u	private loans from the informal banking sector
L_g	government borrowing from the formal private banking sector
L_{cb}	transfers from the central bank to the government
m	formal bank deposits
p	domestic price level
R	reserves of formal banks
R_u	reserves of informal banks
S_p	private savings
T	government tax revenue
u	informal bank deposits
W	net private wealth
x	exports
y	production
y_d	disposable income
Y^d	aggregate demand
Y^s	aggregate supply

Exogenous Variables

δ	rate of depreciation
Π^*	expected (and actual) world rate of inflation
A^*	(real) foreign aid denoted in foreign prices
h_f	the required reserve ratio of the formal banking sector
h_u	reserve ratio of the informal banking sector
i_b	nominal rate of return on bonds
i_m	nominal rate of return on formal bank deposits
i_k	nominal rate of return on private capital
i_u	nominal rate of return on informal bank deposits
p^*	world price level

The Non-bank private Sector

The real budget constraint for the non-bank private sector, which determines in the simulations the demand for foreign currency, is specified as:

$$Y_d + \Delta L_p + \Delta L_u - C_p - \Delta b - \Delta k - \Delta m - \Delta u = \frac{ep^*}{p}\Delta f^*$$

Disposable income is defined as:

$$y_d = y - T + (i_b - \pi^e)b_{-1} + (i_m - \pi^e)m_{-1} + (i_u - \pi^e)u_{-1}$$

$$+ (e^e + \pi^* - \pi^e)f_{-1} - (i_{lb} - \pi^e)L_{p_{-1}} - (i_{lu} - \pi^e)L_{u_{-1}}$$

Assuming that all cross adjustment coefficients are zero the asset demand equations of the non-bank private sector are given by:

$$\Delta m = \alpha_1 y_d + \alpha_2 W + \alpha_3 \Delta L_p + \alpha_4 (i_m - \pi^e) - \alpha_5$$

$$- \alpha_6 (i_b - \pi^e) - \alpha_7 (e^e - \pi^e) - \alpha_8 (i_u -$$

$$\Delta k = \alpha_{11} y_d + \alpha_{12} W + \alpha_{13} \Delta L_p - \alpha_{14} (i_m - \pi^e) + \alpha_{15} (i_k - \pi^e)$$

$$- \alpha_{16} (i_b - \pi^e) - \alpha_{17} (e^e - \pi^e) - \alpha_{18} (i_u - \pi^e) + \alpha_{19} \Delta L_u - \epsilon_{11} k_{-1}$$

$$\Delta b = \alpha_{21} y_d + \alpha_{22} W + \alpha_{23} \Delta L_p - \alpha_{24} (i_m - \pi^e) - \alpha_{25} (i_k - \pi^e)$$

$$+ \alpha_{26} (i_b - \pi^e) - \alpha_{27} (e^e - \pi^e) - \alpha_{28} (i_u - \pi^e) + \alpha_{29} \Delta L_u - \epsilon_{21} b_{-1}$$

$$\Delta u = \alpha_{51} y_d + \alpha_{52} W + \alpha_{53} \Delta L_p - \alpha_{54} (i_m - \pi^e) - \alpha_{55} (i_k - \pi^e)$$

$$+ \alpha_{56} (i_b - \pi^e) - \alpha_{57} (e^e - \pi^e) + \alpha_{58} (i_u - \pi^e) + \alpha_{59} \Delta L_u - \epsilon_{51} u_{-1}$$

The consumption function is given by:

$$\Delta C_p = \alpha_{41} y_d + \alpha_{43} \Delta L_p - \alpha_{44} (i_m - \pi^e) - \alpha_{45} (i_k - \pi^e) - \alpha_{46} (i_b - \pi^e)$$

$$- \alpha_{47} (e^e - \pi^e) - \alpha_{48} (i_u - \pi^e) + \alpha_{49} \Delta L_u + \epsilon_{41} W_{-1}$$

Private savings and wealth are defined as:

$$S_p = y_d - C_p$$

$$W = W_{-1} + S_p - \delta k_{-1}$$

The Government Sector

The government's budget constraint, determining ΔL_g in the simulations, is given by:

$$C_g + I_g + IP_g - T - \Delta b - \Delta L_{cb} - \frac{ep^*}{p}A^* = \Delta L_g$$

Government consumption, investment and taxes are formulated as follows (for a derivation see Gupta and Lensink, 1996).

$$I_g = \eta_1 \Delta k + \eta_2 y_{-1} - \eta_3 C_{g-1} + \beta_2 \left(\frac{ep^*}{p}A^* + \Delta b + \Delta L_{cb} - IP_g \right)$$

$$C_g = \eta_4 C_{g-1} + \eta_5 y_{-1} - \eta_6 \Delta k + \beta_4 \left(\frac{ep^*}{p}A^* + \Delta b + \Delta L_{cb} - IP_g \right)$$

$$T = \eta_7 y_{-1} + \eta_8 \Delta k + \eta_9 C_{g-1} + \beta_6 \left(\frac{ep^*}{p}A^* + \Delta b + \Delta L_{cb} - IP_g \right)$$

The Banking Sector

The budget constraints of the formal and informal private banks, which determine in the simulations the supply of formal and informal loans, are given by

$$\Delta L_p = (1 - h_f)\Delta M - IP_p - \Delta L_g$$

$$\Delta L_u = (1 - h_u)\Delta u - IP_u$$

Reserves of both banking sectors are equal to a fixed percentage of bank deposits, hence:

$$R = h_f m$$

$$R_u = h_u u$$

Taking into account capital gains (losses) on reserves, net real interest payments of both types of banks are specified as:

$$IP_u = (i_m - \pi^e)m_{-1} - (i_{lb} - \pi^e)(L_{p-1} + L_{g-1}) + \pi^e h_f m_{-1}$$

$$IP_u = (i_u - \pi^e)u_{-1} - (i_{lu} - \pi^e)L_{u-1} + \pi^e h_u u_{-1}$$

The lending rates are determined by the zero-profit condition for the banking system (see *e.g.* Montiel *et al.*, 1993):

$$i_{lb} = (1/(1 - h_f))i_m$$

$$i_{li} = (1/(1 - h_u))i_u$$

The budget constraint of the central bank is written as:

$$\Delta L_{cb} = \Delta R + \Delta R_u$$

The External sector

In rate of change, real exports and real imports denoted in foreign prices are specified as a function of the real exchange rate:

$$\frac{\Delta x}{x_{-1}} = -\eta_{10}(\pi^e - e^e - \pi^*)$$

$$\frac{\Delta imp^*}{imp^*_{-1}} = -\eta_{11}(\pi^e - e^e - \pi^*)$$

Real foreign interest payments, denoted in domestic prices, are defined as

$$IP_f = (e^e + \pi^* - \pi^e)f_{-1}$$

Aggregate demand, aggregate supply, inflation and exchange rates

Aggregate demand is written as:

$$y^d = C_p + C_g + \Delta k + I_g + x - imp$$

Using a Leontief type technology, aggregate supply is determined by

$$y^s = y = \alpha k_T$$

where

$$k_T = k + k_g$$

The capital stock for the government and the non-bank private sector is updated each period by using the begin of period capital stock and the investments of both sectors. A depreciation rate, δ, is taken into account. The goods market is closed by price changes. We assume that expected (and actual) inflation is determined by the equilibrium condition on the goods market.

It can be shown that the balance of payments is automatically in equilibrium in the case where aggregate demand equals aggregate supply and the budget constraints of the other sectors hold. This implies that there are no changes in foreign reserves that might affect domestic money supply.

With respect to the expected devaluation of the exchange rate, we assume that it gradually adjusts to purchasing power parity. This implies:

$$e^e = \eta_{12}(\pi^e - e^e_{-1} - \pi^*) + e^e_{-1}$$

Endnotes

1. The model in this chapter draws heavily from Gupta and R. Lensink (1996).

2. This variable could also represent gold or the stock of land. It may be seen as a composite of highly substitutable assets, which serves as an inflation hedge.

3. See Riddel (1987) and White and Luttik (1994) for a survey of the evidence.

References

Blinder, A.S. and Solow, R.M.. "Does Fiscal Policy Matter?" *Journal of Public Economics,* 1973, 2, pp. 319-38.

Boone, P. *The Impact of Foreign Aid on Savings and Growth.* unpublished. London School of Economics, June 1994.

Gupta, K.L. "Financial Liberalization, Wealth Effects and Private Investmen.". Research Paper No. 93-22, University of Alberta, 1993.

Gupta, K.L. and Lensink, R. *Financial Liberalization and Investment.* New York: Routledge, 1996.

Heller, P.S. " A Model of Public Fiscal Behavior in Developing Countries: Aid, Investment and Taxation." *The American Economic Review,* 1975, 65, pp. 429-45.

Marquez, J. "Bilateral Trade Statistics." *Review of Economics and Statistics,* 1990, 72, pp. 70-7.

Montiel, P. J.; Agénor, P. R. and Haque, N. U. *Informal Financial Markets in Developing Countries.* Oxford: Blackwell, 1993.

Morisset, J. "Does Financial Liberalization Really Improve Private Investment in Developing Countries?" *Journal of Development Economics,* 1993, 40, pp. 133-50.

Ogawa, K.; Saito, M. and Tokutsu, I. "The Flow of Funds Equations of Japanese Non-Financial Firms." *Journal of the Japanese and International Economics,* 1994, 8, pp. 72-105.

Owen, P. D. "Dynamic Models of Portfolio Behavior: A General Integrated Model of Incorporating Sequential Effects." *American Economic Review,* 1981, 71, pp. 231-8.

Riddell, R. *Foreign Aid Reconsidered.* London: James Curry, 1987.

White, H. And Luttik, J. *The Country-Wide Effects of Aid.* Policy Research Working Paper, 1337, 1994.

3

LIBERALIZATION AND GROWTH-ORIENTED STRUCTURAL ADJUSTMENT PROGRAMS:
A Financial Programming Approach for India[1]

M. J. Manohar Rao
University of Bombay, India
Balwant Singh
Reserve Bank of India

The underlying rationale for the current approach to structural adjustment in India is explained in terms of a growth-oriented financial programming model. Control theory is then invoked to design a stabilization package to manage the pace at which the exchange rate and interest rate equilibrate with attempts to modify the impact of the liberalization process on foreign exchange reserves so that the possibility of stagflation is avoided.

Broadly speaking, a structural adjustment program comprises a set of economic measures designed to achieve broad inter-related short-run macroeconomic targets. The fundamental objective of all such programs is to provide for an orderly adjustment of both macroeconomic and structural imbalances so as to increase economic growth and reduce inflation while maintaining a sustainable balance of payments position.

The rationale for the current approach to macroeconomic stabilization in India can be explained in terms of "financial programming" which is the theoretical mainstay of nearly all IMF-supported adjustment programs. A financial program includes a set of balance sheet accounting identities which imposes the necessary constraints on policy measures intended to achieve specified targets. The actual mathematical solution of the resulting program is referred to as financial programming.

The basis for financial programming was articulated and formalized principally by Polak (1957) whose model is considered to be the most influential piece of work in macroeconomics after the General Theory of Keynes, especially as it currently forms the cornerstone of most IMF supported programs and policy prescriptions.

While the approach outlined in that paper still forms the basis of most structural adjustment programs recommended by the IMF, several events in the 1970s, notably the switch to a system of floating exchange rates amongst major currencies and the sharp increases in real interest rates in international credit markets, have implied that the design structures of financial programming models which have been adopted by many countries have changed in an attempt to absorb many of the developments that have taken place in the study of open-economy macroeconomics.

While a few attempts were made to integrate these two sectors by Mohsin Khan and his associates at the IMF, these writings have been relatively inaccessible. In this context, with the probable exception of Bacha (1990) and Khan, Montiel and Haque (1990), there have hardly been any authoritative and readily accessible source on such a merged Bank-Fund framework, thereby pre-empting any meaningful debate on its content.

While most discussions on macroeconomic stabilization, based on such a growth-oriented financial programming methodology, have assumed that fiscal austerity, competitive real exchange rates, sound financial markets and deregulation provide the conditions for a resumption of growth, Dornbusch (1990) has argued that there is a possibility of stabilization resulting in stagnation because structural adjustment is only a necessary but not a sufficient condition for growth.

Needless to say, even if the current liberalization process that has been initiated in India does result in the resumption of growth (as it currently seems to be doing), there is little assurance that such a resumption will not translate itself once more into rising current account deficits and the subsequent run on reserves. These past trends in the Indian economy have raised several interesting, albeit unanswered, questions regarding the optimal mix of stabilization policies that need to be pursued in order to avoid such a possibility.

As all these issues have not yet been fully recognized by orthodox economics, the paper discusses the real and monetary aspects of short-run structural adjustment using growth-oriented financial programming analysis based on a flow-of-funds methodology. In doing so, we deal with the specific characteristics of the Indian economy and not with general issues underlying stabilization policies, thereby addressing ourselves to the fact that adjustment programs need to be tailored to the circumstances of the countries where they are being applied.

The policy issues that have to be studied within the current Indian context are related to the following questions: (1) What are the essential steps to ensure monetary stabilization and fiscal adjustment? and (2) What policy coordination measures are necessary to ensure sustainable growth without rising inflation or increasing deficits?

Thus, any design of policy for the Indian economy will have to evaluate the following four elements in order to decide which of these are most likely to play a central role in the long-run success of a stabilization effort: (1) the desired levels of inflation and international reserves, (2) the optimal levels of domestic credit and the exchange rate, (3) the appropriate levels of capital flows and investment, and (4) the sustainable levels of fiscal and current account deficits.

Analytical Framework For Macroeconomic Management

A Macroeconomic Consistency Framework

The basic macroeconomic accounting relationship, on which we shall focus, links savings and asset acquisition: for any economic agent, savings plus borrowings must equal asset acquisition. The link between savings and investment (asset acquisition) of a sector and its associated financial transactions with other sectors can be explained using a flow-of-funds accounting format.

Such a framework, which explains the intersectoral transactions in an economy, can be represented in the form of a consistency matrix. The four sectors identified for this purpose are: the government sector, the private sector, the external sector and the monetary sector. As our purpose is to study only the intersectoral links between savings and investment, we have focused attention exclusively on the capital accounts, which highlights the sources and uses of funds of each of the four sectors. The ensuing matrix is far more compact than those suggested in the literature as it excludes intersectoral current accounts transactions which are relevant only if one is analyzing the links between production, income and expenditure.

The government is defined as all levels of government (central and state) as well as public sector corporations funded through the government budget. The nongovernment (private) sector includes the household sector as well as the private corporate sector. The monetary system identified in the consistency matrix includes, both, the Reserve Bank of India (RBI) and all other scheduled commercial banks, as well as private savings banks and other public savings institutions. As we are interested only in the role of the monetary system as an intermediary for channeling savings from one sector to the other, such an aggregation is preferable. However, any study that attempted to analyze how the operations of the RBI would affect money supply through commercial bank regulations, such as cash reserve ratios, statutory liquidity ratios, bank rates, amongst others, would require further disaggregation.

Table 1 presents the capital accounts transactions of such a 4-sector economy, and rows and columns 1 through 5 describe the financing of asset acquisition by the government, private and external sectors through the intermediary of the monetary sector. In all cases, the symbol "d" preceding a variable indicates a one-period change, i.e., $dX=X-X(-1)$.

In row 1 and column 1, government savings (Sg), government borrowings from the monetary system (dDCg), net direct government borrowings from the private sector (dNDBg), and net foreign borrowings by the government (dNFBg) are used to finance asset accumulation by the government sector (Ig). Asset acquisition is of three forms: gross investment, financial assets in the form of loans to the private sector, and the acquisition of foreign assets. The last two items have been netted out from government borrowings from the private sector, and from foreign borrowings of the government, respectively; and, therefore, these items do not appear explicitly as separate entities in the matrix.

Row 2 and column 2 deal with the private sector. Private savings (Sp), borrowings by households from the monetary system (dDCp) and net private borrowings from abroad (dNFBp) are used to finance private investment (Ip), net lending to the government (dNDBg) and new issues of currency and the change in demand/time deposits held by the monetary system (dM).

Table 1: Consistency Accounting Matrix

Sources *(Across)* Uses *(Down)*	Govt. Sector [C1]	Private Sector [C2]	Ext. Sector [C3]	Mon. Sector [C4]	Sectoral Savings [C5]	Total
Govern-ment Sector [R1]		Domestic borr. by govt. dNDBg	Foreign borr. by govt. (dNFBg)	Domestic credit to govt. (dDCg)	Govern-ment savings (Sg)	Govt. savings plus borr.
Private Sector [R2]			Foreign borr. by priv.sec. (dNFBp)	Priv.sec. domes-tic credit (dDCp)	Private sector savings (Sp)	Private savings plus borr.
External Sector [R3]				Foreign exchan-ge assets (dR)	Current account deficit (Z-X)	External savings plus reserves
Mone-tary Sector [R4]		Broad money supply (dM)				Liabili-ties of mone-tary sys.
Sectoral Invest-ment [R5]	Govt. invest-ment (Ig)	Private invest-ment (Ip)				Total invest-ment
TOTAL	Govt. invest-ment	Assets of private sector	Net capital flows	Assets of mon-etary system	Domes-tic plus foreign savings	

Similarly, in row 3 and column 3, the savings of foreign residents or the current account deficit (CAD) plus the proceeds from the acquisition of new foreign exchange assets (accumulation of reserves) by the monetary system (dR) are used to finance the net foreign borrowings of the government sector (dNFBg) as well as the private sector (dNFBp).

Row 4 and column 4 deal with the monetary system. As an intermediary, it acquires liabilities in the form of new domestic currency issues, demand deposits, time deposits, and other liabilities such as treasury bills, and so on (dM). It, in turn, acquires assets in the form of loans to the government sector (dDCg) and the private sector (dDCp), and net foreign assets or international reserves (dR).

Row 5 and column 5 deal with the savings-investment link at the macroeconomic level and indicate that domestic savings, i.e., the sum of government savings (Sg) and private savings (Sp), plus foreign savings (CAD) must finance total investment, i.e., the sum of government investment (Ig) and private investment (Ip).

Flow of Funds versus Market Equilibrium

The procedure in formulating a financial program is to construct a flow-of-funds matrix for each year, so that the pattern of financial transactions is discernible. Based upon such patterns, it is possible to fill in the elements of a flow-of-funds matrix for a future period, consistent with each sector's savings and investment behavior as well as the monetary and fiscal policies likely to be in force. Since such a matrix also interacts with the behavior of income and expenditure flows, its construction often involves an iterative procedure to adjust the initial estimates until overall consistency is achieved.

In Tables 2A-2D, we have set out the flow-of-funds matrices for 1990-91 (i.e., April 1, 1990 - March 31, 1991) as well as the next three years which mark the liberalization phase. All estimates are in Rs. crores at current prices where 'Rs. crores' stands for ten million Indian rupees. (At the current exchange rate which is nearly Rs. 37.75 per US dollar, one crore Indian rupees would amount to roughly 0.275 million US dollars).

In all the tables, reading across rows provides the sources of finance for each sector while reading down columns indicates the uses of finance. *Ex post*, each sector's deficit must be financed and, as such, the sum of the rows is always equal to the sum of the columns. *Ex ante*, these sectoral balances become constraints for modeling sectoral behavior, be it financial or non-financial.

The fundamental difference between the flow-of-funds and the market equilibrium approaches while formulating a model is that sectoral balances are treated as constraints in the former while the latter treats market equilibria as

Table 2A: Flow-of-funds Matrix (1990-91)

	Govt.	Priv.	Ext.	Mon.	Sav.	Total
Govt.	.	dNDBg= 24426	dNFBg= 3181	dDCg = 23042	Sg = 5591	56240
Priv.			dNFBp= 17950	dDCp = 20065	Sp = 120366	158381
Ext				dR = 3763	Z-X = 17368	21131
Mon		dM = 46870				46870
Inv.	Ig = 56240	Ip = 87085				143325
Total	56240	158381	21131	46870	143325	

GDP=532030; g=5.2%; π=10.3% ; (Rs. crores at current prices)

Table 2B: Flow-of-funds Matrix (1991-92)

	Govt.	Priv.	Ext.	Mon.	Sav.	Total
Govt.	.	dNDBg= 30242	dNFBg= 5421	dDCg = 18070	Sg = 10466	64199
Priv.			dNFBp= 10389	dDCp = 16225	Sp = 137907	164521
Ext				dR = 10624	Z-X = 5186	15810
Mon		dM = 44919				44919
Inv.	Ig = 64199	Ip = 89360				153559
Total	64199	164521	15810	44919	153559	

GDP=615655; g=1.1%; π=13.7% ; Rs. crores at current prices

constraints. In the case where market forces and instantaneous adjustments co-exist, these two types of constraints are equivalent, since when all sectoral accounts are balanced all markets must be cleared. However, any market imperfections and lag adjustments would create a situation where sectoral balances are not equivalent to market equilibria. For instance, when credit rationing is in force, the money market cannot be in equilibrium by definition. The resulting disequilibrium in the money market must co-exist with disequilibrium in at least one other market in the economy. In such cases, sectoral balances yield more reliable constraints.

Table 2C: Flow-of-funds Matrix (1992-93)

	Govt.	Priv.	Ext.	Mon.	Sav.	Total
Govt.	.	dNDBg= 33091	dNFBg= 5319	dDCg = 17826	Sg = 14817	71053
Priv.			dNFBp= 14169	dDCp = 28380	Sp = 141113	183662
Ext				dR = 3809	Z-X = 15679	19488
Mon		dM = 50015				50015
Inv.	Ig = 71053	Ip = 100556				171609
TOTAL	71053	183662	19488	50015	171609	

GDP=705566; g=4.0%; π=10.1%; *(Rs. crores at current prices)*

Table 2D: Flow-of-funds Matrix (1993-94)

	Govt.	Priv.	Ext.	Mon.	Sav.	Total
Govt.	.	dNDBg= 39922	dNFBg= 3837	dDCg = 27697	Sg = 10447	81903
Priv.			dNFBp= 25864	dDCp = 20829	Sp = 184032	230725
Ext				dR = 28713	Z-X = 988	29701
Mon		dM = 77239				77239
Inv.	Ig = 81903	Ip = 113564				195467
Total	81903	230725	29701	77239	195467	

GDP=803632; g=3.8%; π=8.2% ; (Rs. crores at current prices)

Flow-of-Funds Matrices and Financial Patterns

Based upon the flow-of-funds matrices presented in Tables 2A-2D, as well as the supplementary information on gross domestic product at current market prices (GDP), the growth rate of real output (g) and the inflation rate (c), the following patterns emerge:

(1) There was a general recession as a result of the liberalization process initiated in 1991-92. However, this is an inevitable consequence of any structural adjustment program aimed at reducing trade deficits (via devaluation) and controlling inflation (via reduced fiscal deficits and monetary expansion).

(2) While there was an initial worsening in the trade balance following the devaluation in July 1991, the current account improved remarkably, dropping to a negligible level in 1993-94; this could be a direct manifestation of the so-called "J-curve" effect.

(3) While the inflation rate rose steeply following devaluation, the rise in prices was checked subsequently, despite the stagnation in growth, as a result of monetary and fiscal discipline.

(4) The process of fiscal correction which started in 1991-92, continued unabated in 1992-93 with public sector savings (Sg) increasing to 2.1 percent of GDP. However, thereafter, the process suffered a sharp setback and public sector savings decreased to 1.3 percent of GDP in 1993-94 reflecting, once again, growing fiscal indiscipline.

(5) With public sector investment (Ig) registering a marginal increase to 10.2 percent of GDP in 1993-94, the contemporaneous decrease in public sector savings implied a widening government investment-savings gap (Ig-Sg) or, equivalently, a widening gross fiscal deficit (GFD) of, both, the central and state governments which increased from 8.0 percent of GDP in 1992-93 to 8.9 percent in 1993-94.

(6) Private savings (Sp) increased sharply from 20.0 percent of GDP in 1992-93 to 22.9 percent in 1993-94. However, over the same period, private sector investment (Ip) fell from 14.3 percent of GDP to 14.1 percent, which is a definite indication of crowding-out.

Adjustment and Crowding-Out

In order to analyze the factors leading to such a crowding-out of private sector investment, we must look at some of its proximate determinants using the flow-of-funds methodology.

(1)   An event which had a profound influence on the pattern of financial transactions and which can be considered as the genesis behind this crowding-out was the unprecedented foreign capital inflows (dNFB) which increased from 2.8 percent of GDP in 1992-93 to 3.7 percent in 1993-94.

(2)   Import compression as a result of low growth rates as well as the lagged effect of the earlier devaluation led to an improvement in the CAD which was barely 0.1 percent of GDP in 1993-94.   Consequently, aggregate investment (I=S+CAD) in 1993-94 was bound to a lower level than what could otherwise have been attained had the CAD been of the same order of magnitude as in 1992-93.

(3)   The negligible CAD together with the increase in capital inflows implied a massive accretion in foreign exchange reserves (dR) amounting to 3.6 percent of GDP in 1993-94 as against barely 0.5 percent in 1992-93.   The consequent pressure on the rupee to appreciate was staved off by the intervention of the RBI in the foreign exchange market.

(4)   This brought into sharp focus the need for an appropriate monetary policy consistent with the exchange rate policy (of holding the nominal exchange rate constant) and it is in this context that the RBI undertook large-scale sterilization through open-market operations to counter the forces of monetary expansion emanating from the accumulation of foreign exchange reserves.   As a result, domestic credit expansion (dDC) decreased from 6.5 percent of GDP in 1992-93 to 6.0 percent in 1993-94.

(5) However, the credit squeeze fell only on the private sector whose entitlement (dDCp/GDP) decreased from 4.0 percent in 1992-93 to 2.6 percent in 1993-94; while that of the public sector (dDCg/GDP) actually increased from 2.5 percent in 1992-93 to 3.4 percent in 1993-94.

(6) This inability to contain government sector credit implied that the overall credit squeeze was not tight enough and, consequently, monetary expansion (dM)

amounted to 9.6 percent of GDP in 1993-94 as against 7.1 percent in 1992-93 fueling inflationary expectations.

(7) The intention of the government to completely phase out its recourse to *ad hoc* Treasury bills implied that it would, in future, need to meet its entire needs from the market as it would cease to have direct credit from the RBI for financing its deficit. This commitment, along with the large-scale open market operations which were carried out to sterilize reserves, implied that market borrowings (dNDBg) increased from 4.7 percent of GDP in 1992-93 to 5.0 percent in 1993-94.

(8) Such a pattern of money-financing (dM) and debt-financing (dNDBg) to cover fiscal deficits implied that the distribution of private sector asset formation was skewed more towards financial rather than physical assets. Thus, while in 1992-93, the ratio of financial asset creation (dNDBg+dM) to physical asset creation (Ip) in the private sector was about 45:55; this ratio switched to 51:49 in favor of financial assets in 1993-94 signaling a crowding-out of private sector investment.

Stabilization and Adjustment

Thus, the most important feature of the stabilization policy implemented in 1993-94 was the sterilization of reserves to minimize the loss of control over the monetary base as a result of intervention. While this would have been possible with a well developed capital market, under the existing circumstances, it would have implied raising domestic interest rates. This could have been a source of large losses to the RBI if there was a substantial difference between the rate at which the RBI was selling debt instruments through open market operations and the rate which it was earning from its reserves. Moreover, there was the danger of still larger capital inflows as a result of the rise in domestic interest rates. In order to avoid these complications, the RBI decided to reduce the interest rate, facilitating increased market borrowings and the consequent pre-emption of resources away from private investment. In order to forestall any further crowding out of private investment, which is a possible reason why the recessionary phase has continued through 1993-94, the government has to bear the major brunt of sterilization by decreasing its indebtedness to the monetary system if the implemented liberalization policies are to result in higher growth.

Financial Programming

A financial program comprises a set of coordinated policy measures intended to achieve certain short-term macroeconomic targets and such financial programs have come to be closely associated with stand-by or extended arrangements of member countries with the IMF. While financial programming has been the common practice for the authorities of many countries, it has yet to receive recognition in India. Our purpose here is to build upon the framework developed above and specify a "growth-oriented" financial programming model (FPM) capable of determining macroeconomic outcomes, in terms of the elements of a flow-of-funds matrix, expected to occur in the absence of policy manipulation and the policy changes required in order to attain pre-specified targets.

A Financial Programming Model For The Indian Economy

Framework. The economy is classified into private, government, foreign and banking sectors. The first three sectors involve income and financial transactions, whereas the income transactions of the banking sector are assumed to be negligible. An increase in the deficit or a reduction in the non-financial savings of a sector will result in an increase (decrease) in its financial liabilities (assets). Furthermore, given its non-financial savings or deficit, a sector can acquire more of one financial asset only at the expense of its holdings of other financial assets or in exchange for additional financial liabilities.

At each period, each sectoral account has to be balanced and, therefore, the model revolves around a set of sectoral budget constraints. In addition, certain behavioral relations are required to explain some of the intermediate economic and financial activities of various sectors, including real output and the price level. All the definitional identities needed to close the model are assumed implicitly.

In Table 3, we have provided a listing of all the 33 variables used in the model of which the first 21 are endogenous, the next 8 are instruments and last 4 are exogenous. (It needs to be noted that all scale variables, unless specified otherwise, are at current prices).

Table 3: List of Variables Used in the Model

Endogenous Variables:

1.	CAD	:	Current account deficit
2.	ED	:	Total external debt of the government
3.	EL	:	Total net external liabilities of the private sector
4.	G	:	Total public sector expenditures
5.	ID	:	Total internal debt of the government
6.	Ig	:	Gross investment of the public sector
7.	Ip	:	Gross investment of the private sector
8.	dM	:	Change in nominal money supply
9.	MD	:	Demand for real money balances
10.	P	:	GDP deflator (1980-81=1.00)
11.	r	:	Rate of interest (3-year term deposit rate)
12.	dR	:	Change in foreign exchange reserves
13.	Sg	:	Gross savings of the public sector
14.	Sp	:	Gross savings of the private sector
15.	T	:	Total public sector revenues
16.	X	:	Exports of goods and net invisibles
17.	XGS	:	Exports of goods and services (excluding investment income)
18.	XIY	:	Net investment income
19.	y	:	GDP at factor cost at constant (1980-81) prices
20.	Ym	:	GDP at current market prices
21.	Z	:	Imports of goods

Instruments:

1.	dDCg	:	Change in domestic credit to the government
2.	dDCp	:	Change in domestic credit to the private sector
3.	E	:	Nominal exchange rate (Rs. per US $)
4.	dNDBg	:	Change in domestic borrowings of the government
5.	dNFBg	:	Change in foreign borrowings of the government
6.	dNFBp	:	Change in foreign borrowings of the private sector
7.	td	:	Direct tax rate
8.	ti	:	Indirect tax rate

Exogenous Variables:

1.	r1	:	Rate of interest on external debt
2.	r2	:	Rate of interest on internal debt
3.	r3	:	Rate of interest on private sector external liabilities
4.	rf	:	World interest rate (LIBOR)

Structural Form. The 21-equation financial programming model is given below:

$$dR = X - Z + dNFBg + dNFBp \tag{1*}$$

$$dM = dDCg + dDCp + dR \tag{2*}$$

$$Ig = Sg + dDCg + dNDBg + dNFBg \tag{3*}$$

$$Ip = Sp + dDCp + dNFBp - dNDBg - dM \tag{4*}$$

$$y = a(1)\, y(-1) + a(2)\, [Ig/P] - a(3)\, [Ig/P]^2 + a(4)\, [(Ig/P).(Ip/P)] \\ + a(5)\, [Ip/P] - a(6)\, [Ip/P]^2 \tag{5}$$

$$\ln MD = b(0) + b(1)\, \ln y - b(2)\, r \tag{6}$$

$$r = c(0) + c(1)\, [rf + dE/E] + c(2)\, \ln y - c(3)\, \ln m(-1) + c(4)\, [dP/P] \\ + c(5)\, r(-1) \tag{7}$$

$$\ln P = \ln M - \theta \ln MD - [1 - \theta]\, \ln m(-1) \tag{8}$$

$$ID = j(0) + j(1)\, ID(-1) + j(2)\, dNDBg \tag{9}$$

$$ED = k(0) + k(1)\, ED(-1) + k(2)\, dNFBg \tag{10}$$

$$EL = EL(-1) + dNFBp \tag{11}$$

$$Sg = T - G \tag{12*}$$

$$T = t(0) + t(1)\, Ym + [td + ti]\, Ym \tag{13}$$

$$G = g(0) + g(1)\, Ym + r2\, ID(-1) \tag{14}$$

$$Sp = s(0) + s(1)\, [Ym - T + r2\, ID(-1)] \tag{15*}$$

$$Ym = [1/(1 - ti)]\, Py \tag{16}$$

$$\ln (Z/E) = z(0) + z(1)\, \ln y - z(2)\, \ln E \tag{17}$$

$$X = XGS - XIY \tag{18}$$

$$\ln (XGS/E) = x(0) + x(1) \ln y + x(2) \ln E \tag{19}$$

$$XIY = r1\ ED(-1) + r3\ EL(-1) \tag{20}$$

$$CAD = Z - X \tag{21*}$$

The model comprises 11 behavioral equations and 10 identities and integrates the foundations of "growth-oriented" financial programming on lines broadly similar to the one adopted in the merged Bank-Fund model.

Of the 21 equations above, 7 of them have been starred (*) to indicate that the solution of the concerned endogenous variable provides one of the 12 non-zero entries in the 4-sector flow-of-funds matrix constructed in Table 1. The remaining 5 entries are provided directly by the exogenous values assumed by dDCg, dDCp, dNDBg, dNFBg and dNFBp. Eqs. (1)-(4) would ensure that all these 12 values are internally consistent.

Eqs. (1)-(4) are the budget constraints for the external, monetary, government and private sectors, respectively.

Eq. (5) is a production function with the following features: (i) it incorporates differential time-varying ICORs (incremental capital-output ratio) for public and private sector investment; and (ii) the interaction term determines whether Ig and Ip are complementary to each other (if $a(4) > 0$) or whether absorptive capacity constraints limit output expansion (if $a(4) < 0$).

Eq. (6) specifies a money demand function which assumes substitution to take place only between money and financial assets.

Eq. (7) is the reduced form equation for the nominal interest rate in a semi-open economy where $[c(1)+c(5)]$ is an index measuring the degree of financial openness of the economy (see Edwards and Khan, 1985).

The specification of the price equation, eq. (8), is based on the assumption that prices equilibrate to adjust nominal money supply (M) to real money stock (m=M/P). Specifically, we have:

$$\ln P = \ln M - \ln m \tag{22}$$

The equation is then closed by assuming that the stock of real money balances adjusts according to:

$$\text{dln } m = \theta \, [\ln MD - \ln m(-1)] \tag{23}$$

where θ is the coefficient of adjustment ($0 \leq \theta \leq 1$). As nominal money supply has already been endogenized, eq. (23) describes an adjustment mechanism for prices which is obtained by substituting eq. (23) into eq. (22) yielding eq. (8) above.

Eqs. (9) and (10) describe how internal and external debt expand in response to increased net domestic and foreign borrowings of the government; while eq. (11) describes how private sector external liabilities expand in response to its increased net foreign borrowings.

Total tax collections (T) are split up into miscellaneous capital receipts (CR), direct taxes (Td) and indirect taxes less subsidies (Ti). Assuming CR to be some fraction, t(1), of GDP at market prices (Ym), and letting td ($=Td/Ym$) and ti ($=Ti/Ym$) represent the direct and indirect tax rates yields eq. (13).

Total government expenditures (G) are split up into public sector consumption expenditure (Cg) and interest payments on internal debt (Iid). Assuming Cg to be some fraction, g(1), of Ym and assuming Iid $= r2 \, ID(-1)$, where r2 is the rate of interest on internal debt and ID(-1) is the lagged stock of internal debt yields eq. (14).

Private sector savings are assumed to be some fraction, s(1), of personal disposable income (Yd). Defining Yd as:

$$Yd = Ym - T + Iid \tag{24}$$

and substituting the expression for Iid obtained above yields eq. (15).

Defining Ym as the sum of gross domestic product at current factor prices (Py) and indirect taxes less subsidies (Ti), i.e.,

$$Ym = Py + Ti \tag{25}$$

and replacing Ti by its definition, i.e., Ti=ti.Ym, yields eq. (16).

Eqs. (17) and (19) assume that total imports of goods and exports of goods and services (in terms of US dollars) i.e., Z/E and XGS/E, depend on real income and the nominal exchange rate. Thus, the elasticities of nominal imports (Z) and nominal exports (XGS) with respect to the nominal exchange rate (E) are 1-z(2) and 1+x(2), respectively.

Net investment income (XIY) is split up into government interest payments on its external debt (Ied) and private sector interest payments (including profits and dividends) on its external liabilities (Iel). Assuming that: Ied = r1 ED(-1) and Iel = r3 EL(-1), where r1 is the rate of interest on external debt and r3 is the rate of return offered by the private sector on its liabilities, yields eq. (20).

Eqs. (12), (18) and (21) which define public sector savings, total exports and the CAD, respectively, help to effect model closure.

Estimated Form. All the behavioral equations were estimated using annual time-series data spanning the 24-year period 1970-71 to 1993-94. As 1991-92 (which marks the beginning of the liberalization phase in the Indian economy) represents a structural break, these parameters were estimated on a time-varying basis using the Kalman filtering and smoothing recursion algorithms which were modified appropriately to model parameter evolution more precisely (see Rao and Singh 1995). We have provided below only the final Kalman smoother estimators of each equation for 1993-94 which would forecast the conditional means of each of the concerned endogenous variables for 1994-95 based on all available data.

The final set of equations was:

$$y = 0.8426 \; y(-1) + 0.8338 \; (Ig/P) - 0.00006931 \; (Ig/P)^2$$
$$+ 0.0000531 \; (Ig/P).(Ip/P) + 1.1150 \; (Ip/P) - 0.0000194 \; (Ip/P)^2 \quad (26)$$

$$\ln MD = -10.3495 + 1.8324 \ln y - 0.0292 \; r \quad (27)$$

$$r = -38.1489 + 0.0540 \; [rf + dE/E] + 5.4894 \ln y - 2.0874 \ln m(-1)$$
$$+ 6.8609 \; [dP/P] + 0.4594 \; r(-1) \quad (28)$$

$$\ln P = \ln M - 0.7705 \ln MD - 0.2295 \ln m(-1) \quad (29)$$

$$ID = 2610.6 + 1.0736 \; ID(-1) + dNDBg \quad (30)$$

$$ED = -275.77 + 0.9979\ ED(-1) + 0.8210\ dNFBg \tag{31}$$

$$T = -2476.3 + 0.0452\ Ym + [td + ti]\ Ym \tag{32}$$

$$G = -1922.6 + 0.1200\ Ym + r2\ ID(-1) \tag{33}$$

$$Sp = -7561.7 + 0.2746\ [Ym - T + r2\ ID(-1)] \tag{34}$$

$$\ln(Z/E) = -40.1660 + 4.2997\ \ln y - 1.4838\ \ln E \tag{35}$$

$$\ln(XGS/E) = -3.8802 + 0.8957\ \ln y + 0.2179\ \ln E \tag{36}$$

Eq. (28) indicates that the current index of financial openness for the Indian economy is 0.5134 on a scale ranging from 0 (completely closed economy) to 1 (completely open economy). This index provides some information, hitherto unavailable, on the actual degree of integration of the Indian capital market with the world financial markets.

The model was then simulated over the post-liberalization phase in an attempt to estimate the equilibrium rates of interest. The results indicated that the rate of interest should have been raised, not in 1991-92, but rather a year later in 1992-93, and it should have been decreased, not in 1992-93, but rather in 1993-94.

We also estimated the relationship between the real equilibrium rate of interest and the real growth rate over this period. Given that theory predicates a long-run relationship between these two variables (with eventual congruence), the results are interesting; a pattern seems to be emerging over the post-liberalization phase with both these variables converging together almost in lock-step sequence.

Financial Programming within the Framework of Optimal Control

The idea of control theory is to derive an optimal policy capable of steering the economy towards its desired targets (see Rao 1987). To do so, one has to initially specify an objective function which evaluates the loss, incurred as a result of any deviations between the actual values of the instruments and targets from their desired levels, associated with each policy. Given such a loss function and an estimated dynamic model, we can find an optimal policy choice (sequence) that minimizes welfare loss over a given time horizon.

By specifying an objective function, the estimated FPM was formulated in terms of a nonlinear control problem and solved using Generalized Algebraic Modeling Systems (GAMS) to derive alternative macroeconomic policies for 1994-95. These optimal solutions, unlike conventional financial programming exercises, required no further consistency checks. A series of optimal control runs were executed involving: (i) the growth rate, inflation rate, interest rate and foreign exchange reserves as the primary targets; and (ii) the exchange rate, tax rates, domestic credit allocation and market borrowings as the primary instruments.

The two most important results that we obtained were: (i) that the existing nominal exchange rate was unsustainable; and (ii) that it would depreciate to around Rs. 34.31 per US dollar by the end of 1994-95 and reserve accumulation (dR) would decrease to Rs. 23623 crores by then (see Rao and Singh 1995, p.98). Set against the backdrop of (a) the remarkable stability of the nominal exchange rate at Rs. 31.37 per US dollar for almost 18 months since July 1993 and (b) the surge in foreign exchange accretion to almost Rs. 28713 crores in 1992-93 (see Table 2D), both these predictions did seem rather far-fetched at that time but were later on borne out almost precisely when the exchange rate depreciated to Rs. 31.97 per US dollar in March 1995 (and continued to depreciate thereafter towards the predicted value; the exchange rate currently (February 1996) is well over Rs. 38 per US dollar) and reserve accretion amounted to about Rs. 23298 crores in 1994-95 (the reserve accretion rate currently (February 1996) is well under Rs. 5468 crores). As far as the second prediction was concerned, the forecast error was less than 1.4 percent!

The model also predicted a 5.4 percent real growth rate and a 10.9 percent inflation rate for 1994-95. According to the RBI Annual Report (1994-95), the actual growth rate for 1994-95 was 5.3 percent while the actual inflation rate was 10.9 percent. The equilibrium rate of interest for 1994-95 worked out to be 10.64 percent, implying that the 3-year term deposit rate, which was then 10 percent, was more than half a percentage point below its equilibrium level. In this context, it is interesting to note that the RBI raised the rate of interest in February 1995 and April 1995 by one percentage point each time thereby restoring equilibrium and ensuring a positive real (*ex-post*) rate of interest.

As far as the rest of the primary instruments were concerned, the results suggested that any optimal policy required to accommodate stabilization with growth needed to increase (stabilize) private (public) sector savings via reduced (increased) indirect (direct) taxes. Such a policy, together with two key elements; (i) a greater allocation of domestic credit to the private sector and (ii) reduced market borrowings, would increase private sector investment considerably thereby resulting in higher output growth. Under the circumstances, even a slightly higher order of monetary expansion would not be very inflationary. With the required depreciation of the exchange rate being of the order of around 10 percent, moderately higher capital inflows would be needed to finance the desired level of investment.

In Table 4 we have provided the flow-of-funds matrix for 1994-95 based on the latest available data in order to highlight some of the important policy switches that were implemented and their resulting consequences.The matrix indicates that there is a clear switch in the pattern of domestic credit allocation in 1994-95, with the entitlement of the private sector being almost 5.5 percent of GDP as against only 2.6 percent in 1993-94. Thus, the first key element of the optimal policy package has been implemented as a result of which private sector investment is now 15.6 percent of GDP as against only 14.1 percent in 1993-94. However, with external assistance being relatively of the same order of magnitude as in 1993-94, the government is offsetting its reduced dependence on the monetary system by resorting to increased market borrowings which amounted to 5.4 percent of GDP as against 5.0 percent in 1993-94. As increased market borrowings, coupled with the rise in interest rates, is bound to adversely affect public sector savings in the future, it is of utmost importance to implement even the second key element of the optimal policy package. This would help to contain fiscal deficits and thereby ensure that a successful fiscal adjustment program complements the ongoing monetary stabilization process.

Table 4: Flow-of-funds Matrix (1994-95)

	Govt.	Priv.	Ext.	Mon.	Sav.	Total
Govt.	.	dNDBg= 51088	dNFBg= 3947	dDCg = 18498	Sg = 15986	89519
Priv.			dNFBp= 25888	dDCp = 51881	Sp = 214662	292431
Ext				dR = 23298	Z-X = 6537	29835
Mon		dM = 93677				93677
Inv.	Ig = 89519	Ip = 147666				237185
Total	89519	292431	29835	93677	237185	

GDP=945278; g=5.4%; π=10.9% ; Rs. crores at current prices

Conclusions

Much of the theoretical debate in the literature on structural adjustment programs focuses on the relationship between the GFD and the CAD. From [R5] and [C5] of Table 1, we have:

$$(Sg - Ig) + (Sp - Ip) = -CAD \qquad (37)$$

Based upon eq. (37), which shows that improvements in the CAD can take place only if sectoral savings rise relative to sectoral investment, Dornbusch and Helmers (1986) concluded forcefully that policies which do not affect savings cannot be expected to improve the external balance.

However, eq. (37) can also be written as follows:

$$Ip = Sp - (Ig - Sg) + CAD = Sp - GFD + CAD \qquad (38)$$

Eq. (38) indicates that increases in external savings offset public sector dissaving, thereby pre-empting the crowding out of private sector investment.

Now, if the government deficit is corrected, will that eliminate the trade deficit? Based upon the results of Feldstein and Horioka (1986), the answer is "No", because their evidence indicates, just as forcefully, that cutting the budget deficit (thereby increasing the national savings rate) will only increase investment with very little impact on the external deficit.

Thus, whether changes in the savings rate are reflected primarily in the external balance, *à la* Dornbusch and Helmers, or in investment levels, *à la* Feldstein and Horioka, become a policy issue of great practical relevance to the Indian economy.

Thus, any effort to study this issue must examine the factors which caused these deficits in the first place. The CAD as well as the GFD are usually linked within a general equilibrium framework because their basic proximate determinants --mainly the rates of inflation and growth--are themselves endogenous variables. Thus, any meaningful analysis of these deficits would require that their fundamental causes be specifically identified, because the general equilibrium nature of the problem is not merely a theoretical fine point. The conclusion of most economists who have studied these issues is that the twin deficits are largely the result of the development strategies being followed by the country as well as the macroeconomic policies pursued by its major trading partners. Therefore, reducing these deficits would probably, although not necessarily, entail a significant reversal of these policies in order to correct the imbalances.

The literature provides three lines of approach for analyzing responses towards such imbalances. The conventional method usually involves an eclectic model in which trade and fiscal flows are determined by price and income flows. Another approach is known as dual-gap analysis which can be expanded into a three-gap model (see Taylor 1994). In such a framework, one can view these imbalances as reflective of the savings-investment behavior of a nation.

A third strand of thought involves the neoclassical model of public debt which provides a theoretical analysis of the implications of funding a public sector deficit by borrowing from abroad. Studies based upon the open-economy characteristics of such a model have indicated that the adjustment towards a higher external debt implied by a higher public debt is shown to involve an extended period of current account deficits followed by an initial government budget deficit. This result involves the use of foreign savings (and therefore current account deficits) to supplement domestic savings both during the initial period of the government deficit as well as during subsequent periods, when domestic savings are depressed by taxes which are used to service the higher debt. In fact, such an analysis of the interaction between the debt, the fiscal deficit and the current account deficit reflects the more-or-less conventional view in government and academic circles of the relationship that seems to exist between the twin deficits in most countries, including India.

The fact that the Indian CAD did very nearly correct itself in 1993-94 has less to do with the dynamics of debt accumulation than with the fact that the import growth rate was moderate (as a result of a relatively stagnant economy) and that the persistent upward pressure on the rupee as a result of the large capital inflows was staved off by the intervention of the RBI in the foreign exchange market. As a result, there was very little movement in the nominal exchange rate and therefore the economy was not operating on the envelope of a series of shifting "J-curves" which often mask improvements in the actual CAD.

However, such an exchange rate policy of intervention did raise a major problem of monetary management because the resulting increase in foreign exchange reserves, by increasing money growth, put considerable upward pressure on the inflation rate. To the extent that (nominal) exchange rate stability co-existed with inflation, there was a steady appreciation in the real exchange rate which was bound to adversely affect the CAD sooner or later.

This is precisely what happened in 1994-95 with the CAD increasing to almost 0.7 percent of GDP from 0.1 percent in 1993-94. The situation has further exacerbated in the current year (1995-96) with the result that the nominal exchange rate, after remaining stable for almost 2 years, has depreciated by almost 15 percent in the last six months despite the intervention of the RBI. Its impact on the CAD would depend on how rapidly trade volumes react to the changes in prices and incomes as well as the lag with which exports and imports would respond to the depreciating real exchange rate.

All this implies that external resources could well be a continuing feature of the Indian transition and it may not be possible to envisage a zero balance in the current account in the foreseeable future. Thus, it will be necessary to determine a sustainable CAD for a specified level of the debt-income ratio and an assumed growth rate of income and inflation rate contingent upon the stabilization policy being followed.

Using financial programming techniques, the study specifies a merged Bank-Fund framework capable of analyzing all these measures, and charting out the stabilization policy needed to manage the pace at which the exchange rate and the interest rate equilibrate, together with attempts to modify the impact of the liberalization process on foreign exchange reserves so that they corroborate with market-dictated outcomes. Such a gradualist path would lower the probability of stagflation since the inflation and growth effects of these adjustments would be absorbed smoothly. The resulting monetary stabilization and fiscal adjustment strategy should produce high growth, stable inflation and a sustainable trade balance.

If, however, for any reason, such a fiscal adjustment program does not prove feasible, then the effects of any other monetary stabilization policy aimed at correcting these imbalances would be considerably attenuated.

Endnote

1   This paper is a revised version of DRG Study 10, "Analytical Foundations of Financial Programming and Growth-Oriented Adjustment" prepared by the authors as part of the DRG Studies Series of the Reserve Bank of India.

References

Bacha, E. L. "Three-gap model of foreign transfers and the GDP growth rate in developing countries." *Journal of Development Economics*, 1990, vol. 32, pp. 279-96.

Dornbusch, R. "Policies to move from stabilization to growth." *Proceedings of the World Bank Annual Conference on Development Economics*, Washington, D.C.: World Bank, 1990.

Dornbusch, R. and Helmers, F.L.C.H. *The Open Economy: Tools for Policymakers in Developing Countries.* Washington, D.C.: World Bank, 1986.

Edwards, S. and Khan, M. S. "Interest rate determination in developing countries." IMF Staff Papers 1985 32, pp. 377-403.

Feldstein, M. And Horioka, C. "Domestic savings and international capital flows." *Economic Journal,* 1982, vol. 92, pp. 317-27.

International Monetary Fund. *The Monetary Approach to the Balance of* Payments. Washington, D.C.: IMF, 1977.

International Monetary Fund. *Theoretical Aspects of the Design of Fund-*Supported Adjustment Programs: A Study. Washington, D.C.: IMF, 1987.

Khan, M. S.; Montiel, P. J. and Haque, N. "Adjustment with growth: Relating the analytical approaches of the World Bank and the IMF." *Journal of Development Economics,* 1990, vol. 32, pp. 155-79.

Polak, J. J. "Monetary analysis of income formation and payments problems." IMF Staff Papers, 195, 4, pp. 1-50.

Rao, M. J. M. *Filtering and Control of Macroeconomic Systems.* Amsterdam: North-Holland, 1987.

Rao, M. J. M. and Singh, B. *Analytical Foundations of Financial Programming and Growth-Oriented Adjustment.* Bombay: Reserve Bank of India, 1995.

Taylor, L. "Gap models." *Journal of Development Economics,* 1994, vol. 45, pp. 17-34.

4

THE MONETARY DYNAMICS OF ECONOMIC INTEGRATION

Paul Deprez
University of Manitoba, Canada
Johan Deprez
California State University, Long Beach, USA

The process of regional economic integration is currently beset by serious problems in achieving monetary and financial integration, an integrated monetary unit or stable exchange rates, and uniform monetary policy. These problems can trace their roots to policies established under stable conditions and analyses based on models based in money neutrality. This chapter analyzes these fundamental issues by using Keynes' model of a monetary production economy, thereby rejecting any form of money neutrality. It is found that current processes of monetary economic integration tend to lead to divergent growth paths among member states and need to be replaced by monetary structures that undermine speculative financial activity, if mutually beneficial and convergent economic growth is to be achieved.

The modern process of regional economic integration, involving the European Union (EU), the North American Free Trade Agreement (NAFTA), smaller regional attempts, and general globalization based on the General Agreement on Trade and Tariffs (GATT) and the new World Trade Organization (WTO), is currently being beset by serious problems emanating from the monetary realm. There are problems in achieving monetary and financial integration through a general process of liberalization as reflected in the occurrence of financial crises and the failure to meet inflation, debt, and deficit targets[1], of establishing an integrated monetary unit or stable exchange rates as shown by repeated devaluations or wild exchange rate fluctuations, and of creating a uniform monetary policy that is to the benefit of all member nations and supports other economic policy components of the economic union. These problems can trace their roots to policies initially established under stable monetary conditions without the current conditions in mind, and to economic analyses based on theoretical models that assume some important form of money neutrality.

In contradistinction to the standard models stands Keynes' model of a monetary production economy in which all forms of *a priori* money neutrality are rejected. This chapter analyzes the fundamental issues revolving around monetary integration by using this more appropriate model. It is found that current processes of monetary economic integration, by allowing for monetary and financial speculation, tend to lead to divergent growth among member states that, as such, necessarily undermine the efforts of peripheral countries to meet integration criteria. Consequently, current processes need to be replaced by a monetary structure that undermines speculative financial activity, creates a stable monetary environment, and establishes monetary integration as a leading element of economic integration, if such economic integration is to be mutually beneficial and lead to convergent, sustainable, and mutually reinforcing growth.

This chapter initially describes the general nature of a monetary production economy and which specific considerations are to be brought to bear on the problems at hand. Given these theoretical foundations, an interpretation is then given of the monetary components of the modern process of economic integration. The third section points to the systematic problems that come out of this process and that can be expected to persist. The final major section puts forth certain monetary policies and structures that would allow for effective economic integration.

A Keynesian Theoretical Foundation

Keynes' general theory provides a fully integrated model of the determination of output, income and employment, and the impact of monetary conditions and financial markets on these variables. This monetary production economy–as opposed to the classical real-exchange economy–is one within which money is not *a priori* neutral in both the short run and the long run (Keynes, CWJMK, XIII, pp. 408-409). Consequently, it is an ideal tool from which to address the impact of the monetary changes in the process of economic integration. If one were to use the usual macroeconomic models that assume long-run money neutrality, such monetary changes would not matter in the end for the patterns and levels of output, employment, and income coming out of economic integration.

As certain authors like Townshend (1937) and Kaldor (1939) quickly realized, Keynes' general theory provides for a complete monetary theory of value of which the classical perspective is but one special subset. In Chapter 17 of *The General Theory of Employment, Interest, and Money* (Keynes, CWJMK, VII, pp. 222-244), Keynes argued that the relative monetary values of all assets are determined by four considerations. These are (1) the yield of the asset measured in terms of itself, q; (2) the carrying cost of the asset measured in terms of itself, c; (3) the liquidity premium of the asset measured in terms of itself, l; and (4) the appreciation / depreciation of the asset measured in terms of the monetary unit, a. This gives the total return expected of an asset measured in terms of itself—*the own-rate of own-interest*—as equal to q - c + l (Keynes, CWJMK, VII, pp. 225-227).

The *own-rate of money-interest* or *subjective* rate of return is then equal to q - c + l + a. This expected subjective rate of return is the sum of the expected *objective* rate of return, q - c + a, plus the liquidity premium, l, which adds the subjective component. Under perfect competition, these expected subjective monetary rates of return of the different assets tend to equalize. Consequently, Keynes' monetary equilibrium means that the objective rates of return on assets will be different. The objective rate of return on assets with a lower liquidity premium will be higher than the objective rate of return of assets with a higher liquidity premium. Under a (neo-)classical equilibrium of a real-exchange equilibrium, these objective rates of return would equalize, in that such a model has no room for the logical inclusion of liquidity premia. This difference is the fundamental cause for equilibrium at less than full employment being the logical outcome in Keynes' theory and being impossible in the classical vision.

It is a simple extension to arrive at a theory of prices in a multi-currency system. Measured in terms of one of the currencies in the system, perfect competition operates to equalize all the subjective rates of return in this "world" system, creating price structures and world trade patterns different from what is usually assumed (Deprez, 1995). Exchange rates are determined by (1) the net yield of holding particular deposits, including any transaction costs associated with liquidating a position; (2) the expected relative appreciation/depreciation of the particular currency; and (3) the relative liquidity premia of the two currencies. This is simply the interest rate parity theorem with liquidity premia included.

In a flexible exchange rate system agents can hold currencies–just as they hold other financial assets–with a primary focus on expected appreciation. These desires are driven by pure expectations, once one acknowledges a system of true uncertainty (cf. Davidson, 1992). This means that the needs for monies to carry out international trade can easily take a back seat to speculative actions. In fact, currency speculators and market makers do dominate international financial markets (cf. Harvey, 1993). In such a system exchange rates are not a reflection of relative purchasing power or any other set of considerations emanating from the productive realm of economies.

Keynes (CWJMK, VII, p. 293) rejected basic orthodox analyses that focus on the comparison on long-run equilibria in favor of the *shifting equilibrium model*. Within this fully dynamic version of Keynes' general theory (Kregel, 1976) decisions and actions build upon past history to create an ever-changing present in light of an uncertain future. Each historical step is taken within a short-period context and destroys the conditions needed to approach a long-run equilibrium. Consequently, any impact of monetary conditions on real outcomes in one period are not transitory carry over to the next and form the basis for building new decisions and outcomes. This sequential process further means that there is no underlying long-run equilibrium for the economy as a whole, or for growth and exchange rates in particular.

A Keynesian Interpretation of the Monetary Dynamics of Integration

In reviewing monetary and exchange rate policies with respect to the post-World War II economic integration process, it is useful to make a clear distinction between the situation under the Bretton Woods agreement and what happened in the post-Bretton Woods period. Under the Bretton Woods system the world operated under what was essentially a Unified Monetary System (UMS). Following Davidson (1992, pp. 80-82) this category includes a multi-currency system where exchange rates are fixed and expected to remain fixed. Such a system operates as if there is a unified means of exchange. Only the unit of account changes as one moves between regions.[2] With the breakdown of Bretton Woods, the world moved to a Non-Unified Monetary System (NUMS) (Davidson, 1992, p. 81). Within such a system there is *exchange rate uncertainty* (Davidson, 1992, p. 83), meaning that exchange rates can vary and are not expected to remain at their current values.

The Bretton Woods agreement attempted to keep exchange rates between the world's major trading countries within certain margins by fixing exchange rates in relation to the U.S. dollar (US$) and the latter's fixed rate convertibility into gold (35 US$ per oz. of gold). Under such an imposed UMS there is very little room for currency market pressures to challenge the set exchange rate. Because there is no, nor can there be, meaningful expected appreciation or depreciation of currencies, the expected appreciation/depreciation term, a, has a zero or negligible value. In that money in its narrowest definition has a zero yield (Keynes, CWJMK, VII, p. 227), there is also no difference in net yields to have an effect on exchange rates. The more one moves toward interest-bearing accounts and other financial assets, the more yield differentials come into the story. Within a UMS international, differences in net yields of real goods reflect differences in production conditions, demand conditions, and the expectational elements that create production, pricing, and expenditure decisions, and do not involve plays on exchange rate variations (cf. Deprez, 1995). What is left to put pressure on exchange rates are relative differences in liquidity premia.

Differences in liquidity premia reflect standard differences in the characteristics of assets, the organization of markets, and the general state of liquidity preference. Beyond that the differences in liquidity preference are set by the degree to which contracts are denominated in different currencies and the transaction costs of moving between them. If there are key currencies for settling trade and other transactions, then these will carry the higher liquidity premium. Under a given UMS institutional structure these differences can be expected to be quite stable. Hence, trade and related considerations dominate the realm of international financial circulation, with speculative considerations taking a back seat. On this basis one can argue that under the Bretton Woods system, the amount of speculative pressures on exchange rates and international financial dealing were quite limited. This is in part reflected in the relative success in keeping the system working.

Given that context, when the Treaty of Rome establishing the European Economic Community was signed in 1957, the signatories expressed very little concern about exchange rates and their degree of stability. In fact, the text of the Treaty of Rome contains no clauses or references relating to monetary and exchange rate issues. In essence, exchange rates and the other monetary elements of the integration were viewed as non-issues. At that time the main emphasis within the European Union was on issues such as trade, reducing wherever possible the dependence on non-union imports, the free circulation of goods, services, capital and labor within the Union, the transferability of social benefits and the elimination of regional disparities.

But for all its apparent stability, the Bretton Woods system did break down. As European and other economies recovered from the Second World War and became serious international trading powers again; there resulted changing economic power structures, persistent trade deficits or surpluses established themselves, and large US$ reserves were accumulated by certain countries. In essence the Bretton Woods system was shown to lack a mechanism by which trade surpluses and accumulated reserves would be recycled in order to keep economies healthy and prevent the buildup of serious imbalances. As Davidson (1992-93, pp. 154-155) reminds us, such a mechanism was a key part of Keynes' unimplemented suggestions for Bretton Woods.

This situation did two things. *First*, the large amount of US$ reserves held outside the U. S. and the improving relative economic position of major economies relative to the U. S. precipitated a relative movement away from the US$ as a key currency and a key reserve asset. In other words, there was a shifting of the relative liquidity premia away from the preference of holding US$ and assets denominated in US$ to other currencies, assets denominated in other currencies, and gold. This change in relative liquidity premia put downward pressure on the US$ and led to portfolio shifts away from US$ assets.

Second, with many economists calling for flexible exchange rates as a mechanism to deal with the built-up trade imbalances and portfolio shifts, expectations of exchange rate revaluations started to develop. Consequently, these expectations of the depreciation/appreciation of currencies compounded the pressures coming from the changing liquidity premia that were being put on the official exchange rates. From May 1971 onward problems worsened as a result of the strong speculative pressures on the US$ and the crisis reached a high when on August 15, 1971 the American government announced the suspension of the gold convertibility of the US$. Indeed, from that moment onward other countries no longer needed to maintain the dollar parity of their currency within agreed upon or conventional margins, opening the door for the final breakdown of Bretton Woods and the relative devaluation of the US$.

Once one moves to a Non-Unified Monetary System (NUMS) (Davidson, 1992, p. 80-82) with the breakdown of Bretton Woods, a Pandora's Box of possibilities is opened up in terms of the role of speculation and its impact on the world economy. A NUMS is a system that employs various nominal units of account in the formulation of contracts within which the exchange rates between these units are flexible and are expected to vary. Within a NUMS, there is *exchange rate uncertainty* (Davidson, 1992, p. 83). This means that (1) all revenues and costs denominated in "foreign" currencies are subject to this central type of uncertainty; (2) the yields and costs associated with all holding assets denominated in "foreign" currencies are subject to this uncertainty; and (3) all assets denominated in "foreign" currencies are susceptible to exchange-rate based appreciation or depreciation in their values. Within a NUMS, liquidity premia can vary between the different monies in existence. In that the liquidity of any asset depends upon the existence of well-organized, orderly spot markets (Davidson, 1994, p. 54), there are likely to be significant and changing differences in the liquidity premium associated with different currencies and assets denominated in different currencies.

With the breakdown of the Bretton Woods UMS and the development of a global NUMS a number of central patterns developed. In terms of policy creation and development one has seen a perpetual conflict between attempts to create exchange rate stability and reduce the associated uncertainties and the perspective that all variability is fine and only reflects the "market" generating internationally optimal outcomes. Working beside this conflict has been a general development of the international monetary and financial mechanisms and institutions of speculation.

An immediate example of the stabilization attempts was the creation on December 18, 1971 of a new system of parities in relation to the US$ as a result of the Smithsonian Agreement. The Agreement saw also a devaluation of the US$ and the revaluation of the European currencies. Moreover, the Agreement also stipulated that the margins of fluctuation of other currencies against the US$ would be set at 2.25 percent on either side of the US$-parity.

But, the Smithsonian Agreement failed to halt the fundamental shift that was taking place. European central banks considered US$ reserves less and less desirable. This was made abundantly clear when on April 10, 1972 the member-states of the European Community decided to keep the spread between the parity between any two of their currencies within a 2.25 percent range on either side of the parity. That range was also the authorized margin between the European currencies and the US$. They also decided to use only European currencies if intervention was needed to keep their currency inside the new snake. This meant that the central banks could reduce their US$ balances since the need for them was now sharply reduced.

The new system, aimed at stabilizing the exchange rates would, over the years, prove to be a source of confusion, frustration and in-built distortions. First of all, between 1972 and 1978 a number of countries entered the system while a number of them left; in some cases, such as Norway and France, there were repeat performances. Secondly, the set margins of fluctuation have led to major distortions with respect to balance of payments considerations.

The whole system quite quickly led to anomalies that created serious problems and serious tensions between the various European partners. Because of the limitations the system imposed on the margins of fluctuation, both the Spanish peseta and the French franc became overvalued in relation to the German mark, while the latter should have been revalued in order to reflect its true position and value in relation to the two other currencies. Hence, the system had the tendency to obscure the "real" balance of payments between countries. The result has been that within the European Community we gradually see two groups of currencies developing, each with divergent monetary policies. The first group comprises countries that have both strong surpluses in their balance of payments as they relate to other partners in the Community and strong trade relations with Germany. These countries have been gradually aligning their currencies with the German mark and the German monetary policy, while arguing that the parities between the European currencies participating in the snake should be re-assessed. The other group comprises the countries whose intra-community trade has been in deficit and among the latter both France and the United Kingdom are the most prominent. More recently and with the Treaty of Maastricht the European Union, under impulse of Germany, tacked on another condition for participating in the single European currency system: only countries than kept their deficits below the 3-percent-of-GDP-level qualify for participation.

In partial contrast stands the situation prevailing with the North American Free Trade Agreement (NAFTA). The main difference between NAFTA and the European Union lies in the fact that the European Union has attempted and is attempting to undo some of the problems that arose from the post-Bretton Woods situation via mechanisms creating exchange rate fixity, while NAFTA has taken the post-Bretton Woods situation for granted and attempts to achieve economic integration without putting in place measures aimed at creating exchange-rates stability and accepts instead the appropriateness of "market" results. Exchange rates between the three national currencies have been subject to very sharp fluctuations, with the last upheaval a scant two years in the past. While some of the currency variability may have been the reflection of inherent weaknesses in the economy such as Mexico, one cannot deny that strong speculative forces have influenced that variability.

The post-Bretton Woods period also witnessed a rapid and substantial development of international speculative institutions and mechanisms. As Harvey (1991; 1993) has convincingly argued, the determination of exchange rates has very little to do with enterprise and is dominated by speculative activity. Only a small percentage of foreign exchange market transactions are based on the current needs for trade and the production of output. The speculative activity itself is dominated by the activities of foreign exchange rate dealers. This is an increasingly dominant pattern aided by the development of internationally integrated financial markets and trading institutions that are active world wide.

The combination of financial market liberalization and economic integration is contradictory. The integration process asks for exchange rate stability while at the same time creating a process toward the use of certain key currencies. This latter tendency creates changing liquidity premia and puts pressure on exchange rates. In a context of integrated and well-developed financial markets, these pressures are compounded by speculative activity. This creates a cumulative process away from the stable exchange rate goals of economic integration.

In the UMS, Bretton Woods period, there was little focus on the monetary elements of economic integration. The latter NUMS, post-Bretton Woods period, brought to the fore monetary and exchange rate issues, though they were often treated as add-ons to the real trade considerations of economic integration. Policies in the post-Bretton Woods period have also exhibited a tension between a desire to let market forces set exchange rates, as well as generate other monetary and financial dynamics, and a desire for stability and predictability.

Monetary Integration and Economic Growth

Keynes' theory of value has a central ramification for the operation of capitalist economies. The inclusion of liquidity premia means that real assets – key among which is fixed capital – require a higher expected objective rate of return than money and financial assets if they are to be deemed economically desirable. Hence, under conditions where investment projects can be ranked in a declining fashion according to their expected rates of return, a particular rate of interest on money means that there will be less investment projects undertaken when one includes liquidity considerations (Keynesian conditions) as compared to the situation of ignoring such considerations (Classical conditions). If the classical conditions correspond to a level of investment consistent with full employment, then the lower level of investment under the Keynesian conditions dictate an equilibrium at less than full employment. The degree of unemployment increases as money and financial assets carry a higher liquidity premium relative to fixed capital. That is the fundamental conclusion coming out of Keynes' general theory.

Within a UMS, it was argued above that there are no or only small differences in the liquidity premia associated with different currencies. In a UMS the monies act as one. The comparison of investment projects to the rate of interest is similar in all countries. Differences in the rate of investment between countries arise from differences in the long-term expectations of profitability. So differences of expected costs, sales, productivity, and the uncertainty thereof determine international differences in the desired rates of investment and the resulting rates of growth. This holds independent of the ability of transnational investment to occur. Actual rates may be impacted by other constraints, like the access to finance.

When one extends this analysis to contrasting international growth rates within a NUMS, some important insights can be obtained as to monetary causes of differential growth. Within a NUMS there can be significant differences in the liquidity premia associated with different currencies. If fixed capital in all countries of the model has proportionally lower liquidity premia than their corresponding monies, then differences in the liquidity premia of the currencies will translate into differences in the rates of return required of fixed capital to make investment economically desirable. The required rate of return of fixed capital in countries whose currencies have high liquidity premia are higher than these rates of return in countries with currencies carrying low liquidity premia relative to fixed capital. Adjusting for differences in long-term expectations and productive capacity, this means that there will be less investment and lower economic growth rates in the countries where a large premium is put on liquidity.

One category of sources of differential liquidity premia between countries includes differences in economic performance, expectations of future performance, inflation, and other instabilities. All these can put a premium on liquidity and result in less productive investment being undertaken. Some of the problems arising from international economic integration can result in imbalances and uncertainties in the areas mentioned above that will result in a greater preference for liquidity. A cumulative process of increased uncertainties can occur, leading to a greater preference for liquidity resulting in lower investment. The lower profits emanating from that reinforces the shift toward financial assets and money and away from real investment.

The expected variability of exchange rates within a NUMS means that the investment in all assets – real or financial – is valued in a way that includes the expected variation in exchange rates. Profits are more desirable if received in an area whose currency is expected to appreciate. The required rate of return on fixed capital in a country that is expected to experience currency devaluation is higher than that required in a strong currency area. Hence, adjusting for all other relevant factors, this means that there will be lower investment and growth in the weak currency countries.

As argued above, the process of international monetary integration leads to a systematic pattern of changing exchange rates. The international liberalization of trade creates a tendency towards the use of one or a small group of currencies for transactions purposes. These key currencies have associated with them increasing liquidity premia as the globalization of trade progresses. This creates a relative depreciation of currencies and financial assets that are not part of the key group.

The international liberalization of financial markets and capital flows makes such flight to liquidity easier to carry out and contributes to the divergence of the liquidity premia. This financial liberalization gives greater influence to the speculators and traders in the world's financial centers. Hence, the expectations of appreciation and depreciation, as well as the judgment of relative liquidity premia, that enter into the determination of relative prices of international financial assets belong to these major speculators and traders. Consequently, there is a tendency of self-fulfilling prophecies and of downward spirals of currency values.

This means that less investment takes place in the countries that are also experiencing devaluation pressures arising from the lower liquidity premium of their currency. This lower investment means lower rates of growth. Thus the pattern of movement toward certain key currencies creates devaluation pressures on other currencies and creates conditions for lower rates of growth in this latter group of countries. Consequently, monetary integration creates a double problem for all but the countries that form the financial centre.

This monetary theory of exchange rates means that exchange rates and the values of financial assets fluctuate independent of real production considerations. As a matter of fact, the process of globalization causes a particular pattern of changing values. This pattern is generally to the benefit of centre economies and detrimental to periphery economies.

Illustrations of these types of dynamics can be found in the European process of integration discussed in the previous section. The NAFTA process also illustrates many of the theoretical points made in this paper. Briefly, the real conditions for significant growth in Mexico existed. But, the monetary component of the integration has caused an increased reliance on the US$ and US$-denominated securities. When speculative forces caused a run away from Mexican securities, it resulted in a significant devaluation in the Mexican peso. Similar speculative forces have put pressure on the Canadian dollar. These events and the expectation that such a trend will continue have created the situation that higher rates of return are required on fixed capital investment in Mexico and Canada than in the United States. Consequently, investment rates are lower in Mexico and Canada, as are growth rates. This monetary dynamics has prevented real economic forces from creating a convergent pattern of growth. The monetary dynamics has protected the economic health of the United States – the centre country in this context – in a manner inconsistent with real productive and cost considerations.

The Policy Requirements for Effective Economic Integration

The policy implications coming from this analysis can be captured in the sentiment that the international monetary structures, institutions, and rules that exist and that are created matter profoundly to the kind of effects that the liberalization of international trade will have on international growth, relative economic development, and the patterns of international trade. It means that the current tendency to liberalize trade before one creates truly international monies and financial institutions is putting the cart before the horse. The process of monetary integration itself creates a tendency towards volatile and divergent exchange rate that persist in a downward spiral. The devaluation pattern of certain currencies and the ancillary uncertainties put an important dampening effect on investment in those countries, resulting in lower growth rates, causing economic performance to negatively diverge in peripheral countries from what occurs in the centre countries. If globalization is going to have positive benefits for all, then setting up the right monetary environment is a necessary precondition.

Such a monetary environment is one that effectively creates a UMS with fixed exchange rates that are truly expected to remain fixed and where financial speculation is strongly kept in check. Under these conditions the real trade and productivity can flourish and not be buried by speculative activity. This stability of exchange rates translates into higher investment activity and higher economic growth rates. In other words, the *de facto* conditions that existed in the early days of European economic integration are what lend themselves to effective economic integration.

The creation of an international central bank with an international currency, as well as policies and structures that push surplus areas to buy from deficit areas or that promote growth in growth deficient areas would be the ideal. Such ideas were raised by Keynes in the context of the discussion leading to Bretton Woods and, more recently, by Paul Davidson. The international currency supplants all the national currencies. By doing so, it effectively creates a UMS. A well-supported international money becomes the key currency. All national currencies primarily lose liquidity value with respect to this international money, instead of establishing their own hierarchy with a particular pattern of changing exchange rates. The mechanism to recycle trade surpluses has the dual effects of maintaining sales, employment, profits, and general economic health in the deficit areas, thereby enhancing the stability in such areas in terms of investment and the value of their money, and of being a clear signal that real trade activity is what is important as opposed to speculative financial activity.

A second-best solution is a set of policies aimed at insulating financial markets from each other by imposing capital controls, at clearing international capital flows through central banks, increasing the domestic requirements of the financial assets held by domestic financial institutions, and generally making it harder for large-scale flight of money towards key currencies and key-currency denominated financial assets. In other words, if one accepts that flexible exchange rates are—to some degree—the context that one has to deal with before a full integration of an economic region, then it is financial liberalization that must take a back seat to trade and ancillary integration. In fact, as the "real" integration proceeds and increases negative monetary pressures, there is a need to *decrease* the degree of financial liberalization. This is only logical in that economic integration means a reduction in economic diversity and a wiping out of monetary and financial heterogeneity. Policies must help this process for economic integration to be effective and equitable.

A frequently discussed proposal is to put a tax on financial transactions (Tobin, 1978). The basic idea is to make such transactions costly so that there is less speculative content in foreign exchange and financial market transactions. As Davidson (1992-93) has pointed out, there are certain serious problems with the idea. The key is that such a tax does not fundamentally change the international environment of speculation, nor dampen the differential pressures on exchange rate, nor generate trade flows in support of deficit areas.

There will only be effective results if there is tax that succeeds in differentiating between domestic and international transactions. If this is done then one again achieves some degree of differentiation between national financial markets. Such taxes also need to succeed in increasing investment in real goods—a much more difficult proposition. While such taxes can affect the relative net yields between assets, they do nothing in terms of the shifting pattern of relative liquidity premia and of appreciation/depreciation of assets that was pointed to above as a major cause of the problem.

In the end there are severe limitations to any solutions that are market-based by providing certain incentives or disincentives to international financial speculative transactions. Certain market-based reform may be a step in the right direction, but it is the normal operation of markets in a NUMS that generates instability and divergent economic growth rates. What needs to be done is institutional reform to move towards an effective UMS where stability is important and the speculative impact on investment and growth is expunged to as large a degree as possible. As Keynes (CWJMK, VII. p. 159) reminds us;

> Speculators may do no harm as bubbles on a steady stream of enterprise. But the position is serious when enterprise becomes the bubble on a whirlpool of speculation. When the capital development of a country becomes a by-product of the activities of a casino, the job is likely to be ill-done.

Endnotes

[1] Inflation, debt, and deficit targets are a central component of the Maastricht II plan for monetary integration of the European Union.

2. A pure UMS is where the same unit of account is used across all relevant regions.

References

Davidson, Paul. *International Money and the Real World.* 2d. ed. New York: St. Martin's Press, 1992.

_____. "Reforming the World's Money." *Journal of Post Keynesian Economics*, Winter 1992-93, 15 (2), pp. 153-79.

_____. *Post Keynesian Macroeconomic Theory.* Aldershot, England: Edward Elgar, 1994.

Deprez, Johan. "Technology and the Terms of Trade: Considering Expectational, Structural, and Institutional Factors." *Journal of Economic Issues,* June 1995, 29 (2), pp. 435-42.

Harvey, John T. "A Post Keynesian View of Exchange Rate Determination." *Journal of Post Keynesian Economics,* Fall 1991, 14 (1), pp. 61-71.

Harvey, John T. "The Institution of Foreign Exchange Trading." *Journal of Economic Issues*, September 1993, 27 (3), pp. 679-98.

Kaldor, Nicholas. "Speculation and Economic Stability." *The Review of Economic Studies,* 1939, in F. Targetti and A. P. Thirlwall, eds., *The Essential Kaldor*, New York: Holmes & Meier, 1989.

Keynes, John M. *The Collected Writings of John Maynard Keynes.* London: MacMillan and Cambridge, Cambridge University Press, 1971-83. Volumes are referred to as CWJMK followed by the volume number.

Kregel, Jan A. "Economic Methodology in the Face of Uncertainty." *Economic Journal,* 1976, 86 (342), pp. 209-225.

Skidelsky, Robert. *John Maynard Keynes: The Economist as Savior 1920-1937.,*New York: Allen Lane, The Penguin Press, 1994.

Sraffa, Piero. "Dr. Hayek on Money and Capital." *Economic Journal,* March 1932, 42, pp. 42-53.

Tobin, James. "A Proposal for International Monetary Reform." *Eastern Economic Journal,* 1978, 4, pp. 153-59.

Townshend, Hugh. "Liquidity-Premium and the Theory of Value." *Economic Journal,* March 1937, 47 (185), pp. 157-69.

5

EU, ASEAN AND NORTH AMERICAN INTEGRATION:
Lessons from Their Degrees of Integration

Maria Sophia Aguirre
Catholic University of America, U.S.A.

This paper contrasts the EU, ASEAN and NAFTA integrations, analyzing their institutional integration, their implementation, and their impact on growth and financial markets of the member countries. In particular, the paper studies whether different degrees of financial integration affect the reception and transmission of spillovers effect inside and outside blocs. Although more detailed structural specifications are found for Europe and North America, ASEAN's style of integration has improved the Pacific countries' trade, growth and financial markets, and it provides important information for the achievement of economic integration. It suggests that when trade agreements exist with heavy capital investment within the bloc, faster growth and financial stability are achieved.

Since the creation of the European Monetary System (EMS) the member countries have increased their degree of coordination. Furthermore, at the same time that the European Union (EU) developed, other regions followed the trend toward regionalization of their international trading systems. Such is the case with Japan and the newly industrialized countries (NIC) which signed the Association of South East Asian Nations (ASEAN) Treaty in 1995 and with the North American bloc (NA) that signed the North American Free Trade Agreement (NAFTA) in 1993. While the EU has progressively integrated multiple dimensions through explicit institutional arrangements, NA and NIC have limited themselves to a formal trade integration which they have undertaken in different ways.

The literature studying the consequences of integration for policy and economic development of member countries is very extensive at both the theoretical and the empirical levels[1]. All agree that economic convergence in the EU has imposed serious restrictions on monetary and fiscal policies for the member countries which, in turn, have led to recession. There is also strong evidence that within the EU, inflation, exchange rate, and interest rate volatility decreased because of integration. Thus, results seem to suggest that cooperative action, although recessionary in the beginning for the less developed countries within the bloc, allowed an improvement in the welfare of the member countries[2].

Yet, increases in government indebtedness levels, especially after 1990, as well as the crisis in the foreign exchange markets in 1992-1993, showed the strong pressures and costs that market participants can impose on countries' official exchange rates when lack of credibility rises and an expectation of exchange rate realignments develops in the economic agents[3]. Countries participating in the Exchange Rate Mechanism (ERM) of the European Monetary System (EMS), as well as those that peg their currency to the European Currency Unit (ECU), lost large amounts of reserves and were forced to borrow funds in an effort to support each other's currencies and avoid devaluations. Just to mention a few countries, during the attack of the franc, the Bundesbank sold $30 billion in one day and England, during the attack against the pound, spent $70 billion on September 6 alone. A similar credibility crisis was faced by Mexico in December of 1994 which forced the US to lend $25 billion to Mexico. In all cases, a negative impact was experienced on the economies within and outside these blocs. It is this spillover effect inside and outside the blocs with different degrees of integration that is the matter of analysis in this paper. In particular, the paper studies whether different degrees of financial integration affect the reception and transmission of these spillovers.

In the first part of the paper, the EU, ASEAN and NAFTA processes of integration are compared. An econometric analysis follows to determine the timing of the sudden changes of some economic variables' conditional variance as a measure of volatility and spillover effect between 1983 and 1995. The paper concludes with a discussion of the results. Although the integrations are different in nature, a comparison of their style of integration provides an interesting lesson for the implementation of economic integration. Particularly, when trade arrangements exist with heavy capital investment within the bloc, faster growth and financial stability are achieved without high levels of indebtedness or official foreign reserve losses. Furthermore, the volatility of the financial variables shows contemporary and consecutive changes in variance within and across blocs which suggest volatility spillover effects. The effects of this spillover within each bloc member, however, are smaller the less integrated the financial system is.

Blocs and Their Degrees of Integration

Table 1 presents a summary of the process of integration that shaped each of the three blocs under study in this section.

The European Union (EU)

Even before the formation of the customs union, the EU was not a particularly open region because its major trading partners were mainly other European countries. Trade creation and trade diversion effects of the union expanded rapidly after integration. In real terms, intra-bloc trade grew by 42% between the first quarter of 1986 and the third quarter of 1994, with a strong shrinkage in the growth trend after the 1992 exchange rate crises. In spite of this, integration still is not complete. Labor mobility is still not free, and there remain differences in tax structures, as well as in health and safety regulations. Furthermore, real investment and technology transfer have been scarce, after the initial increase through mergers and joint ventures in 1985. Intra-bloc direct investment grew until 1970 but it declined thereafter, with the exception of Italy and Germany. This same behavior is reflected in the GDP. In the 1960s, the EC experienced real growth (on average, real GDP grew by 4.8%) while from the 1970s on, it experienced slow growth and rising unemployment.

The track record of the EMS has been mixed. Inflation differentials have declined as well as exchange rate and interest rate volatility. As of 1992, all national inflation rates, with the exception of Italy, were below the German level. Thereafter, however, most of the countries were above Germany with the exception of Finland, Belgium, and France. Interest rate volatility also decreased since 1985 with a reversal during the ERM crisis of 1992-1993 and thereafter[4]. The periodic currency realignment has not managed to avoid misalignments of currencies against the German mark, the strongest currency in the bloc, and ended with the crisis in the exchange rate market late summer and early fall of 1992 and continued through 1994.

Table 1: Process of Integration

BLOCK		AGREEMENT	OUTCOMES
European Union	1951	*Treaty of Paris*	Established the European Coal and Steel Community. Signed by Belgium, France, Germany, Italy, Luxembourg and the Netherlands
	1957	*Treaty of Rome*	Formed the European Economic Community (EC). It aimed at the "transformation of an integrated market for the free movement of goods, services, capital and people."
	1962	*CAP*	EC adopted the Common Agricultural Policy (CAP).
	1971	*Werner Report*	Proposed three-phase program to reached a fixed exchange rate and an integrated Federal European Bank.
	1973		Denmark, Ireland, UK joined the EC.
	1979		Eight original participants of the European Monetary System began to mutually peg their currency (Exchange Rate Mechanism-ERM).
	1981		Greece joined the EC.
	1985	*White Paper*	Aimed at eliminating several non-tariff obstacles.
	1986	*SEA*	Council of Ministers adopted the Single European Act (SEA). The European Union (EU) was formalized and December 1992 was set for the complete removal of all market restrictions. It contained three main elements: Harmonization of domestic regulations, promotion of coordination in scientific and the technological research, and encouragement of competition. Portugal and Spain joined the EC.

Table 1: Process of Integration (Continued)

BLOCK	AGREEMENT	OUTCOMES
	1988	EU authorized the liberalization of capital movements by December 1990. Extensions were given until 1992 for Spain, Portugal, Ireland, and Greece.
	1989 *Delors Report*	Aproved in March. Determined a three-stage transition to full monetary Union: Coordination of monetary policy and the incorporation of all EU members into to the ERM. Creation of the European Central Bank and narrower exchange rate intervention margins by 1994., and fixed exchange rate parities and adoption of an European Currency together with the transfer of macro policy to the community by 1997. Spain joined ERM.
	1990	UK joined ERM.
	1991 *Maastricht Treaty*	Heads of State agreed to create a monetary union by 1997. Sweeden joined EU and ERM.
	1992	UK and Italy abandoned the ERM.
	1995 *Treaty of Madrid*	Heads of States agreed to delay the creation of the Monetary Union to January 1999. In addition, they set 1998 as the date to rule which nations can participate in the monetary union, 1999 to fixed the currencies, and 2002 to issue notes and coins.
ASEAN	1985-1990	Japan started a large scale investment in some countries of South East Asia: Singapore, Taiwan, Hong Kong, and South Korea. These countries became known as the Newly Industrialized Countries (NIC).
	1990	Japan reduced trade barriers towards NIC.
	1990-present	Japan and NIC started investing in the rest of South East Asia.

Table 1: Process of Integration *(Continued)*

BLOCK		AGREEMENT	OUTCOMES
	1992	*ASEAN Summit Singapore*	The Association of South-East Asian Nations (ASEAN) formalized the intention of forming the ASEAN Free Trade Area (AFTA) by 2007.
	1995	*ASEAN/NICTreaty*	Consolidated the trade agreement among ASEAN members.
NAFTA	1985	*CUFTA*	The Canacian-US Free Trade Agreement (CUFTA) was signed. It incorporated US trading law s reciprocity (replicated in the art.19 of NAFTA), intellectual property rights, and regulations regarding rule of origin.
	1993	*NAFTA*	The North American Free Trade Agreement (NAFTA) was ratified by the US Congress, going into effect in January of 1994. It sat the schedule of tariff reductions over fifteen years. The tariff reduction schedule for NAFTA was set over a 15 years period. Products in which all three countrieswere already internationally competitive, were reduced immediately. Products that needed short term protection were given five years, and less stable products were given ten years. Finally, more sensitive products, such as corn and sugar, were given fifteen years. An important part of NAFTA was the side agreements that mostly dealt with environmental policies and standards to reduce and clean up pollution, as well as with labor laws. It also set the year 2000 to incorporate full participation of foreign banks in the Mexican Banking Industry. For the first years foreign banks are only able to participate in 8% of the Mexican banking industry. This will increase graduallY to 15% by 1999 and, after the year 2000, there will no be limit. Yet, the level of regulation does not indicate the intent of a systematic monetary integration of the kind followed by the EU. Since NAFTA, several Central and South American countries have asked North America to join NAFTA or to agree on preferential trade for some of their products.

Exchange rate overshooting creates significant risk for those engaged in international trade and investment activities since they are exposed to medium-term exchange rate movements. By combining policy coordination with exchange rate realignment, the EU sought to reduce this intra-trade cost. With Germany being the stronger currency in the area and having the lowest level of inflation, one way in which the success of the goal of macroconvergence can be tested is by observing the alignment of nominal and real EU currencies *vis a vis* the German mark.

Figure 1 shows the nominal and the real exchange rate *vis a vis* the mark, for eleven member countries of the EMS between January 1980 and October 1995. The period leading to December 1990 shows an increasing alignment between the real and the nominal exchange rate, thus reflecting efforts of the EC members towards convergence as proposed by the Delors Report. After the initial alignment of December 1990, and with the exception of Germany and the UK, all countries show increasing misalignments between nominal and real exchange rates, especially after 1992. While Belgium, France, Denmark and Netherlands, the most developed countries in the region, show overvalued currencies *vis a vis* the mark, the less developed countries within the bloc show undervalued currencies. Sweden and Italy also have undervalued currencies but the misalignment is smaller than the former. Results show that macroconvergence was not obtained in the less developed countries and the more developed countries defended their exchange rate stability at the cost of large losses of central banks' reserves and, especially after 1990, increased government debt[5]. At the same time, and particularly after 1990, the volatility of the portfolio investment increased, confirming large speculative capital activity in the European financial market. This activity further contributed to exchange rates misalignments.

Clearly, the EU initiatives to create an integrated financial market are closely related to their economics as well as their process of monetary integration. The arguments for and against this policy, have been studied elsewhere[6] and range from burden sharing to currency-substitution effects to policy credibility. For the purpose of this paper, let us note that this combination has succeeded in decreasing volatility in interest and exchange rates, but that large central bank interventions and levels of indebtedness were required to achieve this goal. In spite of this, countries have been unable to maintain official exchange rate levels in alignment and they could not avoid their devaluations when the market reacted to it. Although the target zone principle remains in place, this only has held at a 30% (±15) band which is large enough to make these currencies indistinguishable from a floating system.

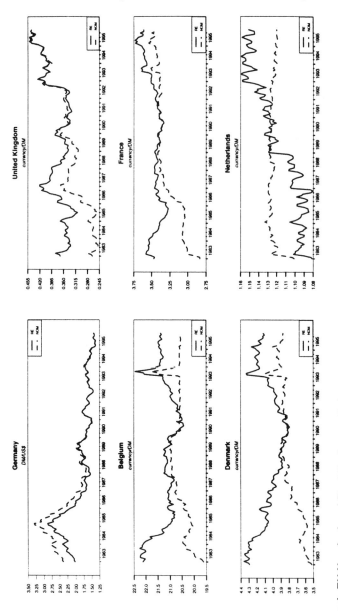

Figure 1: EU Nominal and Real Exchange Rates

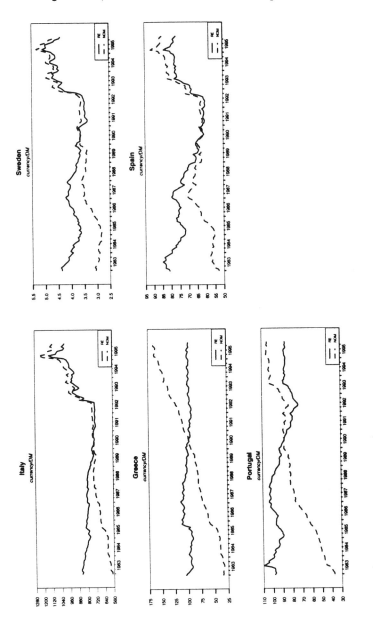

Figure 1: EU Nominal and Real Exchange Rates *(Continued)*

The Association of South East Asian Nations (ASEAN)

The Newly Industrialized Countries (NIC) interregional integration grew rapidly in the second half of the 1980s to consolidate with the agreement signed with ASEAN in 1995. Japanese firms responded to the combination of a closed Europe and the Plaza Agreement by reallocating operations throughout Asia. The aim was not only one of reducing costs but of integrating the region as well as serving American and European markets. As a consequence, South Korea and Taiwan have been transformed from agrarian to industrial economies, and Hong Kong and Singapore have developed their financial markets as well as their industry. Furthermore, these countries, together with Japan, have led direct investments in other countries of ASEAN, especially in Indonesia, Thailand, and Malaysia[7].

As in Europe, trade protectionist policies have also been used in NIC. These protectionist measures, however, when compared with other countries where income substitution policies exist, had both lower and less variable rates across sectors. Intra-regional trade among ASEAN countries in 1994 was three and a half times the trade of 1985, the leading countries being Japan, Korea, Taiwan, Singapore, Indonesia and Malaysia. In addition, these countries collectively experienced trade surpluses. Japan, Singapore, and Korea used their excess domestic savings for global investment. This capital movement has facilitated the development of financial centers in South East Asia, and especially in Hong Kong and Singapore. Thus, until last year when a formal agreement was signed, "the process of regionalization of the Pacific *[has been]* driven by economics, with investment as their driver and (..) a very little *[formalized]* institutional development."[8]

Their financial integration has followed this same characteristic: no explicit institutional arrangement exists. In Figure 2, it can be seen that the two principal countries in the area, Korea and Singapore, have suffered misalignments *vis a vis* the Japanese yen (the strongest currency in the bloc). Korea shows it since 1991 while Singapore shows undervaluation after 1993. This last country alignment has neither been a consequence of the introduction of an exchange rate arrangement nor of central banks' manipulation, but of market adjustments. The misalignment of the 1990s could be explained by the growing role of these countries in the financial markets of the region through both portfolio and direct investment, as well as the increase of European portfolio investments after 1993. Volatility in other macroeconomic variables however, have remained high. Interest rate volatility, in spite of having decreased since 1985, is still larger than in the EU. Direct and portfolio investment volatility in the region has increased. The latter increased as

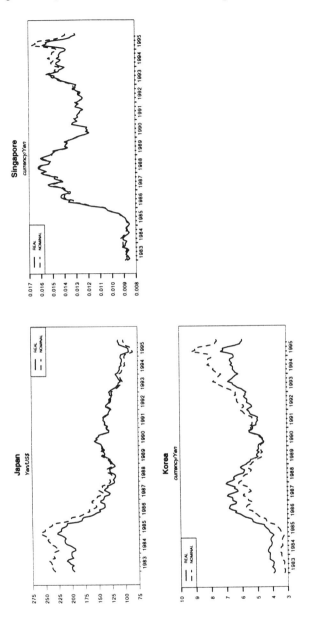

Figure 2: NIC Nominal and Real Exchange Rates

integration consolidated and became strong during the 1992-1993 EMS crisis, suggesting the presence of speculative capital in Asian financial markets. NIC direct investment has increased as well.

As in the case of the EU, the development of an Asian integrated financial market has been closely related to their economic integration but with no formalized financial agreement. For the purpose of this paper, let us note that, as for the EU case, this regional integration has succeeded in decreasing volatility on interest and exchange rates but to a lesser degree than in Europe. In addition, exchange rate alignments across the major players in the region has been maintained without central bank interventions or high levels of indebtedness. Finally, trade as well as portfolio and direct investment have increased during the 1990s to reach other less developed countries in the region, specially Malaysia and Indonesia.

The North American Free Trade Agreement (NAFTA)

Different from the ASEAN case and similar to the European case, economic integration between Canada and USA was already a reality before the Canada-United States Free Trade Agreement (CUSFTA) and NAFTA. Almost 80% of Canadian exports came to the US and about 70% of their imports were American. Canadian exports, however, constitute only about 20% of US trade. Like Canada, Mexico is highly integrated with the US (about 70% of Mexico's international transactions take place with the US), although it constitutes only 3% of US trade. Since 1986, intra-regional trade has grown more rapidly reflecting the impact of CUSFTA first, and then NAFTA[9].

The proportion of American foreign direct investment in Mexico and Canada is high (about 64%), but the US corporations do not have the integrated investment strategy that Japan and the NIC countries have toward the rest of ASEAN. Canadian and Mexican funds in the US are mainly speculative. For the Canadian and the US cases, direct investment has been mainly negative while portfolio investment has increased after 1986. Mexico's direct investment as well as portfolio investment had been steadily low until the end of 1991. The combination of financial and trade liberalization, the high returns offered by the Tesobono and the Cetes, together with a loose US monetary policy and the announcement, in the Spring of 1990, of the intent to sign an agreement between the US and Canada, contributed to an abrupt increase of portfolio investment after 1991. Mexican capital returned to this country. The lack of direct investment in Mexico is reflected in the fact that the rapid growth of less developed countries that took place in the NIC and now taking place in ASEAN, did not take place in Mexico.

Figure 3 depicts the Canadian and Mexican exchange rates *vis à vis* the dollar. They have behaved differently. While the Mexican peso has been largely overvalued until 1990, it has been undervalued since then. The misalignment became worse after the 1994 financial crisis and the trade off has been, as for the case of some of the European countries, the loss of reserves and recession. The pronounced misalignment in 1986 corresponds to the drastic fall in the price of oil that shocked the economy, causing inflation to increase to 106% in 1986 and to 160% in 1987, while output growth fell from 3.6% to 1.7% in the same period. The behavior of the Canadian dollar has varied. During the first half of the 1980s it was overvalued, but it became progressively aligned in the second half until its completion in the 1990s. Since 1993, it became overvalued again.

No clear links can be derived from the North American bloc financial activity. Yet some similarities in the behavior of intra-regional trade, direct and portfolio investments and interest rates volatility are found with respect to the other two blocs. North America presents characteristics similar to the NIC in that no formal institutional arrangements were intended in their financial integration. Two main differences can be pointed out. The first is that Mexican and Canadian capital in the US are not intended as long term investments but behave in a speculative manner. The second is that the development of the NA countries' financial market has not been closely related to their economic integration.

All three blocs have a strong developed country as a center from which economic and financial integration is promoted and which has an important role in the stability of the bloc. Thus, this country affects, although in different degrees according with the degree of integration, the economic and financial development of the other members countries of the bloc. These strong countries are Germany for the EU, Japan for the ASEAN, and the US for North America.

Although with different styles of integration, the EU and the NIC/ASEAN integrations have contributed towards real growth within their regions. The developments of the past ten years, however, suggest a more successful support of economic growth and integration in one case than in the other. Japan's, and later Korea's and Singapore's heavy capital and portfolio investment within the bloc, fostered and continues to foster faster growth within the region and a lower cost of maintaining financial stability than in blocs where there is full integration as is the case of the EU. At the other extreme, the NA can serve as an example of the

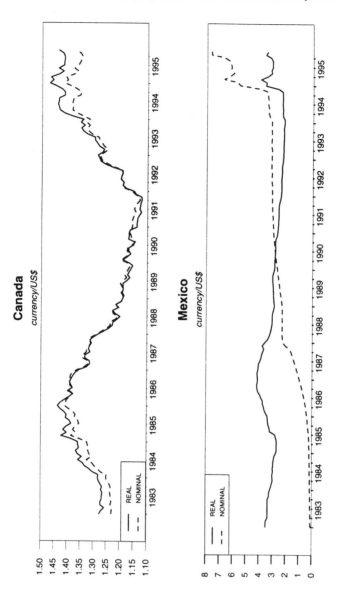

Figure 3: NAFTA Nominal and Real Exchange Rates

consequences for growth when direct investment does not accompany economic integration.

Econometric Analysis

Transmission of volatility changes within and across blocs could cause serious structural adjustment costs because of their effect on trade and capital markets. It is intended, therefore, as part of economic and financial integration, to decrease the volatility within the member countries as well as the isolation of other countries' exchange rate and interest rate volatility. In order to test how successful the different degrees of integration have been in the above goals, sudden changes in conditional variances of economic variables can be calculated and then compared with countries of the same bloc, and countries outside it.

Inclan and Tiao (1992), developed the Iterative Cumulative Sum Square (ICSS) algorithm, to calculate sudden changes in the unconditional variance under the assumption that these changes take place at unknown points in time. Let the cumulative sum square of a series of uncorrelated random variables $\{a_t\}$ with zero means and variance s_t^2, t = 1,2,...,T be:

$$C_k = \Sigma_{t=1}^k a_t^2$$

and let

$$D_k = \frac{C_k}{C_T} - \frac{k}{T}$$

where k = 1,..., T and $D_0 = D_T = 0$ be the centered (and normalized) cumulative sum squares. The plot of D_k against k oscillates around zero for series with homogeneous variance. When there is a sudden change in variance, the plot of D_k will exhibit a pattern going out of some specified boundaries with high probability. These boundaries are obtained from the asymptotic distribution of $\max_k |D_k|$ assuming constant variance, which is available because D_k is asymptotically a Brownian Bridge. The asymptotic 95th percentile of $\max_k |D_k|$ is 1.36[10]. When there are changes in variance, D_k slope shows drastic changes, even a change in sign, creating a peak or a trough according to whether the variance changes to a smaller or greater value respectively. The algorithm iterates successive applications of D_k to pieces of the series, dividing consecutively after a possible change point is found.

One could argue that the sudden changes in unconditional variance are due to external shocks rather than being inherent in the dynamics of the series, or that both phenomena are present. Simultaneous changes in variance across blocs may support the first, while contemporaneous changes within the bloc can be used as support of the second. A third possibility is that changes in the variance may be caused by dynamics inherent in the series and that these changes are transmitted to other countries or blocs as external shocks. The size of D_k, the timing, and its sign can help in providing this information.

The series analyzed by this procedure are monthly nominal exchange rates, nominal interest rates, central banks foreign reserves, direct and portfolio investments, net government borrowing, and intra-regional trade. To have some element of comparison before and after the integrations, and to avoid the oil crises of the 1970s and 1982, the period covered is January 1983 to August 1995. When quarterly data is used, the period covered is 1983 - 1994. The countries included are the EU members (Portugal, Germany, United Kingdom, Netherlands, France, Spain, Belgium, Denmark, Italy, Sweden, Greece, and Ireland), three from Asia (Japan, Korea, and Singapore), and the three NAFTA members.

Tables 2 through 7 show the change points obtained with the ICSS algorithm. Exchange rates (Table 2) reflect significant changes during 1983 within Europe and across blocs, although in this last case only in some countries. While changes within Europe are both simultaneous and consecutive (as in the case of the Netherlands, Ireland and Germany), the impact on Singapore's and Canada's exchange rates was not felt until June of 1983. NIC and NAFTA capture the effect of the Plaza Accord in 1985 simultaneously, while in some countries of the EU this effect can be contemporaneously found but with less significance. The adoption of the Single European ACT (SEA) also caused shifts in variances in several European countries and the impact extended to NIC but no effects were present in NA. All blocs reflect the impact of the 1987 crash as well, although with less intensity in EU except for those countries, as could have been expected, with stronger currencies and more developed financial markets such as France, UK and Belgium. Volatility within the EU decreased overall until 1992 when the exchange rate crisis took place. 1992-1993 variance change points in the EU are both simultaneous across countries and sequential within and across countries as well. The countries that show greater volatility are the stronger countries in the bloc and since November of 1992, Ireland and Portugal. The changes in volatility did not spillover into NA

Table 2: Change Points for Nominal Exchange Rates
(Exchange Rates Are Calculated Against the German Mark, Yen and Dollar for Jan.1933 - Aug.1995)

MO/YR	EU											NIC		NA		
	GR	SD	IT	DK	FR	UK	IR	PO	NE	BE	SP	KO	SI	CA	ME	TO
2-6/93			*	*	*		*	*	*		*		+	*		9
8-10/83			*	+	*	*				*		+		+		7
5/84				+		+							+			3
7-9/85	*			+			+		+	*	*	*	+			8
3-6/86				*	*		*	*	*			*	+			7
12/86												+	*		*	3
6-11/87				*	*	+	+		*			+	*	*	+	9
2-4/88			*				*		*			+	+	*	*	7
5-7/89				+			*					+				3
9/90						+		*				+	+	+	+	6
5/91				+	*	+	+						*			5
7/92	*		*	*	*	+	*	*	*		+	+	*			11
8/92				*	+	+	*	*			+	+	*			8
9/92		*	+							*						2
11-12/92		*		*	*	*	*	+	*			*				7
4-6/93			*	*	*	+	*	+	*	*	+	*	*			11
7-8/93			*	*	*	+	*	*		*	*					8
10-11/93					+	*	*		*							4
12/93				*	+											2
11-12/94			*			+	*								*	3
1-2/95			+	*			+		+							4
3/95							*		*							2
Total	2	2	8	8	12	12	11	13	6	13	9	10	13	8	5	

*significant at 5%, + significant at 10%

countries. The 1992 shift in variance for Canada reflects the political instability due to the referendum that took place at the time[11]. For the case of the Asian countries, spillover effects are seen which reflect the movements of portfolio balances to the area. The impact of the 1992 crises, however, is less significant than in Europe or NA. During 1994 and 1995, overall exchange rate volatility decreased in all blocs. In Europe, however, some shifts of variance took place, especially in the less developed countries within the bloc (Portugal, Spain, and Ireland).

For Korea and Singapore, D_k behaves similarly in its size and timing after 1985. Canada's matches Asia almost every time while not all impacts were transmitted to Mexico, reflecting the isolation of the second country's financial market as well as its exchange rate misalignment. EU shows more changes on unconditional variances than NIC in the 1990s while the reverse holds for the 1980s. NA shows the lowest volatility. As for the countries that suffered the largest number of changes in Europe, they are those that had the stronger currencies or those that are less developed within the bloc. It is not a coincidence, therefore, that Belgium, France, the Netherlands and UK, which have been long supporters of the EMS, show the most number of D_k. Furthermore, the lower significance of the shift in the UK during 1993 reflects the decision of this country, as in the case of Italy, to abandon the ERM at that time. For the two countries of Asia, both shifts are high, reflecting the alignment to Yen that they followed, while for NA there is a clear difference between Canada and Mexico.

Interest rates (Table 3) show low volatility for the EU during the 1990s with the exception of the 1992-1993 crisis. At the time, as previously mentioned, interest rates were used by many countries to defend their currency. Most of the shifts in volatility for the case of Europe reflect domestic monetary policy effects with the exception of the UK (13 change points), whose financial market activity also affected its volatility. During August-September 1993, all countries display significant D_k. Spillover effects were present across blocs. NIC shows higher volatility (12 change points) in the interest rates and in most cases all three countries display them simultaneously. For NAFTA, no clear pattern can be seen until 1991. This was to be expected given that there was no coordinated trade or financial integration until that time. An exception is 1988 when the US shift of variance extended to these and the Asian countries. Thereafter, Mexico and Canada show simultaneous changes in variances. Once again, the effect of the Plaza agreement can be seen in the NIC and NAFTA but not in the EU. The crash of 1987 is also reflected in the exchange rate behavior although the spillover effect into the other blocs was not as strong as in the case of the exchange rate.

Table 3: Change Points for Nominal Interest Rates
(Money Market Interest Rates for January 1983 - August 1995)

MO/YR	EU												NIC			NA			TO
	GR	SD	IT	DK	FR	UK	IR	PO	NE	BE	GE	SP	KO	JA	SI	CA	US	ME	
4/83		*	+								+			*		+			5
6-9 /83			*						+	+		*	*	+	*			+	8
2-5/84					+	*				*		*	*		+	+	+	*	8
9-12/84		+	*		*	+				*			*				*		7
4-5/85						*				*	*	*		+			*	*	7
7-9/85													+	*	*	+			4
2-6/86		*	*			*	*	*			*		*	+	*			*	10
1-2/87						*					*		*		*				4
4-5/87						*							+		*		*	*	5
10-11/87		+				*					+			*		+	*	*	7
2/88									+	*						+			3
9-11/88			*			+							*	*	*	*	*	*	8
4-5/90						+							*		*	*		*	5
2-6/91						*	*						+	*		*		*	6
10-12/91																*		*	2
5-6/92						+				*			*		*	*		*	6
12/92									*	*		*	*					*	5
6-7/93						*	*	*		*	*	*	*				+		8
8-9/93	+	+	+	+	+	+	+	*	+	+	+	+	+	+	+	*	+	+	18
11-12/93				+		+	+	*	+						*		+		7
2 /94						*									*		*		3
11-12/94			*				+										*	+	4
1 /95				+		*									+				3
5/95						*	*								*				3
	1	3	7	2	4	13	9	6	5	8	9	6	13	12	11	12	9	14	

*significant at 5%, + significant at 10%

It has been argued that removing or reducing exchange rate volatility can induce a rise in interest rate volatility and therefore cause an adverse effect in the welfare of consumers[12]. This argument follows from inverting a standard exchange-rate equation and noting that interest rate is the only major variable in the system that fluctuates. The answer to this critique has been that policy credibility reduces speculative attacks on the exchange rates allowing interest rate volatility to be reduced as well.

Results for EU as well as for NIC and NA confirm this last position. Overall, the EU interest rate volatility is significantly lower (eliminating the UK, average change points is 5) than for NIC or NAFTA's (whose averages are 12). It increased, however, as the credibility of the ERM was questioned. At the same time, Korea's interest rate volatility has increased as its alignment with regard to the yen has deteriorated while Singapore, whose exchange rate alignment has been maintained *vis a vis* the yen, closely follows Japanese interest rate volatility. Canada and Mexico, instead, reflect high interest as well as exchange rate volatility as could have been expected given their low degree of financial integration and the lack of credibility prevailing in the Mexican financial market. The history of political and economic instability, which was aggravated by the vents of Chiapas and several assassinations, accentuated the lack of credibility. Finally, D_k for interest rates tend to precede D_k for exchange rates by one to three months suggesting a lag effect between these two variables.

Table 4 shows the results for central banks foreign reserves. EU changes are simultaneous to or have one month lag with exchange rate volatilities of the same country. For the most developed countries, this coincidence also occurs with the volatility of other less developed country members, which suggests intervention to keep the exchange rate of these countries within the bands stipulated so to avoid an exchange crisis to develop. This behavior is also found during the exchange crisis. Whenever the deviations were close to the band, the central bank intervened to bring the exchange rates into the band. After 1993, and with the exception of the stronger currency countries in the EU, the larger exchange rate margins permitted these countries not to use the foreign reserve for this purpose. For the case of NIC, changes in reserves are simultaneous. The Plaza Agreement as well as the Louvre Accord impacts are again reflected by D_k for NIC and NA, as well as for Germany. This was expected due to their heavy interventions in the market to appreciate the yen. This was also the case for the 1987 crash but its effects were heavily felt in Europe as well. Once again, the 1992-1993 crisis displays D_k in all blocs although with some lags within and across blocs.

Table 4: Change Points for Central Bank Foreign Reserves
(Official Foreign Currency and Securities Holdings for Jan.1983 - Aug.1995)

MO/YR	GR	SD	IT	DK	FR	UK	IR	PO	NE	BE	GE	SP	KO	JA	SI	CA	US	ME	TO
					EU								NIC			NA			
5-8/83	+				+		+	•	•		+		+		+	•		+	10
10/83					•		+				+			+				+	5
1-5/84	•	+	+		•	•	+	•	•	+		•		•		+		•	13
1-3/85		•			+		•	+		+			+						6
5/85			•										•	•					3
6-12/85	+				+	•			•	+	+		+	•	•	•	•	+	12
3-6/86	•		•		•	•			•	+	•		•	•	•	+		+	12
9-11/86									+	•						•		•	4
2-9/87	•		•				+	•	•			+	•	•		•	•	•	11
11/87			+		•	•		•	•	•	•	•			•	•		•	11
5-8/88					•						•								2
3/89									•				•	•	•			+	5
7-9/89			•		+					+	•		•	•		•	•	•	9
4-8/90					•				•	+	•			•			•		6
6-9/91	•								+	+	•	+	•		•				7
4-8/92		+			•		•	•	•	•	•	•			•	+		+	11
10-12/92					•		•	+	•	•			•	•	•			+	9
3-6/93					•	•	•		+	•		+	+	•	+	+			10
9/93	+	+	+	+	+	•	•	+	+	•	+	+	+	+	+	+	•	+	18
11-12/93	•			+	•	+			+				+		+				7
2-3/94									+	+								+	3
9-11/94					•				+				+	•					4
5/95					•	•													2
Total	8	4	7	2	17	8	6	9	13	15	13	10	14	13	11	11	5	14	

*significant at 5%, + significant at 10%13

No pattern can be derived from NA except for defensive policy interventions followed independently by each country to align their currencies *vis a vis* the dollar during this time. Overall variance is larger in Asia than in EU and NA. An important difference exists in the source of these variances however. For the NIC, D_k increases in the second part of the 1980s reflecting the large expansion of reserves that all these countries experience as a consequence of their trade surplus. In Europe, the largest number of change points corresponds to the Netherlands, France, Germany and Belgium, reflecting their support of the ERM at the cost of their own reserves. For the case of NA, the reverse case holds. Canada and Mexico show large variations while the US does not. Thus, while in Europe exchange rate alignments within the defined margins have been sustained by central bank reserves, in Asia this has not been required.

Portfolio investment displays higher volatility than direct investment for all countries (Table 5). In the EU, volatility decreased after 1986 to increase again in the third quarter of 1990. The Louvre Accord and the crash of 1987 are exceptions. The shifts in variances on portfolio investment coincides with the shifts in the exchange rates, reflecting the presence of speculative capital. An exception to the high volatility behavioral pattern is shown for Greece. This is due, however, to the capital controls that this country has had. Direct investment, on the other hand displays low numbers of change points. On average and with the exception of Germany, EU D_k has been three. In most cases their significant level is only 10%. The increases of direct investment are found mostly between 1984 and 1987 and after 1990 and they took place in the most developed countries within the region. Portugal, Spain, Ireland and the Netherlands have the lowest quantities of D_k. This reflects low investment in these countries. Between 1984 and 1987, some firms reallocated their investment within Europe so as to consolidate their production in a common market[13].

Japan and Korea show simultaneous and similar size changes in D_k for direct investment until the 90s, when Korea started to invest in other countries of South East Asia. In addition, the simultaneous direct investment changes show opposite direction between Japan and Korea. Portfolio investment shows the same sign, especially after 1988, reflecting financial integration and outside bloc portfolios, as it was the case during the 1992-1993 crises. In both Asian countries, shifts in direct investment almost double those in Europe. This suggests an important difference in the patterns of investments between these two blocs. The less developed country, in this case Korea, shows large direct investment activity. And the developed country, Japan, not only invested within its own country but it

Table 5: Change Points for Portfolio and Direct Investment
(Quarterly Data for I-1983 to IV-1994)

Mo/Yr	GR	SD	IT	DK	FR	UK	IR	PO	NE	GE	SP	KO	JA	CA	US	ME	TO
								EU					NIC		NA		
IV-83					•	+						•				•	4
II-84							•		•			++	••	•	++•	•	5/2
IV-84			++		•		•	•			+	•					5/1
I-85					•++												1/1
II-85				+			+		•				•		+		5
IV-85					•		•				+	+		•	••	•	6/1
II-86		+	•••	+••								+••					4/3
III-86						++	+		++	•				+	••		3/3
I-87		++	••		•	•		•		•••		•••		•	•	•	8/4
II-87						•			•	•							3
IV-87		•	+		•			•	•	•					++	+	7/1
IV-88						•+				••		•	•	•	++		4/3
II-89			•		•	•						••	••	•			4/2
I-90	••				••	++		•		••		•	•				3/4
III-90			+				+		•	•	•	••	•			•	7/1
I-91				++			++						••		+		3/1
II-91	++			••	•	•			•	•			•	••			5/3
IV-91			•		•				•	•		•	•		••		6/1
II-92			•		•					•						•	4
III-92	•	••	•	•			•	++	•		•	•		•			8/2
IV-92		••		•	•	•	+	•	+	+	•		•	•			10/1
I-93			+		++		•		•					+			4/1
II-93			•	•	•	+	•					•	•				7
III-93			+	•	•	+	•	•		++	•	••	•			••	8/3
IV-93	•					+	•										3
I-94					•								•				2
III-94	+					+			••			+••			++	+	4/3
IV-94						+	•				••				••	•	3/2
Total	3/2	2/3	10/3	5/3	9/3	13/2	11/1	10/2	10/2	10/4	7/1	11/7	10/5	9/1	4/8	9/1	

PI=*,** and DI= -,-- significant at 5% and significant at 10% respectively mainly invested in the less developed countries. Finally, for NA, some simultaneous changes of D_k are observed but no real pattern can be derived. The simultaneous shifts, however, can be attributed to favorable conditions in the US financial market that led to inflows of capital from Mexico and Canada. Such was the case during the fourth quarter of 1985 and the first quarter of 1987. As in all previous cases, the 1992 crisis was felt in Canada and the US but not in Mexico. Finally, as in the case of Europe, we find large D_k in portfolio investment and very low D_k (only one change point) in the direct investment of the less developed countries while the US has eight shifts.

Net government borrowing activity for the different blocs shows different patterns across countries (Table 6). The largest activity is found in the NIC countries and this varies between the 1980s and the 1990s. While the shifts between 1986 and 1988 reflect Japanese lending to NIC, the 1990s reflect these countries' lending activities to other less developed ASEAN countries. In the case of Europe, the borrowing increased between 1984-1986 for most countries, reflecting the efforts of monetary discipline and economic convergence before and after 1985. Most of this increased activity, however, is only significant at the 10% level. Since 1990, borrowing activity has increased rapidly, especially during 1992-1993. This reflects a combination of government deficits and exchange stabilization activity. Belgium and Italy show the largest volatility; both countries were heavily affected by the 1992-1993 crises. For NA, no pattern can be derived between countries. This is to be expected since no systematic integration exists between these countries except for trade. The US change points timing, however, suggests borrowing activity during 1985 when the Plaza Agreement was implemented. Also, during 1993, the US increased its borrowing activities. An additional important factor is that the increasing borrowing activity of the 1990s shows a growing portion of short-term financing used for foreign exchange operations.

Finally, Table 7 shows the change points for intra-regional trade. It is not until the third quarter of 1989 that simultaneous changes in D_k are shown across blocs, reflecting the effect of a united Europe as well as the Asian market across blocs. This is supported by the presence of significant D_k across blocs on the second and third quarters of 1992. Less volatility is found during 1983 and 1984 than in later years, when trade integration started in Europe and Asia.

Europe shows the lowest number of D_k that are simultaneous to their exchange rate's D_k. This is to be expected given the ERM. The number of D_k per bloc is similar for NAFTA and NIC. In the case of NAFTA they are contemporaneous with the exchange rate's D_k as is the case for the second quarter

Table 6: Change Points for Net Government Borrowing
(Government Net Borrowing, January 1983 - July 1995)

	EU							NIC		NA		
MO/YR	IT	FR	UK	IR	NE	BE	GE	KO	SI	CA	US	TO
11-83	+							+				2
2-84			+									1
9-84						+						1
4-85					+							1
12-84				+								1
7-85											•	1
11-85	•		•							•	+	4
2-86				•								1
6-86			+	+					•			3
4-87	+											1
8-87								•				1
11-87									•			1
10-88							+	•	•			3
4-89	•											1
7-89		+										1
12-89								•				1
1-90											•	1
4-90							•					1
6-90						•						1
4-91					•							1
11-91									•			1
12-92								•				1
1-2/92	•	•							•			3
4-5/93	•					•	•		•			4
7-9/93					•	•		•			•	4
12-93						•						1
6-94		+										1
11-94								•				1
Total	5	3	3	3	3	5	3	7	6	1	4	

•significant at 5%, + significant at 10%

Table 7: Change Points for Intraregional Trade

(Intraregional Trade, I-1980 to IV-1994)

YEAR	EU	NAFTA	NIC	TOTAL
I-83		+		1
II-83			*	1
IV-83		*		1
II-85			*	1
III-85	+	*	*	3
IV-85			+	1
II-86		*	*	2
IV-86		*		1
IV-87	*			1
I-88		*	*	2
II-89	*	*	*	3
I-90			*	1
III-90	*			1
III-91	*	*	*	3
II-92	*	*	*	3
I-93		*	*	2
III-93		+		1
I-94			+	1
TOTAL	6	11	12	29

of 1986, or they are subsequent to CUSFTA and its implementation as is shown in the third quarter of 1985 and first quarter of 1988. NIC's intra-regional trade D_k also are contemporaneous with the exchange rate's D_k and they reflect the impact of direct investment activity as well. In spite of the effects of appreciation of the yen after the Plaza Agreement, Asian intra-regional trade continued to grow after an initial decrease in the last quarter of 1985 and second quarter of 1986; confirming the relationship between trade, exchange rate volatility, and direct investment. Finally, the effect of the 1992-1993 crisis is reflected on all three intra-trade blocs as well. The institutional arrangements in place in the three blocs were not able to isolate the disturbances that originated in Europe, but they absorbed it.

The combination of simultaneous unconditional variance changes across blocs, with consecutive changes within blocs, seems to confirm as its source both external shocks as well as inherent dynamics in the macroeconomic variables studied for each bloc. Furthermore, external shocks and inherent dynamics within blocs seem to have more effect on the stability and growth of the member countries the higher the degree of integration.

Conclusions

A comparison of the EU, ASEAN and NA has allowed us to derive some lessons from their degree of integration. While the institutional development of these three blocs has some factors in common, it also has marked differences. Europe's institutional development shows a more systematic and deeper level of integration, while Asia has the lowest institutional development but the most effective integration. As in the case of Europe, though, developments in Asia's financial market has been closely related to their economic integration but without a formalized process. Both the EU and the ASEAN integrations have contributed towards real growth within their regions. Yet, Japan's strategic investment behavior has allowed the NIC countries to grow more rapidly than the less developed countries in Europe. This, in turn, has facilitated the maintenance of financial stability within the bloc without losing reserves or increasing their level of indebtedness. On the other hand, NA serves as an example of the consequences for growth when financial integration does not accompany economic integration and investment does not take place in the less developed countries.

The behavior of the interest rate, the exchange rate, foreign reserves, portfolio investment and net borrowing suggests that exchange rate alignments and policy credibility are key for the success of deeper integration like the EU or the successful integration of South East Asia. Financial variables show contemporary changes in variance across blocs, which suggests volatility spillover effects independent of their degree of integration. The effects of this spillover within each bloc member, however, are smaller the less integrated the financial system is. Examples of such an event are the 1987 crash in the U.S. as well as the 1992-1993 exchange rate crisis in Europe.

Computable general equilibrium models have been used to study the effects of integration within and across different blocs[14]. They generally find a positive expansion of intra-regional trade as well as welfare effects[15]. As for the effects across blocs, they find positive or negative results depending on how the model approaches the interplay between trade diversion, capital flows, and changes in the terms of trade.

The solutions for the model suggest that preferential liberalization, without international factor mobility, tends to reduce the volume of trade among blocs, which in turns deteriorates the terms of trade across blocs. When international capital mobility is allowed, the results are the opposite.

Thus, these analyses underline the importance of capital flows in determining the final outcome of an economic integration, results which are consistent with the experience shown by ASEAN versus EU or NA. The determining factor for increasing welfare is the intra-bloc investment. For both NA and EU a more intensive and integrated investment strategy within their blocs are advisable. They have reached a state in which they need a more active involvement of intra-bloc capital and technology transfer to stimulate growth.

Endnotes

1 Some good reviews of the research undertaken are Giavazzi *et al* (1988), Branson *et al* (1990), Barfield and Perlman (1991), Lustig *et al* (1992). On a more theoretical level see Young (1991), Rivera Batiz and Romer (1991), Bachus and Kehoe (1992). For data analysis, see Yannopoulos (1990), Obsfield (1992), Mussa (1993), Ibarra (1995), and Obstfeld and Rogoff (1995) .

2 It may be argued that decreases in volatility do not necessarily correspond to welfare improvements, but to the reduction of misalignment in the exchange rate. Yet, empirical evidence exists suggesting that exchange-rate volatility causes trade-reduction. See Akhtar and Hilton (1984), Cushman (1986). This paper supports this position and adds to the intra-trade reduction-argument a negative cross-bloc spillover effect.

3 For a more detailed analysis of these events see Mussa (1993), Rose and Svensson (1994), and Obstfeld and Rogoff(1995).

4 On September 16, 1992, Sweden Central Bank (Sveriges Riksbank) raised its marginal overnight lending rate to 500% and the Bank of London increased the base lending rate twice, from 10% to 12% and then, to 15%. The LIBOR increased from 10.4% to 28.9% during the same period. Similarly, the Banco D'Italia during the 1994 speculative attack, raised the discount rate by 50 basis points. In all cases, the interest rate was used as a monetary policy tool against the speculative attack of their currency.

5 As of December 1995, government gross debt as percentage of GDP in the EU country members ranged from the lowest of 53.4% in the United Kingdom to the highest of 138.3% in Belgium. The average value for the whole EU was 79.9%. The same average in 1990 was 58%.

6 See Branson *et al* (1990).

7 Differences among the countries' production are pronounced, however. South Korea exports mainly finished products, while Taiwan has specialized in the production of components for computers and consumer electronics. Singapore exports finished electronic goods produced by foreign multinationals. For a more detailed study of trade components within the NIC, see Ahearn and Dibble (1992) and Ostry (1992).

8 Ostry 1992, p.261.

9 During 1994, intra-regional trade increased by 9.2% most of which (7%) corresponds to an increase of US exports to Canada and Mexico.

10 Inclan, 1993.

11 Mussa (1993) argues that the Canadian exchange rate crisis that developed in October 1992 was independent of the EU crisis and that had no effects elsewhere. Political uncertainties in fact were present at the time due to the constitutional referendum scheduled for October 26. It could also be argued that the Canadian case was a combination of both, internal as well as external factors. Expectations of EU members' currency devaluations, could had reinforced the political uncertainty that developed at the time.

12 See Artis and Taylor (1988) for a more detailed study of this argument.

13 Yannapoulos (1990) analyses the dynamics of direct investment during this time.

14 For a review of some computable general equilibrium models undertaken see Weintraub (1992).

15 These welfare effects tend to be larger in models that adopt increasing returns to scale than in those based on constant returns to scale.

References

Ahearn, R. and Dibble, A. "The Role of the Asian NICs in the 1990s," in C. Barfield. and M.. Perlman, eds., *Capital Markets and Trade: the United States Faces a United Europe*, AEI Press, Washington, D.C, 1991.

Akhtar, M. and Hilton, R.S. "Exchange Rate Uncertainty and International Trade: Some Conceptual Issues and New Estimates for Germany and the United States." *Federal Reserve Bank of New York Research Paper,* n. 8403, 1984.

Artis, M. and Taylor, M. "Exchange Rates, Interest Rates, Capital Controls and the European Monetary System: Assessing the Track Record," in F. Giavazzi and M. Miller, eds., *The European Monetary System*, Cambridge University Press, Cambridge, 1988.

Backus, D. and Kehoe, P. "Trade and Exchange Rates in a Dynamic Competitive Economy." *Federal Reserve bank of Minneapolis Working Paper*, n. 348, 1992.

Barfield,C. and Perlman, M. *Capital Markets and Trade: the United States Faces a United Europe*, AEI Press, Washington, D.C.,1991.
Branson, W.; Frankel J. and Goldestein, M. eds. *International Policy Coordination and Exchange Rate Fluctuations*, Chicago: University of Chicago Press, 1990.

Cushman, D. "Has Exchange Risk Depressed International Trade? The Imapct of Third Country Exchange Risk." *Journal of International Economics*, 1986, vol. 18, pp. 47-66.

Garber, Peter and Spencer, Micheal. "Foreign Exchange Hedging and the Interest Rate Defense." *IMF Staff Papers*, 1995, vol. 42, pp. 491-515.

Giavazzi, F. and Miller, M. *The European Monetary System*, Cambridge University Press, Cambridge, 1988.

Inclan, Carla. Use of Cumulative Sums of Square for Restrospective Detection of Changes of Variance. Preceedings of American Statistical Association Conference, 1993.

Lustig, N., B. Bosworth and Lawrence, R., eds., *North America Free Trade: Assessing the Impact*. The Brookings Institute, Washington, D.C, 1992.

Mussa, Michael. "A Note on Macroeconomic Causes of Recent Exchange Market Turbulence." Working Paper, Research Department., International Monetary Found, 1993.

Obsfield, Maurice. "The Effectiveness of Foreign-Exchange Intervention: Recent Experience, 1985-1988," in Frankel Branson and Goldstein, eds., *International Policy Coordination and Exchange Rate Fluctuations,* NBER, Washington D.C, 1990.

Obsfield, Maurice and Rogoff, Kenneth. "The Mirage of Fixed Exchange Rates", *Journal of Economic Perspectives,* Fall 1995, vol. 9, pp. 73-96.

Ostry, Sylvia. "Discussion," in N. Lustig, B. Bosworth, and R. Lawrence, eds., *North America Free Trade: Assessing the Impact,*The Brookings Institute, Washington D.C., 1992.

Rose, Andrew and Svenson, Lars E. O. "European Exchange Credibility Before the Fall." *European Economic Review,* June 1994, vol. 38, pp. 1185-216.

Rivera Batiz, L. and Romer, P. "Economic Integration and Endogenous Growth." *The Quarterly Journal of Economics*, May 1991.

Weintraub, Sidney. "Modeling the Industrial Effects of NAFTA," in N. Lustig, B. Bosworth, and R. Lawrence, eds., *North America Free Trade: Assessing the Impact*, The Brookings Institute, Washington, D.C, 1992.

Yannopoulos, George. "Foreign Direct Investment and European Integration: The Evidence from the Formative Years of the European Community." *Journal of Common Market Studies,* 1990, vol. 28, pp. 235-259.

Young, Alwyn. "Learning by Doing and the Dynamic Effect of International Trade." *Quarterly Journal of Economics,* 1991, vol. 106, pp. 369-405.

6

SPECULATION-LED DEVELOPMENT IN THE THIRD WORLD[1]

Ilene Grabel

Graduate School of International Studies, University of Denver, USA

This chapter presents a post-Keynesian interpretation of the consequences of financial liberalization (FL) programs in less developed countries (LDCs). It is argued that FL can lead to a particular kind of development, "speculation-led economic development," which is characterized by a preponderance of risky investment practices and shaky financial structures. In addition, FL is likely to induce an increase in directly unproductive profit-seeking activities, a greater likelihood of financial crises, a misallocation of credit and, ultimately, diminished rates of real sector economic growth. Given the likelihood of these outcomes (as well as their realization in LDCs that have implemented FL), FL programs are argued to be a poor foundation for stable and sustained real-sector economic growth, especially in the context of resource-scarce LDCs.

Many Latin American and Asian-Pacific countries initiated abrupt and comprehensive financial deregulation programs in the 1970s and 1980s. These "financial liberalization" (FL) programs were undertaken as part of broader liberalization strategies in less developed countries (LDCs). By all accounts these experiments failed, especially in the Southern Cone of South America and in the Philippines. They were widely associated with low levels of productive investment, savings and economic growth, a flourishing of speculative activities, dramatic increases in nonperforming bank loans, and financial crises necessitating government bailouts of failed financial institutions.

The striking similarity of experience across many countries suggests the need for a unified theoretical explanation of the likely effects of FL, one that can account for these stylized facts. An adequate understanding is also necessitated by the current trend toward liberalization in the former socialist countries (FSCs), and by the continuing sway that FL has today over economic advisers and policymakers in LDCs.

The disappointing FL record provoked a reconsideration, among neoclassical economists, of the manner in which the earliest FL experiments had been undertaken. McKinnon (1988, 1991), a pioneer of neoclassical FL theory, has recently begun to reinterpret the disappointing outcomes of the Southern Cone FL experiments through the lens of new-Keynesian theory. In a similar vein, Balassa (1990-1), Galbis (1993), and Kapur (1992) emphasize the need to continue *temporarily* some financial regulations in order to resolve the problems of moral hazard and adverse selection, and the need to institute a healthy macroeconomic environment as preconditions of *eventual, successful FL*. But despite the twenty year maturation of neoclassical FL theory, the essential policy implication that derives from the original work of McKinnon (1973) and Shaw (1973) remain intact. Neoclassicals continue to argue that a properly implemented FL program will induce a virtuous cycle of increased savings, investment, and economic growth, and eliminate opportunities for what Bhagwati (1982) terms "directly unproductive profit-seeking" (DUP) activities endemic to government regulation.

In this chapter I will argue that the incorporation of new-Keynesian insights into neoclassical theory fails to salvage the case for FL, particularly because it provides an unsatisfactory framework for understanding the FL experiences of LDCs. As a consequence, it also fails to shed light on the likely outcomes of future FL programs in LDCs or in FSCs.

To date the most sophisticated critique of FL has emerged within structuralist theory. While neoclassicals contend that FL is *growth-promoting*, structuralists argue that FL in LDCs is *growth-impeding* because it induces adverse macroeconomic effects (such as stagflation) and a reduction in the supply of loanable funds (see Taylor, 1991). The post-Keynesian interpretation advanced here argues that FL is ultimately *growth-distorting* despite variations in specification, implementation, and timing. This is because FL promotes new opportunities for DUP activities and thereby misallocates credit toward speculative activities, with destabilizing macroeconomic effects. In short, FL is likely to induce what will be called "speculation-led economic development" characterized by a preponderance of risky investment practices, shaky financial structures, and ultimately by lower rates of real-sector growth than would otherwise prevail.

The alternative perspective presented here incorporates the new-Keynesian concepts of adverse selection and credit rationing into a thoroughly post-Keynesian theoretical framework.[2] It will be argued that this perspective is better able to account for the actual experiences of LDCs with FL, and may also provide a basis for evaluating the likely consequences of nascent FL programs.

The conclusions of the post-Keynesian interpretation of FL are contrasted with those of neoclassical and structuralist theories of FL in table 1.

The argument advanced here is sufficiently general as to be of relevance to FL in developed countries (DCs) and in FSCs. It is my aim, however, to argue that in the context of resource-scarce LDCs, speculation-led development is a particularly poor foundation for sustained and stable long-term economic growth.

Table 1. Neoclassical, structuralist, and post-Keynesian interpretations of the effects of financial liberalization in LDCs.

Neoclassical Perspective
A properly specified, implemented, and timed FL program: *(1) induces a virtuous cycle of increased savings, investment, and economic growth; (2) eliminates opportunities for directly unproductive profit-seeking behaviors endemic to government regulation; and (3) is growth-promoting.*
Structuralist Perspective
Regardless of specification, implementation, and timing, a program of FL: (1) induces a vicious cycle of stagflation; (2) reduces the availability of loanable funds; and (3) is growth-impeding.
Post-Keynesian Perspective   ("Speculation-led Economic Development")
Regardless of specification, implementation, and timing, a program of FL: (1) induces risky investment practices, shaky financial structures, and ultimately lower rates of real-sector growth than would prevail in the absence of liberalization; (2) introduces new opportunities for directly unproductive profit-seeking activities; and (3) is growth-distorting.

Recently Keynesian and Kaleckian-inspired interpretations of FL experiences in LDCs have emerged (Akyuz, 1991; Burkett and Dutt, 1991; Dutt, 1990-1). These accounts acknowledge that unproductive activities may be fueled by FL (Dutt, 1990-1:229-30). But this insight is under-exploited, as the focus of this work is on the real sector effective demand and distributional problems that may attend FL. While these real sector problems are no doubt important, this work does not address the central financial concerns raised here. Hence, this paper is intended to complement earlier Keynesian- and Kaleckian-inspired treatments of FL.

The chapter is organized as follows. The following section reviews briefly the key components of the analytical framework and discusses the methodological issues involved in drawing new-Keynesian insights into a post-Keynesian framework. The third section puts forth a post-Keynesian interpretation of the consequences of FL in LDCs. To the extent possible, the empirical relevance of this framework to the experiences of LDCs will be discussed. The paper concludes with a discussion of the implications of this work for FL theory and policy in LDCs and FSCs.

Theoretical Foundations of Speculation-led Development

This analysis relies on the post-Keynesian theory of endogenous expectations formation and the related theory of financial fragility. In addition, the new-Keynesian concepts of adverse selection and credit rationing are appropriated into a post-Keynesian framework. These Keynesian-inspired literatures have been developed to analyze the operation of financial markets in DCs. To date, the insights of these Keynesian literatures have not been thoroughly absorbed into the financial development literature; nor have models of FL been articulated that incorporate these insights into a post-Keynesian framework.

Endogenous Expectations Formation and Financial Fragility

Post-Keynesian theory highlights the endogeneity of expectations on the demand- and supply-sides of financial markets.[3] Endogeneity of expectations stems from the inherent fundamental uncertainty regarding the present and future expected-return/risk profiles of investment projects. Rational agents are influenced by conventional wisdom in their decision-making. But conventional wisdom is not static. Over the course of the business cycle, for example, agents' evaluations of what constitutes reasonable investments change, and these changes may be mutually validated by market participants. The pressure to join in a speculative frenzy may stem from agents' evolving boom-euphoric expectations and/or competitive pressures to engage in profit-seeking activities. The combined effects of "expectations-induced" and "competition-coerced" (Crotty, 1993) pressures mean that agents on both sides of the financial market may be drawn to participate in and abet high-risk investment activities. This adventurism, moreover, is likely to be self-propelling (Keynes, 1936; Minsky, 1986:238).

A concrete manifestation of these expectations-induced and competition-coerced market dynamics is what Minsky (1986) identifies as the tendency for financing patterns to become more precarious over the course of the business cycle. As a boom unfolds, agents may move toward "speculative financing," the short-term financing of long-term investment projects. This pattern of financing makes agents vulnerable, as the viability of projects depends on favorable short-term interest rates. Hence, the financial system becomes increasingly fragile.

Adverse Selection and Credit Rationing

The informational assumptions of new-Keynesian theory are quite different from those of post-Keynesian theory. In the post-Keynesian view, fundamental uncertainty prevails on the demand- and supply-sides of financial markets. For new-Keynesians, uncertainty is asymmetric in that it prevails only on the supply-side. Borrowers are assumed to have perfect knowledge of the expected-return/risk profiles of their projects. But knowledge of the profile of individual borrowers is not available to lenders. Instead, lenders are assumed to have knowledge of the true probability distribution of risk/return for all borrowers as a group. With this limited knowledge, lenders are able to compute a functional relationship between the loan rate of interest and expected return, taking into account the probability of default.

The asymmetry of information is particularly problematic when interest rates are high. Investment projects for which expected returns (and risk levels) are low are not viable at high borrowing costs, leaving only those projects that have higher expected returns and high- and low-risk profiles. Thus, under conditions of high interest rates, lenders confront a deterioration in the *average* "quality" of loan applicants, when measured by the risk profile of their investment projects. In the absence of information that would enable lenders to distinguish between borrowers with lower- and higher-risk projects, lenders must choose randomly (or, in the presumed case of market clearing, meet all demand emanating) from this "adverse" pool of borrowers. This is known as "adverse selection" (Akerlof, 1970). Implicit in this approach is the assumption that lenders cannot enforce prudent behavior upon borrowers. The information problem discussed here has particular force in LDCs because of the combined effects of lender inexperience and the underdevelopment of financial markets and associated technologies (Stiglitz, 1989).

In recognition of the adverse selection problem, lenders are assumed to ration credit. By restricting interest rate increases, lenders attempt to prevent the deterioration in the quality of the borrowing pool. Credit rationing is posited as a rational response by risk-neutral lenders to asymmetric information and enforcement problems. The *static* new-Keynesian credit rationing argument is presented in figure 1.

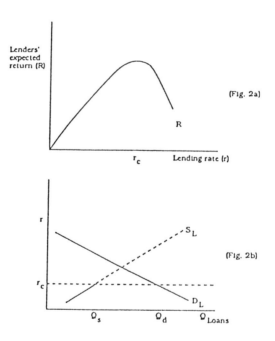

Figure 1. New-Keynesian (static) credit rationing.

Figure 1a presents the loan interest rate/expected return relation in which the expected return on loans falls as the interest rises beyond some critical interest rate, r_c, due to the deterioration in the average quality of the borrower pool. Figure 1b shows that there is an excess demand for loanable funds at the (quoted) market interest rate.[4]

Methodological Concerns

The idea of speculation-led economic development that is developed in the next section appropriates the new-Keynesian concepts of adverse selection and credit rationing into a post-Keynesian model. But it may be argued that post- and new-Keynesianism are incompatible. These paradigms have been elaborated separately--and are characterized by different informational assumptions and dynamics--despite their common origins in Keynes' work. Is this appropriation therefore legitimate? If so, what is to be gained by it?[5]

On its own, post-Keynesian theory is valuable for its focus on endogenous expectations formation in a dynamic setting that evolves over real time, its ability to handle historical and institutional specificity, and its consideration of the incentive and reward structures that motivate agents. These insights allow us to explain why certain types of investment projects flourish and are validated in some historical moments rather than others. Here, they will guide the effort to specify how economic activity might change in the wake of FL.

The post-Keynesian approach may nevertheless be enriched by the incorporation of new-Keynesian insights regarding the relationship between the quality of the borrower pool (and the likelihood of default) and the price of credit. This relationship is consistent with a post-Keynesian framework as long as it is understood that it is *not stable*, and that lenders do not have true knowledge of it, even in a probabilistic sense.[6] Instead, lenders' assessment of the relationship between current interest rates and *future* default rates is founded upon conventions and best guesses, which change with changing sentiments. Moreover, we must recognize that the actions of lenders actually *alters* the functional relationship between loan rates and default rates: the tightening of credit at critical junctures may reduce economic activity and profit rates, and thereby undermine the financial solvency of borrowers.

What will be called here "dynamic credit rationing" provides a microfoundation for the likely response of lenders to the problems associated with lending at high interest rates, one that is not only consistent with post-Keynesian theory, but which contributes to a sharper specification of the demand and supply sides of the credit market. Critically, this incorporation preserves post-Keynesian theory's dynamism, its historical and institutional insights, and its focus on decision-making under conditions of fundamental uncertainty.

Speculation-led Development

The FL programs implemented in LDCs have had three main components[7]: an increase in real deposit and loan interest rates to their free market level; the deregulation of existing financial institutions, and especially the dismantling of channels of governmental influence over credit allocation; and the creation of new types of privately-owned financial institutions, instruments, and markets.[8] These changes may have important demand- and supply-side effects. For clarity of exposition, we will consider these related effects in turn.

Demand-side Effects

The regulatory and institutional changes wrought by FL are likely to effect three reinforcing developments on the demand-side of financial markets: 1) higher loan interest rates attract an adverse class of borrowers; 2) institutional innovations generate new opportunities for short-term, speculative practices, which will be exploited by a broad class of investors; and 3) the interest rate spread is likely to increase, biasing investment toward short-term speculative activities.

High Interest Rates.   Drawing on new-Keynesian theory, it can be seen that the high cost of borrowing, coupled with the institutional changes attending FL, may affect the composition (and volume) of investment projects undertaken.For simplicity, and as a first approximation, we assume that investment projects may be broadly classed as having three possible risk/expected-return profiles: low expected-return/low-risk (type A), high expected-return/low-risk (type B), high expected-return/high-risk (type C). This typology of investment projects is presented in table 2.[9]

Table 2. Typology of investment projects, pre-financial liberalization.

		RISK	
		Low	High
EXPECTED	*Low*	*Type A Projects*	...
RETURN	*High*	*Type B Projects*	*Type C Projects*

An important change in the composition of projects occurs with FL and the concomitant increase in interest rates. High borrowing costs will discourage all but type B and C projects. In other words, type A or "prudent" projects are no longer viable at high loan rates (given their low expected return). The types of projects viable under FL are represented in table 3.

Table 3. Typology of investment projects, post-financial liberalization.

		RISK	
		Low	High
EXPECTED	*Low*	...	...
RETURN	*High*	*Type B Projects*	*Type C Projects*

Given the changes in the composition of investment projects that remain viable under high interest rates, lenders are faced with a deterioration in the average quality of the borrower pool. This result is not dependent upon assumptions regarding asymmetric information, but rather is an outcome of changes in the cost of loanable funds. This adverse pool of projects might include various forms of speculative activities such as leveraged buyouts of industrial enterprises and secondary and tertiary financial investments, and generally what Minsky (1986) might refer to as Ponzi finance schemes. Hence, the likelihood that lenders fund type C projects increases following FL. Indeed, this deterioration in the quality of the borrower pool obtained widely following Southern Cone and Asian FL (e.g., Diaz-Alejandro, 1985; Urrutia, 1988).

In the new-Keynesian view, credit rationing would be expected to emerge in this context. However, a post-Keynesian interpretation of credit rationing allows us to see that lenders either might not ration credit or they might decrease the *degree* of rationing as their expectations evolve endogenously in the context of a speculative boom (see supply-side dynamics below).

Institutional Innovations and Speculation.   Modern financial markets are especially prone to speculation (see Carter, 1991-2). Investors are encouraged to part with capital by virtue of the security provided by liquidity (Keynes, 1936). Financial instruments afford the apparent protection of instantaneous withdrawal of funds by transforming illiquid real sector investments into highly liquid financial claims. Liquidity allows each investor to shuffle ownership among competing assets (or "churn") in response to changes in moods, rumors, etc., or to flee to cash in the event of trouble.

Liquidity also amplifies the tendency for changes in valuations in financial markets. Rewards from trading can be immediate and large. The successful investor can realize substantial gains by anticipating future sentiments of other market participants. The proliferation of financial instruments expands these opportunities by multiplying the possibilities for the churning of assets. Every change of sentiment creates opportunities to outguess the market, to buy the favored instrument the day before others reshuffle their assets.

A corollary of these opportunities is the diminution of the duration of financial "commitments." The relative independence of financial asset values from underlying "fundamentals" imparts extreme price variability. The successful financial investor need be little concerned with the long-term profitability of the firms whose equities she/he trades (especially to the degree that new assets appear that bundle equities of diverse corporations, that anticipate future events, etc.) (Keynes, 1936:ch.12).

But these same attributes also ensure that market participants will be driven to shorten their time horizons for defensive purposes. The forces that reward the player who anticipates market behavior penalizes severely the investor who lags behind. The laggard is forcibly reminded that the apparent security which liquidity provides for any individual investor evaporates in the context of a general flight. The net effect may be to punish the investor who takes a long-term view.

With these attributes of financial markets in mind, it is apparent that the flowering of instruments and institutions that accompany the "regime shift" to FL *expands* type C opportunities. The financial deepening that attends FL expands these opportunities by creating instruments that transform ownership of claims on illiquid real assets into extremely liquid positions, and by installing institutions that facilitate trading. FL therefore amplifies the pressure to speculate as the opposite side of the coin that expands the opportunity to do so.[10]

The dramatic changes heralded by FL, moreover, represent a regime shift of the sort likely to be associated with ruptures in the structure of conventional wisdom regarding investment risk.[11]   Under such circumstances, market participants look out on an as yet unlived "new era" which promises greater reward and lower risk. Thus, a more sanguine evaluation of type C projects may be expectations-induced. In this manner, type C projects can come to play a more important role in overall economic activity.

Combined with this expectations-induced shift, there is likely to be an element of competition-coerced profit-seeking among financial and erstwhile non-financial corporations. Both types of firms, ranging (for example) from insurance to manufacturing enterprises, may feel compelled to chase the higher returns available through financial speculation, and they may come to divert resources from their primary activities to the financial arena. Such practices may be seen by corporate managers as a substitute for the corporation's traditional economic activity, or as a means to enhance the firm's financial position to further its competitive position within its traditional sector.   In either event, a critical manifestation of the new mood among market participants is increasing borrowing to finance short-term financial speculation. The net effect of these demand-side changes is a preponderance of type C activities. This has been a universally noted phenomenon in the Southern Cone, Philippine, Indonesian, Malaysian and Turkish FL experiments (Sundararajan and Balino, 1991; Cho and Khatkhate, 1989; Rittenberg, 1990). It has been reflected in run-ups in stock and real estate prices and the expansion of Ponzi and secondary and tertiary activities following FL.

Increasing Interest Rate Spread.   The typology of investment projects developed previously (see table 3) warrants further attention. We can now distinguish between those projects with long-term horizons and low liquidity, and those with short-term horizons and high liquidity. This, of course, separates real sector investment in plant and equipment (by non-financial firms) from financial sector investment (by financial or non-financial firms or individuals) in the context of liquid financial markets.[12]   While financial investments are not always independent of real sector investments, the latter tend to be less liquid and have longer gestation periods. To the degree that the financial sector is more prone to speculation and asset price fluctuations (for the reasons explored above), this typology correlates with the former: type B projects have long-term and type C projects have short-term horizons (see table 4).

We have heretofore treated summarily the interest rate effect of FL. It remains to investigate this issue. In the wake of FL there are two mutually reinforcing factors that increase both the *spread* between long and short-term lending rates, and the mean lending rate.[13] First, as speculative activity increases relative to total economic activity, there is likely to be a consequent increase in

Table 4. Typology of investment projects (with time horizons), post-financial liberalization.

		RISK	
		Low	*High*
EXPECTED	*Low*	...	...
RETURN	*High*	*Type B Projects (long time horizon)*	*Type C Projects (short time horizon)*

asset price volatility (see Grabel, 1995). Under these circumstances, banks may be expected to value less securely the assets put up as collateral by prospective borrowers. Hence, *ceteris paribus*, banks will be expected to exact a higher risk premium in the form of higher interest rates, especially in the case of long-term debt. Non-financial corporations that seek long-term financing directly through the issuance of bonds are also likely to pay this risk premium, as purchasers demand protection from increased volatility.

Second, in the course of a euphoric boom, bankers may be expected to develop a preference for short-term lending so that they will recoup the funds quickly in order to be able to take advantage of the new opportunities available in the immediate future. Short-term lending also provides better protection against the cost effects of future increases in the market deposit interest rate that follow from increased competition for funds. Hence, the spread is likely to rise following FL.

To the extent that limited medium and longer term credit existed prior to FL, there is some evidence that its real cost rose more rapidly than that of short-term credit (Urrutia, 1988; Cho and Khatkhate, 1989). This may have reflected an increasing risk premium on long-term lending coupled with lender preference for short-term lending (Federer, 1993). But insofar as most long-term credit was subsidized and allocated by the government prior to FL, it is difficult to assess empirically the precise degree to which changes in expectations and risk premia, rather than the decrease in government lending, accounts for this change.

An increasing spread benefits type C projects at the expense of type B. Type C borrowing is less long-term interest rate elastic than type B borrowing, as a consequence of the shorter time horizon involved. Non-financial firms will find it increasingly expensive to secure financing for capital formation; they might be expected to respond by cutting back on the demand for credit altogether or shifting their use of borrowed funds to type C activities. Alternatively, such firms might be induced by the rising spread (or, to the degree that it occurs, by credit rationing in this market) to seek funds in the short-term market to finance long-term investment projects (Minsky, 1986). But this increases the susceptibility of real-sector investment to interest rate shocks, exposing it to increasing risk. Type B projects are thereby transformed into type Cs, inducing increasing real-sector fragility. Together, these changes suggest that there are strong demand-side forces inducing development to become what I call "speculation-led."[14]

Supply-side Effects

The supply-side effects remain to be specified. Why would lenders choose to validate the "animal spirits" of this adverse class of borrowers in the context of a regime shift to FL? Three reasons will be offered here separately; these will then be drawn together in a dynamic argument.

Conventional Wisdom and the Critical Interest Rate.   Once one adopts a post-Keynesian approach to new-Keynesian credit rationing it is evident that the degree of lenders' credit rationing may change endogenously as conventional wisdom and institutional structures evolve. Credit rationing is then an historically dynamic process.[15]

Given the combined effects of expectations-induced changes in lending practices and the availability of new instruments fostered by FL, there is likely to be an upward adjustment in the critical interest rate (potentially causing a decrease in the *degree of credit rationing*) following FL. In the context of boom-euphoric expectations, lenders are likely to increase the (critical) interest rate at which they expect loan returns to fall because of increasing defaults. This buoyancy in lenders' expectations during the FL experiments has been widely noted (Diaz-Alejandro, 1985; Cho and Khatkhate, 1989).[16] This dynamic view of lenders' credit rationing is represented in figure 2.

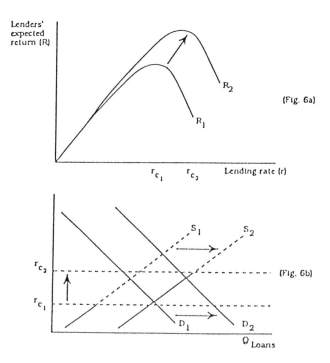

Figure 2. Dynamic credit rationing following liberalization.

As figure 2a shows, lenders' expected return/interest rate relation shifts as expectations evolve endogenously and the institutional climate changes. Figure 2b depicts the supply of and demand for credit, which also shift as expectations of lenders and borrowers evolve. R_1 represents the interest rate/expected return curve that obtains in "normal times." Note that even in normal times there may be some excess demand for credit because asymmetric information might inhibit some lending by risk neutral lenders. R_2 depicts a boom, such as that which may be fostered by FL. Here lenders have substantially increased the critical interest rate. Moreover, the supply of and demand for credit increases as lenders and borrowers seek to exploit perceived profit opportunities. Under these circumstances the likelihood that credit will be rationed is diminished.

Competition-coerced Lending.   Combined with the expectations-induced changes in credit rationing behavior discussed above, the competitive pressures unleashed by deregulation serve to dampen credit rationing (Keynes, 1936; Minksy, 1986). A financial institution that does not validate the new speculative activities in the context of a boom may face slower growth of its capital base and a loss of market share. Financial institutions are compelled to finance investment projects and to reduce their reserve margins in ways that might be unacceptable in a less competitive climate. In this context, even formerly prudent financial institutions may be impelled toward speculative financing. These institutions may also be driven to abandon financing of real-sector activities.[17]

Internal Incentive Structures and Risk.   These market pressures are reflected *internally* in firms in what Crotty (1994) terms the "asymmetric reward structure." In the context of financial institutions, the asymmetric reward structure means that lenders/money managers are "rewarded" for riding speculative waves and indeed are compelled to engage in these activities in order to cement their institutional positions. Additionally, government bailouts of failed financial institutions may provide an additional incentive for adventurism by lenders (and borrowers) during the boom.

A Post-Keynesian Interpretation of FL

The regime shift to FL is likely to effect important changes on the demand- and supply-sides of the economy. On the demand-side, the risk profile of the projects presented for financing increases due to adverse selection and enforcement problems (which are exacerbated by lending under high interest rates). Compounding this deterioration of the borrower pool is the increasing institutional opportunities for type C projects, coupled with the expectations-induced and competition-coerced motivations for pursuing them. Additionally, the increasing interest rate spread, a consequence of the increasing asset price volatility and the concomitant decline in the security of collateral, may discourage type B projects (which are relatively elastic with respect to long-term interest rates) or transform them into type C projects through changes in financing patterns.

At the same time, supply-side changes combine to compel lenders to validate and encourage the adverse class of investment projects likely to flourish following FL. Specifically, the shift in conventional wisdom regarding lending practices, boom-euphoric expectations, and the increasingly competitive climate of the financial sector combine to reduce the degree of credit rationing following FL. Moreover, the tendency for type C projects to dominate type B projects will be exacerbated and reinforced by the asymmetric reward structure internal to lending institutions. In the context of FL, then, the economy's aggregate risk profile increases and speculative projects come to dominate other types of projects. This is consistent with the stylized facts of LDCs' FL experiences in the 1970s and 1980s.

Note that when the speculative bubble collapses (figure 2), borrowers may witness a reduction in the critical interest rate, with the effect of sudden credit rationing. In this situation, the critical interest rate falls and loanable funds begin to dry up, reflecting lenders' increased conservatism. If the decline in the supply of credit precedes the decline in the demand for credit, lender pessimism will increase the chances that credit will be rationed at precisely that point when it is most needed by distressed borrowers in order to avert collapse.[18] This effect on credit supply has been documented in the case of the failed LDC experiments (Urrutia, 1988; Cho and Khatkhate, 1989).

Consequences of Speculation-led Economic Development

Speculation-led development may have several consequences. *First*, the economy suffers rising ambient risk levels as a result of the preponderance of type C projects (DeLong et al., 1989:681; Snowden, 1987). This makes the returns on all assets riskier, and thus reduces the volume of investment (Federer, 1993). Increasing ambient risk levels may have accounted for the decline in overall investment following FL in many LDCs.

Second, the economy becomes more susceptible to financial crises, with spillover effects in the real sector (cf. DeLong et al., 1989:687). A variety of "surprise" macroeconomic events can threaten fragile financial structures, inducing bank distress and loan defaults (Wolfson, 1986, 1990). Profit expectations may deteriorate and banks may reduce lending, inaugurating a "credit crunch." Hence, the real sector may pay a high price for FL (Minsky, 1986). The bank collapses and lending cutbacks that marked the end of several FL experiments may be a case in point (Sundararajan and Balino, 1991).

Third, the economy is forced to bear an increase in DUP activity. Even if speculation is privately profitable and price stabilizing, it may be detrimental (Kemp and Sinn, 1990). If the social costs of speculation outweigh the private gains, then these activities may be DUPs since they do not directly increase the flow of new goods and services in the short run.[19] Contrary to neoclassical political economy, removing the government from financial markets *may induce new DUPs as private sector agents expend resources in seeking out profitable opportunities for speculative trading*. Indeed, a rise in the proportion of DUP to non-DUP activity has been widely noted in wake of FL (Diaz-Alejandro, 1985; Cho and Khatkhate, 1989).

Fourth, FL discourages low-risk, low-expected return investments with long time horizons. High borrowing costs discourage type A projects, while the pressures and rewards brought to bear on the market undermine type B investments. Coupled with this relative increase in type C investments, there may be an absolute increase in these projects. Thus, credit may be misallocated to the detriment of economic growth. Indeed, it is widely recognized that credit was directed away from long-term real sector projects following FL.

Implications for Financial Liberalization Theory and Policy

FL may very well distort the character of economic development and fail to provide the conditions for stable and sustained real sector development. FL programs should therefore not be part of LDC or FSC strategy.

But are the adverse effects of FL described here inevitable? Certainly, institutions that allocate credit to industrial investment through non-market channels could insulate firms and/or sectors from increased financial volatility and instability.[20] The performance of the Japanese *keiretsu* over the past decade is instructive in this regard. Paradoxically, such extra-market institutional relations may be thought of as the private sector analogue of the public sector regime that the FL prescription is designed to eliminate. It may be that this arrangement--of liberalized finance coupled with extra-market private investment institutions--is therefore practically incompatible and ultimately unsustainable.

The critique of FL developed here does not in and of itself call forth a particular alternative regime. It does not follow, for example, that the only option available is a return to the previous regime of "financial repression." Rather, the regulatory options available to financial policymakers are vast and nuanced. The challenge ahead is to discover and explore alternative regulatory regimes which are compatible with broader developmental and social objectives in LDCs and FSCs alike.

Endnotes

1 This is a shortened and revised version of the author's "Speculation-led Economic Development: A Post-Keynesian Interpretation of Financial Liberalization Programmes in the Third World," which originally appeared in the *International Review of Applied Economics* 9(2) (1995):127-49. The author is especially indebted to James Crotty, Gerald Epstein and J. Mohan Rao for their comments on earlier versions of this paper. The author also wishes to thank an anonymous referee, Paul Burkett, George DeMartino, Gary Dymski, Don Goldstein, David Levine, Eric Nilsson, Bob Pollin, Ellen Tierney, Howard Wachtel, and participants in the GSIS faculty seminar for their comments. Jeff Judge provided excellent research assistance.

2 The methodological issues raised are addressed below.

3 These insights are developed in Keynes (1936) and Minsky (1986). See also Crotty (1994) and Davidson (1991).

4 Stiglitz (1987) uses a backward bending supply curve for loans. This approach is not followed here because lenders do not supply credit at interest rates beyond r_e. Hence in the credit rationing diagrams included here, the points on the supply curve above r_e should not be taken as effective supply loci, in that they can not obtain in the face of credit rationing.

5 Fazzari (1992) and Wolfson (1995) also make a case for drawing some new-Keynesian insights into a post-Keynesian framework.

6 In a post-Keynesian framework, even borrowers do not have perfect information regarding their project's risk/expected-return profiles. I thank James Crotty for this point.

7 A fourth component of some FL programs is the opening of the capital account. The likely effects of this opening are not addressed here, but they would exacerbate the problems identified. For example, increased levels of external indebtedness and capital flight contributed importantly to the problem of financial fragility in LDCs.

8 Of course the precise specification of FL programs differed across countries. For a complete description of these programs, see Cho and Khatkhate (1989), Diaz-Alejandro (1985) and Sundararajan and Balino (1991).

9 Cf. Stiglitz's (1987:10-1) labor market classification.

10 The relationship between financial and real investments should be made clear. While the "new issues" equity and bond markets are often (but not always) coterminous with real investment by industrial corporations, secondary and tertiary markets are not necessarily directly (or even indirectly) related to real investment. While both new issues and secondary market activity increase with FL, the secondary market experiences more dramatic growth and "deepening" and tends to become a site of increased short-term trading. Thus, FL may be expected to induce a dramatic increase in financial sector activities that are not directly related to real sector investment.

11 This is explicit in post-Keynesian theory (see fn4).

12 Certainly, financial instruments are not necessarily short-term. A long-term bond is one example of a long-term financial commitment. But while the obligation of the issuer of the bond is necessarily long-term, the commitment of the purchaser is not so constrained provided a developed financial market exists.

13 The spread is also affected by expectations concerning future short-term interest (and inflation) rates and lenders' liquidity preferences, in accordance with expectations and liquidity premia hypotheses of the term structure (Cox et al., 1981).

14 There may be times when boom-euphoric expectations lead to a reduction in the spread (perhaps because banks overvalue collateral) as a result of the growing optimism about long-term prospects (Keynes, 1936). The "volatility effect" presented here would operate in the opposite direction. At any particular moment, optimism might outweigh volatility, or vice versa. When optimism outweighs volatility, the spread will not rise. In this context, the arguments relating to speculation-led development are not compromised. The increased fragility of the macroeconomy still obtains due to the other demand-side changes discussed previously. When the volatility outweighs the optimism effect, the likelihood of speculation-led development is reinforced.

15 Guttentag and Herring (1984), Jaffee and Stiglitz (1990:215-6), Stiglitz (1987:13-14), and Wolfson (1995) also argue that lenders' credit rationing may evolve as expectations change. These works do not, however, pursue dynamic credit rationing in the context of the triggering mechanism of FL.

16 Credit rationing has not been tested in LDC markets. See Driscoll (1991) and Wolfson (1995) for such tests in DC markets.

17 In the Southern Cone countries another factor leading to the validation of borrowers' adventurism was the existence of *grupos* or financial-industrial complexes (Burkett and Dutt, 1991).

18 In the face of distress, borrowers might initially increase their demand for credit in order to compensate for a shortfall in returns (in a manner analogous to Wolfson's (1986) "necessitous demand for credit"). In this case, we might expect a dramatic increase in interest rates followed immediately by severe credit rationing.

19 This is especially the case when the majority of financial trading is in the secondary rather than the new issues market. Whether the increased income that may emanate from DUP activity in the short run *eventually* results in higher levels of productive activity is unclear. Under a FL regime it is not at all evident that the increased income flowing from DUPs will be expended on non-DUP (i.e., productive) activities.

20 This issue is explored at length in Grabel (1996).

References

Akerlof, G. A. "The Market for 'Lemons': Quality Uncertainty and the Market Mechanism." *Quarterly Journal of Economics,* 1970, vol. 84, no. 3, pp. 488-500.

Akyuz, Y. "Financial Liberalization in Developing Countries: A Neo-Keynesian Approach." UNCTAD, Discussion Paper No. 36, 1991.

Balise, B. "Financial Liberalization in Developing Countries." *Studies in Comparative International Development*, 1990-1, vol. 25, no. 4, pp. 56-70.

Bhagwati, J. "Directly Unproductive Profit-Seeking Activities." *Journal of Political Economy* 1982, vol. 90, no. 5, pp. 998-1002.

Burkett, P. and Dutt, A. K. "Interest Rate Policy, Effective Demand, and Growth in LDCs." *International Review of Applied Economics* 1991, vol. 5, no. 2, pp. 127-53.

Carter, M. "Uncertainty, Liquidity and Speculation: A Keynesian Perspective on Financial Innovation in Debt Markets." *Journal of Post Keynesian Economics* 1991-2, vol. 14, no. 2, pp. 169-182.

Cho, Y. J. and Khatkhate, D. "Lessons of Financial Liberalization in Asia: A Comparative Study." World Bank Discussion Paper, No. 50, 1989.

Cox, J.; Ingersoll, J. and Ross, S. "A Re-examination of Traditional Hypotheses About the Term Structure of Interest Rates." *Journal of Finance* 1981, vol. 36, no. 4, pp. 769-799.

Crotty, J. "Are Keynesian Uncertainty and Macropolicy Compatible? Conventional Decision Making, Institutional Structures, and Conditional Stability in Macromodels," in P. Minsky; G. Dymski and R. Pollin, eds., *New Perspectives in Monetary Macroeconomics: Explorations in the Tradition of Hyman,* Ann Arbor: University of Michigan Press, 1994.

_____. "Rethinking Marxian Investment Theory: Keynes-Minsky Instability, Competitive Regime Shifts, and Coerced Investment." *Review of Radical Political Economics* 1993, vol. 25, no. 1, pp. 1-26.

Davidson, P. "Is probability theory relevant for uncertainty? A Post-Keynesian perspective." *Journal of Economic Perspectives* 1991, vol. 5, no. 1, pp. 129-44.

De Long, J. B.; Shleifer, A.; Summers, L. and Waldmann, R. (DSSW). "The Size and Incidence of the Losses From Noise Trading." *Journal of Finance* 1989, vol. XLIV, no. 3, pp. 681-696.

Diaz-Alejandro, C. "Good-Bye Financial Repression, Hello Financial Crash." *Journal of Development Economics* 1985, vol. 19, pp. 1-24.

Driscoll, M. "Deregulation, Credit Rationing, Financial Fragility and Economic Performance." OECD Department of Economics and Statistics, Working Paper, No. 97, 1991.

Dutt, A. "Interest Rate Policy in LDCs: A Post-Keynesian View." *Journal of Post Keynesian Economics* 1990-91, vol. 13, no. 2, pp. 210-232.

Fazzari, S. "Keynesian Theories of Investment and Finance: Neo, Post, and New," in S. Fazzari and D. Papadimitriou, eds., *Financial Conditions and Macroeconomic Performance*, Armonk, NY: ME Sharpe, 1992.

Federer, P. "The Impact of Uncertainty on Aggregate Investment Spending: An Empirical Analysis." *Journal of Money, Credit, and Banking* 1993, vol. 25, no. 1, pp. 30-45.

Galbis, V. "High Real Interest Rates Under Financial Liberalization: Is There a Problem?" IMF Working Paper, No. 7, 1993.

Grabel, I. "Savings, Investment an Functional Efficiency: A Comparative Examination of National Financial Complexes," in R. Pollin, ed., *The Macroeconomics of Finance, Saving, and Investment*, Ann Arbor: University of Michigan Press, forthcoming 1996.

_____. "Assessing the Impact of Financial Liberalisation on Stock Market Volatility in selected developing countries." *Journal of Development Studies* 1995, vol. 31, no. 6, pp. 903-17.

_____. "The Political Economy of Theories of 'Optimal' Financial Repression: A Critique." *Review of Radical Political Economics* 1994, vol. 26, no. 3, pp. 47-55.

Guttentag, J. and Herring, R. "Credit rationing and financial disorder." *Journal of Finance* 1984, vol. 32, no. 5, pp. 1359-82.

Jaffe, D. and Stiglitz, J. "Credit rationing," in B. Friedman and F. Hahn, eds., *Handbook on Monetary Economics*, Amsterdam: North-Holland, 1990.

Kapur, B. "Formal and Informal Financial Markets and the Neostructuralist Critique of the Financial Liberalization Strategy in Less Developed Countries." *Journal of Development Economics* 1992, vol. 38, pp. 63-77.

Kemp, M. and Hans-Werner Sinn. "A Simple Model of Useless Speculation." NBER Working Paper, No. 3513, 1990.

Keynes, J. M. *The General Theory of Employment, Interest, and Money.* NY: Harcourt Brace Jovanovich, 1936.

McKinnon, R. I. *The Order of Economic Liberalization: Financial Control in the Transition to a Market Economy.* Baltimore: Johns Hopkins University, 1991.

____. "Financial Liberalization and Economic Development: A Reassessment of Interest-rate Policies in Asia and Latin America." International Center for Economic Growth, 1988.

___. *Money and Capital in Economic Development.* Washington, DC: Brooks Institution, 1973.

Minsky, H. P. *Stabilizing an Unstable Economy.* New Haven: Yale University, 1986.

Rittenberg, L. "Investment Spending and Interest Rate Policy: The Case of Financial Liberalization in Turkey." *Journal of Development Studies* 1990, pp. 151-67.

Shaw, E. S. *Financial Deepening in Economic Development.* NY: Oxford University Press, 1973.

Snowden, P. "Financial Market Liberalisation in LDCs." *Journal of Development Studies* 1987, vol. 24, no. 1, pp. 83-93.

Stiglitz, J. "Financial Markets and Development." *Oxford Review of Economic Policy* 1989, vol. 5, no. 4, pp. 55-68.

_____. "The Dependency of Quality on Price." *Journal of Economic Literature* 1987, vol. 25, pp. 2-48.

Sundararajan, B. and Balino, T. eds., *Banking Crises*: Cases and Issues. Washington, D.C.: IMF, 1991.

Taylor, L. *Lectures on Structuralist Macroeconomics*. Cambridge: MIT Press, 1991.

Urrutia, M., ed. *Financial Liberalization and the Internal Structure of Capital in Asia and Latin America*, Hong Kong: UN University, 1988.

Wolfson, M. *A Post-Keynesian Theory of Credit Rationing*. Mimeo, Department of Economics, University of Notre Dame, 1995.

_____. "The Causes of Financial Instability." *Journal of Post Keynesian Economics* 1990, vol. 12, no. 3, pp. 333-355.

_____. *Financial Crises*. Armonk: M. E. Sharpe, 1986.

7

GLOBALIZATION AND DEVELOPMENT:
Lessons from the Peripheral Countries of the European Union

Eleni Paliginis[1]

Middlesex University, UK

Globalization and European integration had important but disparate effects on countries of the European Union. States, at an intermediate level of development, such as Spain, Portugal, Ireland and Greece experienced a weakening of their domestic structures. Policies for convergence within the EU did not have the desired effects. The aim of this paper is to discuss the process of Globalization and assess the possibilities for endogenous or exogenous development in countries at an intermediate stage of their development.

The European Union has undergone a series of transformations and expansions since its original conception in the late 1950s. In its original form it was a free trade area between six core European countries with very similar socio-political structures. In the 1980s it experienced a very significant process of widening and deepening. The membership rose to twelve countries and the Single European Market was created. Policies were directed towards the restructuring of European capital, convergence between member countries and the creation of a more cohesive Community.

The expansion in the 1980s to the Southern European countries created heterogeneity, as countries at an intermediate stage of development and with more diverse social and institutional arrangement joined the Community. They all had a GDP per capita lower than 75% of the EU average, a large and inefficient agricultural sector and weak domestic capital. The creation of the Single European Market in 1992, which involved the free movement of capital, goods and labor, was intended to strengthen European capital. As most of the weak industries were in the periphery, the effects of the restructuring were disproportionate. The Single European Market, operating between countries at an unequal level of development, could not assist, at least in the short run, the development of the periphery and could not contribute towards convergence. Within a more integrated global economy, nonetheless, the competitiveness of economies becomes essential and continuous dependence on support from national governments impossible.

This chapter examines the process of globalization within a European context. More specifically, it concentrates on the effects of EU membership on the weakest members of the Community. After an initial discussion of the conditions for convergence and the economic structures of the weak countries there will be an evaluation of the effects of the Single market. Indices such as the GDP per capita growth, the level of unemployment and the Balance of Trade will be used as indications of these effects. This will be followed by an examination of the impact of EU policies in these regions and the requirements and prospects for endogenous or exogenous growth. The paper will conclude with an appraisal of existing policies and recommendations for policies in the near future.

Conditions for Convergence in the EU Periphery

Developments in the 1980s led to the creation of dualistic structures within the EU. The incorporation of countries at different levels of economic development and the subsequent abolition of all internal protection of their domestic markets was a high risk strategy. The neo-classical model predicted that the openness of the economy, the free play of the market and the lack of state protection could generate the necessary movements of capital and labor which could stimulate production and hasten economic development. Convergence between core and periphery would have been the anticipated effect. Other models of development nonetheless came with alternative predictions. In the theory of cumulative accumulation Myrdal (1963) put forward the hypothesis that spatial differences do not tend to disappear over time, as the neo-classical model would have predicted, but instead they tend to persist and widen. Capital and labor tend to migrate towards the prosperous regions, setting in motion cumulative effects. In this model, dynamic economies of scale lead to increasing returns in the developed economies, aggravating the initial disequilibrium between core and periphery. In a similar manner Kaldor (1972) sees that dynamic increasing returns to scale induce higher productivity and rate of growth in the faster growing economies, making it progressively harder for the others to catch up. The engine of growth, according to Kaldor, is the manufacturing sector as this the only one which could generate increasing returns.

The Myrdal/Kaldor thesis attaches a particular importance to the development or restructuring of the manufacturing sector in the process of development. In the EU periphery, this process could be achieved either with the assistance and development of domestic capital or by the attraction of foreign capital into the country.

Post-Fordist theories (Piore & Sabel 1984) examined the possibilities for an endogenous development. As a result of market and technological changes in the 1970s and serious support form the local authorities, smaller and more flexible units of production developed. They could respond faster to market changes by producing customized products and reorganizing both labor relations and distribution networks. They could create 'niches' and exploit their uniqueness. Their 'smallness' was their advantage. They represented the engine of growth. Decentralized forms of organization of production and transfer of control from central to local Government are characteristics of this model. Further, within a globalized mode of production dependency solely on local markets was not necessary. Their flexibility, local connections and lower costs of operation could attract the co-operation of Larger Scale Enterprises (LSEs) and Multinational Enterprises (MNEs). Developments in regions, such as Emilia-Romagna in Italy, in the 1970s, based on Small and Medium Enterprises (SMEs) showed the possibilities for an endogenous form of growth based on the development of local resources.

Endogenous development enhances local endowments and is embedded with local culture and customs. Despite these advantages, exogenous development based on the operation of multinational enterprises is increasingly perceived as the way to economic development. Their access to capital and new technology bridges the gap between the requirements for development and the lack of endowments of these countries. Employment, improvements in balance of payments and training of the local labor force and management are cited as the main advantages. However, competition with domestic companies in the sector of their operation and lack of links with local firms are some of the shortcomings. Because of this a third path has been identified. An interaction of indigenous and exogenous opportunities may be the way forward. Assistance to the creation of clusters of local industries in areas where there is a national comparative advantage may be the way to generate links between the MNEs and local capital and generate spin-offs.

Research and Development (R&D) could play an important role in enhancing endogenous development. It facilitates the modernization of companies, making them able to innovate, upgrade their products, improve managerial skills and close the productivity gap between core and periphery. R&D does not necessarily involve original research. Peripheral countries, to the extent that they could adopt research to their indigenous needs, could have an advantage over the core countries. "In technology or organization, as well as in science, learning and imitating is typically cheaper and faster than is the original discovery and testing" (Gomulka 1987). The effect of technology is to fuel growth but the diffusion of it ultimately brings to an end the advantage to the innovator (Schumpeter 1939). R&D is important for the modernization of the peripheral economies and thus for convergence.

Economic Structures: *Core and Periphery*

The fast economic development, in the post-war period, of the original EU countries, (formerly EEC) France, Germany, Italy, Luxembourg, Belgium and Netherlands as well as the UK and the Nordic countries, (core countries) could be attributed to the restructuring of these economies and the dominant role of a Fordist type of production. The Southern European countries (Spain, Greece, Portugal) and Ireland were not part of the Fordist development. They were not only geographically on the periphery of Europe, but they lagged behind in the ongoing economic transformation. Their economies were dominated by a large and unproductive agricultural sector and a fragmented capital (Arestis & Paliginis 1993). The divergence between core and periphery became more pronounced and this was consistent with the Myrdal/Kaldor thesis.

By the late 1960s, persistently high levels of employment in the core countries led to a rise in the social wage and, linked with exogenous factors such as the oil crisis, led to a reduction in the level of profit and a quest for its restoration. There was a restructuring of production within the core countries and a relocation of capital from core to periphery. Within Europe there was a relocation of capital from the core countries to the Southern periphery and Ireland to take advantage of cheaper labor and/ or by-pass high tariffs in them. This relocation, together with Keynesian policies, contributed to a period of fast economic development and low levels of unemployment in the periphery (Lipietz 1987).

Despite these improvements in the late 1960s and early 1970s period, the peripheral economies remained at an intermediate level of development, with serious structural problems. They all possessed an agricultural sector considerably larger and more inefficient than the EU average, a GDP per capita lower than the EU average and serious structural problems of unemployment or underemployment. While for the EU12 the share of employment in agriculture, in 1992, was 6% and the value-added in this sector 3%, the equivalent values for the peripheral countries are significantly different. The respective figures for Spain were 10% and 4%, Portugal 12% and 4%, Ireland 14% and 8% and Greece 22% and 16%.

Furthermore, the manufacturing sector was dominated by small and fragmented capital in areas of low value added such as food, drinks and textiles. In Greece, 40% of the employment was generated in units of less than ten individuals (Papandreou, 1991) and the average size of firms in 1986 was 4 to 5 employees (Katseli, 1990). Similarly, in Spain, in the same period, 80% of companies in the manufacturing sector were employing less than 10 workers and only 0.2% more than 500, (Vinals 1990). As official EU statistics do not even quote companies with less than 20 employees, it is impossible to know the equivalent figure for the EU12. Lack of possibilities for work in the industrial sector inflated the numbers of self-employed. In 1992, the level of the self-employment was 32.6% in Greece, 19% in Ireland, 17.4% in Spain and 22.9% in Portugal. The equivalent level for the EU12 was 13.8%, (European Network for SME Research 1995).

The period from 1986 (starting date for EU membership of Portugal and Spain) to 1993 indicates limited evidence for convergence. The rate of growth of GDP shows that, with the exception of Ireland, initial differences tended to disappear and we have a convergence towards the EU12 average, Figure 1. This index partly justifies Myrdal's hypothesis. As the rate of growth of GDP converges, there is no apparent trend towards a convergence of GDP per capita between core and periphery, as the neo-classical model would have predicted. For this to take place, the rate of growth in the periphery should remain consistently higher than in the core over a number of years.

Similarly, examining the level of unemployment over the same period we see that there is no indication of convergence between core and periphery. While the trends are similar, the gap between them remained the same, Figure 2. In 1993, the level of unemployment in Spain was 21.3% and Ireland 18.4% while the EU12 average was 10.4%. Contrary to the predictions of the neo-classical school and Myrdal there was no labor migration. Linguistic and cultural differences inhibited labor movement. Consistently lower figures for unemployment in Greece and

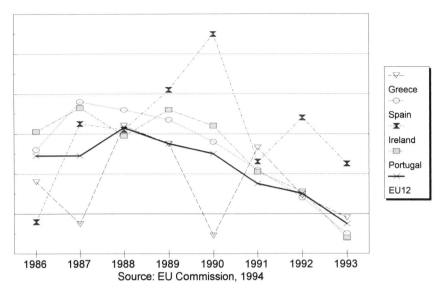

Source: EU Commission, 1994

Figure 1. Rate of Growth of GDP, 1986 - 1993

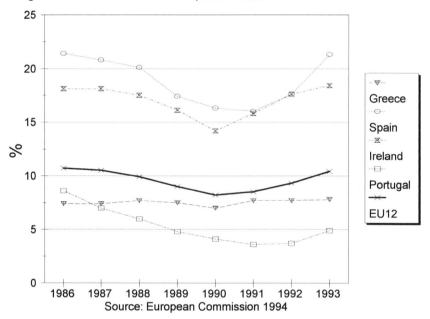

Source: European Commission 1994

Figure 2. Unemployment Rates, 1986 - 1993

Portugal may be an underestimation of the real level, partly due to differences in Social Protection. Such variances are fully discussed in European Commission 1995. On the other hand, differences in the structure of the real economy may also be partly responsible for these differences in unemployment rates. While clothing, textiles and footwear (labor intensive industries) represent 23% of both the Portuguese and Greek exports; in Ireland and Spain these sectors represent only 8% and 19% respectively. Chemicals and machinery (capital intensive) represent 46% of exports in Ireland and 51% of exports in Spain (Barry & Hannan 1995). The industrial operations, particularly of MNEs, in these countries tend to concentrate in relatively capital intensive areas.

The balance of trade depicts a similar picture. While for the EU12 the Import/Export ratio remained almost unchanged between 1986 and 1992, for the three out of the four peripheral countries this ratio is considerably higher than the EU average. Ireland, because of the successful attraction of MNEs, exhibits a ratio lower than the EU12, Figure 3.The Single European Market (SEM) had significant trade creation and trade diversion effects.

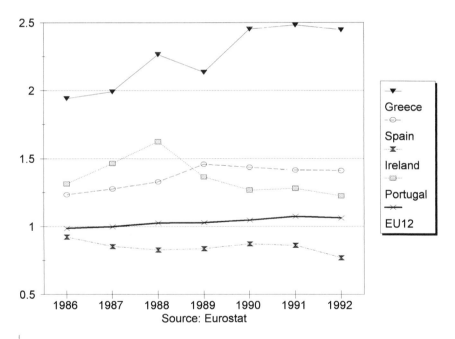

Source: Eurostat

Figure 3. EU Balance of Trade. Imports/ Exports. 1986 - 1992.

The Single European Market.

Low rates of growth and high levels of unemployment in the EU as a whole in the early 1980s were attributed to the growing globalization of production and global competition. A process of restructuring of the EUwas considered essential. This entailed the restructuring of the EU capital but also the development of the EU periphery. Competitiveness, economic convergence and social cohesion, not at a national but at EU level, were the main aims.

The Single European Market, initiated in 1986 but in operation since 1992, represented an EU attempt to liberalise, restructure capital and increase its efficiency and competitiveness relative to the US and Japanese capital. The restructuring of capital involved the support, at an EU level, of strategic industries, such as electronics or information technology. Research and Development was earmarked as the means for strengthening European capital. Partly funded and coordinated now by the EU, it assisted the collaboration between EU countries and between companies enabling winners to emerge. Research projects such as *ESPRIT* (European Strategic Programme for Research and Development in Information Technology) were examples of the new direction of the EU.

The restructuring and liberalisation of the markets necessitated regulation and control and could only be achieved through a partial transfer of sovereignty and political power from the nation state to the EU. It entails the *hollowing out* of the nation state (Jessop, 1994). In the 1980s global competition led to a declining ability of the nation state to control the economy through traditional economic policies on tariffs, exchange rates and capital movements. As traditional methods to fight unemployment through Keynesian policies became weaker, governments' focus switched from social cohesiveness to global competitiveness. The EU provided a framework for the protection of workers' fundamental social and economic rights, without nonetheless providing social protection at an EU level.

For the peripheral countries these changes are of special importance. The restructuring and rationalisation of capital, initiated by the SEM, aimed to strengthen large companies while adversely affecting non-competitive ones. The concentration of uncompetitive SMEs in the periphery was exposing them to disproportionate consequences. The SEM intensified the Europeanization of production.

At a political level, although the *hollowing out* of the nation state was universal it had disproportionate effects on the periphery. The relative loss of power to follow independent economic policies and the partial transfer of this responsibility to supranational institutions is at least controversial. It pre-assumes that these institutions now express a collective will towards this aim. But the will is not collective; instead, there remain conflicting and antithetical interests within the Community and the ability of the nation states to promote them is directly related to their economic and political power.

Policies for the Development of the European Periphery

In the mid 1980s it was felt that the future of the European Union depended on the rigour and competitiveness of the European economy. The changes introduced through the SEM could strengthen EU capital but it was recognized that it could further accentuate the divergence between core and periphery. A programme for the development of the European periphery was conceived which aimed to create the preconditions for endogenously and/or exogenously determined development.

EU Policies for the Development of the Periphery.

The EU is qualitatively different from alternative free trade formations such as the North American Free Trade Agreement (NAFTA), as convergence and social cohesion in the EU are among its objectives. Regional policies were mainly intended for the development of the European periphery, the 'lagging regions'. The Structural Funds (SF) of the EU, consisting of Regional, Social and Agricultural (restructuring only) Funds, were reformed and enhanced in 1989 to assist the development of 'lagging regions' (Objective 1) and regions in core countries suffering from industrial decline (Objective 2). 'Lagging regions' were defined as the ones with a GDP per capita less than 75% of the EU average. The prospects for the creation of an Economic and Monetary Union (EMU) by the end of the century led to an enhancement of the Structural Funds by the Cohesion Funds, for the period 1993-99. In 1993, the Structural and Cohesion Funds represented 3.3% of GDP for Greece, 1.5% for Spain, 3.1% for Ireland and 3.3% for Portugal. Although these EU contributions may appear reasonable, the overall structure of contributions is skewed towards the core countries. In 1993, the CAP commanded 53.6% of the EU budget vs. 24.7% for the Structural Funds, while only 24% of the CAP was directed to the four peripheral countries, although 34% of the economically active population in agriculture lived there.

Although the Structural Funds represent a desire for the improvement of the European periphery, they have not succeeded in bringing the desired effect as they are quantitatively insufficient and qualitatively not fully appropriate for the industrialisation of the periphery. They concentrate on the development of the infrastructure, the development of which is a necessary but not sufficient condition for the industrialisation of these countries. The modernisation of industries in the peripheral countries, their ability to innovate and develop managerial or other skills will depend to a large extent upon their ability to carry out R&D. Thus, more positive assistance, such as assistance with R&D, could be more fruitful. It is instructive, thus, to examine the expenditure, private and public, that core economies undertake as a percentage of their GDP, Figure 4.

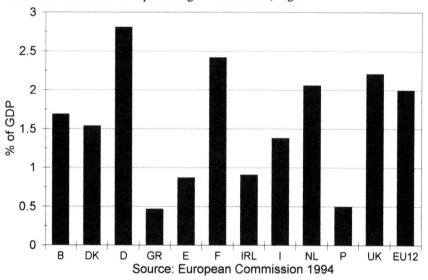

Source: European Commission 1994

Figure 4: Gross Expenditure on R&D as a % of GDP, 1990

The measures cover a wide spectrum of R&D such as Science Parks, Universities, training programmes etc. All the peripheral EU countries have levels of expenditure well below the EU average. In Greece this level is 0.47% of GDP, in Portugal, 0.50%, Spain 0.87% and Ireland 0.91%. The EU12 average was 2.00% (European Commission, 94). In peripheral countries neither the state not the private sector can afford to fund research. Thus, the extent to which the Structural Funds (SF) offset this imbalance is an indication of their contribution to the development of these countries. In fact, the SF do not correct this anomaly. Structural assistance for R&D from the EU is skewed towards the depressed regions of core countries rather than to the periphery. While, 9.3% of SF, are directed towards R&D for Objective 2 (depressed regions in core countries), Objective 1 (mainly the peripheral EU countries and few lagging behind regions from the developed ones) receive only 2.7% of SF for this purpose. In particular, R&D represents 1% of SF in Greece, 2% in Spain, 2.4% in Portugal and 4% in Ireland. On the other hand the average expenditure from the SF for R&D in the core countries is 9.3%, Figure 5.

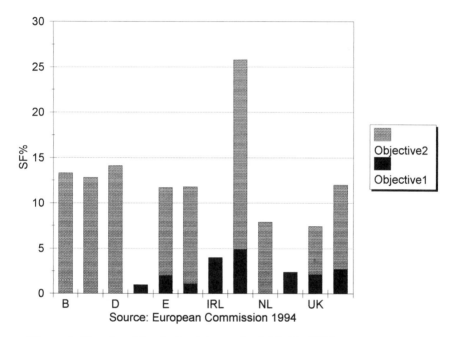

Figure 5. Structural funds Assistance for R&D, %, 1994

MNEs and the Development of the Periphery

MNEs are considered very influential factors in the developmental process. They bring capital and expertise, become *growth poles* by creating linkages with domestic capital, employment, assisting the acquisition of skills, supporting local

R&D and transferring technology, thus setting in motion Myrdal's principle of *cumulative causation*. In fact, MNEs, in an effort to decrease uncertainty with respect to their global operations, could enter forms of restructuring such as downsizing, outsourcing or subcontracting, thus becoming a catalyst for local business and employment.

The European Commission does not have a specific policy towards MNEs. Nonetheless, through its policy on tariffs and quotas and the definition of a minimum local content, it has indirectly influenced their behaviour. Indeed, plans for the SEM, the structural changes of the 1980s, affected the location and the type of expansion of MNEs.

Dunning (1988) in his "eclectic theory" sees three main factors as influential in a company going multinational, the OLI factors (ownership, location, internalisation). While the OLI factors summarise the reasons behind a company's decision to go multinational, they do not provide an overall explanation of the geographical destination of FDI. Other factors such as the *institutional thickness* of a country are equally important. Institutional thickness refers to a strong institutional presence in the form of financial institutions, development agencies, local authorities etc. as well as to local, social and cultural factors which could influence growth. All of them together determine economic success (Amin & Thrift, 1994).

The interaction of the OLI factors and *institutional thickness* made the core EU countries very attractive locations for MNEs. The increased globalization of production in the 1980s, together with the moves towards the creation of a Single European Market, increased the multinational activities of Japanese and US capital in EU. This could be seen as a result of two main strategies by the US and Japanese capital; first an effort to protect export markets from different forms of trade barriers, and second a desire to gain access to information and technology needed to upgrade and rationalize domestic operations. Neither US nor Japanese capital were particularly interested in low cost operations, thus, the main areas of operation of MNEs were the core countries of the EU and Ireland. Between 1986-1991 the four peripheral countries have collectively received 14% of the total external FDI in EU (European Commission 1994). The UK, with 46% of total inward (external) FDI was the main beneficiary.

The role of MNEs as *growth poles* in the periphery depends very much on the type of companies attracted and their linkages with domestic capital. A substantial distinction exists between *cost-driven* companies, in the pursuit of lower production costs, and *performance* companies, which derive their advantages from product excellence and seek the appropriate location for this purpose (Amin & Tomaney, 1995). The peripheral countries are further differentiated with regard to the OLI factors and *institutional thickness.* Such differences led to a disproportionate attraction of MNEs to countries within the periphery and to varied effects on their path of development.

Ireland, as a result of language, a young and well-educated work force, tax concessions from the government and cultural affinities, was an attractive location for US multinationals. From a very early stage, it decided to base its development in the attraction of inward FDI. The Industrial Development Authority (IDA) was set up in 1969 to organize and promote the growth of FDI as a matter of national policy. Multinational companies, mainly from the UK and the USA were attracted into Dublin and Cork. By the late 1980s the USA accounted for a third of the total multinational subsidiaries in Ireland. Electronics was the industry favored by US multinationals, followed by the pharmaceutical industry. As Jacobson and Andreoso (1990) argue, one of the attractions of the pharmaceutical industry, particularly the manufacture of active ingredients, was that the latter have a more deleterious effect on the environment than the final product. The *country-specific advantage* of Ireland was its less rigorous implementation of environmental legislation.

Ireland is regarded today as the tiger economy of the EU. Among the peripheral EU countries Ireland has exhibited the highest rate of growth and a balance of trade better than the EU average. The more positive performance of the Irish economy in relation to the rest of the EU periphery is related to the successful attraction of FDI. Nonetheless, the early decision to attract MNEs was at the cost of the development of domestic capital and has led to the dependence of the Irish economy on MNEs. The fourth Periodic Report on the Regions of the EC, as quoted in Amin & Tomaney (1995), says:

> while foreign investment could be a catalyst for local business....there is also the risk of creating a dependent economy. The Irish experience is very instructive in this respect where the new activities from outside have not forged links with the domestic sector, resulting in a kind of dual economy where the growth of a competitive sector of national firms have not been stimulated significantly.

The Culliton Report (1992) on Industrial Policy in Ireland, (not implemented) aimed to establish a better balance between inward and domestic capital by switching some of the state expenditure on grants from the MNEs to the promotion and assistance of clusters of local firms.

In Greece, geographical peripherality and lack of *institutional thickness* are the most important factors explaining the very small involvement of MNEs in the country. There is an outmoded financial and banking system, a political system based on favouritism and clientelism, a lack of a skilled labour force and frictional unemployment, with very high unemployment among graduates. Growth rates have remained very slow and the performance of the industrial sector remained weak.

In both Spain and Portugal, their incorporation into the EU in 1986 led to an increase of FDI mostly from the EU countries, and from some US companies. As Spain is the largest peripheral country, FDI were mostly of a *market seeking* nature, concentrating in the already developed regions such as Madrid, Catalunya and Valencia where cost of labour was already high. Nonetheless, although labour cost increased by 30% between 1986 and 1992, wages were still lower than in the core EU countries (Gual & Martin, 1995).

The very low wages in Portugal (the lowest in EU) made this country attractive to *cost-reducing* FDI, mainly from the UK, while geographic peripherality and low educational achievements created problems in attracting *performance* firms. This was confirmed by a study by Amin & Tomaney (1995), which showed that most of the MNEs in Portugal, such as recent investment by Ford - VW, GM and Blaupunkt, are greenfield investments of a semi-skilled assembly nature for export purposes. There was almost a total lack of local research facilities and few linkages with domestic capital.

In the case of Spain and Portugal increased multinational activity in the late 1980s coincided with a period of expansion in the EU. From the 1990 onwards there is a general decline in FDI in peripheral Europe. In Spain, FDI decreased from $13,984mn. in 1990 to $8,144 mn in 1993 (International Financial Statistics 1995). An initial upsurge of FDI in Portugal, following EU membership, was followed by a fall in FDI in the 1990s from $2,610mn in 1990 to $1,301mn in 1993 (op. cit.). Similar movements were experienced in the other countries. This fall was the outcome of both a depression in EU and the changes in Central and Eastern European (CEE) countries.

Experience from the MNEs in the peripheral countries shows that they could, in some cases, assist the development of the manufacturing sector and, through a process of cumulative causation, play an important role in the process of development. Nonetheless, for this process to occur, linkages are needed with the domestic capital, and national or EU policies may be important in stimulating these developments.

Endogenous growth

Exogenous growth based on the role of the MNEs is in some cases difficult to achieve because of the geographical peripherality of the country or the fears of dependency that this type of growth may create. Even in the most successful case of Ireland, scepticism arises out of the dependence of the economy on MNEs and the extent of subsidization of foreign capital at the cost of local capital. Industrial policies in the early post-war era had traditionally concentrated on the strengthening of the local firms as a means to promote endogenous development.

Developments in regions based on SMEs, such as in Emilia-Romagna in Italy in the 1970s, showed the possibilities for an endogenous form of growth based on the development of local resources. Modernisation of SMEs and, at times, close co-operation with large enterprises and MNEs open the way of a more balanced development and a better use of internal resources. Emilia-Romagna represents a desirable model of endogenous development. Its success was the result of internal factors such as proximity to a very developed industrial sector in North Italy and very supportive local government. Although these factors may be exceptional, they provides an example of a region which developed by taking advantage of its special circumstances.

In most other countries in the periphery, very weak industrial structures, linked with the lack of institutional thickness, make domestic companies uncompetitive both externally and increasingly internally. Within a globalized world it becomes increasingly difficult to isolate these economies and fully protect them. As O'Donnell (1993) argues, regional development therefore necessitates a careful articulation of endogenous and exogenous opportunities in order to create opportunities within the global economy. In this respect selection and assistance of SMEs which have the potential to develop, either of their own or in co-operation with MNEs, may be a way forward. National or local government assistance could be a way to assist the development of these areas.

Conclusion

The EU periphery was suffering from serious structural problems at the time of joining the EU in the 1980s. At the end of the 1980s, the EU had the dual, but contradictory aims, to restructure the European capital and assist the development of the periphery. The effect of the Single European Market was to weaken further the domestic capital in the periphery. EU regional policies, although they represented a serious attempt to assist the periphery, did not manage to reverse the trend.

The development of the periphery depends on the existence of a coherent restructuring of the industrial set-up in these countries. Although endogenous development may be preferable, as it does not create dependency and has more spin-off effects on the economy as a whole, the case of Ireland showed the possibilities and dangers of development based on MNEs. Fast growth, but high unemployment and lack of links with local industries were some of the effects. When purely endogenous policies cannot operate, because of the structural problems, then policies aiming to co-ordinate the operation of MNEs with selected sectors of domestic companies may be the solution. Selected assistance to SMEs through national, local and EU efforts could allow these companies to play an important role in the developmental process. R&D funds could assist the upgrade and modernisation of local companies and create the basis for their successful co-operation with MNEs.

Endnote

1. I would like to thank Professor P. Arestis, Professor J.P. Dunne, M. Walsh and an unknown referee for very helpful comments on an earlier version of this paper.

References

Amin, A. and Thrift, N. "Living in the Global," in A. Amin & N. Thrift, eds., *Globalization, Institutions and Regional Development in Europe,* Oxford: Oxford University Press, 1994.

Amin, A. and Tomaney, J. *Behind the Myth of European Union.* London: Routledge, 1995.

Arestis, P. and Paliginis, E. "Divergence and Peripheral Fordism in the European Community." *Journal of Economic Issues,* 1993, 27, pp. 657-65.

Barry, F. and Hannan, A. "Multinationals and Indigenous Employment. An "Irish Disease?" Working paper 13, University College Dublin, 1995.

Culliton, J. *A Time for Change: Industrial Policy for the 1990s.* Report of the Industrial Policy Review Group, Dublin, 1992.

Dunning, J. H. *Explaining International Production.* London: Unwin Hyman, 1988.

European Commission. *Competitiveness and Cohesion: trends in the regions.* Fifth Periodic Report on the Social and Economic Situation and Development of the Regions in the Community, Luxembourg, 1994.

European Commission. *Social Protection in Europe,* Luxembourg, 1995.

EIM,European Network for SME Research. *3rd Annual Report. The European Observatory for SMEs,* The Netherlands, 1995.

Gual, J. and Martin, C. "Trade and Foreign Direct Investment with Central and Eastern Europe: Its Impact On Spain," in R. Faini and R. Portes, eds., *European Union Trade with Eastern Europe,* London, 1995.

Gomulka, S. "Catching Up," in M. Milgate and P. Newman, eds., *The New Palgrave: A Dictionary of Economics,* Vol. II, J. Eatwell, London: Macmillian, 1987.

International Financial Statistics. IMF, Washington, D.C., 1995.

Jacobson, D. and Andreoso, B. "Ireland as a Location for Multinational Investment," in A. Foley and M. Mulreany, eds., *The Single European Market and the Irish Economy,* Institute of Public Administration, Dublin, 1990.

Jessop, B. "Post-Fordism and the State," in A. Amin, ed., *Post-Fordism: A Reader,* Oxford: Blackwell, 1994.

Kaldor, N. "The Irrelevance of Equilibrium Economics." *The Economic Journal,* 1972, vol. 82, pp. 1237-55.

Katseli, L. "Economic Integration and the Enlarged European Community," in C. Bliss and J. Braga de Macedo, eds., *Unity with Diversity in the European Economy: The Community's Southern Frontier,* Cambridge: Cambridge University Press, 1990.

Lipietz, A. *Mirages and Miracles* Verso. London, 1987.

Myrdal, G. *Economic Theory and Underdeveloped Regions.* London: Methuen, 1963.

O'Donnell, R. "Ireland and Europe. Challenges for a New Century." Policy Research Series Paper 17, Dublin: Economic and Social Research Institute, 1993.

Papandreou, N. "Finance and Industry: The Case of Greece." *International Review of Applied Economics*, 1991, vol. 5, pp. 1-23.

Piore, M. and C. Sabel. *The Second Industrial Divide: Possibilities for Prosperity*, New York: Basic Books, 1984.

Schumpeter, J.A. *Business Cycles*, London: McGraw Hill, 1939.

Vinals, J. "Spain and the EC 1992 Shock," in C. Bliss and J. Braga de Macedo, eds., *Unity with Diversity in the European Economy: The Community's Southern Frontier*, Cambridge: Cambridge University Press, 1990.

8

GLOBALIZATION'S IMPLICATIONS FOR INDONESIA:
Trade Policy, Multinationals, and Competition

William E. James
East-West Center, USA
Eric D. Ramstetter
Kansai University, Japan

Indonesia has become increasingly outward-oriented in its growth strategy since the early 1980s. This chapter examines the role of private domestic and multinational enterprises in the growth of non-oil manufacturing value-added and exports in Indonesia based on compilations of establishment-level survey data. Foreign multinationals and private domestic firms alike have responded to trade liberalization in a manner consistent with Indonesia's comparative advantage. The composition of exports is gradually shifting towards more sophisticated electrical and non-electrical machinery and it appears that multinationals are playing a significant, if not dominant, role in this process.

Global trade liberalization will be accentuated by reductions of tariff and non-tariff barriers (NTBs) brought about by the Uruguay Round Agreement. Moreover, the expanded coverage of international economic transactions by the multilateral trading system will have a significant impact on the way the global economy functions. International business competition will be stimulated by the lowering of protective barriers and by moves to harmonize rules governing competition within global and regional trading regimes. Moreover, national treatment of foreign investment, improved intellectual property protection, and more effective dispute resolution mechanisms will provide a more predictable climate for multinational business operations.

The implications of these changes for newly liberalizing and low income developing countries that are opening up to international trade and investment are vigorously debated. In Indonesia the terms of the long-running debate, between the "economists" (technocrats) on the one hand and the "engineers" (interventionists) on the other, on the role of the state in the pattern of industrial and trade development have been influenced by the rise of global economic interdenpendence ("globalization"), "new trade theory", and the revisionist views about the lessons to be learned from the East Asian experience.

Those engaged in the policy debate in Indonesia have seen several swings of the policy pendulum. From the mid-sixties until 1972, the economist/technocrats reigned supreme and set about putting Indonesia's economic house in order. However, during the oil boom years (1973-1983), the influence of the economists waned as trade and industrial policy became increasingly *dirigiste*. With the collapse of oil prices and revenues in the mid-eighties, the pendulum swung back in favor of the economists. The reforms have been so successful since then that a consensus in favor of deregulation appears to exist in the government. Nonetheless, with the cabinet formed in 1993, there has been a perception that the influence of the "engineers" favoring selective state interventions to influence the allocation of economic resources, like Science and Technology Minister B.J. Habibie, have become stronger and the influence of more market-oriented technocrats weaker. Thus, a large number of market distortions have been maintained to promote strategic sectors of industry and to protect monopolies in certain commodities.

The nuances of the policy debate in Indonesia have been influenced by the undeniable rise in global interdependence that has been shaped as much by technological advances as by the global advance of free market economics. Almost all observers regard adjustment to the "globalization phenomenon" as inevitable, whether or not they believe the likely outcome of the changes to a more open and rules-based system of international economic activities to be positive or negative in their net effects on developing countries.

How do we evaluate the outcome of far-reaching changes in the global trading rules? What methodologies or models are the most appropriate for determining the distribution of the gains and the costs of adjustment between countries and among groups within countries? With increasing interaction of international investment and trade flows, including trade in services, an improved understanding requires additional theoretical and empirical research. In recent years, numerous studies on the likely impact of the recently concluded Uruguay Round Agreement on various groups of developing and developed countries have been undertaken. Studies of the welfare effects of trade liberalization in various countries have also proliferated. However, these studies usually rely on models that are subject to shortcomings in the data and specification errors.[1] In-depth empirical study of the economic activities of multinational and domestic industrial enterprises is likely to lay the basis for an improved understanding of the impacts of global trade and investment openness on the industrial structure and trade of newly liberalizing developing countries.[2] Indonesia makes an ideal case study. It has progressively implemented structural adjustment reforms since the mid-eighties, including far-reaching liberalization of its trade and foreign investment policies.[3] In addition, as Aswicahyono, Bird and Hill (1994) point out:

> "Indonesia provides a suitable case-study: its policy reforms from the mid 1980s were decisive, and its industrial data base is relatively sophisticated."

In this chapter, we examine the changes in the structure of industry and trade brought about by the increasing openness of the Indonesian economy to international trade and investment flows. In particular, we seek to present empirical results on the role of multinational firms in the Indonesian economy in terms of their share in value-added in non-oil manufacturing, direction and share of exports and imports in sales, and some related measures of firm activity.

Recent Economic Trends and the Policy Debate

It is apparent that economic growth in recent years has been led by non-oil manufacturing (Table 1). Prior to 1987 manufacturing as a whole (including oil and gas refineries) grew faster than non-oil manufacturing, however, since 1987 the reverse has been the case. Trade performance has also clearly been influenced by the changing economic policy environment. Since the far-reaching reforms of the mid-eighties, export growth in real terms has accelerated with non-oil export growth more than doubling in 1987-1992 compared with 1983-1986. Real import growth was negative between 1983-1986 but recovered in 1987-1991 before slackening somewhat between 1992 and 1994.

Table 1: Growth Rates of GDP, GDP Deflators, Merchandise Trade, Merchandise Trade Prices, Nominal FDI, Exchange Rates, and Population *(Percent)*

Variable	75-83	83-86	1987	1992	1993	1994
Real GDP	7.4	5.1	4.9	6.5	6.5	7.3
Real GDP Expenditure Components						
Priv. Consumption	9.1	2.4	3.3	2.9	5.8	5.8
Govt. Consumption	9.8	4.6	(0.2)	5.8	0.1	2.9
Fixed Investment	11.8	3.2	5.5	4.9	5.7	12.6
Exports	0.7	4.2	14.6	14.7	6.6	7.3
Imports	13.6	0.5	2.0	6.6	4.4	13.3
Real GDP Industry Components						
Agriculture	4.0	3.8	2.1	6.7	1.4	0.3
Mining	3.6	0.4	0.3	(1.9)	2.2	5.3
Oil & Gas	NA	0.3	0.3	0.3	0.3	0.3
Manufacturing	13.5	14.0	10.6	9.7	9.3	11.1
Non Oil Manuf.	NA	12.2	11.4	11.0	11.6	12.0
Other	10.6	5.0	6.1	7.8	8.6	8.6
GDP Deflator	16.8	4.5	15.8	7.3	9.1	6.6
Deflators for GDP Expenditure Components						
Priv. Consumption	13.2	7.8	10.0	5.7	10.1	9.8
Govt. Consumption	15.0	7.0	4.0	12.4	20.2	1.3
Fixed Investment	15.2	5.0	18.5	5.6	4.5	6.8
Exports	26.3	(3.8)	30.3	7.0	4.9	3.3
Imports	12.3	1.9	30.3	7.5	6.3	1.1
Deflators for GDP Industry Components						
Agriculture	15.8	7.9	14.6	6.4	8.3	11.3
Mining	21.9	(11.0)	49.6	(3.0)	0.6	(5.4)
Oil & Gas	NA	(11.7)	53.7	(2.1)	1.7	(7.6)
Manufacturing	15.6	5.4	11.3	8.2	9.1	10.4
Non Oil Manuf.	NA	7.1	16.3	10.1	8.6	12.0
Other	14.8	7.7	9.9	9.8	11.1	5.6
Real Merchandise Trade Flows						
Export	3.1	5.1	6.9	16.7	12.9	11.6
Non Oil Export	NA	12.3	28.8	27.2	12.1	11.6
Import	10.9	(10.5)	20.8	6.1	4.8	11.6
Nominal FDI, Balance of Payments Estimates						
Flows	3.8	7.6	91.3	24.8	16.0	NA
Stocks From 1970	19.5	17.3	26.7	35.8	30.5	NA
US $ / Rupiah	(9.3)	(10.8)	(22.0)	(3.9)	(2.7)	(3.4)
Population	1.9	2.1	2.2	1.7	1.7	1.6

Notes :
For 1975, private consumption includes changes in stocks but for 1983-1994, changes in stocks are excluded. Real trade flows estimated with World Bank price indices for 1975 with wholesale price indices for 1983-1994 (all indices defined as 1 for 1983). All prices and values defined in rupiah, translated from US$ estimates where necessary.
Source: Asian Development Bank (1985).
    Bank Indonesia (various years a, various years b),
    Biro Pusat Statistik (various years a),
    World Bank (1994),
    International Monetary Fund (1995, various years).

Major devaluations were undertaken in 1983 and again in 1986. The devaluations were accompanied by administrative reforms. The first major reform was to hire a private Swiss firm--Societe Generale de Surveillance (SGS)--to conduct pre-shipment inspection of imports, replacing the corrupt and inefficient customs service. The second major change was to become a signatory to the GATT subsidies code and to replace GATT-illegal export subsidies with a duty drawback and exemption program. These administrative changes were followed by measures to replace non-tariff barriers (NTBs) with tariffs. Foreign investment regulations were relaxed, a negative list was adopted, and the number of sectors which were restricted or closed to foreign direct investment (FDI) was progressively reduced. These real sector reforms set the stage for the rapid growth of FDI inflows and stocks (Table 1). The stability of the real exchange rate was maintained through steady nominal depreciation of the rupiah and by controlling the rate of inflation to single digits.

In recent years (1993-1995) non-oil/gas export performance has deteriorated, with nominal growth decelerating from 28% in 1992 to 16% in 1993 and 12% in 1994. While non-oil/gas exports improved in 1995 (growing by 14% in the first 9 months over the same period the previous year), a surge in imports drastically reduced the merchandise trade surplus and led to a ballooning of the current account deficit. The current account balance was -$3.3 billion in 1994 (1.9% of GDP), and in 1995, it is conservatively estimated to rise to -$6.4 billion (3.4% of GDP). The deficit in the current account in Indonesia is relatively minor (as a percent of GDP) when compared with neighboring countries such as Malaysia and Thailand.

The deterioration of export performance has not led to any reversal of deregulation policies. Indeed, the May 1995 deregulation package cut tariffs by an average of 5 percentage points so that the simple average tariff declined from around 20% to 15% according to World Bank estimates (Condon and Fane, 1995). Further, the package commits Indonesia to a time bound schedule of tariff reduction, so that tariffs on almost all manufactured goods (excluding the automotive sector) will be between zero to10% by 2003. However, there is some concern that further policy reform may be constrained. For example, Indonesia appears to have recently retreated from its stated position of advocacy of universal coverage of trade policy reform in ASEAN (and, by implication, in APEC) as it sought to withdraw 15 "sensitive" agricultural items from its temporary exclusion list for the ASEAN Free Trade Agreement (AFTA) common effective preferential tariff (CEPT) scheme and to place these items instead on a list of sensitive (excluded) items. Indonesia reached a temporary compromise with its ASEAN partners that effectively extends the protection of these items (including rice, sugar, wheat flour, cloves, milk and dairy products among others) until 2010. It has also been announced that Indonesia will continue to pursue its high-technology industrial promotion policies in the aero-space industry and other strategic industries under the control of the Minister of Science and Technology. Finally, in the May 1995 package, some sectors were added to the negative list of sectors where FDI is banned or restricted.

These developments do not necessarily constitute a trend away from liberalization. They do indicate that the policy debate is far from resolved. At the center of the present debate is the issue of comparative advantage versus competitive advantage and the interpretation of the elements of successful policy (including the question of an activist industrial policy) in East Asia.

Changing Trade Structures and Comparative Advantage

The concept of competitive advantage has been juxtaposed against one of the best established concepts in international economics: the law of comparative costs or what is sometimes called the law of comparative advantage. There are two potentially important differences between the two concepts. First, those using the concept of competitive advantage often imply that trade is driven by absolute price differentials by focusing on single commodity or single industry comparisons across countries (Porter, 1990), while the principle of comparative advantage demonstrates definitively that it is differences in relative prices that determine the patterns of trade. In this respect, the concept of competitive advantage must either be defined explicitly in terms of absolute prices or it is simply wrong. However, this point is not intuitive and is often forgotten by policy makers who focus only on the industry they are concerned with and forget that they must think about that industry relative to others.

Second, analysts using the concept of competitive advantage (Porter, 1990) often imply that government promotion of competitiveness in strategic industries is a worthy policy goal and this is a siren's call that is hard for policymakers to resist. On the other hand, economists that use the concept of comparative advantage have a tendency to emphasize the costs of such protectionism (Warr, 1994), though there also are a number of economists that have argued that protection of infant industries, that is industries in which costs can be lowered simply by expanding production or through the accrual of learning effects, can be beneficial (Wade,

1990; Amsden, 1989). Moreover, in the last two decades trade theory has become increasingly concerned with strategic trade policies, policies that resemble infant industry protection in that they protect selected industries in an attempt to lower costs, expand market share, and/or extract larger rents by facilitating expanded production in the presence of economies of scale or accelerating the accumulation of learning effects. Other economists are also quick to point out, however, that such policies result in the government giving market power to firms, and thus create strong motives for rent-seeking behavior (Krueger, 1987; Nasution, 1996).

These economic juxtapositions miss a key and powerful element of the concept of competitive advantage, that experiences of successful individual firms and "clusters" of firms in selected industries have large impacts on how the pattern of comparative advantage evolves over time.[4] On the other hand, in its most commonly taught form, the law of comparative advantage holds that nations will tend to produce and export those goods that are more intensive in factors of production that are relatively abundant or in which they have relatively large technological advantages, and to import those goods the production of which requires intensive use of factors of production that are relatively scarce or in which their technology is relatively poor.[5]

Although this theory is static and is less useful for predicting trade patterns where most trade is with countries of similar technology levels or factor endowments (e.g., trade among most developed economies), it is quite useful for predicting the sort of industries that will be export-oriented within a country such as Indonesia, where the majority of trade is with countries of dissimilar factor endowments and technology levels. Moreover, assuming a country does not have the power to control world prices, an assumption that is reasonable for the vast majority of developing economies, the theory provides a powerful basis for understanding why the static costs of protection can be astronomical by highlighting the role of the internal allocation of a nation's resources. In the context of Indonesia and similar countries, the theory of comparative advantage also explains the early stage of "export-push" where exports of primary commodities and standardized labor-intensive manufactured items are important.

In Indonesia, the oil and gas sector was paramount as it accounted for the vast majority of exports. Non-oil manufacturing exports have grown particularly rapidly in recent years. If one disaggregates manufacturing exports by 3-digit ISIC industries, non-oil manufactured exports, which comprised but 11 percent of total exports in 1983, grew rapidly to account for 55 percent of total exports by 1992 (Table 2).

Table 2: Total Exports *(US$ millions)* **and Shares of Total Exports by Industry** *(Percent)*

Industry	1975	1983	1986	1990	1992
TOTAL EXPORTS	7,102	21,152	16,075	25,674	33,861
SHARES OF TOTAL EXPORTS					
Manufacturing	12.3	15.8	29.1	47.1	58.1
Petroleum Refineries	5.7	4.5	5.7	4.6	3.6
Other Oil & Coal	0.0	0.0	0.0	0.0	0.0
Non Oil Manufacturing	6.5	11.3	23.4	42.4	54.5
Food (ISIC 311)	3.3	1.5	2.3	2.9	3.6
Food (ISIC 312)	0.0	0.1	0.2	0.3	0.2
Beverages	0.0	0.0	0.0	0.0	0.0
Tobacco	0.2	0.1	0.1	0.3	0.4
Textiles	0.0	0.6	2.1	5.6	9.5
Apparel	0.0	0.7	3.0	5.8	8.5
Leather	0.0	0.0	0.1	0.3	0.2
Footwear	0.0	0.0	0.0	0.1	0.2
Wood	0.5	3.8	8.9	12.9	12.3
Furniture	0.0	0.0	0.0	0.4	0.6
Paper	0.0	0.0	0.2	0.8	1.0
Printing, etc.	0.1	0.0	0.0	0.2	0.3
Industrial Chemicals	0.0	0.4	1.2	1.8	1.8
Other Chemicals	0.3	0.2	0.4	0.6	0.6
Drugs & Medicines	0.2	0.1	0.1	0.1	0.1
Rubber	0.0	0.0	0.1	2.0	3.4
Plastics	0.0	0.0	0.1	1.4	2.3
Pottery	0.0	0.0	0.0	0.1	0.2
Glass	0.0	0.0	0.1	0.4	0.4
Other Non Metalic	0.0	0.0	0.3	0.4	0.4
Ferrous Basic Metals	0.0	0.0	0.4	1.0	0.9
Non Ferrous Basic Metals	0.7	2.7	2.8	2.3	1.6
Metal Products	0.6	0.1	0.1	0.9	1.2
Non Electric Machinery	0.0	0.0	0.0	0.1	0.6
Office & Computing	0.0	0.0	0.0	0.0	0.4
Electric Machinery	0.1	0.7	0.4	0.8	2.6
Radio & Television	0.1	0.7	0.3	0.5	2.0
Transport Machinery	0.2	0.0	0.1	0.5	0.7
Shipbuilding	0.1	0.0	0.1	0.2	0.1
Motor Vehicles	0.1	0.0	0.0	0.1	0.2
Precision Machinery	0.1	0.0	0.0	0.2	0.3
Miscellanious Manufac.	0.0	0.2	0.3	0.5	0.8

Sources: Australian National University (1995);
International Monetary Fund (1995).

Among the manufactured exports, textiles, apparel, wood, paper, rubber and plastic products as well as electrical machinery have shown the most impressive growth rates.[6] However, despite the rapid growth in all these categories, only three traditional labor- and resource-intensive industries, textiles, apparel, and wood, combined to account for over half of non-oil manufacturing exports.[7] Imports have also undergone structural change (Table 3). The rising shares of non-electrical machinery, electrical machinery and precision machinery are noteworthy as is the continued large share of chemicals. Although we have no parallel estimates of factor endowments with which to correlate these trade data, it is clear that the relative abundance of natural resources, oil and gas, wood, rubber, among others, and a relatively cheap work force are major factors behind the pattern of exports. Likewise, the relative backwardness of Indonesian technology combined with the relative scarcity of capital are important factors behind the pattern of imports.

These observations are reinforced by examination of changes in indices of revealed comparative advantage (RCAs) for the years 1975, 1983 and 1986-1992 (Table 4). For manufacturing and non-oil manufacturing as a whole there has been a decided reduction in comparative disadvantage.[8] These data also indicate that Indonesia has gone from a position of revealed comparative disadvantage to one of revealed comparative advantage in several labor-intensive and resource-based industries: textiles, apparel, wood, and rubber. It also has maintained its comparative advantage in petroleum refineries and has recently gained a comparative advantage in the downstream plastics products industry. On the other hand, despite a long history of protection and promotion, comparative disadvantage remains in the chemicals and transportation equipment industries, particularly in motor vehicles. For a number of years in the 1980s, there was a revealed comparative advantage in non-ferrous basic metals, but this position has been reversed in recent years. Of some interest is the rise in the RCAs for electric machinery and miscellaneous manufacturing indicating that these industries may be moving toward a position of revealed comparative advantage in the next decade or so.[9]

The changes observed in RCAs have clearly been influenced by the policy changes that were introduced in the mid-eighties. The removal of many trade restrictions allowed firms to source inputs at closer to world prices and the lessening of the sectoral biases that existed in the previous decade made it easier for factors of production to be reallocated in favor of the labor- and resource-intensive industries in which Indonesia now has a comparative advantage. In this respect, it is important to emphasize that a fundamental message of the law of comparative advantage is that international trade is usually win-win. More importantly, analyses

Table 3: Total Imports *(US$ millions)* **and Shares of Total Imports by Industry** *(Percent)*

Industry	1975	1983	1986	1990	1992
TOTAL IMPORTS	4,770	16,352	10,718	21,837	27,280
SHARES OF TOTAL IMPORTS					
Manufacturing	63.2	69.5	58.5	75.3	72.4
Petroleum Refineries	3.5	15.7	3.7	3.6	3.6
Other Oil & Coal	0.1	0.1	0.1	0.1	0.1
Non Oil Manufacturing	59.6	53.7	54.8	71.5	68.6
Food (ISIC 311)	5.7	3.5	1.6	1.6	2.4
Food (ISIC 312)	0.3	0.3	0.4	0.7	0.5
Beverages	0.1	0.1	0.1	0.1	0.1
Tobacco	0.1	0.0	0.0	0.0	0.1
Textiles	2.0	0.8	1.0	2.9	3.2
Apparel	0.1	0.1	0.1	0.1	0.1
Leather	0.0	0.0	0.0	0.4	0.8
Footwear	0.0	0.0	0.0	0.0	0.0
Wood	0.1	0.0	0.0	0.1	0.1
Furniture	0.2	0.1	0.1	0.3	0.2
Paper	0.8	1.4	1.6	1.6	1.8
Printing, etc.	0.2	0.2	0.3	0.6	0.5
Industrial Chemicals	10.8	7.7	11.0	12.4	10.2
Other Chemicals	1.2	1.3	1.9	1.9	1.9
Drugs & Medicines	0.5	0.6	0.6	0.6	0.6
Rubber	0.6	0.4	1.0	0.7	0.7
Plastics	0.5	0.6	1.0	1.6	1.4
Pottery	0.0	0.0	0.0	0.1	0.1
Glass	0.2	0.2	0.4	0.4	0.3
Other Non Metalic	1.2	0.6	0.7	0.5	0.5
Ferrous Basic Metals	6.8	5.0	4.2	5.4	4.8
Non Ferrous Basic Metals	0.8	0.8	1.1	1.6	1.5
Metal Products	4.1	4.4	2.6	3.1	4.5
Non Electric Machinery	8.7	11.5	10.3	17.8	15.0
Office & Computing	0.3	0.4	0.6	0.9	0.5
Electric Machinery	5.0	4.9	5.1	5.3	8.2
Radio & Television	2.9	3.2	3.1	3.6	5.8
Transport Machinery	9.0	8.1	8.2	9.7	7.4
Shipbuilding	0.9	1.6	1.7	1.3	2.0
Motor Vehicles	5.9	4.3	4.9	6.0	3.7
Precision Machinery	0.8	1.2	1.3	1.7	1.6
Miscellanious Manufac.	0.2	0.2	0.3	0.4	0.4

Sources: Australian National University (1995);
International Monetary Fund (1995).

Table 4: Indices of Revealed Comparative Advantage by Industry

Industry	1975	1983	1986	1990	1992
Manufacturing	0.17	0.22	0.37	0.59	0.72
Petroleum Refineries	1.38	0.82	1.77	1.74	1.71
Other Oil & Coal	0.00	0.00	0.06	0.01	0.01
Non Oil Manufacturing	0.09	0.17	0.31	0.55	0.69
Food (ISIC 311)	0.49	0.29	0.44	0.69	0.82
Food (ISIC 312)	0.10	0.21	0.37	0.49	0.31
Beverages	0.00	0.00	0.00	0.04	0.03
Tobacco	1.16	0.29	0.37	0.85	1.12
Textiles	0.01	0.20	0.65	1.77	2.96
Apparel	0.02	0.34	1.05	1.85	2.37
Leather	0.02	0.06	0.17	0.46	0.39
Footwear	0.00	0.00	0.00	0.12	0.20
Wood	0.44	3.45	8.34	11.34	11.20
Furniture	0.01	0.02	0.05	0.52	0.76
Paper	0.00	0.02	0.10	0.35	0.47
Printing, etc.	0.25	0.00	0.01	0.27	0.41
Industrial Chemicals	0.00	0.07	0.18	0.27	0.30
Other Chemicals	0.17	0.12	0.18	0.26	0.22
Drugs & Medicines	0.22	0.08	0.11	0.08	0.05
Rubber	0.00	0.03	0.16	2.48	3.96
Plastics	0.06	0.02	0.08	1.28	1.80
Pottery	0.00	0.00	0.03	0.39	0.76
Glass	0.01	0.10	0.17	0.78	0.79
Other Non Metalic	0.00	0.07	0.49	0.73	0.67
Ferrous Basic Metals	0.00	0.01	0.12	0.31	0.31
Non Ferrous Basic Metals	0.29	1.20	1.40	1.02	0.86
Metal Products	0.20	0.02	0.06	0.32	0.42
Non Electric Machinery	0.00	0.00	0.00	0.01	0.05
Office & Computing	0.00	0.00	0.00	0.00	0.11
Electric Machinery	0.02	0.10	0.05	0.10	0.28
Radio & Television	0.03	0.17	0.07	0.10	0.34
Transport Machinery	0.02	0.00	0.01	0.04	0.05
Shipbuilding	0.03	0.00	0.08	0.20	0.14
Motor Vehicles	0.01	0.00	0.00	0.01	0.02
Precision Machinery	0.04	0.00	0.02	0.07	0.12
Miscellanious Manufac.	0.01	0.10	0.17	0.29	0.46

Sources: Australian National University (1995);
International Monetary Fund (1995).

based on the concept of comparative advantage in countries like Indonesia, where the explanatory power of the factor endowments approach to comparative advantage is relatively high, can demonstrate most clearly how much Indonesia has lost from previous protection, and correspondingly how large the benefits of liberalization have been.

This important message may get lost when the notion of competitive advantage is used without due consideration to the importance of comparative advantage. Specifically, the often espoused idea that interventions to restrict trade can lead to gains, even in an moderately sized economy such as Indonesia, at the expense of other nations, receives an unrealistic degree of credibility.[10] Although some interpretations of industrial policy experience in Japan, Korea, and Taiwan argue that government interventions dictated the course of industrial and trade development, more balanced interpretations of those experiences show that the more effective policy interventions actually reinforced existing patterns of comparative advantage.[11]

In Indonesia, as in other developing economies, there are those who focus on the concept of competitive advantage and are attracted to the idea that an early push toward technology and capital-intensive industries can create competitiveness in so-called strategic sectors. The problem with this approach in a developing economy such as Indonesia is that it requires a concentration of a developing nation's relatively scarcest resources on industries that may not attain a comparative advantage even in the long-run. Moreover, relatively abundant resources such as labor tend to be neglected and under-utilized in such an approach.

Competitive advantage has provided insights that are useful to the strategy of individual firms competing within a certain market or markets. The decision to develop differentiated products rather than to focus on keeping costs down for standard products is an example of where competitive advantage can help firms. Porter (1990) shows that it is the adoption of a single strategy focussed on development of differentiated products that gives successful firms their competitive advantage, and demonstrates that such firms do best globally when they emerge from a vigorously competitive domestic market. Competitive advantage places its explanatory emphasis on what determines commercial success of individual firms in the competitive global market place. However, it cannot tell us anything about the efficient allocation of resources at the national level.

Should policies aimed at influencing the composition of production and exports be adopted as a national development strategy as those who focus on competitive advantage suggest? What happens to central policy issues such as maintenance of sound macroeconomic policies? Changing composition of exports and production is a consequence rather than a cause of national development (Warr 1994). Removing restrictions on international trade often fosters more rapid economic growth and development, which in turn leads to a changing composition of exports. This is precisely what we believe has happened in Indonesia since deregulation began in earnest in 1986 and, in our view, it is acceleration of the liberalization process that will create the largest probability that Indonesia's economic development will continue at a rapid pace in the future as well.

Foreign Multinational Firms and Competition in Indonesian Manufacturing

Another important aspect of Indonesia's economic performance since the mid-1980s has been the large increases in FDI noted above. Accordingly, foreign multinationals have been asserted to have played a key role in the rapid growth of Indonesian manufacturing during this period. This section thus examines the role of foreign multinationals in Indonesian manufacturing, with particular attention given to their role in facilitating increased international competitiveness in Indonesian industries. The statistical basis of these analyses is a series of industrial surveys that have been conducted by Biro Pusat Statistik and are available on unpublished diskettes, from which it is possible to compile a number of indicators by industry and ownership category from 1975 forward. In this study, we rely on compilations of these data by Anas (1995), Aswachiyo, Bird and Hill (1995), and Pangestu (1995), because the former two sources provide estimates of foreign shares of value added covering the longest time span known to be available and because the latter provides the only known trade estimates from this source.[12]

In compiling the data on ownership a problem encountered is that seven categories of ownership are identified in some years.[13] Aswicahyono and Hill (1995, p. 146) assert that the foreign and foreign-private groups can reasonably be classified as unambiguously foreign because control usually lies with foreign partners in foreign-private joint ventures. Correspondingly, the series from Aswicahyono, Bird and Hill (1995) given in Table 5 is consistent with this definition, giving the foreign share at 18 percent for this year. The estimates from Anas (1995) given in Table 6 indicate a somewhat larger foreign share for 1985, 21 percent, and a difference of similar magnitude is observed between estimates of foreign shares for 1975, 21 percent versus 23 percent.[14]

Table 5: Value Added in Indonesia's Manufacturing Establishments by Ownership *(Total in Billions of Rupiah, Shares in Percent)*

Year	National Accounts Estimates Total at Market Place	Industrial Statistics Estimates				
		Total at Market Place	Total at Factor Cost	Govt. Share	Private Share	Foreign Share
ALL MANUFACTURING, INCLUDING OIL AND GAS						
1975	1124	NA	NA	35	45	19
1976	1453	NA	NA	34	41	25
1977	1817	NA	NA	34	41	26
1978	2420	NA	NA	33	44	23
1979	3311	NA	NA	39	40	21
1980	5288	NA	NA	35	43	22
1981	7067	NA	NA	36	42	22
1982	7482	NA	NA	39	41	20
1983	9896	NA	NA	39	43	19
1984	13113	NA	NA	47	40	14
1985	15503	NA	NA	46	41	13
1986	17185	NA	NA	42	44	14
1987	21150	NA	NA	40	46	15
1988	26252	NA	NA	40	46	14
1989	30323	NA	NA	38	46	16
1990	38910	NA	NA	37	48	15
NON OIL MANUFACTURING						
1975	NA	NA	483	27	50	21
1976	NA	752	646	25	46	28
1977	NA	949	775	26	46	29
1978	NA	1,222	1,006	25	50	26
1979	NA	1,602	1,288	26	48	25
1980	NA	NA	2,128	18	54	28
1981	NA	NA	2,713	19	53	28
1982	NA	3,394	2,970	20	54	26
1983	7,666	4,579	3,379	22	55	24
1984	9,394	8,111	4,474	26	56	19
1985	11,216	8,067	7,204	25	57	18
1986	13,301	9,348	8,343	25	57	18
1987	17,233	11,279	10,238	26	57	18
1988	21,278	13,874	12,646	26	57	17
1989	24,876	19,046	16,919	24	56	19
1990	31,621	25,156	22,830	22	59	19
1991	39,145	29,893	28,124	NA	NA	NA
1992	47,836	41,397	39,346	14	61	21

Notes :
Industrial statistics' estimates refer to establishments with 20 or more employees.
Shares for 1992 estimated as the ratio of shares for 1992 and 1985 from Anas
(1995) multiplied by the corresponding 1985 shares from Aswicahyono, Bird,
and Hill (1995) and repeated in this Table.
*Sources: Anas (1995, p. 749); Aswicahyono, Bird, and Hill (1995, p. 11);
             Asian Development Bank (1985);
             Biro Pusat Statistik (various years a, various years b, various years c)
             c); United Nations Statistical Division (1993).*

Table 6: Value Added in Indonesia's Manufacturing Establishments by Industry and Owner *(Total in Billions of Rupiah, Shares in Percent)*

Industry	Total 1985	Total 1992	Govt. Share 1985	Govt. Share 1992	Private Share 1985	Private Share 1992	Foreign Share 1985	Foreign Share 1992
Non Oil Manufacturing	8,226	35,219	20	11	59	63	21	25
Food (ISIC 311)	855	4,569	38	23	54	70	9	7
Food (ISIC 312)	202	1,215	18	9	57	65	25	26
Beverages	109	395	0	0	29	26	71	74
Tobacco	1,338	4,217	0	0	94	96	6	3
Textiles	792	4,092	10	4	59	75	31	21
Garments	120	1,528	1	2	96	73	2	25
Leather Products	16	176	5	6	65	67	30	28
Footwear	37	1,078	0	0	37	43	63	57
Wood Products	714	3,867	15	1	72	87	13	11
Furniture	21	467	0	0	94	93	6	7
Paper Products	132	1,447	33	3	55	67	12	30
Printing & Publishing	108	546	11	28	84	68	5	4
Industrial Chemicals	495	2,604	70	25	14	26	17	48
Other Chemicals	463	1,215	4	5	56	59	40	36
Rubber Products	392	1,229	10	10	80	66	10	24
Plastics Products	204	910	0	1	42	91	58	9
Pottery & China	29	231	1	1	94	70	5	29
Glass Products	112	351	4	3	15	58	81	39
Cement	274	760	33	32	33	20	34	48
Other Non Metalic	19	82	7	1	82	91	11	8
Structural Clay Products	19	147	7	3	93	92	0	5
Other Non-Metallic	529	2,562	77	NA	10	NA	13	NA
Basic Metals	NA	1,887	NA	74	NA	17	NA	9
Ferous	NA	675	NA	3	NA	18	NA	80
Non Ferrous	330	1,510	10	3	62	61	28	36
Fabricated Metals	90	537	35	21	26	46	39	32
Non Electric Machinery	315	1,916	11	24	46	30	43	46
Electric Machinery	478	3,279	11	12	69	68	20	20
Transport Machinery	5	62	0	25	67	61	33	14
Miscellanious	31	409	3	0	56	45	41	55

Notes :
Estimates refer to establishments with 20 or more employees.
Source: Anas (1995), p. 749.

Potential sources of differences in the estimates are the sampling methodology used or the definition of value added employed. Published estimates of value added in 1985 were 7,204 billion rupiah at factor cost and 8,067 billion rupiah at market prices (Table 5 and Biro Pusat Statistik, various years-b).[15] However, the estimate given by Anas (1995) is 8,226 billion rupiah (Table 6) which differs from the published estimate. Unfortunately, no estimates of total value added that correspond to the shares for 1975-1990 in Table 5 are given in the original source. It appears that the definitions and/or samples employed in Tables 5 and 6 are somewhat different. Thus, caution is necessary when interpreting these figures.[16]

Having identified potential discrepancies between the various compilations used here, there are nonetheless at least two interesting patterns that estimates of foreign shares in value added (Tables 5 and 6) reveal.[17] First, in the aggregate, foreign shares of non-oil manufacturing were relatively high in 1976-1983 (24-29 percent) but declined steeply to 17-19 percent in 1984-1990.[18] An attempt to extrapolate this series to 1992 by multiplying the ratio of the 1992 and 1985 shares given from Anas (p. 749, c.f., Table 6) and the 1985 ratio in Table 5 yields an estimate for 1992 of 21 percent, markedly higher than estimates for 1984-1990, but still a good deal below estimates for 1976-1983. Thus, despite the elimination or moderation of a number of restrictions on foreign multinationals and a large increase in FDI flows, much of it in manufacturing, the share of foreign-controlled firms in manufacturing production has not increased as much as might be expected and remains below the levels reached in 1976-1983.[19] However, the growth of real production in foreign firms was probably somewhat higher in the post-1985 period and the declining share of foreign firms is best viewed as a result of the relatively rapid growth of private firms rather than slow growth in foreign firms.[20] Policy reforms have apparently led to the largest production increases in private firms and facilitated continued rapid increases in foreign firms, but have led to reduced growth in production by state owned enterprises.

Second, the pattern of foreign shares is somewhat different in Indonesia than in other East and Southeast Asian economies such as Malaysia and Thailand. Perhaps the starkest contrast in this respect is that foreign firms are still relatively small in Indonesia in the three major machinery industries (nonelectric, electric, and transport machinery), accounting for only 30 percent of the value added in these industries and only 19 percent of value added in all foreign manufacturing plants in 1992 (Table 6). In contrast, in Thailand in 1990, corresponding shares of sales were 62 percent and 42 percent, respectively, and in Malaysia in 1991, corresponding shares were 79 percent and 44 percent, respectively, when measured in terms of fixed assets.[21] However, it should be noted that the share of these three industries in total value added of foreign firms has risen steadily from 9 percent in 1975 and 15 percent in 1985. Thus, although these industries still account for a relatively small portion of foreign firm activity in Indonesia, their share in the total has been rising quickly.

Of the 29 (1975 and 1985) or 30 (1992) 3-digit industries listed in Table 6, only 11 of them had foreign shares of 25 percent or greater in 1975, but this number increased gradually to 14 in 1985 and 17 in 1992. Foreign involvement has been relatively large with foreign shares of over 50 percent in beverages (1985, 1992), footwear (1975, 1985, 1992), other chemicals (1975), rubber (1975), plastics (1985), glass (1985), and miscellaneous manufactures (1992) and moderately large with shares of 39-50 percent in some of these industries (other chemicals in 1985, glass in 1992, miscellaneous manufacturing in 1985) as well as in basic chemicals (1992), cement (1992), fabricated metals (1975), and electric machinery (1975, 1985, 1992). Foreign shares rose steadily in beverages, basic chemicals, cement, and miscellaneous manufacturing, and fell continuously in footwear, wood products, and other chemicals, but fluctuated, often in a wide range, in the majority of the industries identified in Table 6.   These fluctuations result in part because Indonesia's industrialization is still in its early stages and many industries are thus still quite small, and in part because some of the foreign firms are quite large relative to their industries in Indonesia. Moreover, these fluctuations make it dangerous to generalize about the roles of foreign firms in Indonesia. However, it is clear that foreign firms have played and continue to play important roles in a number of industry groups, including industries where the importance of knowledge-based intangible capital is thought to lead to a large multinational presence (e.g., chemicals, electric machinery), as well as industries typically thought to be labor-intensive (e.g., textiles, garments, footwear, miscellaneous manufactures) and natural resource-intensive (e.g., metals, rubber).

Relative to total value added of foreign firms, calculated from the foreign shares and value added estimates in Table 6, the largest industries were tobacco (30 percent of the total), textiles (11 percent), other chemicals (11 percent), fabricated metals (7 percent), and electric machinery (7 percent) in 1975. By 1985, the leading industries were textiles (14 percent), other chemicals (11 percent), electric machinery (8 percent), plastics (6 percent), and transport machinery (6 percent). In 1992, they were basic chemicals (14 percent), electric machinery (11 percent), textiles (11 percent), basic metals (ferrous plus nonferrous, 8 percent), and transport machinery (7 percent). Viewed from this perspective, the pattern of foreign multinationals' production is becoming more typical of the patterns in other Asian economies with electric machinery, transport machinery, and basic chemicals occupying a larger portion of this production in recent years. Moreover, there are indications that electric machinery, in particular, has continued to grow especially rapidly with a number of new investments by large Japanese firms in this industry.[22]

Although the growth of foreign firms in terms of value added has been perhaps slower than one might expect, given the scope of liberalization in Indonesia between 1985 and 1992, the growth of foreign firms has apparently been much more rapid if measured in terms of exports (Table 7). In only two years, from 1990 to 1992, in all non-oil manufacturing the share of foreign firms in Indonesian exports increased from 22 percent to 32 percent.[23] Moreover, by 1992 foreign firms' shares exceeded 50 percent in a wide range of industries: beverages, footwear, nonferrous basic metals, metal products, nonelectric machinery, electric machinery, transport machinery, precision machinery and miscellaneous manufactures. Correspondingly, the export propensities of foreign firms increased rapidly in 1990-1992, from 17 percent to 36 percent in non-oil manufacturing. For foreign firms in 1992 export propensities were extremely high (76 percent or larger) in garments, footwear, nonferrous basic metals and miscellaneous manufactures, and also exceeded 50 percent in wood and electric machinery. For private firms, export propensities also increased markedly in 1990-1992, from 19 percent to 24 percent, and were also relatively high (above 40 percent) in 1992 in 4 of the 6 industries with high export propensities for foreign firms, nonferrous basic metals and electric machinery being the two exceptions. Thus, although the recent policy reforms may not have led to a large increase in foreign firm presence per se, they do appear to have led to rapid export growth in both foreign and private firms.

It is also remarkable that import propensities are generally much higher in foreign firms compared to local firms, especially local private firms (Table 8). However, in the 1986-1992 period, import propensities changed relatively little, increasing from 53 percent to 57 percent in foreign firms and from 36 percent to 37 percent in government firms, while declining from 25 percent to 23 percent in private firms. For foreign firms, import propensities exceeding 50 percent were observed in roughly half of all individual industries (14 of 26 in 1986, 15 of 29 in 1992). Notably, 5 of the 6 industries with high export propensities in 1992 were among the industries with high import propensities, wood being the only exception. Other industries in which foreign firms had import propensities of over 50 percent in 1992 were basic chemicals, other chemicals, pottery and china, glass, other nonmetallic minerals, ferrous metals, basic metals, metal products, nonelectric machinery, transport machinery, and precision machinery. Note that many of these

Table 7: Shares of Exports and Export Propensities in
Manufacturing Establishments by Ownership and Industry

Industry	Shares of Exports					
	Government		Private		Foreign	
	1990	1992	1990	1992	1990	1992
Non Oil Manufacturing	8	4	70	63	22	32
Food (ISIC 311)	11	7	86	86	3	7
Food (ISIC 312)	38	17	52	40	10	43
Beverages	0	0	100	34	0	66
Tobacco	17	0	82	100	1	0
Textiles	3	2	75	64	21	34
Garments	1	2	88	53	11	45
Leather Products	0	2	100	82	0	15
Footwear	0	0	60	44	40	56
Wood Products	0	1	87	86	13	13
Furniture	1	0	83	95	17	5
Paper Products	0	5	44	78	56	18
Printing & Publishing	10	0	90	75	0	25
Basic Chemicals	38	44	21	19	41	37
Other Chemicals	8	3	78	72	13	25
Rubber Products	7	1	70	85	24	14
Plastics Products	0	0	90	85	10	15
Pottery & China	0	1	36	73	64	27
Glass Products	46	6	54	88	0	6
Cement	28	90	72	10	0	0
Structural Clay Products	0	0	100	28	0	72
Other Non-Metallic Minerals	1	0	71	87	29	13
Basic Metals	NA	NA	NA	NA	NA	NA
Ferous	58	47	37	24	5	29
Non Ferrous	0	0	3	12	97	88
Fabricated Metals	0	2	23	18	77	80
Non Electric Machinery	0	0	36	46	64	54
Electric Machinery	0	0	36	24	64	76
Transport Machinery	11	0	5	31	84	69
Precision Machinery	0	5	95	45	5	50
Miscellaneous	0	0	64	32	36	68

Table 7: Shares of Exports and Export Propensities in Manufacturing Establishments by Ownership and Industry (Continued)

Industry	Exports Propensities					
	Government		Private		Foreign	
	1990	1992	1990	1992	1990	1992
Non Oil Manufacturing	10	10	19	24	17	36
Food (ISIC 311)	5	5	15	24	4	14
Food (ISIC 312)	55	56	15	11	8	33
Beverages	NA	0	4	5	0	10
Tobacco	73	2	1	7	0	0
Textiles	10	8	15	16	19	36
Garments	44	77	39	45	59	81
Leather Products	0	24	47	36	10	27
Footwear	32	0	48	73	64	76
Wood Products	9	41	47	54	56	61
Furniture	34	36	46	63	72	37
Paper Products	0	12	7	19	20	17
Printing & Publishing	1	0	2	5	0	22
Basic Chemicals	10	16	10	7	11	10
Other Chemicals	15	2	6	4	1	2
Rubber Products	18	10	51	59	38	34
Plastics Products	0	0	9	11	10	26
Pottery & China	0	9	5	24	22	21
Glass Products	29	36	4	35	NA	4
Cement	5	6	29	2	0	0
Structural Clay Products	0	0	1	1	0	40
Other Non-Metallic Minerals	1	0	7	9	20	13
Basic Metals	NA	NA	NA	NA	NA	NA
Ferous	11	14	12	11	2	36
Non Ferrous	NA	0	2	15	56	85
Fabricated Metals	0	17	3	6	18	35
Non Electric Machinery	0	0	1	4	2	4
Electric Machinery	1	0	9	22	23	53
Transport Machinery	3	0	0	2	2	13
Precision Machinery	NA	11	13	11	1	32
Miscellaneous	0	0	13	43	25	78

Source. Pangestu (1995), Tables 11A, 12A.

Table 8: Import Propensities in Manufacturing Establishments by Ownership and Industry

Industry	Government 1986	Government 1992	Private 1986	Private 1992	Foreign 1986	Foreign 1992
Non Oil Manufacturing	36	37	25	23	53	57
Food (ISIC 311)	2	11	13	6	26	18
Food (ISIC 312)	0	0	16	18	23	22
Beverages	1	0	11	7	56	37
Tobacco	13	77	16	4	26	36
Textiles	43	38	24	20	53	47
Garments	6	3	22	23	NA	86
Leather Products	63	17	11	12	11	47
Footwear	NA	0	6	45	7	79
Wood Products	0	0	2	3	2	4
Furniture	0	0	5	2	22	1
Paper Products	54	6	44	38	57	19
Printing & Publishing	66	47	10	16	46	23
Basic Chemicals	56	55	50	43	76	77
Other Chemicals	49	40	48	37	72	57
Rubber Products	16	0	4	13	28	25
Plastics Products	0	46	46	65	56	32
Pottery & China	25	66	49	61	14	73
Glass Products	54	52	40	35	81	55
Cement	38	2	29	6	19	9
Structural Clay Products	18	38	28	48	15	35
Other Non-Metallic Minerals	17	5	10	35	NA	67
Basic Metals	58	NA	19	NA	78	NA
Ferous	NA	97	NA	41	NA	50
Non Ferrous	NA	94	NA	62	NA	64
Fabricated Metals	21	16	46	17	67	67
Non Electric Machinery	50	55	47	48	81	87
Electric Machinery	97	88	68	54	76	77
Transport Machinery	81	62	55	45	85	66
Precision Machinery	0	53	34	18	91	90
Miscellaneous	10	0	62	35	81	58

Source. Pangestu (1995), Tables 11A, 12A.

are industries where multinationals are expected to be concentrated and where Indonesia has yet to develop a revealed comparative advantage (c.f., Table 4).

In Table 9, an attempt to go one step beyond the foregoing descriptive analysis is made by presenting the correlation coefficients among measures of trade propensities, foreign shares of value added, as well as four-plant concentration ratios for the roughly 30 3-digit industries covered in the previous tables.[24] Looking first at correlations among export propensities themselves, there were positive and statistically significant correlations (at the 0.05 level) among propensities for foreign and private plants in both 1990 and 1992, as well as for foreign plants in the two years with the change in private plant export propensities in 1990-1992. The correlation between government plants in 1992, on the one hand, and private plants in either year and foreign plants in 1990 were also positive and significant. Thus, in the early 1990s, the pattern of export propensities appears quite similar in foreign and private plants, with some evidence that government plants became similar in this respect with a lag.

Often one finds high dependence of firms on imported intermediate goods in the production of exports. In this context, it may be surprising that correlations between import propensities and export propensities are often negative, and that all significant correlations are negative. Significant correlations are concentrated in relationships involving export propensities of private plants; the correlation between the changes in export and import propensities for government plants being the only exception to this. However, among import propensities themselves, there are a number of significant and positive correlations of interest, most notably among all types of plants in 1986 and again in 1992. In other words, in a static sense, patterns of import propensities had greater similarity across ownership groups than patterns of export propensities. Moreover, the similarity is apparently dynamic as well, as import propensities in 1986-1992 were negatively and significantly correlated with import propensities in 1986 for all ownership groups.[25] It is likely that import dependence may be decreasing as local sources of intermediate inputs are located. This would also help explain the negative correlations found between export and import propensities.

As indicated above, the relationships between trade propensities and foreign shares of value added in this cross section are apparently very weak with only two correlations being significantly different from zero; the positive correlation between the foreign plant import propensity in 1986, the change in the foreign share in 1975-1985, and the negative correlation between this foreign share and the change in the import propensity of foreign firms in 1986-1992. On the other hand,

Table 9: Correlation Coefficients among Measures of Trade Propensities, Foreign Shares of Value Added, and Concentration Ratios

Variable	X92G	X9290G	X90P	X92P	X9290P	X90F	X92F
X92G							
X9290G	0.51						
X90P	0.46	0.23					
X92P	0.39	0.12	0.82				
X9290P	0.02	(0.11)	(0.01)	0.57			
X90F	0.43	0.22	0.64	0.83	0.57		
X92F	0.27	0.27	0.40	0.56	0.41	0.73	
X9290F	(0.08)	0.12	(0.28)	(0.19)	0.07	(0.23)	0.50
M86G	(0.29)	0.01	(0.27)	(0.27)	(0.06)	(0.29)	(0.26)
M92G	(0.34)	(0.29)	(0.57)	(0.45)	0.04	(0.30)	(0.10)
M9286G	(0.10)	(0.49)	(0.30)	(0.15)	0.18	(0.13)	(0.04)
M86P	(0.27)	0.08	(0.58)	(0.39)	0.14	(0.33)	(0.09)
M92P	(0.34)	0.01	(0.44)	(0.20)	0.29	(0.01)	0.18
M9286P	(0.05)	(0.10)	0.24	0.29	0.16	0.30	0.17
M86F	(0.28)	0.05	(0.60)	(0.42)	0.12	(0.40)	(0.21)
M92F	(0.11)	0.00	(0.28)	(0.12)	0.19	(0.01)	0.19
M9286F	(0.06)	(0.17)	0.31	0.29	0.07	0.25	0.30
V75F	(0.17)	(0.31)	0.09	0.28	0.37	0.23	0.07
V85F	(0.18)	(0.09)	(0.11)	0.02	0.19	(0.14)	(0.03)
V92F	(0.15)	0.06	(0.06)	0.05	0.17	0.19	0.27
V8575F	0.00	0.20	(0.17)	(0.23)	(0.16)	(0.33)	(0.09)
V9285F	0.12	0.17	0.15	0.06	(0.12)	0.20	0.15
C75	(0.10)	(0.13)	(0.11)	0.06	0.26	0.02	(0.09)
C85	(0.30)	(0.42)	(0.33)	(0.16)	0.20	(0.32)	(0.23)
C92	(0.29)	(0.41)	(0.48)	(0.41)	(0.03)	(0.36)	(0.20)
C8575	(0.19)	(0.29)	(0.21)	(0.24)	(0.13)	(0.33)	(0.13)
C9285	0.09	0.07	(0.18)	(0.40)	(0.45)	(0.35)	(0.39)

Variable	M92G	M9286G	M92P	M9286P	M86P	M92F	M9286F	V75F
M92G	0.54							
M9286G	(0.49)	0.47						
M86P	0.45	0.56						
M92P	0.38	0.55	0.68					
M9286P	(0.17)	(0.12)	(0.44)	0.35				
M86P	0.41	0.44	0.68	0.35	(0.51)			
M92F	0.30	0.41	0.50	0.54	0.02	0.58		
M9286F	(0.02)	0.09	(0.19)	0.21	0.53	(0.52)	0.39	
V75F	0.09	0.07	0.02	0.22	0.24	(0.22)	0.14	0.50
V85F	0.11	0.07	0.27	0.24	(0.04)	0.33	0.21	(0.06)
V92F	0.23	0.00	0.33	0.26	(0.23)	0.27	0.32	0.10
V8575F	0.02	(0.01)	0.21	0.01	(0.25)	0.46	0.05	(0.47)
V9285F	0.07	(0.25)	0.02	(0.13)	(0.19)	(0.18)	0.07	0.18
C75	0.38	0.21	0.27	0.37	0.07	0.20	0.50	0.35
C85	0.30	0.38	0.18	0.23	(0.04)	0.22	0.25	0.20
C92	0.10	0.60	0.19	0.21	(0.17)	0.25	0.15	(0.09)
C8575	(0.12)	0.14	(0.14)	(0.23)	(0.13)	(0.02)	(0.39)	(0.25)
C9285	(0.35)	0.09	(0.14)	(0.33)	(0.22)	0.17	(0.26)	(0.53)

Table 9: Correlation, Coefficients among Measures of Trade Propensities, Foreign Shares of Value Added, and Concentration Ratios *(Continued)*

Variable	V75F	V85F	V92F	V8575F	C75	C85
V85F	0.34					
V85F	0.34					
V92F	**0.41**	**0.65**				
V8575	**(0.60)**	**0.55**	0.18			
V9285	0.02	**(0.57)**	0.25	**(0.50)**		
C75	0.36	0.31	**0.63**	(0.06)		
C85	0.07	0.20	0.30	0.10	**(0.67)**	
C92	(0.11)	0.18	0.14	0.26	**(0.42)**	**0.85**
C8575	**(0.39)**	(0.17)	**(0.50)**	0.19	**(0.52)**	0.28

Variable definitions are as follows:

X90G	= export propensity, 1990, government plants
X92G	= export propensity, 1992, government plants
X9290G	= export propensity, 1992 less 1990, government plants
X90P	= export propensity, 1990, private plants
X92P	= export propensity, 1992, private plants
X9290P	= export propensity, 1992 less 1990, private plants
X90F	= export propensity, 1990, foreign plants
X92F	= export propensity, 1992, foreign plants
X9290F	= export propensity, 1992 less 1990, foreign plants
M86G	= import propensity, 1986, government plants
M92G	= import propensity, 1992, government plants
M9286G	= import propensity, 1992 less 1986, government plants
M86P	= import propensity, 1986, private plants
M92P	= import propensity, 1992, private plants
M9286P	= import propensity, 1992 less 1986, private plants
M86F	= import propensity, 1986, foreign plants
M92F	= import propensity, 1992, foreign plants
M9286F	= import propensity, 1992 less 1986, foreign plants
V75F	= foreign share of value added, 1975
V85F	= foreign share of value added, 1985
V92F	= foreign share of value added, 1992
V8575F	= foreign share of value added, 1985 less 1975
V9285F	= foreign share of value added, 1992 less 1985
V75F	= four-firm concentration ratio, 1975
V85F	= four-firm concentration ratio, 1985
V92F	= four-firm concentration ratio, 1992
V8575F	= four-firm concentration ratio, 1985 less 1975
V9285F	= four-firm concentration ratio, 1992 less 1985

Bold indicates a significant correlation exists (at the 0.05 level)

Note:	Correlation coefficients between variables in the first panel and X90G, X9290F are not shown as none were significant. In the middle panel for the same reason correlation coefficient with M86P are not shown, and in the third panel, coefficient for V9285F and C92 are also not show for the same reason.

there are a number of significant relationships among trade propensities and four-plant concentration ratios taken from Anas (1995, p. 753). Of these relationships, the negative relationships between concentration ratios and export propensities for all ownership groups in 1992 are notable, though only the relationship involving private plants is significant. Of perhaps more interest, however, is the dynamic dimension with the change in concentration ratios in 1985-1992 being negatively and significantly correlated with export propensities in 1992 for both foreign and private plants and the change in export propensities in 1990-1992 for private plants.

In contrast, the correlation between the change in concentration and government export propensities was positive, though weak and insignificant. Significant correlations involving concentration and import propensities were far less common, with a positive relationship between concentration and government import propensities in 1992 and a negative relationship between the change in concentration in 1985-1992 and the change in foreign import propensities in 1986-1992 being the major items of interest in this regard.

There are also a couple of interesting correlations observed among foreign shares and concentration ratios themselves. Among foreign shares, reflecting the large changes in the patterns of foreign shares described above, there are negative and significant correlations between changes in foreign shares and the shares at the beginning of the period involved (e.g., 1975-1985 and 1975), and between changes in 1975-1985 and 1985-1992. Among concentration ratios, there are positive and significant correlations between ratios for all three years but negative correlations between changes in concentration and concentration at the beginning of the period involved (e.g., 1975-1985 and 1975). Moreover, there are no significant static relationships among foreign shares and concentration, though correlations are positive. However, changes in concentration are negatively correlated with foreign shares at beginning of the period in question, with the relationship being significant for the change in concentration in 1975-1985 and the foreign share in 1975. This suggests that, although a large multinational presence may have contributed to greater concentration in a static sense, it led to greater competition over time.

Conclusions

To sum up the analysis of the roles of foreign multinationals, we find evidence that the patterns of foreign multinationals' shares in production in Indonesian manufacturing have changed markedly over the last two decades, with increasing concentration in the machinery industries traditionally dominated by multinationals. Second, patterns of trade and trade propensities differ in important respects from patterns of production in foreign multinationals, and the correlation between trade propensities and shares of value added are very weak. Third, private and foreign firms often display similar patterns of export propensities, and patterns of import propensities are similar in all ownership groups. Fourth, concentration ratios are usually negatively correlated with export propensities and positively correlated with import propensities in a static sense, but negatively correlated with changes in import propensities. Fifth, there are weak indications that large foreign presence contributes to concentration in a static sense but to greater competition in a dynamic sense. The results indicate that greater openness to international trade and investment have strengthened the Indonesian private manufacturing sector and its international competitiveness. Both foreign-owned or controlled and domestic private firms have become more export-oriented and the pattern of manufactured exports increasingly reflects Indonesia's comparative advantage.

Combined with the trade analysis of the preceding section, these patterns suggest that if liberalization of the trading environment is continued or accelerated, sectors in which Indonesia has developed a revealed comparative advantage over the last decade, namely textiles, apparel, wood, rubber, and plastics, are likely to remain the industries with the largest export shares and the most pronounced revealed comparative advantage for some time to come. Moreover, should there be a retrenchment of policies and a return to higher levels of protection, it is these industries that would undoubtably suffer the most. On the other hand, it is also important to emphasize that liberal trading policies will not lock Indonesia into this pattern of comparative advantage. Rather, growth will lead to increased labor costs and a gradual shift toward more capital- and technology-intensive industries. Moreover, openness to foreign multinationals already appears to be leading toward reduced comparative disadvantage in an important industry that is, at the same time, labor intensive and technology intensive, electrical machinery. It also seems reasonable to expect a comparative advantage to emerge in this industry in the next decade as it has in many other Southeast Asian countries. However, in more sophisticated machinery and chemical industries, it is unlikely that even the most heavy handed intervention could foster a revealed comparative advantage in less than two decades, and even if that goal could be achieved, the costs of such efforts would definitely be astronomical.

Appendix

Table 1: Four-firm Concentration Ratios
in Manufacturing Establishments by
Industry

Industry	1975	1985	1992
Non Oil Manufacturing	38	35	34
Food (ISIC 311)	13	11	20
Food (ISIC 312)	36	15	19
Beverages	69	42	43
Tobacco	47	68	75
Textiles	12	9	13
Garments	48	16	17
Leather Products	44	32	25
Footwear	87	55	22
Wood Products	14	8	12
Furniture	24	16	11
Paper Products	53	40	39
Printing & Publishing	34	36	35
Basic Chemicals	72	52	41
Other Chemicals	25	19	15
Rubber Products	32	17	24
Plastics Products	21	17	32
Pottery & China	92	49	36
Glass Products	78	72	68
Cement	66	51	52
Structural Clay Products	15	57	48
Other Non-Metallic Minerals	50	23	30
Basic Metals	70	81	NA
Ferous	NA	NA	64
Non Ferrous	NA	NA	74
Fabricated Metals	29	19	20
Non Electric Machinery	56	29	29
Electric Machinery	62	29	25
Transport Machinery	56	44	45
Precision Machinery	46	49	64
Miscellaneous	53	49	30

Note :
Percentages of industry output accounted for by four
largest establishments.
Source: Anas (1995), p. 753.

Endnotes

1.For example, an OECD study (Golden and Knudsen 1990) that was widely cited in Indonesia as evidence that the Uruguay Round 1994 Agreement would have negative effects on Indonesia used 1985 as the base year for the economic structure of Indonesia including its trade patterns. In 1985, non-manufactures accounted for nearly 80 percent of Indonesia's exports. By the year the Uruguay Round was completed, however, manufactured goods were over 50 percent of exports. The study therefore exaggerates the negative effects of agricultural trade liberalization (Indonesia is a net grain importer) and grossly understates the beneficial effects of reduced barriers to manufactured exports for Indonesia.

2.Aswicahyono, Bird and Hill (1994) point out that while there is no dearth of literature on the effect of economic reform and liberalization on economic performance, there is very little, if any, solid empirical research on the effects of liberalization on industrial structure, ownership, concentration, and productivity.

3.From 1973 to 1985, Indonesia adopted more restrictive trade and foreign investment regulations under a state-led import substitution industrialization strategy. For this reason the World Bank reclassified Indonesia from being "moderately outward oriented" in 1965-1973 to being "moderately inward oriented" from 1973-1985 (World Bank 1988). The decline in international oil prices from 1982 to 1985 and the collapse in 1986 forced Indonesia to adopt policies aimed at attracting investment including FDI into export-oriented manufacturing (Hill 1995).

4.This point may be more relevant to firms operating mainly in the markets of the advanced industrial countries where development of new products and technologies is more important to overall economic performance than in less developed countries. For an entertaining essay from the perspective of the professional economist see Warr (1994).

5.The factor endowments-related part of this statement is the well-known Heckscher-Ohlin explanation of why comparative costs differ across countries while a simple statement of the technology-related part can be found in the works of Ricardo.

6.We use ISIC classifications rather than the usual SITC classifications for compatibility with the production and trade data presented in the next section of the paper. Because we use the ISIC based data compiled by the Australian National University, export and import shares and totals may differ from SITC based data from the Central Bureau of Statistics.

7.Note that the textiles, apparel, and rubber estimates appear to have substantial footwear exports included with them. Corresponding estimates of non-oil manufactured export shares in 1992 are textiles and apparel 34.7 percent, footwear 7.7 percent, and wood 22.1 percent (Department of Trade 1994).

8.The RCA index is calculated as $(XIi/XI)/(XWi/XW)$ where XI and XW are total merchandise exports for Indonesia and the world, respectively, and XIi and XWi are exports of industry i for Indonesia and the world, respectively. An RCA index of greater than 1 implies that Indonesia exports relatively large amounts from industry i and is interpreted as an ex post expression that Indonesia has comparative advantage in that industry. Similarly, an RCA index of less than 1 implies a comparative disadvantage for Indonesia.

9.Note that these two industries, especially electric machinery, have become important export industries for other labor-abundant Asian economies.

10.Under some conditions this is also a conclusion that may be derived from the "new international economics" (Helpman and Krugman 1994 and Krugman 1993).

11.For a so-called revisionist interpretation of these experiences see Wade (1990). For a more balanced interpretation see Smith (1995).

12.A fundamental problem faced by these studies and others like them (e.g., Hill 1988, 1991; Pangestu 1991) is that the coverage of the industrial surveys has tended to become more complete over time. This is illustrated, for example, by the rise the in ratio of non-oil manufacturing value added reported in industrial surveys to corresponding estimates from the national accounts (both at market prices) from 54-60 percent in 1983-1984 to 65-72 percent in 1985-1988 and 76-80 percent in 1989-1991 and 87 percent in 1992 (calculated from Table 5). Largely as a result of the improvements in coverage in recent years, estimates for a number of earlier years have been revised to compensate for low coverage in those years and it is our understanding that the estimates presented here use these revised series. For this reason we have chosen to use these estimates over previous estimates found in Hill (1988, 1991) and Pangestu (1991).

13.For 1985, for example, Aswicahyono and Hill (1995, p. 146) report the percentage shares of each respective group in total value added as government=0.4, (local) private=55.8, foreign=1.3, government-private joint ventures=0.4, government-foreign joint ventures=0.5, private-foreign joint ventures=17.1, and government-private-foreign joint ventures=24.7.

14.As pointed out by Aswicahyono and Hill (1995, pp. 146-147) there are large problems in classifying government-foreign and government-private-foreign joint ventures, some of which are very large, and this is a potential source of difference between these estimates.

15.The estimated shares of value added in Aswicahyono, Bird and Hill (1995) are consistent with estimates of manufacturing value added provided by Aswicahyono and Hill (1995, p. 146). For 1985 the figure reported in the latter source is 7,154 billion rupiah, which differs from the published estimate given in our Table 5.

16.Note that the compilations of trade shares and propensities given below come from yet another source, Pangestu (1995), further underscoring the need for caution in interpreting the data presented in this section.

17.Also see Hill (1988, 1991) and Pangestu (1991).

18.These shares are based on the time series estimates of Aswicahyono, Bird and Hill (1995) given in Table 5.

19. On a balance of payments basis, nominal FDI flows increased at an average annual rate of less than 4 percent in 1975-1983 and 8 percent in 1983-1986 but at rates ranging from 16 percent to 91 percent in 1987-1993 (Table 1). Data on the stock of realized foreign investment from Bank Indonesia (various years a, 1987/88 issue) and Anas (1995, p. 743) indicate that the share of manufacturing in the total was rather stable, 66 percent at year end 1987 and 64 percent at the end of April 1994.

20. In non-oil manufacturing, the estimates in Table 5 imply that the production of foreign firms grew at 29 percent per year in 1975-1985 and 27 percent in 1985-1990, while estimates in Table 6 indicate an identical growth rate in 1975-1985 but a slightly lower growth rate in 1985-1992, 26 percent. The value added deflator for all manufacturing, including oil and gas, increased 14 percent annually in 1975-1985, versus 9 percent annually in 1985-1990 and 1985-1992 (Table 1 and its sources). Corresponding inflation rates for non-oil manufacturing cannot be calculated for 1975-1983 but were 10 percent annually in both 1985-1990 and 1985-1992 (Table 1 and its sources).

21. Data for Thailand come from the numbers underlying Figure 1 in Ramstetter (1994); note that calculations from unpublished data underlying Table 3 in this source also indicate that these shares are similar in terms of value added. Malaysian data taken from Ramstetter (1995, Table 2). Note also that the patterns observed in Malaysia and Thailand are similar to those observed in a number of Asia's Newly Industrializing Economies; see Lee and Ramstetter (1991) for evidence on Korea, Ramstetter (1991) for evidence on Singapore, and Ramstetter (1992) for evidence on Taiwan.

22. Using data as of October 1994 from Toyo Keizai (1995), at least 12 Japanese affiliates fall in this category.

23. The shorter time frame here is a result of data availability, the industrial surveys having only recently included questions on exports and Pangestu (1995) being the only known compilation of these data.

24. Two additional disclaimers are necessary here. First and most importantly, this analysis should not be construed to imply the existence of meaningful economic relationships among all the variable pairs in Table 9 as there are clearly a number of relationships in that table that are either of little or no analytical significance. Moreover, even when meaningful relationships are involved, the strength and significance of the observed correlation may be misleading as the effects of related variables are not accounted for as would be the case in more formal models. In other words, the analysis is perhaps best viewed as suggestive with respect to the types of relationships involved in a more complete modelling effort, the lack of definitiveness deriving primarily from the lack of information on a number of important variables involved in the relationships (e.g., factor intensities and prices). A second less serious problem is that sample sizes differ somewhat for different pairs of variables due again to data availability problems and the fact that there are no plants in some categories.

25. Similarly export propensities in 1990 were negatively correlated with changes in 1990-1992 for all ownership groups but the correlation was only significant in government plants and was very close to 0 in private plants.

References

Amsden, Alice. *Asia's Next Giant: South Korea and Late Industrialization.* New York: Oxford University Press, 1989.

Anas, Titak. "Industri Manufaktur Indonesia: Perjalanan Lima Puluh Tahun," in Bantarto Bandor, J. Kristiadi, Mari Pangestu, and Onny S. Prijono, eds., *Refleksi Setengah Abad Kemerdekaan Indonesia,* Jakarta: Center for Strategic and International Studies, pp. 738-761 (in Indonesian), 1995.

Asian Development Bank. *Key Indicators of Developing Member Countries of ADB.* Vol 16 (April issue). Manila: Asian Development Bank, 1985.

Aswicahyono, H.H. and Hill, Hal. "Determinants of Foreign Ownership in LDC Manufacturing: An Indonesian Case Study." *Journal of International Business Studies,* 1995. Vol 26, No. 1, pp. 139-158.

Aswicahyono, H.H.; Bird, Kelly and Hill, Hal. "What Happens to Industrial Structure When Countries Liberalize? Indonesia Since the Mid-1980s." Economics Division Working Paper SEA 95/2, Research School of Pacific Studies, Australian National University, 1995.

Bank Indonesia. *Annual Report.* 1980/81 to 1994/95 issues. Jakarta: Bank Indonesia, various years, a.

_____. *Financial Statistics.* Jakarta: Bank Indonesia, various years, b

Biro Pusat Statistik. *National Income of Indonesia.* 1983-1988, 1986-1991, 1987-1992, and 1988-1993 issues. Jakarta: Biro Pusat Statistik, various years, a.

_____. *Statistik Indonesia (Statistical Yearbook of Indonesia,* 1980/81, 1984, 1988, 1989, 1991, 1992 issues. Jakarta: Biro Pusat Statistik, various years, b.

_____. *Statistik Industri.* Vol. 1, 1990, 1991, and 1992 issues Jakarta: Biro Pusat Statistik, various years, c.

Department of Trade. *Trade Statistics.* April 1994, Jakarta.

Condon, Tim and Fane., George. "Measuring Deregulation in Indonesia." Conference of Economists, University of Adelaide, September, 1995.

Golden, I. and Knudsen, O. eds., *Agricultural Trade Liberalization.* Paris: Organization for Economic Cooperation and Development, 1990.

International Monetary Fund. International Financial Statistics., September CD-ROM. Washington, D.C.: International Monetary Fund, 1995.

Helpman, Elhanan and Krugman, Paul. *Trade Policy and Market Structure*. Cambridge: The MIT Press.

Hill, Hal. *Foreign Investment and Industrialization in Indonesia*. Singapore: Oxford University Press, 1988.

_____. "Multinationals and Employment in Indonesia." Multinational Enterprises Programme Working Paper No. 67. Geneva: International Labour Office, 1991.

Krugman, Paul. "Free Trade: A Loss of (Theoretical) Nerve?" *American Economic Review*, 1993 Vol. 83, No. 2, pp. 362-66.

Lee, Chung H. and Ramstetter, Eric D. "Direct Investment and Structural Change in Korean Manufacturing," in Eric D. Ramstetter, ed., *Direct Foreign Investment in Asia's Developing Economies and Structural Change in the Asia-Pacific Region*, Boulder, Co: Westview Press, pp. 105-141, 1991.

Nasution, Anwar. "Survey of Recent Developments." *Bulletin of Indonesian Economic Studies*, 1995, August, pp. 3-40.

_____. "Market Mechanism and Government: The Case of Indonesia Following the Economic Reforms Since the 1980s." Conference on the World Economy in Transition, Hitotsubashi University, Tokyo, Japan, February, 1996.

Pangestu, Mari, "U.S. Direct Investment in Developing Asia and Structural Adjustment in U.S. Manufacturing Industry," in Eric D. Ramstetter, ed., *Direct Foreign Investment in Asia's Developing Economies and Structural Change in the Asia-Pacific Region*, Boulder, Co: Westview Press, pp. 35-64, 1991.

_____. "Trade, FDI and East Asian Integration: An Indonesian Case Study." paper presented at the Workshop on Trade and FDI: Underpinnings of East Asian Integration, 19-20 May 1995, Institute of Southeast Asian Studies, Singapore, 1995.

Porter, Michael, *The Competitive Advantage of Nations*. New York: The Free Press, 1990.

Ramstetter, Eric D., "The Macroeconomic Effects of Direct Foreign Investment in Singaporean Manufacturing: A Macroeconometric Study," in Mitsuru Toida, ed., *ASEAN, Ajia NIEs no Keizai Yosoku to Bunseki (III)--Heisei Ninendo ELSA Hokokusho--* [Economic Forecasts and Analyses for ASEAN and the Asia NIEs (III)--1990 ELSA Annual Report--], Tokyo: Institute of Developing Economies, pp. 49-138, 1991.

_____. "The Macroeconomic Effects of Inward Direct Investment in Taiwan: A Multifirm Econometric Analysis," in Mitsuru Toida and Daisuke Hiratsuka, eds., *Ajia Kogyoken no Keizai Bunseki to Yosoku (I)* [Projections for Asian Industrializing Region (I)], Tokyo: Institute of Developing Economies, pp. 53-154, 1992.

_____. "Comparisons of Japanese Multinationals and Other Firms in Thailand's Non-oil Manufacturing Industries." *ASEAN Economic Bulletin*, vol 11, no. 1, pp. 36-58, 1994.

_____. "Characteristics of Multinational Firms in Malaysia: A Time Series Perspective" in Mitsuru Toida and Daisuke Hiratsuka, eds., *Ajia Kogyoken no Keizai Bunseki to Yosoku (IV)* [Projections for Asian Industrializing Region (IV)], Tokyo: Institute of Developing Economies, pp. 95-171, 1995.

Smith, Heather. "Industry Policy in East-Asia." *Asian-Pacific Economic Literature*, May 1995, pp. 17-39.

Toyo, Keizai. *Kaigai Shinshutsu Kigyo Soran: Kigyoubetsu Hen (A Comprehensive Survey of Firms Overseas, by Firm)*, 1995 issue. Tokyo: Toyo Keizai (in Japanese), 1995.

United Nations Statistical Division. *General Industrial Statistics*. diskette. New York: United Nations, 1993.

Wade, Robert. Governing the Market: Economic Theory and the Role of the Government in East Asian Industrialization. Princeton University Press, 1990

Warr, Peter G. "Comparative and Competitive Advantage." *Asia-Pacific Economic Literature*, November 1994, Vol. 8, No. 2,, pp.1-14.

World Bank. *World Development Report*. New York: Oxford University Press, 1988.

World Bank. *The East Asian Miracle*. New York and London: Oxford University Press, 1993.

9

TECHNICAL DIFFUSION AND CONFUSION

Michael Bradfield[1]
Dalhousie University, Canada

An emphasis on high tech development reflects limited definitions of both development and technology. Attracting "state of the art" multinational corporations only perpetuates relationships that can be harmful to development. The goals of development need to be clear to set the context for development policy. When development is defined as growth and growth assumed to depend on "value added" exports, high tech products are seen as crucial. Multinationals become the source of the technologies "necessary" for development. While presented as a short term catalyst, the long term consequences are dependence, inequality, and lost opportunities for real development. On the other hand, if development is defined in terms of self-reliance, sustainability, and equity and if technological change is appropriate to achieving these goals, alternative strategies can be effective.

Most policy makers equate growth with development. Growth is seen to depend on exports and therefore on international competitiveness. Technological change becomes "the key to the magic kingdom of regional development and national competitiveness" (Walker 1985:226). High tech promises high value added exports, growth, and presumably employment and higher wages. Since high tech production is seen to be large scale, sophisticated, and capital-intensive, it is conceded to be the domain of the multinationals. They have the research labs and they have the market dominance to profit from their R and D. Therefore, the theory goes, technological diffusion must move from the developed to the developing: if a country wishes to develop, it must rely on foreign technology and foreign investment.

But this logic relies on a chain of assumptions with many weak links produced by twisting basic principles. Basic principles are examined to indicate that reliance on exports, high tech, and multinational corporations is a dysfunctional approach to development.

Back to the Basics

Growth vs. Development

Growth and development are distinct phenomena. Growth simply means more output, with institutions and inequities intact, unchallenged, and often exacerbated. Development, on the other hand, is "the structural transformation of an economy such that...it becomes increasingly capable of sustaining its capacity for further expansion out of its own, internal resources" (Lithwick, 1986:110). Development requires changes in institutions, particularly with respect to their impacts on the poorest members of society. By definition, development challenges vested interests. If we equate growth with development, policy fossilizes existing economic and social relations and ignores the potential trade-offs between material vs. political, social, and cultural ends.

The Economic Council of Canada, for instance, specifies the basic goals of society as "*well-being and equity*... The degree of well-being is determined by the extent to which the material, social, cultural, psychological, and other needs of society are met. Equity, on the other hand is an appropriate distribution of well-being among members of society" (1977:11) [italics in original]. Nonetheless, the Council restricts its focus to the material, to the *"ultimate* goal ... to improve income and employment opportunities" (ibid:18) [emphasis added] and where there is a conflict between jobs and wages, to jobs alone (ibid:19).

A focus on market growth further separates growth from development since it ignores vast amounts of unpaid activity, primarily women's work, that contributes so much to the welfare of society, particularly in developing countries (Waring, 1988). Growth policies designed for the market economy are often disastrous for non-market activities, for the people engaged in them, for the social relations interwoven with them, and for the natural environment (Ibid.). But even on its own terms, growth policies may not promote an increase in market employment, or in wages, particularly when predicated on exports of high tech products.

Why Export?

Those who promote export-led growth carry the burden of proof - they must show that they are not simply neo-mercantilists arguing for exports to create jobs.

Trade is trade - exports finance imports. An export-led growth strategy is therefore simultaneously an import-dependent strategy, unless a temporary increase in exports is necessary to finance the import of needed goods to promote long term development.

If exports are necessary to finance the import of foreign capital, why is foreign capital needed? Often foreign capital involves techniques of production which are inappropriate (Cuadrado et al., 1983:118), especially for labor surplus regions. In other cases, foreign capital is necessary to produce exports, but that still does not explain what will be done with the export earnings. How do the exports meet local needs that could not be met directly, from local production?

Further, to claim that only trade and technology promote welfare (Macdonald, 1985) is to assume full employment--an economy using all of its productive capacities must either expand those capacities (with technology) or surmount them (through trade). But an economy with unemployment can grow without new technologies or trade, using unemployed resources.

The unemployed are usually seen as problems but they also represent part of the solution. They are an untapped resource that could meet more needs. Growth does not need the stimulus of foreign demand for exports. Unemployed economies need to make effective the demands (i.e., to meet the needs) of their poorest citizens.

Thus it must always be remembered that trade enhances consumer utility and only co-incidentally employment or even growth. At best, welfare will be increased when imports offset exports.

Why Import Technology?

Could local needs be met effectively with local good produced by current techniques? Delays in switching to new techniques are often cited as evidence of incompetence and resistance to change. But which technique is more productive depends on context, and the context varies dramatically between developed and developing countries. Moreover, using an older technology may be efficient because the fixed costs of the older technology have already been incurred (Bradfield, 1988:217-220).

If technological change emanates from developed regions, then technology is generated in regions with high incomes, skilled labor, and abundant capital. The preferred technical trajectory substitutes relatively cheap capital for expensive labor (Mainwaring, 1994:212)--technical change is likely to be capital-intensive (Duchin, 1991:8). This is not the only possible trajectory but it is the most profitable, in developed countries. Once the technological trajectory is chosen, "Innovation slowly constrains and narrows the field of future technical endeavors. The direction of innovative interactions therefore tends to be stable..." (Debresson, 1991:79). Stability, however, does not have to mean inevitability. Nor does it imply superiority, even under the conditions of its initial adoption. The literature contains many examples of inferior technologies which determined technological trajectories, such as the narrow gauge railway, FORTRAN, and the QWERTY keyboard (Burns, 1989:126).

Is the technical path of the developed regions appropriate for the developing regions? As shown below, the capital-intensive technology of developed countries will exacerbate rather than narrow income differentials between high and low income regions. If the developed countries determine the technological trajectory for all, their preferred paths will be least helpful to lagging regions. These regions would be better off, in the long run, choosing their own technological paths.

Despite all of the above, "...so attractive is the image of a high technology future that politicians and officials...are inevitably drawn toward it..." (Hall, 1985:49). There is an "overstressing of *science*" and an emphasis on "Big Business" (Fach and Grande, 1991:46) [italics in the original] which lead to the assumption that development hinges on attracting foreign investment to bring high tech industries, R&D capacity, and spin-off benefits. But peripheral regions lack the conditions to make the high tech route effective: a strong financial base (Hilpert, 1991:21), major universities and research units, existing high tech industries, and local wealth and entrepreneurship (Castells, 1991:13).

Ultimately, a successful foreign investment is, almost by definition, an unsuccessful development project. "[E]ven if mobile industry *could* still be steered in sufficient quantity... it would still not be contributing to, and indeed may be further reducing, the capacity of the recipient regions to generate *self-sustaining* economic growth..." (Gillespie, 1983:2) [italics in the original]. It adds to a sense of dependence on foreign investment, on foreign technology and foreign expertise. It often has weak linkages with the local economy and generates few direct spin-offs. The profits, and their capacity for assisting further investment, are externally controlled.

Projects or People?

The fascination with big science assumes that significant scientific achievements and their applications are the product of the expensive R&D projects of the big corporations. But scientific breakthroughs are usually the result of the work and insights of a few people, often working alone or in small groups in universities and government labs. Creative people find the structured research of large firms too confining (Cohen and Noll, 1991:21) and set up their own firms to go in new directions. Moreover, the bulk of corporate research is on development, not the primary research that many find most stimulating (Buswell, 1983:14). Primary research is risky since it is uncontrolled as a research project and unpredictable as to its commercial pay-offs. Thus, individuals as well as university and government researchers continue to play a significant role in high tech developments.

Another reason for the importance of research outside the large corporate R&D environment is that the bulk of technological change is incremental (Berra and Gastaldo, 1991: 100). A scientific breakthrough is the beginning, not the end. It creates a new field on which many can play. No matter how esoteric or expensive, once a discovery is made, lesser labs and minds can push it in a myriad of directions and applications. A technology strategy need not, indeed should not, focus on a "big bang" breakthrough, but rather on small applications (Walker, 1985:237-240).

A related point is that technological change is seldom a sophisticated, highly technical phenomenon. New products and processes are developed by minor alterations of what already exists. They reflect workers or consumers responding to an identified need. These people may have specific skills but often the major ingredient is their curiosity and determination. Each innovation may be small and mundane but the cumulative effect is our modern technology.

Fewer Jobs But Better Wages?[2]

An imported, capital-intensive production technique may be inappropriate to the developing country's current wage/rental ratio and excess labor conditions, but development changes underlying conditions. By capital-deepening, will imported techniques raise wages and assist development? This neo-classical prediction can be questioned on its own terms.

Take an industry competitive in its factor and product markets, using a Cobb-Douglas production function:

$$X = P_q.Q = P_q.A.(C.K)^{\alpha}.(B.L)^{1-\alpha} \tag{1}$$

where X is the value of the physical output, Q, P_q is the price of output, A, B, and C are the neutral, labor-specific, and capital-specific efficiency co-efficients, respectively, K and L are the inputs of capital and labor, respectively, and α is the production function parameter.

A change in α represents technical change, a change in the techniques of production. Changes in A, B, or C represent changes in the knowledge base, i.e., technological change. Of course, the change in technique reflects the discovery of a new way of producing Q, and therefore also picks up the effects of technological change.

In a competitive industry, each firm exhausts all economies of scale; the production function must be homogeneous of degree one. For the competitive firm, P_q is given. This may be true for some regional markets - even for the national industry if international markets set prices. On the other hand the national market and large regions may face a downward sloping demand curve for their output of Q. For them, P_q would be a function of the level of output. The efficiency co-efficients, A, B, and C, are assumed exogenous to both the firm and the industry.

Equilibrium in the capital market requires that capital be hired until the marginal revenue product of capital is equal to its cost:

$$r.P_k = \partial X/\partial K = \alpha.P_q.A.C^{\alpha}.B^{1-\alpha}.k^{\alpha-1} \tag{2}$$

where r is the rate of interest (the cost of financial capital), P_k is the cost of a unit of physical capital, and k is the capital/labor ratio, K/L. Re-arranging equation (2), the equilibrium capital/labor ratio can be expressed as:

$$k_e = (\alpha.P_q.A.C^\alpha)^{1/(1-\alpha)}.B.(r.P_k)^{1/(\alpha-1)} \tag{3}$$

Similarly, labor market equilibrium means that the wage is equal to the marginal revenue product of labor:

$$W_e = \partial X/\partial L = (1-\alpha).P_q.A.C^\alpha.B^{1-\alpha}.k_e^\alpha \tag{4}$$

Substituting from equation (3) for the capital/labor ratio in (4), the equilibrium wage rate can be expressed as:

$$W_e = (1-\alpha).(\alpha^\alpha.P_q.A.C^\alpha)^{1/(1-\alpha)}.B.(r.P_k)^{\alpha/(\alpha-1)} \tag{5}$$

In words, the underlying conditions and the capital market equilibrium determine the equilibrium capital/labor ratio. These same underlying conditions and the equilibrium capital/labor ratio determine the equilibrium wage. The (unspecified) labor supply will then determine how many people are willing to work in the industry at the equilibrium wage and hence the size of the industry.

Taking differentials, noting that $d \log V = V^* = \Delta V/V$, from equation (5), we can express W_e^*, the rate of change in the equilibrium wage rate, as

$$\begin{aligned} W_e^* = (1-\alpha)^* &+ 1/(1-\alpha).[\alpha.\alpha^* + P_q^* + A^* + \alpha.(C^* - r^* - P_k^*)] + B^* \\ &+ [d(\alpha/\{1-\alpha\})].\log\alpha + [d(\alpha/\{1-\alpha\})].\log(C/r.P_k) \\ &+ [d(1/\{1-\alpha\})].\log.(P_q.A) \end{aligned} \tag{6}$$

Since $d(\alpha/\{1-\alpha\}) = d(1/\{1-\alpha\}) = d\alpha/(1-\alpha)^2 = -(1/\{1-\alpha\}).(1-\alpha)^*$, the rate of change in the equilibrium wage can be expressed as

$$\begin{aligned} W_e^* = (1-\alpha)^* &+ 1/(1-\alpha).[\alpha.\alpha^* + P_q^* + A^* + \alpha.(C^* - r^* - P_k^*)] \\ &+ B^* - [(1-\alpha)^*/(1-\alpha)].\log(\alpha.P_q.A.C/rP_k). \end{aligned} \tag{6'}$$

The effects of $(1-\alpha)^*$ and of $\alpha^*.\alpha/(1-\alpha)$ in equation (6) are not only opposite but equal. The algebra of this is relatively straightforward. The expression $(1-\alpha)$ changes when α changes:

$$\Delta(1-\alpha) = -\Delta\alpha \tag{7}$$

and therefore

$$\Delta(1-\alpha)/(1-\alpha) = [-\Delta\alpha/(1-\alpha)].\alpha/\alpha \tag{7'}$$

or, $(1-\alpha)^* = -\alpha^*.\alpha/(1-\alpha)$ [Q.E.D.]   (7")

Thus $(1-\alpha)^*$ cancels out the $\alpha^*.\alpha/(1-\alpha)$ of equation (6) and it becomes

$$W_e^* = 1/(1-\alpha).[P_q^* + A^* + \alpha(C^* - r^* - P_k^*)]$$
$$+ B^* - [(1-\alpha)^*/(1-\alpha)].\log(\alpha.P_q.A.C/r.P_k). \quad (8)$$

The sign of the last argument of equation (8) is impossible to evaluate since $[(1-\alpha)^*/(1-\alpha)]$ is negative when technical change is capital-intensive ($\alpha^* > 0$), and $\log(\alpha.P_q A.C/rP_k)$ will be positive or negative depending on which is larger, the numerator or the denominator, respectively.

Since some of the effect of the change in the production function parameter, α, cancels out in equation (8) and the remaining effect is indeterminate, increases in the equilibrium wage are not guaranteed by changes in the production technique, i.e., by changes in α. Indeed, depending on the factor intensity of technical change and on the value of $\alpha.P_q.A.C$ relative to $r.P_k$, the effect of technical change may be to lower equilibrium wages. Thus, capital-deepening technical change need not raise the wage rate.

A more capital-intensive technique raises the equilibrium capital/labor ratio which increases the marginal physical product of labor. However, the concomitant change in the production function parameter lowers the marginal product of labor for any given capital/labor ratio. The two effects are contradictory; the effect of capital-intensive technical change on wages is therefore indeterminate.

Foreign Investment -- For Real?

The debate over foreign investment is often unproductive because there is a failure to distinguish between real and financial investment. Real investment may be necessary to overcome particular bottlenecks or weaknesses in an economy-- foreign machinery, technology transfer, or expertise may be crucial to a development strategy. The investment boom will be in foreign countries. Nonetheless, foreign investment is often touted as the key to stimulating a lagging economy even (especially) when the real investment capacity employed is domestic.

But when foreign investment is financial (when foreign funds are used to finance real domestic investment), there is a "Kierans" effect: the job creating effect may be zero or negative because of the exchange rate effects of foreign finance.

The inflow of foreign funds increases the demand for the domestic currency on international exchange markets as foreign funds are converted to domestic funds to hire domestic resources for investment. While the real investment creates jobs, the increased demand for domestic currency raises the exchange rate and makes domestic exports more expensive and imports cheaper. This crowding out of net exports (Mahdavi, 1995:128) means the decline in the foreign trade balance equals, and offsets, the stimulus to the economy from the foreign-financed domestic real investment. The net job effect depends on the labor-intensity of the investment goods industry relative to the export and import-substitution industries which suffer from the higher exchange rates.

Figure 1 can be used to illustrate these effects. If initially there are only import and export flows between countries, the international money market demand, D(x), for a country's currency ($) is a function of the demand for its exports. Similarly, the supply of the country's currency on the international money market, S(m), is to buy imports. The initial exchange rate of Y units of foreign currency per $ of local currency is determined at point A, and exports equal imports.

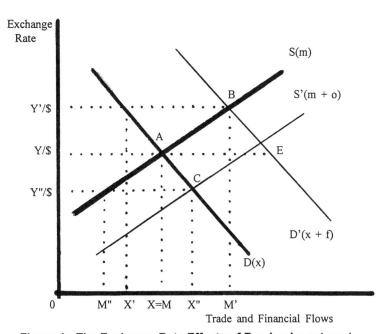

Figure 1: The Exchange Rate Effects of Foreign Investment

If foreign funds flow in to finance real domestic investment, the foreign demand for dollars is increased by "f", the financial demand; and the exchange rate is raised to Y'/$. With the higher exchange rate, exports fall to X' and imports rise to M'. There is a current account balance of payments deficit of M' - X', the necessary shift in trade to effect a real transfer equal to the foreign financial investment. The attempt to create jobs by foreign financial investment destroys them in exporting and import-competing industries. The investment financing crowds out net exports. The decline in net exports offsets the stimulatory effects of the foreign finance in terms of both jobs and money supply effects.

In the long run, principle and interest must be paid out; the supply of domestic currency increases by "o", the outflow of debt servicing costs. The equilibrium moves to C where exports exceed imports by X" - M", equal to the debt servicing costs. This export surplus creates jobs but the real benefit, the increase in output, goes to foreigners. The exchange rate must fall by enough to generate this real transfer to foreigners. If the Kierans effect, the investment-induced exchange rate rise, damaged the country's export capacity, export demand would be diminished and the exchange rate fall would be still greater.

In other words, there is a Kierans[3] effect with foreign financial investment similar to the "Dutch Disease" caused by an increase in primary products exports. In both cases, the inflow of foreign funds drives up the exchange rate which puts export and import-substitution industries at risk. If the inflow lasts long enough, the at-risk industries suffer permanent damage to their competitiveness. When the inflow of foreign funds ceases and the exchange rate falls, the at-risk industries may not recover.[4]

Could the Kierans effect be avoided if the central bank buys up the excess foreign currency on the international exchange market? The increase in the supply of domestic funds would match the increased foreign demand and the exchange rate need not be affected by the foreign financial investment. (This would be represented by a shift to point E in Figure 1.) This is possible but then it is the central bank which finances internal investment, and it is the foreign investors who control it! If the central bank provides the funds, why not do it to promote domestic ownership and control? That will enhance independence whereas foreign control increases dependence.

Technology and Equity

What is the implication of the technical trajectory chosen to promote growth and equity? It can be easily shown that a capital-intensive option will increase capital's share of output.

Figure 2 depicts the capital and labor inputs used to produce the output X_i most efficiently. A budget of $Y allows the firm to hire any of the combinations of capital and labor along the isocost line KL.

The least cost combination of capital and labor to produce output X_i is K_i and L_i, respectively. If technical change leads to a new, more capital-intensive, production technique, it can be represented by the isoquant X_n tangent to KL closer to K. The optimal combination of inputs for producing X_n would be K_n units of capital and L_n workers. With existing capital and labor prices, the capital/labor ratio has risen; $K_n / L_n > K_i / L_i$. Assuming that the new production technique is superior to the old (i.e., $X_n > X_i$), firms will gradually shift to the new production technique.

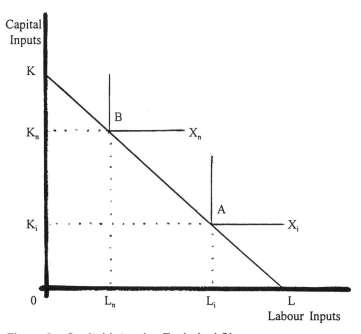

Figure 2: Capital-intensive Technical Change

The relationship between the geometry of Figure 2 and factor shares can be seen from the fact that $K = \$Y/P_k$ and $K_i = (\$Y - L_i \cdot W)/P_k$, i.e., K_i, the amount of capital used, equals the total budget less the money spent on labor divided by the price of capital. Therefore,

$$K_i = \frac{\$Y - L_i \cdot W}{P_k} = \frac{\$Y}{P_k} - \frac{L_i \cdot W}{P_k} = \frac{\$Y}{P_k} - \frac{L_i \cdot W}{P_k} \cdot \frac{\$Y}{\$Y}$$

$$= \frac{\$Y}{P_k} - \frac{L_i \cdot W}{\$Y} \cdot \frac{\$Y}{P_k} = \frac{\$Y}{P_k} \cdot \left(1 - \frac{L_i \cdot W}{\$Y}\right) = \frac{\$Y}{P_k} \cdot \left(1 - \pi_l\right) = \frac{\$Y}{P_k} \cdot \left(\pi_k\right)$$

(9)

where π_l is the percent of the budget spent on labor, i.e., labor's share of output since the value of the output must be equal to the expenditures on inputs if there are no economic profits, and π_k is the rest, capital's share, so that $\pi_k + \pi_l = 1$.

We can take K_i as a fraction of K from the above expression to find capital's share:

$$K_i / K = \frac{\$Y \cdot \pi_k / P_k}{\$Y / P_k} = \pi_k$$

(10)

Thus, when technical change is capital-intensive, capital's share of output rises.

Since capital-intensive technical change increases capital's share of output, it exacerbates inequities in the distribution of income. Wealth income is highly concentrated. Capital-intensive technical change therefore increases the share of output going to the wealthy. If the new production is owned domestically, internal inequities are increased. If the new production is foreign-owned, international inequities are increased by more capital-intensive production methods. One of the fundamental goals of development, equity, is subverted while at the same time employment falls, *ceteris paribus*. Moreover, there is no guarantee that those still working will have higher wages.

This impact on the functional distribution of income from a more capital-intensive technique is in addition to its effect on wage rate disparities. From equation (4), the differences in wage rates between two regions or two countries, i and j, can be expressed as

$$W_{ij} = (P_{xij} \cdot A_{ij})^{1/(1-\alpha)} \cdot C_{ij}^{\alpha/(1-\alpha)} \cdot B_{ij} \cdot (r_{ij} \cdot P_{kij})^{\alpha/(\alpha-1)}$$

(11)

Equation (11) delineates the role played by product price (P_x), by neutral (A), by capital-biased (C), and by labor-biased (B) efficiency differences, and by capital costs (r and P_k) in determining long run wage differences. Equilibrium does not imply the equalization of wages as long as underlying factors affecting prices or efficiency levels are different in different countries.

Differences in production technique will affect the equilibrium wage relative. If region i has a small (e.g., five percent) advantage in each of the factors of equation (11), it becomes

$$W_{ij} = [(1.05).(1.05)]^{1/(1-\alpha)}.(1.05)^{\alpha/(1-\alpha)}.(1.05) [(1.05).(1.05)]^{\alpha/(1-\alpha)}$$
$$= (1.05)^{(3+2\alpha)/(1-\alpha)} \tag{12}$$

If α has a value of 1/3 in equation (12), the equilibrium wage relative is

$$W_{ij} = 1.05^{11/2} = 1.31. \tag{13}$$

However, if the production technique were more capital-intensive, for instance, if α were 1/2, then (12) becomes

$$W_{ij} = 1.05^8 = 1.48. \tag{14}$$

Thus, the higher capital-intensity of the production technique, with a given set of underlying variables, requires a higher equilibrium wage relative--the disadvantages of the underlying variables must be offset by a progressively lower wage the more capital-intensive the production function.

Relative factor prices in the developed nations make it profitable to choose a capital-intensive technical trajectory but this generates greater differences in relative wages if it is adopted by the developing countries. It is only in correcting the underlying disadvantages that wage gaps can be closed.

Reality Check

A high tech growth strategy lacks a strong theoretical basis if the goal is self-reliance, sustainability, and equity. The high tech strategy is further weakened when a dose of reality is added to the theory. The importance of individuals and the incremental nature of technological change help explain one of the stylized facts of recent decades--despite quantum leaps in technology, growth in employment continues to be in the small and medium sized enterprises (Hilpert and Ruffieux, 1991:69; Neumann 1991:210). Where are the links between big science, big business, and economic stimulus?

Even if a high tech strategy is "successful", it may have smaller benefits and greater costs than predicted. Benefits are reduced by the higher import content of foreign subsidiaries and by their use of inappropriate technologies. R&D parks may be "cathedrals in the desert" (Hansen 1992:103) with virtually no local linkages.

Moreover, there are major costs to foreign investment. If a company's technology gives them an advantage, they will use it to maximize subsidies from regions desperate for jobs and technology. This "industrial blackmail" (King et al., 1993:591) is rampant. OECD subsidies to multinationals cover up to 50 per cent of the "foreign" investment (Amin and Smith, 1986:51). If developed regions are manipulated by the multinationals, what more must others do to be in the running?

Countries with large multinational branch plants are subject to continuing demands, for further financial subsidies, or for the erosion of environmental, labor, or health and safety standards (Ettlinger, 1992:117). If a plant is a major employer, it has leverage over governments and over its workers. There can be significant political costs as domestic politics are shaped by and for foreign investors (Castells, 1991:31).

In addition, "competitive tax cutting and competitive subsidization for investment by national governments...must ultimately work in favor of a redistribution towards profits" (Cowling ,1986:36). Equity in the distribution of income is again thwarted.

Despite the costs, attracting high tech industry does not guarantee high tech jobs nor increased technical capacities (Amin and Goddard, 1986:12). High tech products, such as computers, may require continuing R&D, but this usually occurs at the head office (Neumann, 1991:198), not at the subsidiary in a developing country. Sub-assembly operations employ low skilled people and often have few linkages with the local economy.

Thus, economic reality suggests that whatever benefits are theoretically possible, the net benefits of a high tech growth strategy are dubious. It is important, then, to recognize and develop alternative strategies.

Alternatives

Once big science, big business, and foreign investment are seen in context, development policy is freed to consider technological diffusion alternatives to the large corporations of developed countries. More appropriate strategies and technologies would allow a region to build up firms and industries which, because they would be small, would leave the local economy with greater diversity, stability, and autonomy.

Technology - Appropriate to what?

Development through appropriate technology (AT) would be concerned with the local labor force and its health, attitudes, and skills. This would raise wages and also increase the capacity of the economy for technical change (Nilsson 1995). AT should mean developing comparative advantage based on resources and the environment -- natural, built, and social (in the sense of culture, politics, and aspirations).
What is appropriate technology also depends on needs. "A preferable course would be to link [government] R&D investments to new areas of demonstrable public needs--[e.g.] environmental protection where the market clearly cannot address the problem. As industrial policy, a national needs-based industrial approach is a better bet than guessing at winning technologies" (Markusen, 1993:11).

By finding solutions to the local problems, an appropriate technology strategy can meet needs directly and expand the local economy. The process may involve the importation of basic ideas from elsewhere, such as how to convert animal dung to methane or to manufacture cinder blocks to improve the housing stock. It may involve reviving local techniques and past practices which had been replaced by "modern" techniques which ultimately prove unaffordable because of their import requirements or unanticipated side-effects. Of course, it may involve new solutions. Locally generated solutions use more local inputs. Stimulation may also come from export opportunities for the products, for the processes, or for the expertise developed.[6] However, this is a desirable side-effect and should not be the primary expectation of policy.

Of course, what is appropriate is not limited to local skills and needs nor to labor-intensive techniques. Policy should be flexible enough to support high tech ideas even though policy should not make a fetish of high tech.

The Appropriate Strategies

The appropriate strategies for technological development begin with the proposition that there are many people with the needs, ideas, and expertise to develop a multitude of small changes which can be cumulatively significant. The strategies must both elicit these ideas and understand--and remove--the barriers to their implementation.

Ideas are developed in the plant by the people who make the products and understand the production process (Berra and Gastaldo, 1991:91). Networks of producers, suppliers, and customers are also important sources of technological change (Hansen, 1992; Ettlinger, 1992). There are alternatives to large corporate R&D. "Practical inventions do not, as a rule, flow from scientists and little industrial R&D is basic research... Despite all the attention to R&D in the literature, there is little evidence that R&D effort explains technical change..." (Walker, 1985:238). What is needed are alternative institutions to create an environment for success.

This does not deny the potential of research for technical change, but suggests that the focus must be on the technical change and not on the research. Otherwise, policy makers fall into the "high tech trap: [governments] have to go on spending subsidies on a strategy that hardly brings any benefits but they lack the money to engage in economic or employment programmes" (Hilpert, 1991:300). A technology strategy should assist those with ideas but should also develop mechanisms for locally controlled research and development. This may be through government and university research or through community-controlled research facilities such as the Ikerlan unit of the Mondragon co-operatives with their "development from below" (Stöhr and Taylor, 1981).

Technology is one of the means to fundamental ends, not an end in itself. The geographic and institutional sources of technology are important because they determine the technological trajectory and this affects employment, wage levels, and the income distribution, domestic linkages, and the possibilities for building on the technological base. Technological diffusion will be more effective if it is between similar regions than if between developed and developing regions.

The approach to technology should emphasize local control, but this is neither xenophobic nor luddite. It reflects the need to maximize the benefits of new technologies and to minimize the costs. It is based on the assumptions that innovation is incremental and dependent on individuals. To the extent that foreign technologies are imported, they should be adapted to a region's needs and incorporated into its technological base, if technological dependency is to be reduced. Having overcome the confusion of the conventional wisdom, a technology strategy can lead to greater self-reliance, sustainability, and equity.

The discussion of equation (8) makes it clear that capital-intensive technical change does not guarantee that wages will rise but is likely to cause employment to fall. However, improvements in the general level of efficiency, A, in labor's efficiency, B, and even capital's efficiency, C, will increase the demand for labor and raise wages. Achieving these efficiency gains normally takes a long time and involves a number of strategies including improvements in physical infrastructure, in education and health, and in management training. Thus both hard and soft infrastructure expenditures are important.

Labor productivity improvements can also be achieved by institutional changes, e.g., providing more job security and safety through better, and better enforcement of, occupational health and safety legislation. Similarly legislation protecting workers from arbitrary treatment, including technological unemployment, may be important for attitudes and hence for productivity. The promotion of worker co-operatives can achieve impressive results in workers' productivity--and in their receptivity to technical change.

In many cases, wages or incomes do not represent low productivity but rather a situation of monopsony where the worker or primary producer receives a low payment for their effort. Monopsony may be much more serious in depressing returns and employment than the literature suggests (Bradfield, 1990). Thus collective action through labor unions or marketing boards may be necessary to offset the market power exercised by multinationals and others.

Equation (8) also indicates that labor productivity and wages can be increased by dealing with imperfections in product and capital markets. The price received by local producers may be increased by legislation restricting the market power of large firms which marginalise local producers. In the capital market, many firms would benefit by more access to financial capital at reasonable rates. While these approaches take us well beyond the concerns of technological change, they are important to development and need to be part of the many strategies necessary for true development.

Endnotes

1. This paper draws heavily from Bradfield, 1993. The author revised it extensively while a visiting fellow at Monash University where he benefitted from the helpful comments of Robert Rice.

2. This section is taken from Bradfield and Dunn, 1991, which also presents a proof using a CES production function.

3. Eric Kierans, an economist and then Canadian cabinet minister, pointed out that the initial foreign financing of the Mackenzie Valley oil pipeline would drive up the exchange rate and the subsequent energy sales to the US would keep it up, thereby generating both a Kierans effect and the Dutch Disease.

4. There is a worse scenario - when foreign funds come into a country to speculate in currency, in land, or stocks, or for other unproductive activities. Instead of real investment, the country gets "zaitech" investment (Tatsuno, 1991: 220) which generates no jobs but the foreign exchange effects destroy jobs. This is represented in Figure 1 by the shift from the equilibrium at A to B, without any matching increase in domestic investment activity. Zaitech funds respond to increases in domestic interests rates which cut off real domestic investment.

5. To equate labor's share of the firm's expenditures to labor's share of output is to assume there are no excess profits - i.e., there is perfect competition. In addition, the straight line isocost assumes perfectly competitive input markets - the monopsonist's isocost is concave to the origin because its marginal cost of labor is rising (Bradfield, 1988).

   With a Cobb-Douglas production function, capital and labor shares of output are equal to the production function parameter α and $(1-\alpha)$, respectively. The analysis here is general since it is not constrained to a particular specification of the production function. This provides a useful empirical test of the capital-intensity of technical change, since labor's share, by industry, is easily determined. Of course, for changes in labor's share of output to indicate only changes in production technique requires the assumption that excess profits are a fixed fraction of output.

6. An interesting example is Germany, with some of the world's toughest environmental standards. These have forced changes in design and in production processes which have provided additional selling points for products and the possibility of exporting technology (Moore, 1992).

References

Amin, Ash and Smith, Ian . "The Internationalization of Production and Its Implications for the UK," in Ash Amin and John Goddard, eds., *Technological Change, Industrial Restructuring and Regional Development*, London: Allen & Unwin, 1986.

Arthur, W.B. "Competing technologies, increasing returns, and lock-in by historical events." *Economic Journal*, 1989, vol. 99, pp. 116-31.

Berra, Mariella and Gastaldo, Piero. "Science Parks and Local Innovation Policies in Italy," in Ulrich Hilpert, ed., *Regional Innovation and Decentralization: High Tech Industry and Government Policy*, London: Routledge, 1991.

Bradfield, M. "Technological frontiers - the answer to whose questions?" International Conference on Regional Development - The Challenge of the Frontier, Ben Gurion University and UCLA, Dead Sea, Israel, December 27-30, 1993 .

_____. "Long run equilibrium under pure monopsony." *Canadian Journal of Economics*, 1990, vol. 23, pp. 700-704.

_____. *Regional Economics: Analysis and Policy in Canada*. Toronto: McGraw-Hill Ryerson, 1988.

_____ **and Dunn, K.** "An Extended neo-classical muddle of technical change and regional wage disparities." 30th Annual Meetings, Western Regional Science Association, Monterey, Cal., February, 1991.

Buswell, R. J. "Research and Development and Regional Development: A Review," in A. Gillespie, ed., *Technological Change and Regional Development*, London: Pion, 1983.

Castells, Manuel. "High Technology, Economic Restructuring, and the Urban-Regional Process in the United States," in Manuel Castells, ed., *High Technology, Space, and Society*, London: Sage Publications. *Urban Affairs, Annual Reviews*, 1985, vol. 28, pp. 11-40.

Cohen, Linda R. and Noll, Roger G. "Government Support for Commercial R&D," in Linda R. Cohen; Roger G. Noll; J.S. Banks; S.A. Edelman and W.M. Pegram, eds., *The Technology Pork Barrel.* Washington, DC: The Brookings Institution, 1991.

Cowling, Keith. "The Internationalization of Production and De-industrialization," in Ash Amin and John Goddard, eds., *Technological Change, Industrial Restructuring and Regional Development.* London: Allen & Unwin, 1986.

Cuadrado Roura, J. R.; Granados, V. and Aurioles, J. "Technological Dependency in a Mediterranean Economy: The Case of Spain," in A. Gillespie, ed., *Technological Change and Regional Development.* London: Pion, 1983.

Dalhousie University. *Dalhousie Explorer*, 1993, 3.

Debresson, Christian. "Technological Clusters and Competitive Poles: The Case of Canadian Energy," in Jorge Niosi, ed., *Technology and National Competitiveness: Oligopoly, Technological Innovation, and International Competition.* Montreal: McGill-Queen's University Press, 1991.

Duchin, Faye. "Technological Change and International Trade," in Jorge Niosi ed., *Technology and National Competitiveness: Oligopoly, Technological Innovation, and International Competition*, Montreal: McGill-Queen's University Press, 1991.

Economic Council of Canada. *Living Together - A Study of Regional Disparities.* Ottawa: Minister of Supply and Services, 1977.

Ettlinger, N. "Modes of corporate organization and the geography of development." Papers in Regional Science, 1992, vol. 71, pp. 107-26.

Fach, Wolfgang and Grande, Edgar. "Space and Modernity - On the Regionalization of Innovation Management," in Ulrich Hilpert, ed. , *Regional Innovation and Decentralization: HighTech Industry and Government Policy.* London: Routledge, 1991.

Hall, Peter. "Technology, Space, and Society in Contemporary Britain," in Manuel Castells, ed., *High Technology, Space, and Society*, London: Sage Publications. *Urban Affairs Annual Reviews*, 1985, vol. 28, pp. 41-52.

Hansen, N. "Competition, trust, and reciprocity in the development of innovative regional milieux." *Papers in Regional Science*, 1992, vol. 71, pp. 95-105.

Hilpert, Ulrich. "The Optimization of Political Approaches to Innovation - some Comparative Conclusions on Trends for Regionalization," in Ulrich Hilpert, ed., *Regional Innovation and Decentralization:High Tech Industry and Government Policy.* London: Routledge, 1991.

Hilpert, Ulrich and Ruffieux, Bernard . "Innovation, Politics and Regional Development - Technology Parks and Regional Participation in High Tech in France and West Germany," in Ulrich Hilpert, ed., *Regional Innovation and Decentralization: High Tech Industry and Government Policy.* London: Routledge, 1991.

King, I.; McAfeee, R. P. and Welling, L. "Industrial blackmail: dynamic tax competition and public investment." *Canadian Journal of Economics*, 1993, vol. XXVI, pp. 590-608.

Lithwick, Harvey N. "Federal Government Regional Economic Development Polices: An Evaluative Survey," in Kenneth Norrie, ed., *Disparities and Interregional Adjustment.* Toronto: University of Toronto Press, 1986, vol. 64, research studies for the Royal Commission on the Economic Union and Development Prospects for Canada.

Macdonald, Donald *et al.* *Royal Commission on the Economic Union and Development Prospects for Canada.* Ottawa: Minister of Supply and Services, 1985.

Mahdavi, S. "Some empirical evidence on the temporal relationships between foreign inflows and aggregate spending categories in the United States." *Journal of Post Keynesian Economics*, 1995, vol. 18 pp. 125-140.

Mainwaring, Lyn. "Global Development: An Evolutionary synthesis of Classical and Post-Keynesian Perspectives," in Mark A. Glick, ed., *Competition, Technology, and Money - Classical and Post-Keynesian Perspectives.* Aldershot, England: Edward Elgar, 1994.

Markusen, A. "Conversion from a military to a civilian economy: what President-elect Clinton is likely to do." *The Survey of Regional Literature*, 1993, vol. 23, from ECAAR News Network, Winter, 1992, 11.

Moore, C.A. "Down Germany's road to a clean tomorrow." *International Wildlife*, 1992, vol. 22, pp. 20-24.

Neumann, Wolfgang. "The Politics of Decentralization and Industrial Modernization-France and West Germany in Comparison," in Ulrich Hilpert, ed., *Regional Innovation and Decentralization: High Tech Industry and Government Policy.* London: Routledge, 1991.

Nilsson, E.A. "Innovating-by-doing: skill innovations as a source of technological advance." *Journal of Economic Issues*, 1995, vol. XXIX, pp. 33-46.

Stöhr, Walter B. and Taylor, D.R.F., eds. *Development From Above or Below? The Dialectics of Regional Planning in Developing Countries.* Chichester, England: John Wiley and Sons, 1981.

Tatsuno, Sheridan M. "Building the Japanese Techno-State," in Ulrich Hilpert, ed. *Regional Innovation and Decentralization: High Tech Industry and Government Policy.* London: Routledge, 1991.

Walker, Richard A. "Technological Determination and Determinism: Industrial Growth and Location," *in* Manuel Castells, ed. *, High Technology, Space, and Society.* London: Sage Publications. *Urban Affairs Annual Reviews*, 1985, vol. 28, pp. 226-264.

Waring, Marilyn. *If Women Counted.* San Francisco: Harper. 1990.

10

THE ROLE OF INTELLECTUAL PROPERTY RIGHTS IN ECONOMIC GROWTH

David M. Gould
William C. Gruben
Federal Reserve Bank of Dallas, USA

By influencing the incentives to innovate, intellectual property rights protection may affect economic growth in important ways. An important question for many countries is whether stricter enforcement of intellectual property laws is a good strategy for economic growth. This chapter examines the role of intellectual property rights in economic growth, utilizing cross-country data on patent protection, trade regime, and country-specific characteristics. The evidence suggests that intellectual property protection is a significant determinant of economic growth. These effects appear to be slightly stronger in relatively open economies and are robust to both the measure of openness used and to other alternative model specifications.

Explanations of economic growth are increasingly focusing on the power of expected profits to motivate innovation (Grossman and Helpman, 1991; Romer, 1990b). Meanwhile, policymakers debate whether stronger protection of intellectual property will stimulate or retard growth in their countries. If innovation is a principal engine of growth and agents innovate to capture or hold a share of the market they would not retain otherwise, then perhaps protection of intellectual property might boost long-run growth.

An important question, however, is whether intellectual property protection is always consistent with innovation and higher growth. For example, if individuals only innovate to capture or hold a share of the market, they may not increase their rate of innovation with stronger intellectual property rights when their share of the market is already guaranteed. Indeed, some evidence suggests that stronger intellectual property rights protection may not provide a stimulus to innovation in countries that are highly protected from international trade. Using a survey of more than 3,000 Brazilian companies, Braga and Willmore (1991) found that firms' propensities to develop their own technology or to purchase it abroad were both negatively related to the degree of trade protectionism their industries enjoyed. Braga and Willmore's empirical work suggests that, in closed regimes, protecting intellectual property may not increase innovation because the competitive framework there is inadequate to stimulate much innovation. Rivera-Batiz and Romer (1991) offer a theoretical model that suggests similar conclusions. In their model, copying foreign technology is typically more profitable than innovating in a closed-trade regime.

In contrast, open trade regimes may exhibit a stronger linkage between intellectual property protection and innovation. Open trade implies that local firms are more likely to face competition from foreign producers that use the latest technology both in their production processes and in their products. Moreover, local firms that wish to meet this challenge by purchasing technology from abroad may find that weak intellectual property protection at home impedes their efforts. In fact, some evidence suggests that foreign technology-producing firms often refuse to license or lease their latest innovations to firms in countries with weak intellectual property protection in fear that the licensing contract will ultimately be unenforceable (Sherwood, 1990). In a survey of 100 major U.S. firms in six manufacturing industries, Mansfield (1994) found that a country's weak intellectual property rights protection deterred foreign direct investment and joint ventures, especially in research and development facilities.

This chapter examines the role of intellectual property rights in economic growth. We utilize cross-country data on overall levels of patent protection, trade regime, and country-specific characteristics and find that intellectual property protection (as measured by the degree of patent protection) is an important determinant of economic growth. This effect is slightly stronger in relatively open economies than in relatively closed economies and is robust to both the measure of openness used and to other alternative model specifications.

Our findings suggest that market structure may influence the links among intellectual property rights, innovation, and growth. Although our results do not fully capture all market structure subtleties, the findings suggest that the linkage between innovation and intellectual property rights protection may play a weaker role in less competitive markets.

These results have implications for developing countries, especially with regard to trade liberalization under the General Agreement on Tariffs and Trade (GATT) and the push for greater intellectual property rights protection. Many countries, particularly those in Latin America, have been turning away from trade protectionism and moving toward liberalization. While some countries, such as Mexico, are liberalizing and rapidly tightening their intellectual property protection, others are moving more slowly to strengthen intellectual property protection. The implication of this chapter is that while intellectual property rights appear to be positively related to economic growth, trade liberalization accompanied by intellectual property protection may be a slightly stronger conduit for economic growth.

We begin this chapter by looking at how intellectual property rights vary across countries and how they may or may not be related to increased innovation. We then discuss the implications of intellectual property rights protection and innovation in an endogenous growth theory context. Finally, we present our empirical findings on intellectual property rights protection and economic growth.

Intellectual Property Rights Protection

Because products of the intellect are typically non-rival, intellectual property law incorporates the inherent tension between private gain and public welfare. That is, once such a product has been created, it can be used by many parties at little or no additional cost. To motivate innovation, governments try to ensure that inventors can profit from inventing. But protecting innovators too stringently may limit the dissemination of new ideas and, therefore, opportunities for economic growth.[1]

We consider in more detail below the optimal level of intellectual property protection by focusing on the arguments for weak and strong intellectual property protection.

The Case for Weak Protection

Free access to information that agents would otherwise have to pay for is one, but not the only, argument for weak intellectual property protection. Another argument involves the monopolistic behavior that strong protection permits. It has been shown that under some conditions, a monopoly may accumulate patents to preserve its power by allowing the patents to "sleep" so as to deter entry into an industry (Gilbert and Newbery, 1982).

The argument that firms innovate—in part—to secure monopoly power has particularly important implications for developing country policies. Chin and Grossman (1990) demonstrate conditions under which the globally efficient degree of intellectual property protection does not necessarily maximize every country's welfare. Here again, the enforcement of protection mitigates competition and may replace it with monopolistic behavior. In net innovation-consuming countries, the cost of monopolization can more than offset the contribution of stronger intellectual property protection toward stimulating more cost-saving innovations.[2]

Likewise, under conditions presented by Diwan and Rodrik (1991), the net innovation-consuming country will only be motivated to protect intellectual property as long as the type of innovation it demands is different from the type demanded in the net innovation-producing country. If the consuming country has the same demand as the innovating country, the innovating country will develop the technology regardless of whether there is intellectual property rights protection in the consuming country. On the other hand, if the consuming country demands innovations that are very different from those produced by the innovating country, the innovating country will only innovate on behalf of the consuming country if the consuming country protects intellectual property.

From the perspective of net innovation-consuming countries that also wish to encourage innovation at home, another argument against strong intellectual property protection relates to institutional structures in which innovations are produced and distributed. Vessuri (1990) argues that transnational computer corporations located in Brazil were not interested in developing or absorbing local technology because they typically restricted their research and development to home country locations. So, instead of protecting intellectual property, Brazil attempted to foster local innovation by reserving a portion of its market for domestic producers of mini- and microcomputers and their peripherals.[3]

The Case for Strong Protection

Why offer strong intellectual property protection? Survey evidence suggests that, at least in the United States, protection stimulates innovation (Mansfield, 1986) and the social rate of return appears to be considerably higher than the rate of return to the innovator (Mansfield, Rapoport, Romeo, Wagner, and Beardsley, 1977). In a

Brazilian survey, 80 percent of 377 firms said they would invest more in internal research and would improve training for their employees if better legal protection were available (Sherwood, 1990). Mansfield (1994) finds that U.S firms, particularly in the chemical and pharmaceutical industries, limit foreign direct investment in countries with weak intellectual property rights protection.

Moreover, despite arguments that strong intellectual property protection significantly enhances the monopoly power of producers in some markets, it does not appear that patent protection—the strongest form of intellectual property protection—has often prevented competitors from entering markets in developed countries for very long (Evenson, 1990; Levin, Klevorick, Nelson and Winter, 1987). Firms surveyed by Mansfield (1985) believed that, for about half of a selected sample of innovations, patent protection deterred imitation by competitors for only a few months.[4]

An additional case for strong intellectual property protection is that, without it, the technology acquirable may not cost much but it will be old (MacLaughlin, Richards, and Kenny, 1988, 106). Productive processes, on average, will be more backward than in regimes with strong intellectual property protection.[5] A net innovation-consuming country that does not protect intellectual property can affect its firms' ability to purchase technology, even when firms are willing to pay for it. When dealing with firms in such countries, foreign producers of technology are cautious about selling it, out of concern that the prospective buyers may violate purchasing agreements with impunity.[6]

A final motivation for consuming nations to protect intellectual property is that innovation-producing countries may retaliate against those with weak intellectual property protection. Indeed, it has been argued that the recent move of some developing nations toward stronger intellectual property protection may be a direct response to U.S. trade retaliation over the last decade (Gadbaw and Richards, 1988).

Intellectual Property Rights and Economic Growth Theory

While the discussion above suggests much about the interaction between intellectual property rights and innovation, little has been mentioned about the dynamic process of innovation, which is the backbone of many new theories of endogenous growth. So far, the theoretical literature on intellectual property rights, innovation, and economic growth has been quite limited, while the empirical work on economic growth—such as that of Kormendi and Meguire (1985); Barro (1991); Romer (1990a); Mankiw, Romer, and Weil (1992); Levine and Renelt (1992)—has yet to examine the relationship between intellectual property rights and economic growth. This section relates intellectual property rights protection to endogenous growth theories.

Several popular models of endogenous growth are based on the idea that innovation is carried out to make profits on the introduction of new products.[7] But every new product adds to the stock of human knowledge, so the cost of innovation falls as human knowledge accumulates. Thus, the rate of growth of the economy will vary directly with the rate of introduction of new products such as the automobile or personal computer. Moreover, economic growth will also be faster the larger is the stock of human capital or the more conducive the economic environment to the accumulation of human knowledge. By creating an environment conducive to the accumulation of human knowledge, intellectual property rights will tend to increase innovation and economic growth.

Economic growth may also depend on the openness of an economy. The work of Paul Romer (1990b) and Grossman and Helpman (1991, 238-46) suggests that if externalities are international in scope, then economic integration will increase economic growth. With openness, a country's economic growth depends on the stock of world human capital; accordingly, higher stocks of human capital in a country should have only a slight marginal impact on economic growth in that country. Likewise, intellectual property rights protection would also have a small marginal impact on that country's growth rate. However from a global standpoint, human capital accumulation and intellectual property rights protection would be very important to economic growth.

In other endogenous growth models, there is a dynamic sector that exhibits learning-by-doing externalities, spillover effects, or other human-capital-type externalities and a traditional sector that does not.[8] Depending on whether free trade shifts resources toward or away from the dynamic sector, economic growth may increase or decrease. How resources are allocated under free trade depends, of course, on the structure of the model and a country's initial factor endowments. While intellectual property rights protection would clearly enhance growth in those countries that move toward free trade and have a comparative advantage in the high-technology sector, its role in a country with a disadvantage in the high-technology sector would be less important.

Although there are many theoretical models of innovation and growth, and static models of intellectual property rights and income, relatively few studies have modeled the dynamic effects of intellectual property rights and growth. Segerstrom, Anant, and Dinopoulos (1990) examine a dynamic general equilibrium model in which research and development (R&D) activity and, hence, technological change are influenced by the length of patent protection and the height of tariffs. They find that increasing the length of patents in the North (the innovating region) can either increase or decrease R&D activity. Although longer patents increase the return to R&D, they may also mean that more fixed resources will be devoted to producing existing products. Segerstrom (1991) examines the dynamic process of innovation and imitation and conditions under which government lump-sum subsidies to innovation (or imitation) alter the rate of innovation.

Building on the work of Grossman and Helpman (1991), Helpman (1993) models intellectual property rights, innovation, and economic growth as an interaction between countries in the North that innovate and countries in the South that imitate. The stronger the level of intellectual property rights, the less imitation there is in the South. He finds that strong intellectual property rights will increase innovation in the short run as the profitability of innovation in the North increases. In the longer run, however, the rate of innovation actually falls because the North produces more old-technology goods, which takes resources away from innovation.

Although the theoretical literature suggests many possible mechanisms for innovation and growth, it does not suggest any clear-cut relationship between intellectual property rights, trade regime, and economic growth. We attempt to discover the central facts and then suggest a tentative explanation.

Intellectual Property and Economic Growth

The Benchmark Model

Before examining the role of intellectual property rights in economic growth, we first present the results of a basic benchmark growth model. The model utilizes a formulation that is common to many of the recent cross-country empirical examinations of growth.[9] Equation 1 of Table 1 presents the estimation results of the benchmark model.[10] The dependent variable is the average annual real per capita gross domestic product (GDP) growth rate between 1960 and 1988,[11] and the explanatory variables are 1) the log of real GDP per capita in 1960, $\ln(Y60)$; 2)

Table 1: Growth and the Role of Intellectual Property Rights:

OLS Estimation (Dependent Variable: Average yearly per capita GDP growth 1960-1988)

	(1)	(2)	(3)	(4)
Constant	15.650††	14.182††	13.668††	12.150††
	(8.039)	(6.402)	(6.148)	(5.428)
ln(Y60)	-0.846††	-0.865††	-0.922††	-1.042††
	(-3.960)	(-4.058)	(-4.297)	(-4.688)
ln(I/Y)	3.331††	3.276††	3.149††	3.084††
	(8.314)	(8.175)	(7.751)	(7.572)
ln(SEC)	0.828††	0.642††	0.611††	0.414
	(6.261)	(3.393)	(3.239)	(1.912)
ln(LIT60)		0.308	0.339	0.315
		(1.366)	(1.510)	(1.366)
ln(IPROP)			0.425	0.421
			(1.550)	(1.427)
ln(GovCon)				-1.082††
				(-3.092)
ln(ASSN)				-0.037
				(-1.008)
ln(REV)				-0.043
				(-0.982)
AFRICA				-0.618
				(-1.431)
LATAM				-0.547
				(-1.637)
$\overline{R^2}$	0.62	0.63	0.64	0.68
r.m.s.e.	1.13	1.13	1.12	1.06
observations	95	95	95	95

Note: T-statistics in parentheses. ††Significant at the 5% level. †Significant at the 10% level.

physical capital savings, which is the log of the share of investment in gross domestic product, ln(I/Y); and 3) a proxy for human capital savings—the log of secondary-school enrollment rates in 1960, ln(SEC).[12]

The results of the benchmark model are consistent with most recent growth studies. Real GDP per working-age person in 1960 is negative and highly significant, suggesting income convergence conditional on human capital.[13] Physical capital savings and the proxy for human capital savings, ln(I/Y) and ln(SEC), are positive and significant at the 1 percent level, consistent with Levine and Renelt (1992).

Equation 2 of Table 1 examines the role of the stock of human capital, as proxied by literacy rates, in economic growth. We specifically examine the stock of human capital to account for any scale effects that human capital may have in economic growth as suggested by the endogenous growth literature. Our proxy for the stock of human capital is the literacy rate in the early 1960s. As model 2 shows, the coefficient on the stock of human capital, ln(LIT60), has a large standard error but it still contributes to the explanatory power of the model as shown by the higher adjusted R^2. Holding all else constant, the point estimate suggests that a country with a literacy rate in 1960 of 95 percent would have grown about 0.18 percentage points per year faster than a country with a literacy rate of 50 percent. Furthermore, notice that when the literacy rate is included in the benchmark growth equation, the coefficient on human capital savings falls by 0.2 (model 1 versus model 2).[14] This result suggests that both variables, to some degree, may be accounting for scale effects of human capital in economic growth.

Intellectual Property Rights and Economic Growth: *The Results*

Can intellectual property explain any variation in economic growth once human capital and other determinants of growth are held constant? Before we examine this question, we first discuss how intellectual property rights are measured.

Optimally, a complete picture of a country's intellectual property rights protection would include measures of copyright protection, trade secret laws, and patents. But even when one has measures of all of these aspects of intellectual property law, countries may enforce these laws quite differently. Two countries may have identical laws on their books to protect computer software, but one country may turn a blind eye to its local software pirates while the other country does not. Moreover, patent protection may be more important for some industries than others. For example, it is much easier to copy in the chemical and pharmaceutical industry where adopting new technology does not require large capital outlays than in the metals and transportation equipment industries that require much greater outlays (Mansfield 1994). On the other hand, even if a country does not have laws on its books to protect intellectual property, it may nonetheless protect intellectual property by assuming it falls under the same laws as physical property. These are some of the difficulties in obtaining a comprehensive index of intellectual property rights protection.

Rather than attempting to obtain a complete and comprehensive index of intellectual property rights protection, we focus on an aspect of intellectual property protection that is potentially the most important for economic growth—patent protection. The proxy for intellectual property rights we use is taken from an index of patent protection developed by Rapp and Rozek (1990). The index is based on the conformity of each nation's patent laws to the minimum standards proposed in the *Guidelines for Standards for the Protection and Enforcement of Patents* of the U.S. Chamber of Commerce Intellectual Property Task Force.[15] Although the index has its deficiencies, recent survey evidence from U.S. firms is considerably correlated with its rankings (Mansfield 1994).

The index ranks the level of patent protection on a scale of one to six, where one is assigned to a nation having no patent protection law at all and six corresponds to nations whose laws are fully consistent with the minimum standards.[16] For example, the procedure gives a score of two on the patent protection scale for Argentina. Argentina does have a patent law and the duration of protection under the law is 15 years from the date a patent is granted. According to Rapp and Rozek, however, the combination of high inflation and a maximum fine fixed in 1864 means that there is no practical penalty for infringement. Moreover, the law makes no provision for preliminary injunctions. Thus, enforcement is nearly impossible. By contrast, Singapore registers and protects patents under the United Kingdom Patents Act. Compulsory licensing may be granted three years after registration for certain classes of invention when the invention is being neither practiced nor imported. The government retains the right to exclude pharmaceutical patents for its own purposes, but in all other respects patents are enforceable. Singapore, accordingly, is given a score of five on the patent protection index. A problem with the index is that it is based primarily on the laws in force against infringement but not on their enforcement or implementation. Thus, the index will overestimate the level of protection in a country where strong anti-infringement laws are on the books but do not work in practice because of lack of enforcement or other administrative obstacles. Some developing countries, for example, have laws on their books as a carryover from colonial days but do not have a legal system to enforce them.

Table 2 shows the countries in the data set, their level of patent protection, and the average growth rate across countries at each level of patent protection. Without controlling for other important determinants of growth, those countries with the highest level of intellectual property rights protection tended to grow the fastest. However, those countries with the second lowest level of patent protection grew faster on average than those countries in the middle levels of patent protection. Overall, there appears to be a positive but weak relationship between patent protection and economic growth. Many other factors should be taken into account before any conclusions can properly be made.

Table 2: Level of Patent Protection and Average Annual Growth Rate

Country	1 Growth Rate	Country	2 Growth Rate	Country	3 Growth Rate	Country	4 Growth Rate	Country	5 Growth Rate	Country	6 Growth Rate
Myanmar	2.63	Turkey	2.87	Chile	1.03	Portugal	4.50	Austria	3.95	US States	1.94
Angola	-2.73	Argentina	1.10	Colombia	2.27	Costa Rica	2.45	Norway	3.42	UK	2.19
Ethiopia	0.79	Bolivia	1.02	Mexico	2.65	Dominica	2.46	Canada	2.43	Belgium	2.95
Madagascar	-1.75	Brazil	4.60	Nicaragua	1.07	El Salvador	1.31	Japan	6.11	Denmark	2.92
Mozambique	-2.02	Ecuador	2.78	Panama	3.50	Guatemala	1.51	Finland	3.63	France	3.38
Papua New Guinea	0.83	Honduras	1.34	Venezuela	2.20	Haiti	0.28	Greece	4.58	W. Germany	3.36
		Paraguay	2.27	Syria	4.06	Uruguay	0.57	Ireland	2.70	Italy	4.00
		Peru	1.67	Egypt	4.26	Jamaica	1.91	Spain	3.64	Netherlands	3.03
		India	0.77	Bangladesh	0.25	Korea	5.55	Australia	2.33	Sweden	2.61
		Thailand	3.59	Algeria	3.73	Malaysia	3.98	New Zealand	1.76	Switzerland	2.19
				Cameroon	3.58	Nepal	0.91	Trinidad & Tabago	3.31	South Africa	1.65
				Central Africa	-0.54	Pakistan	1.93	Jordan	3.12	Israel	3.63
				Chad	-2.37	Somalia	0.23	Sri Lanka	1.05		
				Congo	3.52	Tunisia	3.32	Philippines	2.29		
				Benin	-0.24	Zambia	-1.43	Singapore	6.62		
				Ivory Coast	1.34			Botswana	7.14		
				Mali	0.30			Burundi	1.71		
				Mauritania	0.08			Zaire	0.19		
				Nigeria	-0.40			Ghana	-0.50		
				Senegal	-0.24			Kenya	1.61		
				Togo	1.77			Liberia	-0.45		
				Burkina Faso	1.61			Malawi	1.30		
								Mauritius	1.68		
								Morocco	2.78		
								Nigeria	0.69		
								Zimbabwe	1.63		
								Rwanda	2.03		
								Sierra Leone	-0.01		
								Sudan	0.14		
								Tanzania	2.25		
								Uganda	-0.17		
Average Growth Rate	-0.38		2.20		1.52		1.96		2.35		2.82

Average annual growth rates are from 1960 to 1988.

Model 3 in Table 1 adds our proxy for the level of intellectual property rights (IPROP) to the benchmark model. As the results indicate, intellectual property rights protection has a positive effect on economic growth but is only marginally significant. Still, despite problems in the measurement of IPROP, the statistical significance of the variable is strong enough to contribute to the explanatory power of the equation. In model 4, its significance level falls only slightly when adding such variables as the amount of government spending, as proxied by the average ratio of real government consumption to real GDP [ln(GovCon)], the degree of political instability, as proxied by the number of revolutions and coups per year [ln(REV)], and the number of assassinations [ln(ASSN)], and dummy variables for sub-Saharan Africa (AFRICA) and Latin America (LATAM).[17]

Figure 1 plots the average yearly growth in real GDP per capita between 1960 and 1988 against (IPROP), holding constant all the explanatory variables in model 3. That is, the figure shows the partial correlation between growth rates and our proxy for intellectual property rights protection. The figure demonstrates the positive relationship between growth and intellectual property rights protection, but also shows the large degree of variation in this relationship.

Problems with Measurement Error

As previously mentioned, the level of patent protection is, at best, a rough measure of the theoretical concept of intellectual property rights protection. Undoubtedly, measurement error is possible because constructing any general measure of intellectual property rights protection requires judgment. A common way to address this problem is to consider our proxy as subject to measurement error and use the instrumental variables technique of estimation. The variables used must be correlated with the independent variable they are instrumenting for, and have to be uncorrelated with the primary regression's error term. Several variables that may qualify for this role are the average duration of patent protection, a set of dummy variables indicating a country's membership in an international convention that sets guidelines for intellectual property rights protection (e.g., the Paris Convention, the Berne Convention, and the International Convention for the Protection of New Varieties of Plants), and a set of dummy variables indicating whether a country has patents for pharmaceuticals, petty patents, food products, chemical products, plant/animal varieties, surgical procedures, and microorganisms and like products.[18] Other country-characteristic variables, such as literacy rates, from the primary regression equation are also included as instruments, but the instruments ultimately

Percent Growth

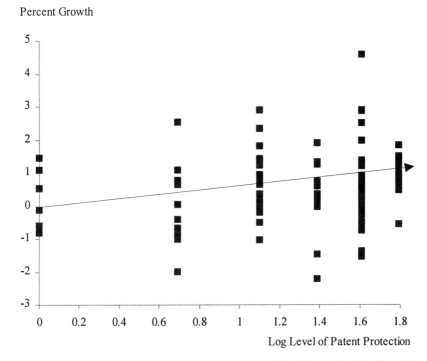

Figure 1: Partial Correlation Between Average Yearly per Capita Growth
(1980-1988) and Level of Patent Protection (from regression (3) Table 1)

chosen were solely determined on the basis of whether they minimized the equation's mean squared error. [19]

An advantage of using an IV approach to deal with measurement error is that it is also a method used to address potential endogeneity problems. Endogeneity may be problematic if rapidly growing economies tend to adopt more stringent intellectual property rights protection after they begin to grow. However, endogeneity may not be much of a problem because the level of patent protection for most countries was established during or before the 1960s, while the dependent variable is based on later data.[20]

Table 3 contains the IV estimates for the four growth equations estimated in Table 1. The data set is smaller because the set of countries with data on the instruments is smaller. When utilizing the IV technique to address the potential problems of measurement error, the results show that intellectual property rights protection becomes significant at the 5-percent level. Moreover, after controlling for the ancillary variables (model 3 versus model 4), the significance level of intellectual property rights protection falls only slightly from the 5-percent level to the 8-percent significance level. However, although this is not a large drop in the significance level, it does raise questions about the importance of intellectual property rights in economic growth. As suggested by the empirical work of Braga and Willmore (1991), a firm's development of technology through R&D may be directly affected by the degree of foreign competition. The following section assesses how our results depend on differences in trade regime.

Intellectual Property in Open and Closed Trade Regimes

How do intellectual property rights influence growth in open and closed economies? Although quite a few multicountry studies have found that closed economies grow less than outward-orientated economies (Krueger, 1978; Bhagwati, 1978; World Bank, 1987; De Long and Summers, 1991; Michaely et al., 1991; Edwards, 1992; and Roubini and Sala-i-Martin, 1992), the way in which intellectual property rights interact with the trade regime and growth has received little attention.[21]

All studies face the challenge of how to measure the degree of outward or inward orientation. Surveys of business opinion, the height of effective tariff rates, black market exchange rate premia, export shares, the growth of export shares, and real exchange rate distortions have all been used (World Bank, 1991). No measure is perfect because the true rate of protection reflects a complicated combination of tariffs, quotas, exchange rate controls, and a host of administrative barriers. We present results based on trade regimes as defined by black market exchange rate premiums, real exchange rate distortions, and a comprehensive index of trade orientation based on several commonly applied indicators of trade regime used in the literature.[22] Export shares or the growth of export shares are not used because of potential inference problems. Export shares reflect the size of a country, and the growth of export shares is itself a complicated endogenous variable reflecting many factors in addition to trade regime.[23]

Table 3: Growth and the Role of Intellectual Property Rights:
Instrumental Variables Estimation

(Dependent Variable: Average yearly per capita GDP growth 1960-1988)

	(1)	(2)	(3)	(4)
Constant	15.822[tt]	14.220[tt]	13.705[tt]	13.075[tt]
	(6.852)	(5.605)	(5.403)	(4.992)
ln(Y60)	-0.857[tt]	-0.916[tt]	-0.990[tt]	-1.201[tt]
	(-3.438)	(-3.653)	(-3.928)	(-4.479)
ln(I/Y)	3.361[tt]	3.352[tt]	3.385[tt]	3.291[tt]
	(6.921)	(6.954)	(7.056)	(6.877)
ln(SEC)	0.835[tt]	0.601[tt]	0.604[tt]	0.429
	(5.388)	(2.717)	(2.748)	(1.551)
ln(LIT60)		0.419	0.374	0.198
		(1.472)	(1.315)	(0.657)
ln(IPROP)			0.938[tt]	1.086[t]
			(1.985)	(1.766)
GovCon				-1.133[tt]
				(-2.648)
ASSN				-0.045
				(-1.070)
REV				-0.054
				(-1.024)
AFRICA				-0.893[t]
				(-1.745)
LATAM				-0.156
				(-0.320)
$\overline{R^2}$	0.57	0.58	0.59	0.64
r.m.s.e.	1.17	1.16	1.15	1.08
observations	79	79	79	79

Note: T-statistics in parentheses. [tt]Significant at the 5% level. [t]Significant at the 10% level.

We begin with one of the most widely used measures of overall trade orientation—black- market exchange rate premiums. Countries with high black-market exchange rate premiums are typically highly distorted and inward oriented. As in De Long and Summers (1991), we summarize the degree of trade orientation by a zero-one dummy variable. We create the zero-one dummy variable because black-market exchange rate premia, although they are good general measures of trade regime, cannot distinguish subtle differences in openness. This is not a problem since we are only interested in a measure of relative openness. Moreover, a binary variable of relative openness helps to elucidate the interactive effects of trade regime and patent protection on economic growth. The dummy variable is assigned zero for open economies—those with black-market premiums greater than the median of the sample—and one for closed economies—those with black-market premiums less than the median of the sample.[24]

Table 4 presents the results on the role of intellectual property rights in open and closed trade regimes. All regressions shown use the instrumental variables technique and the instruments discussed earlier. Because introduction of the trade orientation variable (BMPMED) reduces the size of the data set to seventy-six observations, a reference model of our benchmark growth equation is estimated with the seventy-six-country data set. In comparing the benchmark model 1 of Table 4 with the corresponding model 3 of Table 3, we see that the signs and magnitudes of the coefficients are all similar. The proxy for intellectual property rights (ln(IPROP)) is significant and the size of its coefficient changes little. This finding implies that the original results with respect to intellectual property rights are fairly robust to the countries chosen.

Model 2 of Table 4 includes a term interacting intellectual property rights and the trade orientation variable [ln(IPROP) * BMPMED], as well as intellectual property rights [ln(IPROP)] by itself. By including both variables in the estimating equation, the coefficient on ln(IPROP) represents the effects of intellectual property rights in relatively open trade regimes, and the sum of the coefficients on ln(IPROP) and the interaction term, [ln(IPROP) * BMPMED], represent the effect of intellectual property rights in highly protected trade regimes.

Controlling for differences in trade regimes, we find that ln(IPROP) continues to be statistically significant, and its point estimate increases by about 40 percent to 1.217, while the interaction term itself is negative and insignificant. By summing up the coefficients on ln(IPROP) and [ln(IPROP) * BMPMED], we find that in relatively closed trade regimes the coefficient on intellectual property rights is smaller, only 0.743. These results suggest that intellectual property rights may play a slightly larger role in open economies.

If we assume a moderate level of intellectual property rights protection of 4, the point estimates on ln(IPROP)and [ln(IPROP) * BMPMED] suggest that growth induced by intellectual property rights protection is approximately 0.66

Table 4: Growth: The Role of Intellectual Property Rights and Trade Regime (Black Market Premium > Median of Sample = Closed Regime): *Instrumental Variables Estimation*

(Dependent Variable: Average yearly per capita GDP growth 1960-1988)

	(1)	(2)	(3)	(4)
Constant	13.757††	14.433††	14.737††	13.899††
	(5.272)	(5.338)	(5.296)	(4.902)
ln(Y60)	-1.004††	-1.173††	-1.216††	-1.338††
	(-3.914)	(-3.928)	(-3.911)	(-4.363)
ln(I/Y)	3.368††	3.363††	3.357††	3.349††
	(6.864)	(6.779)	(6.697)	(6.682)
ln(SEC)	0.614††	0.552††	0.554††	0.528†
	(2.680)	(2.320)	(2.303)	(1.695)
ln(LIT60)	0.373	0.493	0.525	0.224
	(1.179)	(1.466)	(1.524)	(0.635)
ln(IPROP)	0.986††	1.217††	1.169††	1.409†
	(2.037)	(2.297)	(2.156)	(1.779)
BMPMED				
* ln(IPROP)		-0.474	-0.382	-0.345
		(-1.141)	(-0.848)	(-0.695)
BMPMED			-0.195	
			(-0.570)	
ln(GovCon)				-1.199††
				(-2.695)
ln(ASSN)				-0.056
				(-1.247)
ln(REV)				-0.032
				(-0.477)
AFRICA				-0.548
				(-0.920)
LATAM				0.009
				(0.018)
$\overline{R^2}$	0.58	0.58	0.57	0.62
r.m.s.e.	1.17	1.18	1.19	1.12
observations	76	76	76	76

Note: T-statistics in parentheses. ††Significant at the 5% level. †Significant at the 10% level.

percentage points higher per year in open versus protected economies. For example, both Korea and Jamaica have an index of intellectual property rights protection of 4, but Korea has much lower overall distortions than Jamaica. Between 1960 and 1988, annual growth in per capita income was 5.6 percent in Korea versus 1.9 percent in Jamaica. The results suggest that 0.66 percentage points of this difference may be attributed to the interaction between openness and patent protection.

Figure 2 plots the partial correlation between growth rates and our proxy for intellectual property rights protection (IPROP) in both open and closed trade regimes. The figure shows how the relationship between growth and the level of intellectual property rights protection varies according to trade regime. Although the relationship is not strong, it shows that the more open the economy, the greater the role of intellectual property rights protection and innovation in economic growth.

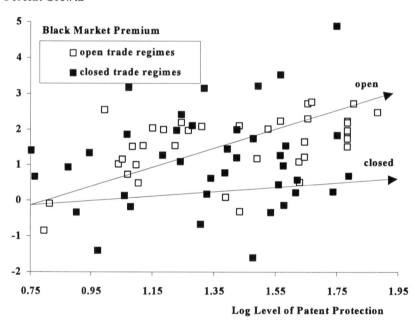

Figure 2: Partial Correlation Between Average Yearly per Capita Growth (1960-1988) and Level of Patent Protection

Model 3 of Table 4 includes the zero-one dummy variable (BMPMED) by itself to account for shift effects due to the trade regime. The results confirm the previous findings. Intellectual property rights are important determinants of growth. The growth effects, however, are only slightly larger in open trade regimes.

Of course, the positive relationship between growth, intellectual property rights, and openness may be sensitive to other factors correlated with trade regime and intellectual property rights. Consequently, we include the ancillary variables discussed earlier: real government consumption as a proportion of real GDP (Govcon), and the degree of political instability, as proxied by the number of revolutions and coups per year (REV), the number of assassinations (ASSN), and Africa (AFRICA) and Latin America (LATAM) dummy variables. After controlling for these other factors, we continue to find that intellectual property rights play a larger role in open trade regimes.

Because the above results may be sensitive to measurement error in trade orientation, we examine trade orientation as defined by two other criteria—real exchange rate distortions and a composite trade regime index.[25] Like black market exchange rate premia, countries with high real exchange rate distortions are typically highly distorted and inward-oriented. The advantage of real exchange rate distortions is that they may be a more general measure of trade orientation. Furthermore, because of data availability, the data set expands to 79 countries.

Table 5 shows the results corresponding to those in Table 4 using Dollar's (1992) measure of trade orientation. (RERMED) is a zero-one dummy variable that is equal to one for countries that have a real exchange rate distortion greater than the median of the sample. These countries are considered relatively closed trade regimes.

Model 2 of Table 5 shows results similar to those found earlier. Our proxy for intellectual property rights continues to be significant and positively related to economic growth in open trade regimes but is less important in closed trade regimes. For this definition of trade regime, the point estimate on ln(IPROP) implies that an open economy with a moderate level of intellectual property rights protection of 4 grew about 1.4 percentage points faster than a closed economy with the same level of intellectual property rights protection, all else being equal. Models 3 and 4 indicate that the results of model 2 are robust to shift effects of trade regime, government consumption expenditures, political assassinations and revolutions, and regional dummies.

Table 5: Growth: The Role of Intellectual Property Rights and Trade Regime (Real Exchange Rate Distortion > Median of Sample = Closed Regime): *Instrumental Variables Estimation*

(Dependent Variable: Average yearly per capita GDP growth 1960-1988)

	(1)	(2)	(3)	(4)
Constant	13.705††	13.889††	13.949††	13.936††
	(5.403)	(4.954)	(4.925)	(4.731)
ln(Y60)	-0.990††	-1.071††	-1.071††	-1.320††
	(-3.928)	(-3.793)	(-3.763)	(-4.298)
ln(I/Y)	3.385††	3.297††	3.324††	3.237††
	(7.056)	(6.193)	(6.108)	(6.138)
ln(SEC)	0.604††	0.477†	0.468†	0.477
	(2.748)	(1.878)	(1.816)	(1.557)
ln(LIT60)	0.373	0.160	0.159	0.001
	(1.315)	(0.472)	(0.467)	(0.001)
ln(IPROP)	0.938††	2.005††	1.986††	1.892††
	(1.985)	(2.468)	(2.420)	(2.114)
RERMED				
* ln(IPROP)		-1.025†	-0.949	-0.961
		(-1.714)	(-1.453)	(-1.373)
RERMED				-0.127
				(-0.299)
ln(GovCon)				-1.166††
				(-2.478)
ln(ASSN)				-0.055
				(-1.175)
ln(REV)				-0.057
				(-0.988)
AFRICA				-0.369
				(-0.543)
LATAM				-0.117
				(-0.219)
$\overline{R}^2$	0.59	0.54	0.54	0.59
r.m.s.e.	1.15	1.27	1.28	1.19
observations	79	79	79	79

Note: T-statistics in parentheses. ††Significant at the 5% level. †Significant at the 10% level.

Table 6 shows the results of the same experiment that was conducted in Tables 4 and 5, with the measure of trade orientation as defined by the composite index of trade regime indicators. The dummy variable (TRD) is assigned zero for open economies—those countries above the median index value for openness—and

Table 6: Growth: The Role of Intellectual Property Rights and Trade Regime (Composite Trade Regime Index) *Instrumental Variables Estimation*
(Dependent Variable: Average yearly per capita GDP growth 1960-1988)

	(1)	(2)	(3)	(4)
Constant	13.705††	15.315††	16.024††	14.274††
	(5.403)	(5.421)	(5.474)	(4.857)
ln(Y60)	-0.990††	-1.211††	-1.301††	-1.344††
	(-3.928)	(-4.139)	(-4.257)	(-4.403)
ln(I/Y)	3.385††	3.247††	3.121††	3.255††
	(7.056)	(6.319)	(5.866)	(6.317)
ln(SEC)	0.604††	0.541††	0.556††	0.474
	(2.748)	(2.296)	(2.312)	(1.583)
ln(LIT60)	0.374	0.302	0.312	0.142
	(1.315)	(0.993)	(1.006)	(0.434)
ln(IPROP)	0.938††	1.308††	1.212††	1.474††
	(1.985)	(2.426)	(2.189)	(2.062)
TRD				
* ln(IPROP)		-0.969†	-0.772	-0.866
		(-1.849)	(-1.392)	(-1.429)
TRD			-0.488	
			(-1.345)	
ln(GovCon)				-1.187††
				(-2.571)
ln(ASSN)				-0.057
				(-1.237)
ln(REV)				-0.010
				(-0.162)
AFRICA				-0.541
				(-0.896)
LATAM				-0.164
				(-0.312)
$\overline{R^2}$	0.59	0.57	0.56	0.60
r.m.s.e.	1.15	1.22	1.25	1.17
observations	79	79	79	79

Note: T-statistics in parentheses. ††Significant at the 5% level. †Significant at the 10% level.

one for closed economies—those countries below the median index value for openness.[26] The results are similar to those in the other tables and are even stronger than previously estimated.

Percent Growth

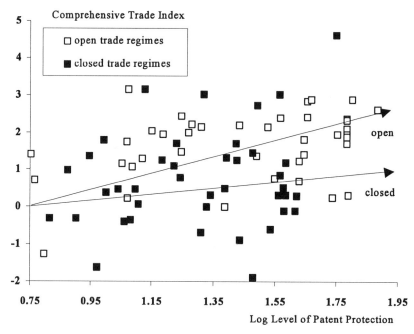

**Figure 3: Partial Correlation Between Average Yearly per Capita Growth
(1960-1988) and Level of Patent Protection (from regression (2) Table 4)**

Figures 3 and 4 plot the average yearly growth in real GDP per capita for open and
closed trade regime, as defined by real exchange rate distortions and composite
index of trade regime indicators. The results are consistent with those shown in
Figure 2 and indicate that the effects of intellectual property rights on growth vary
slightly according to trade regime.

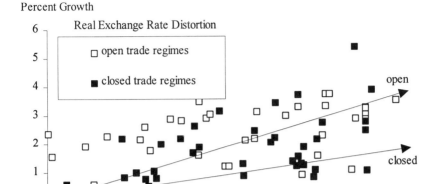

Figure 4: Partial Correlation Between Average Yearly per Capita Growth (1960-1988) and Level of Patent Protection (from regression (2) Table 4)

Conclusion

Although the role of intellectual property rights in economic growth is not clear in recent theory, empirically, we find that stronger intellectual property rights protection corresponds to higher economic growth rates in a cross-country sample. Moreover, a nation's trade policy may influence the degree to which intellectual property rights enhances growth. Although the statistical difference between trade regimes is small, and the results do not capture all market structure subtleties, the findings suggest that the linkage between innovation and intellectual property rights protection may play a weaker role in less competitive, highly protected markets. This is what one would expect if innovation adds less to a firm's market share and profits in less competitive markets.

Under a system of relatively closed markets, we might expect exogenous technology shocks to be more important in determining economic growth than in more open markets. In highly protected, uncompetitive markets, agents are unlikely to innovate much themselves, perhaps preferring to spend their resources on legislative schemes to preserve their market shares.[27] Conversely, under a regime of open markets, we might expect competitive forces to stimulate innovation and intellectual property protection to induce even more of it. An important avenue of future research would be to explore this relationship in greater detail.

Data Source Appendix

Real per capita GDP growth: Least squares estimates of real per capita GDP growth. Source of primary data: Summers and Heston (1991).

Y60: Real per capita gross domestic product in 1960. Source: Summers and Heston (1991).

I/Y: Investment as a share of GDP, 1960-1989. Source: World Bank National Accounts.

SEC: Secondary school enrollment rates, 1960-1989. Source: Barro (1991).

LIT60: Literacy rates in 1960. Source: United Nations (1971).

IPROP: Level of patent protection. Source: Rapp and Rozek (1990).

BMPMED: Dummy variable for black market premium greater than the median of the sample. Source of primary data: Levine and Renelt (1992).

RERMED: Dummy variable for real exchange rate distortion greater then the median of the sample. Source of primary data: Dollar (1992).

TRD: Dummy variable for comprehensive trade index greater than the median of the sample. Source: Gould and Ruffin (1994).

GovCon: Government consumption share of gross domestic product. Source: Levine and Renelt (1992).

ASSN: Number of assassinations per year. Source: Barro (1991).

REV: Number of revolutions and coups per year. Source: Barro (1991).

AFRICA: Dummy variable for sub-Saharan African countries.

LATAM: Dummy variable for Latin American countries.

**Patent coverage used   PHAR: Dummy variable for patents on
in the instrumental   pharmaceuticals.
variable estimation:**
                        FOOD: Dummy variable for patents on food
                                   products.
                        CHEM: Dummy variable for patents on chemical
                                   products.
                        PLANAM: Dummy variable for patents on plant or
                                   animal varieties.
                        SURG: Dummy variable for patents on surgical
                                   procedures.
                        MICRO: Dummy variable for patents on
                                   microorganisms and ike products.
                        PETTY: Dummy variable for petty patents.
                        BERNE: Dummy variable for member of the Berne
                                    Convention.
                        PARIS: Dummy variable for member of the Paris
                                   Convention.
                        UPOV: Dummy variable for member of the
                                   International Convention for the
                                   Protection of New Varieties of Plants.
                        PDUR: Patent duration.
                                   Source: Siebeck (1990).

Endnotes

1. In virtually all countries this problem is addressed by allowing patents to expire after a given time period. It is interesting to note that developing countries have traditionally offered shorter periods of protection for patents than have developed countries.

2. The degree to which the consuming country is motivated not to protect is, in part, inversely related to the relative size of its market.

3. An additional argument against strong intellectual property laws in net consuming countries is that enforcement costs can be very high (Primo Braga, 1990). Foreigners hold the bulk of patents in developing countries, so enforcement costs may simply lead to increased royalty gains for foreigners and greater royalty expenses for nationals.

4. These findings do not completely gainsay the monopolization argument, even though they weaken it somewhat. Schankerman (1991: 28), in an econometric study of French patents (including patents to applicants from Germany, the United Kingdon, Japan, and the United States, as well as France) finds that "the property rights generated by the patent system confer sizeable economic rents on patentees. On the average, these rents are equivalent to subsidy rate to R&D of about 15 percent. Hence patent protection is a significant source of returns to inventive effort, but it does not appear to be the major one."

5. They may also be simpler. A United Nations study notes that if "the technical services, management experience and capital resources as well as other connections of the foreign patentee himself are essential for the introduction of the patented process in the under-developed country, basically the situation is that in one form or other the minimum terms and conditions of the foreign patentee must be met if the innovation is to be brought to the under-developed country" (United Nations, 1964, 50).

6. Sherwood (1990) cites anecdotal evidence in which a Brazilian firm's employees have approached companies abroad to gain cost-effective technology, but that negotiations with the foreign source often came to an abrupt end when the source learned of Brazil's weak protection for innovation. The representative interviewed by Sherwood noted that his employees no longer try to keep up with technological advances abroad, since the information will do them little good.

7. See, i.e., Lucas (1988), Romer (1990b), and Grossman and Helpman (1991).

8. See, for example, Lucas (1988), Rivera-Batiz and Romer (1991), Stokey (1991), and Young (1991). Grossman and Helpman (1991) create a two-factor, three-sector endogenous growth open economy model by including a research and development sector, a high-technology good, and a traditional good.

9. See, for example, Kormendi and Meguire (1985), Barro (1991), Romer (1990a), Levine and Renelt (1992), Edwards (1992), Roubini and Sala-i-Martin (1992), Backus, Kehoe, and Kehoe (1992), and Mankiw, Romer and Weil (1992).

10. The benchmark model utilizes a log-linear formulation for two reasons: 1) it has a basis in Cobb-Douglas production technologies (e.g., Backus, Kehoe, and Kehoe, 1992 and mankiw, Romer, and Weil, 1992), and 2) this model is superior to a simple linear formation in minimizing the mean squared error.

11. Least squares estimates are used because they are less sensitive to the end points of the growth period.

12. See the appendix for a list of all the data sources.

13. Although regressing average growth rates against initial income levels suggests income convergence, it does not necessarily provide statistical evidence of convergence. Quah (1990) and Friedman (1992) note that, because of regression to the mean, a negative relationship between average growth rate and initial income does not necessarily provide statistical evidence of convergence.

14. Utilizing the White test, we could not find evidence to suggest that heteroscedasticity is a significant problem.

15. In constructing their index, Rapp and Rozek (1990) based their procedure on that found in Gadbaw and Richards, (1988), pp 11, 52-55.

16. The original Rapp and Rozek index range was from 0 to 5; however, we adjusted the index to lie in the range of 1 to 6 in order to enable us to perform the same log transformation that we applied to other variables in the equation. Taking a log of this variable, however, did not appreciably change the statistical inferences or sign of the coefficient.

17. Because intellectual property rights are hypothesized to influence economic growth through R&D, one can test whether intellectual property rights protection in the early 1960s is correlated to higher R&D spending in the 1970s and 1980s. Although cross-country data on R&D are extremely limited (only 48 countries in recent United Nations' World Economic Surveys) and are subject to a large degree of error (much of the country data include public with private spending on R&D), we found that the simple correlation coefficient between patent protection and future R&D expenditures as a share of GDP was .504 (significant at the .001-percent level).

When R&D as a share of GDP is included in our basis benchmark model with patent protection, it is significant at the 10-percent level, while the significance of patent protection does not change. The number of observations, however, is only 48.

18. These data are from Siebeck (1990).

19. The first stage IV equation for the level of intellectual property rights was estimated as:

$$
\begin{aligned}
\ln(\text{IPROP}) = \quad & 0.083 & + \quad & 0.061*\ln(\text{LIT60}) & + \quad & -0.111*\text{AFRICA} \\
& (1.398) & & (1.353) & & (-1.797) \\
+ \quad & -0.017*\ln(\text{REV}) & + \quad & 0.213*\text{PETTY} & + \quad & 0.234*\text{CHEM} \\
& (-2.512) & & (2.511) & & (2.821) \\
+ \quad & 0.209*\text{MICRO} & + \quad & 0.038*\text{PDUR} & + \quad & -0.090*\text{BERNE} \\
& (1.423) & & (6.987) & & (-1.423) \\
+ \quad & 0.139*\text{UPOV} & & & & \\
& (1.721) & & & &
\end{aligned}
$$

$\overline{R}^2$ = 0.60, Observations = 79

T-statistics are in parentheses. See data source appendix for variable definitions.

20. Rapp and Rozek show in Table A-1 that present patent law for 71 countries in our 79-country sample was established during or before the 1960s. Although several countries had amendments to their laws after this period, most were minor. The most recent major changes that have taken place in intellectual property laws across countries, such as in Mexico, Korea, Taiwan, and China, took place after the sample.

21. Maskus and Penubarti (1993) find that trade flows are positively related to intellectual property rights protection, although they do not examine the relationship between economic growth and intellectual property rights.

22. The index was created by Gould and Ruffin (1994). Measures of trade orientation that contribute to the index are: outward orientation (Syrquin and Chenery, 1988); overall trade openness and trade intervention (Leamer, 1988); trade orientation 1963-73 and 1973-85 (World Bank Development Report, 1987); effective rate of protection (Barro, 1990); black market premium (Levine and Renelt, 1992); real exchange rate distortion (Dollar, 1992); and the ratio of import taxes to imports (Levine and Renelt, 1992).

23. See also the comments of De Long and Summers (1991).

24. Using a continuous trade regime variable or a binary trade regime variable derived from the mean of the sample does not alter the statistical inferences made.

25. The real exchange rate distortion data are averaged over 1976-1985 and were from Dollar (1992). The composite trade regime index data were from Gould and Ruffin (1994). Real effective rates of protection were also used and strongly confirm the present results.

26. For each trade regime variable that is a component of this index (see footnote 22), countries are ranked according to quartiles. Countries that are the least outward oriented, or most protected, will fall into the first quartile and are assigned a value of one. Countries in the second quartile are assigned a value of two, and likewise for the third and fourth quartiles. The new aggregate trade regime index is calculated by averaging quartile values for each country. For example, if a country has two indicators suggesting it is in the third quartile and once indicator suggesting it is in the fourth quartile, the new indicator takes on a value of 3.333 $(3.333=(3+3+4)/3)$.

27. See Magee, Brock, and Young (1989).

References

Barro, Robert J. "Economic Growth in a Cross Section of Countries." *Quarterly Journal of Economics,* vol. 1991, 106, pp. 407-443,

Bhagwati, Jagdish. *Anatomy and Consequences of Exchange Control Regimes*, Cambridge, Mass: Ballinger Publishing Co., 1978.

Backus, David K.; Kehoe, Patrick J. and Kehoe, Timothy J. "In Search of Scale Effects in Trade and Growth." *Journal of Economic Theory*, 1992, vol. 58, pp. 377-409.

Braga, Helson C. and Willmore, Larry N. "Technological Imports and Technological Effort: An Analysis of Their Determinants in Brazilian Firms." *The Journal of Industrial Economics*, June 1991, vol. XXXIX, pp. 421-433.

Magee, Stephen; Brock, William and Young, Leslie. *Black Hole Tariffs and Endogenous Policy Theory: Political Economy in General Equilibrium,* New York: Cambridge University Press, 1989.

Chin, Judith C. and Grossman, Gene M. . "Intellectual Property Rights and North-South Trade," in Ronald W. Jones and Anne O. Krueger, eds., *The Political Economy of International Trade: Essays in Honor of Robert E. Baldwin.* Cambridge, Mass.: Basil Blackwell, 1990, .pp. 90-107

De Long, Bradford J. and Summers, Lawrence H. "Equipment Investment and Economic Growth." *Quarterly Journal of Economics* , 1991, vol. 106, pp. 407-502.

Diwan, Ishac and Rodrik, Dani. "Patents, Appropriate Technology, and North-South Trade." *Journal of International Economics*, February 1991, vol. 30, pp. 27-48.

Dollar, David. "Outward-Oriented Developing Economies Really Do Grow More Rapidly: Evidence from 95 LDCs, 1976-1985." *Economic Development and Cultural Change*, April 1992, vol. 40, pp. 523-44.

Edwards, Sebastian. "Trade Orientation, Distortions, and Growth in Developing Countries." *Journal of Development Economics,* 1992, vol. 39, pp. 31-59. .

Evenson, Robert E. "Survey of Empirical Studies," in Wolfgang E. Siebeck, ed., Strengthening Protection of Intellectual Property in Developing Countries: A Survey of the

Literature, World Bank Discussion Chapters 112 , Washington D.C.: The World Bank, pp. 33-46, 1990.

Friedman, Milton. "Do Old Fallacies Ever Die." *Journal of Economic Literature*, December 1992, vol. 30, pp. 2129-32.

Gadbaw, Michael R. and Richards, Timothy J. "Introduction," in Michael R. Gadbaw and Timothy J. Richards, eds., *Intellectual Property Rights: Global Consensus, Global Conflict?* ,Boulder, CO: Westview Press, pp. 1-37, 1988.

Gilbert, R. J. and Newbery,D. "Preemptive Patenting and the Persistence of Monopoly." *American Economic Review*, June 1982, vol. 72, pp. 514-526.

Gould, David M. and Ruffin, Roy J. "Human Capital, Trade and Economic Growth." Federal Reserve Bank of Dallas. Research chapter no. 9301, 1993.

_____. "A New Comprehensive Measure of Trade Openness." Federal Reserve Bank of Dallas, Mimeo, 1994.

Grossman, Gene M., and Elhanan Helpman. *Innovation and Growth in the Global Economy*, Cambridge: MIT Press, 1991.

Helpman, Elhanan. "Innovation, Imitation, and Intellectual Property Rights." *Econometrica*, 1993, vol. 61, pp. 1247-1280.

Kormendi, Robert and Meguire, Philip. "Macroeconomic Determinants of Growth: Cross-Country Evidence." Journal of Monetary Economics, September 1985, pp. 141-63.

Krueger, Anne. *Foreign Trade Regimes and Economic Development: Liberalization Attempts and Consequences*, Cambridge, Mass: Ballinger Publishing Co., 1978.

Leamer, Edward E. "Measures of Openness," in R. Baldwin, ed., *Trade Policy Issues and Empirical Analysis*, National Bureau of Economic Research Conference Report Series. Chicago: University of Chicago Press, pp. 147-200, 1988.

Levin, Richard C.; Klevorick, Alvin K.; Nelson, Richard R. and Winter, Sidney G. "Appropriating the Returns from Industrial Research and Development." *Brookings Chapters on Economic Activity* , 1987, vol. 3, pp. 783-820.

Levine, Ross, and Renelt, David. "A Sensitivity Analysis of Cross-Country Growth Regressions." *American Economic Review,* 1992, vol. 82, pp. 942-63.

Lucas, Robert E., Jr. "The Mechanics of Economic Development." *Journal of Monetary Economics*, 1998, vol. 22, pp. 3-42.

MacLaughlin, Janet H.; Richards, Timothy J. and Kenny, Leigh A. "The Economic Significance of Piracy," in R. Michael Gadbaw and Timothy J. Richards, eds., *Intellectual Property Rights: Global Consensus, Global Conflict?* , Boulder, CO: Westview Press, pp. 89-108, 1988.

Mankiw, Gregory N. ; Romer, David and Weil, David N. "A Contribution to the Empirics of Economic Growth." *Quarterly Journal of Economics*, 1992, vol. 107, pp. 107-437.

Mansfield, Edwin; Rapoport, John; Romeo, Anthony; Wagner, Samuel and Beardsley, George. "Social and Private Rates of Return from Industrial Innovations." *The Quarterly Journal of Economics*, May 1977, vol. XCI, pp. 221-240.

Mansfield, Edwin. "How Rapidly Does Industrial Technology Leak Out?" *Journal of Industrial Economics*, December 1985, vol. XXXIV, pp. 217-223.

_____. "Patents and Innovation: An Empirical Study." *Management Science*, February 1986, pp. 173-181.

_____. "Intellectual Property Protection, Foreign Direct Investment, and Technology Transfer." IFC Discussion Chapter 19, The World Bank and International Finance Corporation, 1994.

Maskus, Keith and Penubarti, Mohan. "How Trade-Related Are Intellectual Property Rights?" University of Colorado, mimeo, 1993.

Michaely, M.; Papageorgiou, D. and Choksi, A., eds. *Liberalizing Foreign Trade: Lessons of Experience in the Developing World*, vol. 7, Cambridge, Mass.: Basil Blackwell, 1991.

OECD. "Economic Arguments for Protecting Intellectual Property Rights Effectively." TC/WP (88) 70, Paris: OECD, 1989.

Primo Braga and Alberto, Carlos. "The Developing Country Case For and Against Intellectual Property Protection," in Wolfgang E. Siebeck, *ed., Strengthening Protection of Intellectual Property in Developing Countries: A Survey of the Literature*, World Bank Discussion Chapters 112 ,Washington D.C.: The World Bank, pp. 69-87, 1990.

Quah, Danny. "Galton's Fallacy and Tests of the Convergence Hypothesis." Massachusetts Institute of Technology, (Photocopy), 1990.

Rapp, Richard T. and Rozek, Richard P. "Benefits and Costs of Intellectual Property Protection in Developing Countries." National Economic Research Associate, Working Chapter #3, 1990.

Rebelo, S. "Long-Run Policy Analysis and Long-Run Growth." *Journal of Political Economy*, 1991, vol. 99, pp. 500-521.

Rivera-Batiz, Luis A. and Romer, Paul M. "International trade with endogenous technological change." *European Economic Review*, 1991, vol. 35, pp. 971-1004.

Romer, Paul M. "Human Capital and Growth: Theory and Evidence." *Carnegie Rochester Conference Series on Public Policy*, 1990a, vol. 32, pp. 251-285.

_____. "Endogenous Growth and Technical Change." *Journal of Political Economy*, 1990b, vol. 98, pp. 71-102.

Roubini, Nouriel and Sala-i-Martin, Xavier. "Financial Repression and Economic Growth." *Journal of Development Economics*, 1992, vol. 39, pp.5-30.

Segerstrom, Paul S.;Anant, T.C.A. and Dinopoulos, Elias . "A Schumpeterian Model of the Product Life Cycle." *American Economic Review,* 1990, vol. 80, pp. 1077-91.

Segerstrom, Paul S. "Innovation, Imitation, and Economic Growth." *Journal of Political Economy,* 1991, vol. 99, pp.807-27.

Schankerman, Mark. "How Valuable is Patent Protection? Estimates by Technology Field Using Patent Renewal Data." National Bureau of Economic Research Working Chapter No. 3780, July 1991.

Sherwood, Robert M. *Intellectual Property and Economic Development*, Boulder, Colo.: Westview Press, 1990.

Siebeck, Wolfgang E. *Strengthening Protection of Intellectual Property in Developing Countries: A Survey of the Literature.* World Bank Discussion Chapters 112, Washington D.C.: The World Bank, 1990.

Stokey, Nancy L. "Human Capital, Product Quality, and Growth." *Quarterly Journal of Economics*, 1991, vol. 106, pp. 587-616.

Summers, Robert and Heston, Alan . "The Penn world table (Mark 5): An expanded set of international comparisons, 1950-1988." *The Quarterly Review of Economics*, 1991, vol. 106, pp. 327-68.

Syrquin, Moshe and Chenery, Hollis B. "Patterns of Development, 1950-1983." World Bank Discussion Chapters No. 41, 1988.

United Nations. *The Role of Patents in the Transfer of Technology to Developing Countries. Report of the Secretary General.* New York: United Nations, 1964.

_____. Department of Economic and Social Affairs (1971), *World Economic Survey, 1969-1970*, E/4942 ST/ECA/141, 1971.

Vessuri, H.M.C. "O Inventamos O Erramos: The Power of Science in Latin America." *World Development* , November 1990, vol. 18, pp. 1543-1553.

World Bank. World Development Report 1987, New York: Oxford University Press, 1987.

_____. *World Development Report 1991*, New York: Oxford University Press, 1991.

Young, Alwyn. "Learning by Doing and the Dynamic Effects of International Trade." *Quarterly Journal of Economics,* 1991, vol. 106, pp. 369-405.

11

A NEW APPROACH TO GLOBAL TRADE IMBALANCES

Ravi Batra

Southern Methodist University, USA

Traditionally there have been two main approaches to the balance of payment disequilibrium by a country--the absorption approach and the monetary approach. This paper develops an alternative framework focusing on a country's domestic price level. The orthodox analysis fails to explain the persistence of trade deficits in the United States despite large and regular depreciation of the dollar, whereas a similar exchange depreciation in Mexico resulted in a quick turn around in its trade short fall. The paper shows that a trade imbalance can arise only if the general price level is not the same as the one consistent with balanced trade commercial policies--competitiveness and the production structure may be responsible for such price divergence.

After the Second World War several developing countries experienced balance of payments deficits for many years, whereas the United States enjoyed a persistent surplus. This led to the development of new theories about the payments imbalance. The traditional elasticities approach gave way first to the absorption approach and later to the monetary approach.

With these developments the subject seems to have been closed. But increasing globalization in the world has created new problems in the current accounts of some countries, and the monetary and absorption approaches have failed to offer full explanation. The purpose of this paper is to offer a new approach to the persistence of trade imbalances.

1995 marked the 10th anniversary of the Plaza accord that resumed the depreciation of the dollar. At that time a dollar bought more than 240 yens in the foreign exchange market. In June 1995, it bought less than 85 yens. From all accounts the dollar had depreciated far more than expected and intended, yet the U.S. trade deficit, especially with Japan, was in absolute magnitude as high as ever. According to traditional theories the U.S. deficit should by then have fallen to zero and even turned into a surplus. But that had not happened.

This situation should be contrasted with that of Mexico, where the peso devaluation in December 1994 almost overnight turned the Mexican trade deficit into a surplus.

In order to explain all these developments, the present paper offers a new analysis which may be called the price approach. By definition a country's trade balance is the difference between aggregate spending and aggregate supply, both of which can be shown to be related to the country's internal general price level. At some price level such as P_0, both aggregate spending and production are equal, so that the trade balance is zero. If the country's price level is higher than P_0, its spending is lower and output possibly higher (unless the aggregate supply curve is vertical). Then for $P > P_0$, the country has a surplus; similarly, for $P < P_0$, the country has a deficit.

This way countries with high internal price levels such as Japan, Singapore, Hong Kong tend to have surpluses, whereas relatively low price level countries such as the U.S., Canada, Australia and India tend to have deficits.

Since the focus of this paper is on the market or equilibrium price level, which is the result of the interaction of monetary and fiscal policies as well as technology, the analysis presented in this chapter highlights a wide variety of factors that determine the trade imbalance.

As stated earlier, there are two well known approaches to the balance of payments crisis: the monetary approach and the absorption approach. Both are general equilibrium in nature, and thus superior to partial methods. In the monetary approach, the trade balance disequilibrium is purely a monetary phenomenon, occurring when there is excess demand or supply for money. However, this approach has failed to explain Japan's tendency to have persistent surplus in its current account in spite of an extremely high rate of money growth during the 1970s and the 1980s.

The Absorption Approach

The more popular absorption approach has its own problems, because its proponents often confuse the cause and effect relationships. By definition, real aggregate demand (AD) is

$$AD = C + I + G + (X - M) \tag{1a}$$

$$= A + B$$

where C is consumption, I is investment, G is government spending on final goods and services, X = exports, M = imports, B = balance of payments (BOP) surplus, which may be positive or negative, and A is aggregate expenditure usually called absorption, but is in reality domestic demand, i.e., the demand or spending from the nation's residents. In equilibrium, gross domestic product or

$$GDP = AD \tag{2a}$$

Therefore, from (1a) and (2a)

$$B = GDP - A \tag{3a}$$

According to the absorption approach, given in (3a), the BOP surplus equals real GDP minus absorption; therefore, the causes of the surplus are all the underlying production and spending decisions made in the economy. Since

$$GDP \equiv C + S + T \tag{4a}$$

where S = private saving, and T = tax revenue, then from (1a), (2a) and (4a),

$$D = (I - S) + (G - T) \tag{5a}$$

where $D \equiv -B$ is the balance of payment deficit. Equation (5a) displays a version of the absorption approach that is in special favor today. For any given S and I, the higher the budget deficit of the government, so that $G > T$, the larger the trade deficit, i.e., $M > X$. Hence, the high U.S. budget deficit becomes a cause of the BOP deficit. This is the popular hypothesis of twin deficits.

However, the twin deficit hypothesis suffers from a glaring flaw. The term (G - T) in (5a) does not equal a government's budget deficit, which is given by:

$$\text{Budget Deficit} = G + Tr + G_i - T$$

$$= (G - T) + Tr + G_i \tag{6a}$$

where Tr denotes transfer payments and G_i is interest paid by the government on its debt and deficit borrowing. In fact, in many countries today more than half of total government spending is on interest and transfer payments. Transfer payments are extremely high in developed nations whereas interest payment is large in developing economies. In addition G < T so that (G - T) < 0, and this tends to create a trade surplus, not a deficit, for given S and I. Suppose I = S; then D = G - T < 0, and the country has a surplus.

The interpretation of (5a) in favor of twin deficits also shows that if transfer payments or interest costs raise the budget deficit, there will be no impact on the trade deficit, because they do not even enter into equation (5a). This, to say the least, is a curious implication of the popular hypothesis. Clearly, there is something wrong with the current interpretation.

Similarly, for any given G and T, the lower the S relative to I, the larger the trade deficit. Hence, another cause of the U.S. BOP deficit is said to be the low saving rate prevalent since 1980. Thus, conventional wisdom holds that trade policies of the United States or other countries have nothing to do with the BOP deficit. All that matters is the low American saving rate and high budget deficits. Thus, Hatsopoulos, Krugman and Poterba (1989, p.6) argue that "the current low national saving rate," itself the product of the high budget deficit, is the root cause of the persistent BOP deficit.

When you hear such arguments, the first thing that strikes you is, what about competitiveness and commercial policies? What about product prices in the two countries? They are there, according to the low saving-hypothesis, but only in the background.

This tends to raise a suspicion. Common sense dictates that competitiveness should be in the forefront of any explanation about unbalanced trade. That should be the primary cause, and nothing else. After all, Germany and Japan, the surplus nations of the 1980s, also have had large budget deficits, and while their saving rates are high, there investment levels are also high. They have outcompeted the United States in global markets and that is why they have been mostly surplus nations since the early 1970s.

An Alternative Approach

In this section, I present an alternative approach to the BOP crisis, which is not only a synthesis of the current views, but also gives an explicit role to price levels in global and domestic markets. In my approach, the BOP crisis is not a purely monetary or absorption phenomenon, but purely a competitiveness phenomenon. However, real and monetary factors all enter in the determination of inter-country competitiveness.

Let me present the traditional model first, because from that will emerge a new methodology. The orthodox framework is an open economy aggregate demand-aggregate supply version of the macro model. The AD function is obtained as follows:

$$AD = C + I + \overline{G} + X - M$$
$$= A(Y, i, \overline{G}) + B(q, Y)$$
$$ + - + \phantom{\overline{G}) +} + -$$

(1)

where Y = real GDP, i = rate of interest and $\overline{G}$ is autonomous level of government spending, and

$$q = \frac{e p_m^*}{p_x}$$

(2)

where p_m^* is the foreign currency price of imports, e is the exchange rate and p_x is the local currency price of home goods or exportables; q is sometime called the real exchange rate or the relative price. The signs below the variables indicate how each of them affects A or B. Thus a rise in Y tends to raise A, whereas a rise in i tends to lower A by reducing investment, and so on. In equilibrium, Y = AD. Therefore,

$$Y = A(Y, i, \overline{G}) + B(q, Y)$$

(3)

If we linearize this system, we get:

$$Y = \bar{A} + aY - bi + \bar{B} + \phi q - mY \tag{4}$$

Equation (4) is the well known equation of the IS curve. Here $a > 0$ is the fractional marginal propensity to spend or consume, $m > 0$ is the fractional marginal propensity to import, $\bar{A}$ is autonomous spending, $\bar{B}$ is autonomous trade balance, $\phi > 0$ and $b > 0$ is the investors' response to changes in the interest rate.

The equation of the LM curve is given by:

$$M_d(\underset{-}{i}, \underset{+}{Y}) = kY - hi = \bar{M}/P \tag{5}$$

where k and h are positive constants, M_d is the money demand function, $\bar{M}$ is the supply of money determined by the central bank, and P is the general price level, i.e.

$$P = \theta p_x + (1 - \theta) e p_m^* \tag{6}$$

where θ is the proportion of home spending on exportables. From (4) and (5),

$$Y = \alpha\left[\bar{A} + \bar{B} + \phi q + \gamma \bar{M}/P\right] \tag{7}$$

where $\gamma = b/h$ and

$$\alpha = \frac{1}{s + m + \gamma k} \tag{8}$$

is the autonomous spending multiplier. Equation (7) furnishes the well known AD function derived, for instance, by Rivera-Batiz and Rivera-Batiz (1994, p.466). Here $s = 1 - a$ is the marginal propensity to save. The aggregate supply curve is given by

$$Y = F(P, \bar{K}) \tag{9}$$

where $F_P \geq 0$ and $F_K > 0$, with $\bar{K}$ being the stock of capital.

In (7), a rise in P induced by a rise in p_x reduces the real value of money supply and lowers the BOP surplus as q falls so that exports become expensive and imports relatively cheaper than before. Both these effects tend to lower AD. Similarly, in (9), suppose p_x rises, raising P in the process; in the short-run Y rises, but in the long-run remains constant at natural output. To all this, let us now add the zero BOP equation, i.e.

$$B(q, Y) + \bar{B}(q) + \phi q - mY = 0 \qquad (10)$$

and we have a complete macro model of an open economy with free trade.

Equations (7), (9) and (10) are graphed in Figure 1. Initially, AD_1 is the negatively sloped aggregate demand function, AS_1 is the positively sloped short-run aggregate supply function and BB is the negatively sloped zero trade balance function. A rise in Y lowers the BOP surplus by raising imports. In order to restore B to its zero level, P must fall, so that exports go up or relatively expensive imports come down. In other words, Y and P are negatively related along the BB locus. It may be noted here that a rise in q tends to raise B.

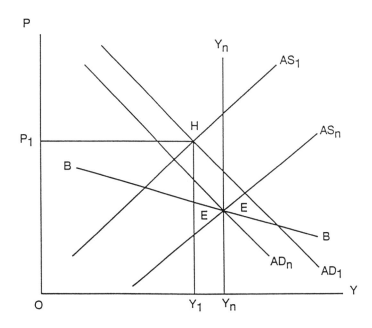

Figure 1: Adjustment to the Trade Deficit

Any point above the BB line means a trade deficit, because then for a given Y, P is higher so that exports are low and imports are high, resulting in the BOP deficit. Point H in Figure 1 is one such point. Here the equilibrium price level is P_1 and equilibrium output is Y_1, which is below the natural output Y_n. The vertical line Y_nY_n is the long-run AS curve.

Does this economy facing trade deficit and some unemployment have a tendency to move toward E where trade is balanced and the economy is at full employment? The answer in theory is yes.

Suppose the exchange rate is fixed. Because of unemployment nominal wages decline and because of the external deficit, money supply shrinks. From the first reason, the short-run AS curve shifts to the right, and from the second, AD curve shifts down. Both lines move until AS reaches AS_n and AD reaches AD_n, all intersecting the BB line at E.

If the exchange rate is variable, the adjustment process accelerates, because the local currency depreciates (or e rises) with the trade deficit, making exports cheaper abroad and imports dearer at home. As a result the external deficit falls and output expands at a faster pace. The disequilibria also vanish at a fast pace.

This is how the BOP analysis is currently presented in most textbooks on international economics. Although the approach deals with all factors, real as well as monetary, it is somewhat clumsy and complex and does not tell us why the trade deficit of the United States has persisted since 1983 in spite of repeated depreciation of the dollar. Conversely, why has the trade surplus in Japan endured despite its torrid money growth, high budget deficit and sharp appreciation of the yen.

Nonetheless, the orthodox model can be simplified and given a sharper focus to obtain the true cause of the BOP crisis. Let us develop the aggregate expenditure (AE) or domestic demand function A. From (1)

$$A = C + I + G \tag{11}$$

But,

$$C = \bar{C} + a(Y - \bar{T}) = \bar{C} + a(A + B - \bar{T})$$
$$I = \bar{I} - bi$$
$$G = \bar{G}$$

where $\bar{C}$ = autonomous consumption, $\bar{G}$ = autonomous government spending and $\bar{T}$ = autonomous tax receipts. From this,

$$sA = \bar{A} - bi + aB \qquad (12)$$

where $\bar{A} = \bar{C} + \bar{I} + \bar{G} - a\bar{T}$ is autonomous spending, as before. However, our BOP and money demand functions are:

$$B = \bar{B} + \phi q - mA \qquad (13)$$

$$M_d(A, i) = kA - hi \qquad (14)$$

suggesting that the transactions demand for money (kA) is linked to total spending, not just real income. This is a better description of the money demand function, because transactions do not occur until income is spent. Similarly, BOP surplus is also better linked to q and spending. In the money market equilibrium

$$kA - hi = \bar{M}/P \qquad (15)$$

so that from (12), (13), (14) and (15)

$$A = \beta\left[\bar{A} + a\bar{B} + a\phi q + \gamma\bar{M}/P\right] \qquad (16)$$

where $\beta = 1/(s + am + \gamma k)$. This is our aggregate expenditure or the AE function. The AD function corresponding to the AE function of (16) can be obtained as follows: since,

$$Y = A+B = A+\bar{B}+\phi q-mA = (1 - m)A+\bar{B}+\phi q$$

Then substituting (16) in this yields:

$$Y = (1 - m)\,\alpha\left(\bar{A}+\gamma\bar{M}/P\right) + \left[1+a\beta(1 - m)\right]\left(\bar{B}+\phi q\right) \qquad (17)$$

his is now the AD function. And as before, the AS function is

$$Y = F(P, \bar{K}) \qquad (9)$$

I have developed the AE function with a purpose. The BOP surplus is the difference between output and AE. Therefore, the BOP analysis is more comprehensible through the AE function rather than the AD function. The AE function also has a negative slope. As P rises $\overline{M}/P$ falls and so does q. Therefore AE declines.

Figure 2 displays the AE line and the short-run AS line. P_0 is the price level that generates a balance in the foreign trade sector, because then AS = AE or domestic supply equals domestic demand. Here Y = A, and B = 0. If the actual price level is different from P_0, there is imbalance in the BOP account. In view of (6), the actual price level may be written as:

$$P_a = \theta \, p_x + (1 - \theta) \, e \, p_m^*(1 + t) \tag{18}$$

where t is the tariff rate. In a small economy, P_a is determined totally by world prices. Otherwise, the actual price level P_a is one that equates AD and AS. If P_0 is not the same as P_a, the external account is unbalanced. For instance, suppose P_a is at P_{US} in Figure 2a. Here equilibrium output is at R, but aggregate spending at S. Therefore RS is the trade deficit. Such is the case in the United States. The equilibrium or the actual price level is so low that there is insufficient output, but excessive spending. What is wrong with the economy is that the price level, for some reason, is out of balance. This may be because of the demand, supply or monetary factors, or because of an improper commercial policy.

Given the AE and AS functions, there are three reasons why P_a may fall below P_0: a fall in e, p_m^* or t. In other words, the trade deficit springs from (1) currency appreciation, (2) improved foreign competitiveness so that ep_m^* falls relative to p_x or (3) a movement toward free trade. The only way to eliminate the deficit is either to raise P_a to the level of P_0 or bring P_0 down to the level of P_a. In order to lower P_0, either AE must fall or AS must expand, and if this is difficult, as has been the case in the United States, a rise in t and/or e are the only alternatives.

By contrast, if the actual price level is at P_j^* , as in Figure 2b, the equilibrium output is at N and spending at M, generating a trade surplus of MN. The equilibrium price level is high relative to the zero trade balance price level of P_0^*, so that it discourages spending but stimulates output, generating a trade surplus in the process. Such is the case in Japan. Thus, the trade imbalance is ultimately a price phenomenon.

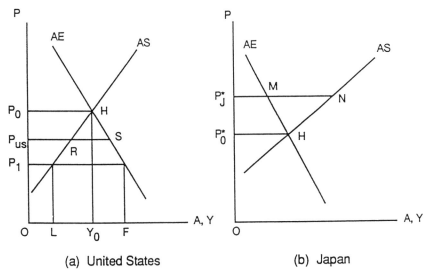

(a) United States   (b) Japan

Figure 2: The Trade Balance Equilibrium

If $G = T$, then the deficit is still the difference between S and I, and if $S = I$, the deficit is still the excess of G over T. But these are not the causes. The explicit cause is the price imbalance. Of course, G, T, S and I along with e and t all affect the price level. But all these factors are in the background, while competitiveness of the country's trading sector is in the forefront.

The importance of commercial policies is clear. A fall in the tariff rate tends to lower P_a, generating a rise in the trade deficit. A rise in the tariff does the opposite. Non-tariff barriers also create a wedge between foreign and domestic prices of imports, thereby raising P_a and hence the trade surplus. Thus, while the trade imbalance is indeed a macro phenomenon, commercial policies also have a role in it. In Japan, the non-tariff barriers tend to keep P_a high, thereby generating surplus tendencies. Similarly, with lower tariffs and barriers to imports, the United States is doomed to the external deficit.

From the AE line, high P_a means low C and hence high S, which, other things remaining the same, tends to create a trade surplus. Similarly, low P_a means high C, low S and a tendency for trade deficits. Thus, in my approach also a trade surplus country is likely to have a high savings rate, but the cause for the surplus is high domestic price level relative to the one consistent with balanced trade.

By contrast, a low saving country is still likely to have a trade deficit, but the cause is that its domestic price level is below the one consistent with balanced trade.

From equation (18) e and t tend to create a divergence between P_a and the balanced trade price. In the United States, the income tax began to replace the tariff rate as early as 1913, and this switch was more or less complete by 1972 when the Kennedy round of the GATT fully went into effect. Ever since then the BOP in the U.S. has been on the decline, although it remained positive in one or two years. The gradual replacement of the tariff by various taxes on income may be called a tax switching policy.

The effect of the U.S. tax switching policy can be easily analyzed. Suppose the tariff is eliminated and replaced by an equivalent income tax such that the tax revenue remains the same. In this case, AE and AS lines are unchanged in Figure 2a but P declines from P_{us} to P_1. The trade deficit widens to LF and the equilibrium output falls to OL. It is now clear that with the help of the AE line, the general equilibrium BOP analysis becomes as simple as the analysis of trade in a partial equilibrium demand-supply diagram for one industry.

If the deficit is eliminated through proper commercial policy, the U.S. output will rise to Y_0. That, of course, is the problem of the day: how to eliminate the trade deficit.

It may be noted here that the process of adjustment to disequilibrium remains the same in my model. For instance, if the economy suffers from unemployment and a trade deficit, both the nominal wage and money supply fall. The AE line shifts down and the AS line shifts to the right until they both intersect each other at a point on the long-run AS curve. If in addition the exchange rate is flexible, the rise in e and the resulting fall in the BOP deficit hastens the movement toward the BOP equilibrium.

Thus, while the adjustment process is the same as before, the explanation is simpler, because now we do not have to bother about the trade balance equation or the BB line in Figure 1. In theory any disequilibrium is corrected by the market forces without any government intervention. In practice, however, this has not happened. Between 1983 and 1993, the United States had a persistent trade deficit, and no one believes that this deficit will disappear anytime soon. So what has impeded the adjustment process?

A Critique of the Current Thinking

The current thinking among international economists is that the persistent U.S. external deficit is the result of high budget deficits and a low saving rate. Let us note at this point that in the traditional view, other things remaining the same, a low saving rate, a high budget deficit, a high level of investment and high money growth tend to raise the trade deficit, while the exchange depreciation tends to lower it.

With these considerations in mind, let us examine Table 1, which presents data about the rate of national saving and gross investment as percentages of GDP, average annual money growth, average budget deficit as a percent of GDP and the cumulative current account balance (BOP surplus) in Japan and the United States during the 1970s and the 1980s.

Table 1. Saving, Investment, Money Growth, Budget Deficit and Current Account Balance in Japan and the United States: 1970s and 1980s

	Japan		*United States*	
	1970s	*1980s*	*1970s*	*1980s*
Average Saving Rate (%)	33.7	32	19.7	16.5
Average Investment Rate (%)	34.5	29.5	20	19
Average Annual Money Growth Rate (%)	16	8.9	10	8
Average Budget Deficit Ratio (%)	2.4	1.7	1	2.8
Current Account Balance (billions of dollars)	31	415	-6	-798

During the 1970s Japan had a cumulative BOP surplus of $31 billion, which rose to $415 billion in the 1980s. By contrast, the United States had a deficit of $6 billion in the 1970s — which is almost balanced trade — and a huge deficit of $798 billion during the 1980s. In the 1970s, Japan had a high saving rate, which tends to create a surplus, but had huge money growth, investment rate and budget deficit, all much greater than those in the United States. On the demand side, high savings were neutralized by high investment. And with high money growth and budget deficits, ordinarily Japan should have had an external deficit. In addition, the yen gradually appreciated during the 1970s. In spite of all this, the country had a BOP surplus. The reason lies in the high level of investment.

Investment is a double edged sword. In the short-run, it raises AE, but in the long-run it raises capital stock and productivity; it also leads to a rightward shift in the AS curve and to a low price level that increases competitiveness. If the rightward shift of the AS curve is very strong, it can overcome the strong upward shift of the AE curve resulting from high money growth and budget deficits, while the stimulus to AE from high investment is offset by the high level of savings.

But this is not the whole story. A strong rightward shift should normally produce a low price level relative to that in other countries, whereas in Japan prices tend to be generally higher than those in the United States and other nations. That is where commercial policy comes in. Through a variety of tariff or non-tariff barriers a country can keep its domestic price level high and yet outcompete other nations in global markets. Thus, the secret behind Japan's persistent and growing trade surplus is its extraordinary rate of investment and a protectionist policy that keeps the domestic price level above that consistent with balanced trade. And high prices keep savings high.

During the 1980s, Japan's investment rate fell slightly, but still remained much higher than the U.S. rate. Compared to the fall in the investment rate, Japan's money growth and the budget deficit ratio fell at a much faster pace. Thus AS continued to expand, but the growth of AE fell. Clearly, it widened the gap between domestic supply and domestic demand. In addition, Japan's export prices fell relative to competing goods produced by other nations, while protectionist policies kept the domestic price level high. That is why during the 1980s, Japan's BOP surplus soared in spite of the massive yen appreciation. Thus, competitiveness and protectionism jointly explain the persistence of Japan's trade surplus.

During the 1970s, the United States had a much lower budget deficit ratio than Japan. The U.S. saving rate was, of course, low but on the spending side, the low saving rate was offset by the low investment rate. U.S. money growth was also much lower than Japan's. All this should have given a trade edge to the United States. But investment and trade policies are the key. Over time low investment produces a leftward shift of the AS curve relative to the AD curve, raising the equilibrium price and reducing a nation's competitiveness. On the other hand, liberal commercial policy tends to bring the domestic price level down, raising spending and lowering output in the process. For these two reasons, the United States had a small deficit even during the 1970s, as P_0 and P_a were close to each other. Actually, the deficit would have been higher, if the dollar had not depreciated (Blecker 1992, ch.3).

During the 1980s the U.S. budget deficit ratio ballooned, while money growth fell only slightly. This raised AE and AD. Since the investment rate changed little, the AS curve shift was slight. Consequently, the trade deficit zoomed in spite of the falling dollar. In view of Japan's experience, it is not the budget deficit or the low saving rate that are the primary cause of the trade deficit. It is the low investment rate, hence low competitiveness, and relatively liberal trade policy that explain the persistence of the American external deficit.

A New Interpretation of U.S. BOP History

An interesting question arises at this point. Currency devaluation is supposed to eliminate the trade deficit. The devaluation of the Mexican peso after December 1994, after all, turned the Mexican deficit into a large surplus within six months. Why did the dollar depreciation then not have a similar effect on U.S. trade? In order to understand this, let us examine U.S. history since the 1930s.

U.S. President Roosevelt began to reduce tariffs after 1932 and by 1950 the average tariff was down to just 15% as compared to the historical average of 45% over 113 years from 1820 to 1933. Initially, the decline in duties was too small to impact the economy, and then came the Second World War during which most industrial nations were virtually destroyed. The United States was the undisputed economic leader in the world until 1965. By then the G-7 countries had recovered, and that is when the U.S. tariff decline began to bite.

Consider Figure 3, which graphs the long-run AS curve, a vertical line at the natural output Y_n. As before, AE is the aggregate spending line. From 1900 to 1975, the U.S. current account balance was in a modest surplus, which means that

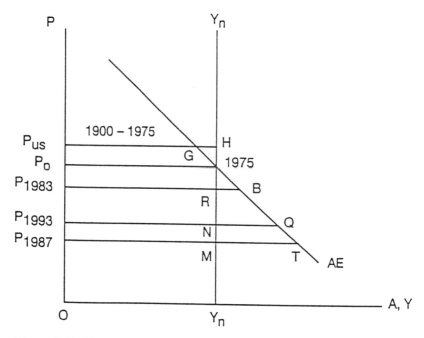

Figure 3: Tariff Decline and the US Trade Deficit

the actual price level (P_{US}) remained above the zero trade balance price level P_0. The BOP surplus corresponding to P_{US} is small at GH. The figure is drawn for just one set of AE and AS curves, because even though the two curves have shifted over time, the existence of the BOP surplus or deficit is still explained by the gap between the actual price level and the zero trade balance price level.

After 1965 the U.S. surplus began to fall, even though the budget deficit was fairly low and the saving rate higher than today's. The reason was that $P_a = P_{US}$ began to decline.

Recall that

$$P_a = \theta p_x + (1 - \theta) \, ep_m^*(1 + t) \tag{18}$$

With other countries investing at a high rate, they began to outcompete the United States in the world market, so that p_m^* fell, and so did P_a. As tariffs had already been lowered, foreign producers found it easy to penetrate the U.S. market. After 1973, however, the exchange rate became flexible, and e began to rise, or the dollar depreciated, enough to keep the current account roughly in balance until 1975 and for the rest of the 1970s. Therefore, P_a is identified with P_{US} in 1975, when there was a rough equilibrium in the current account, and remained so until 1982. At that point tight money policy kept interest rates higher in the United States than in Europe and Japan.

In search of high yield, money poured into America from abroad, sharply raising the global demand for the dollar, which then began to appreciate, i.e., e started to fall. Imports became cheaper and exports became dearer abroad, and the BOP account went into a small deficit in 1983. In terms of equation (18), a fall in e led to a fall in $P_a = P_{US}$, i.e., the actual price level. As P_{US} fell, the deficit began to grow and reached a record high of $160 billion in 1987, represented by MT in the diagram.

Alarmed by the mushrooming U.S. deficit, the G-7 countries met in Paris in 1986 and agreed to bring down the dollar, an effective devaluation. They began to sell dollars in the market for foreign exchange, raising its supply in the process; the dollar began to fall and has been falling ever since. By 1993, the trade deficit had fallen to $110 billion, represented by NQ in Figure 3. In reality

$$e_{1993} = e_{1982}$$

i.e., by 1993 the dollar had depreciated to the level at which the BOP account was roughly zero, as in 1982. Then why does the deficit persist?

There are two reasons. First, because of high rates of investment abroad, there has been a long term decline in U.S. competitiveness, so that foreign prices fell relative to U.S. prices of home goods. Second, foreign producers, eager to preserve their trade surplus and thus their output levels, simply dumped their goods into the American market, which further lowered p_m^*. As a result, P_a did not return to the 1982 level even though the rate of exchange did.

Developing Economies

The BOP approach developed in this chapter has been illustrated with the help of the history of developed economies such as the U.S. and Japan. But the analysis is general and applies to developing countries as well.

Take India for instance. The country has had very large tariffs since its independence in 1947. Why did they produce persistent trade deficits? The reason lies in the domestic production structure wherein state monopolies coexisted with private oligopolies. There was and is very little competition in many important industries. This led to inefficiency and hence a leftward shift of the AS curve relative to the AE line. Even though high tariffs kept domestic import prices and hence the price level high, the oligopolist production structure kept the actual price level below the one consistent with the zero trade balance. This is because that is the only way a trade deficit can possibly occur.

Conclusion

In this paper I have developed a new approach to a country's balance of payments. This may be called a price approach, because it directly deals with the question of competitiveness. In this analysis the trade imbalance arises because the actual domestic price level is different from the one consistent with balanced trade. This may occur because of commercial policies or the domestic production structure.

References

Blecker, R. *Beyond the Twin Deficits*. New York: M. E. Sharpe, 1992.

Hatsopoulos, G.; Krugman, P. and Poterba, J. *Overconsumption: The Challenge to U.S. Economic Policy.* New York: American Business Conference and Thermo Electron Corporation, 1989.

Rivera-Batiz and Rivera-Batiz, L. *International Finance and Open Economy Macroeconomics.* New York: Macmillian, 1985 and 1994.

12

STRUCTURAL MICROECONOMICS OF PRODUCTIVE EFFICIENCY AND STRATEGIC ALLIANCES

Robin Rowley
McGill University, Canada
Renuka Jain
Worcester State College, USA

The microprocessor revolution has changed the nature of production and distribution for large firms, facilitating new dynamic processes of globalization in several ways. We identify some consequences of software advances for managerial activities and flexible organizational structures. In particular, we note (1) weaker managerial limits on economies of scale, (2) major changes in the impact of experience, information and knowledge, (3) various fundamental commitments to continuous change and time-saving innovation, (4) systematic collaboration and inter-firm strategic alliances, and (5) dynamic aspects of global firms and competition. These significant features support a realistic framework for appraising economic organizations from an adaptive and evolving theoretical perspective that can effectively deal with the spatial relocation of economic activities.

Thirty years ago, with surprising foresight, Simon (1967) asked whether it was appropriate to view computer software as a novel factor of production, along with more conventional factors such as labor and real capital equipment. He indicated that software may be a significant factor which was quite distinctive because of its easy storage, retrieval, and replication at modest cost. This question reflected contemporary attempts to come to terms with electronic advances, including those stimulated by a potential parallelism with brain processes, human decisions and inferences--illustrated, for example, in an exploration of computers as "thoughtful scientists" by Kendall (1967), who reappraised statistical inference in light of newer computational developments.

As a productive factor, computer software cannot be merely included in familiar production functions, because it transforms most systems of managerial controls, basic social relations in production, the direction and nature of information flows, and marketing choices, including an involvement in particular markets. Substantial reliance on new software creates pervasive influences which affect the character of capital equipment, some means of managerial and financial control, flexibility in output choices, and organizational structures. Further, the substantial impact of software cannot be explored with conventional notions of marginal productivity, diminishing or increasing returns, competitive equilibrium, and economies of scale. A proper recognition of software requires radical theoretical developments--associated with multiple and variable product lines, economies of scope, strategic interaction, an active management of information flows, geographical contiguity of suppliers, effective governance, and novel perspectives on industrial and corporate structures, for example--and it transforms our understanding of the nature of effective competition, markets and entrepreneurial objectives.

Inertial Forces and Prior Commitment to Competition

The emergence of such radical theoretical developments was stimulated by the failed innovation of contestability, a partial replacement of the invisible hand of Adam Smith by a more visible one--as described and explored in Chandler (1990, 1992), Caves (1980) and Williamson (1981)--and by those fundamental changes in the spatial location and direction of economic activity which we associate with globalization, a dynamic process mediated by the business activities of transnational or global firms and the industrial shadow groups. Beyond such elements, due recognition of the structural impact of new software had to wait for a strong commitment to perfect competition, by many economic theorists, to weaken to a sufficient degree.

The strength of this prior commitment is clearly reflected in a bold assertion of Stigler (1957: 17) by reference to the aftermath of Robinson-Chamberlin innovations in the early 1930s, including the emergence of an empirical approach to industrial structures and firms. Stigler insisted, without qualification, that "the concept of perfect competition has defeated its newer rivals in the decisive area: the day-to-day work of the economic theorist" and thus "today the concept of perfect competition is being used more widely by the profession in its theoretical work than at any time in the past." This assertion should be weighed against a contrary judgement of Hayek (1978: 179), who suggested "it is difficult to defend economists against the charge that for some 40 to 50 years they have been discussing competition on assumptions that, if true of the real world, would make it wholly uninteresting and useless." Such bold judgments were connected to different treatments of economic knowledge, just as the following appreciation of management software will note the intimate role of computers in the acquisition and use of real information, which facilitates and causes fundamental changes in structure.

The inertial forces associated with a commitment to perfect competition and the definitional conditions which have been used to characterize competitive markets (the existence of free and complete information, the absence of effective power, the freedom to enter and exit markets, and the evolutionary adjustments that must quickly remove any above-normal profits) are destructive to a clearer understanding of the competitive world economy which emerged during the last half century. These forces delayed a better consideration of the major structural consequences of a very rapid assimilation of software in production, distribution, financial accounting, and basic intra-firm control mechanisms--in part, because the conventional models of perfect competition always took business structures to be exogenously given rather than endogenously determined within a dynamic evolution of most competitive processes. Economic efficiency too was presumed for an abstract or remote world markedly different from that which could contain any large firms and strategic alliances as we know them. Software developments affected structural choices and thus widened the options and focus of managerial decisions. Further, the generic predictions usually associated with familiar models of perfect competition are obviously insufficient for sensible appraisals of production, distribution, and labor and customer relations for global firms in practice.

Theoretical Omissions and Realistic Inadequacies

The modest weakening of inertial forces in economic theory during the last two decades is illustrated by Goldhar and Jelinek (1985) and Baumol (1991a,b), although their brief flirtation with contestability seems disappointing since it revealed persistent theoretical prejudices rather than a clearer appreciation of the strategic nature of "new competition" (Best, 1990), as normally realized through industrial and corporate restructuring. That a wide scope remains for further theoretical improvement is evident from any comparison of the principal ingredients for realistic views of any competitive and collusive processes (which display the substantial global adjustments now underway) with the usual contents, focus and technical methods in treatments of production by mathematical economists. Fare and Primont (1995), a prominent example of the latter treatments, illustrate technical attachment to duality, homogeneity, convenient curvature properties, and the normal competitive assumptions on which the plausibility of dual concepts must surely depend. But these theoretical elements are effectively challenged by the flexible internal arrangements of modern firms, weaker market boundaries, and the strategic market arrangements affected by an increasing reliance on software and by changing corporate perspectives. An environment in which major cross-border mergers and acquisitions are also commonplace (over 2700 in 1989 alone, and valued in excess of $US 130 billion in that year) is incompatible with a justifiable reliance on such competitive assumptions.

Earlier assumptions of exogeneity and free information are still retained for output portfolios, productive processes and prices, while any dramatic shifts among global markets including complete withdrawal from a market (envisaged in the contemporary benchmarking and re-engineering strategies of large firms, for example) and systemic ignorance are ignored. Economic theorists seem destined to continue a strange practice of first developing abstract theory without much consideration of the world outside their windows, and then seeking empirical applications (without much enthusiasm or real intent to match actual economic phenomena with their hypothetical counterparts) while discounting the value of detailed case histories of business choices. Any structural endogeneity disappears when mathematical tractability, immanent fashionableness and conceptual myopia overwhelm the inclusion of more realistic features. Yet many economists continue to commit basic errors of the third kind in the sense that they pose the wrong questions and assume away some relevant features that are obscured by the 'black-box' firm of most economic theories.

Fortunately, the common negligence of economists is partly overcome by contributions from business-related disciplines. For example, we can now draw on (1) discussions of global marketing, management and business in the recent textbooks of Akhter (1994), Alkahafaji (1995), and Czinkota et al. (1995), (2) treatments of informational infrastructure and supply-chain management, such as that of Strader and Shaw (1994) for agriculture, (3) significant reports for government agencies and international organizations, such as those produced by

Bailey, Parisotto and Renshaw (1993) for the International Labor Office, Howells and Wood (1992) for the Commission of the European Communities, and conference reports such as Bradley, Hausman and Nolan (1993). The contrast between stale approaches to firms in the *American Economic Review* or *Economic Journal* with dynamic and more realistic approaches found in the *Sloan Management Review* or *Harvard Business Review* is especially striking in this context.

Structural Design, Technological Progress and Information

Simon (1967) also asked whether the newly evolving systems of stored computer programs could be fruitfully integrated in a concept for representing technological change. The acceptance of this concept would profoundly alter appraisals of technological progress and the diffusion of new industrial procedures. In line with his better-known treatment of cognitive and behavioral or procedural dimensions of rational choice, and his recognition of the substantial cost of most calculations, Simon suggested that a modern corporation may be best described as a vast information-processing system. From this perspective, production machinery consisting of information-processing items and similar structural features routinely affect the daily management of major networks for both distributing products and coordinating the acquisition of raw materials and control of inventories, including work in progress. Soon after, Simon (1971) extended this perspective to wider issues involving *active structural design* of organizations, business firms and governmental agencies, so that they can better handle the enormous pressures of operating in an information-rich environment.

Simon's probing questions reflected sharp awareness of real institutional evolution. Computers and communication technology permitted greater flexibility to deal with the necessary means of control, newer competitive pressures, comprehensive demands for the management (data collection, analysis, and dissemination) of relevant information, and radical changes in potential delegation of effective authority within individual firms and among members of strategic alliances through local empowerment and intra-group coordination, besides major changes in product specialization and market responsiveness. He pointed economists towards endogenous organizational design and structural issues, in contrast to the normal 'black-box' methods of theoretical inquiry which pervade economic textbooks and professional journals.

The dynamic evolution of structural endogeneity, as directly stimulated by software, cannot be represented within the static classifications of competition (perfect competition, monopoly and oligopoly) or by superficial discussions of returns to scale, the manipulation of familiar neoclassical production functions, and crude representations of technical change. Giving more attention to structural endogeneity is part of a comprehensive development which recognizes 'management' as a primary factor in determining production and distribution, rather than an element hidden by the three conventional assumptions of economists-- persistent profit maximization over an ill-defined interval, no transactions costs for decision making, and a continued participation in all markets as determined by marginal calculations and the coverage of fixed costs.

Microeconomic Foundations of Globalization

Such conventional assumptions obscure some important aspects of spatial location for economic activity and of chosen product lines, which must provide the basic focus of globalization. Their unqualified use prevents a sensitive discussion of the character, consequences and evolution over time of globalization, not least because all transnational or global firms conduct their affairs in imperfect markets and react to basic incentives to internalize activities through a reliance on non-market exchanges (Cowling and Sugden, 1987) as might be anticipated from a simple extension of Coasian notions. Since transnational firms directly provide almost 10 per cent of non-farm jobs worldwide and perhaps up to 20 per cent of such jobs in the industrialized countries, with indirect employment on a similar scale according to some recent estimates from the UN, the persistent failure of economists to recognize the primary characteristics of internal organizations and normal market activities of transnational firms is clearly outrageous and disappointing.

In the consumer-driven world of today, the perceptiveness of Simon's questions is confirmed by an emergence of configurators and other interactive software packages in normal use within *all* large firms. These programs facilitate the scheduling and routine management of resources (MRP, MRPII), integration of multi-plant manufacturing activity (CIM), the attainment of higher overall quality assurance (TQM), collection and use of raw and modified information (MIS) and electronic data interchange (EDI) within firms and among groups of trading partners, leaner production and lower levels of inventories (JIT), a better system of maintenance and less costly periods of down-time (TPM), a partial blurring of earlier market boundaries with vendor-managed inventory systems (VMI) and even shared participation in product development, and organizational learning. They offer additional responsiveness to complex customer demands with respect to speed (QRM) and product choice.

Some configurators are described by Lieberman and Leete (1995) and Bourke and Friedman (1994), while basic descriptions and evaluations of other software packages can be found in *APICS--The Performance Advantage* and other business-related journals on a continuing basis. Such journals also provide some specific accounts of the practical implementation, relative effectiveness and weaknesses of these software packages for individual firms, especially those innovative firms at the forefront for active development of new software applications or benchmark models (such as Ford, Honda, Sony, 3M, L.L. Bean, Wal-Mart, Federal Express, United Parcel Service, Motorola, Disney World, Xerox, General Electric, NEC, Toyota, Texas Instruments, Toshiba, Canon, Hewlett-Packard and their European counterparts). Information processing may also be outsourced as it is by Eastman Kodak, General Dynamics, BP Exploration, Continental Airlines, British Aerospace and various government departments in the United Kingdom.

Nor are the direct benefits of microprocessors limited to a few large and specialized firms based in the main industrialized countries. More than 100 of the top 500 US corporations used on-site or off-site software services provided by Indian companies during 1995, and India has emerged as a major exporting country for software services with a very rapid growth of these exports (absolutely and in relation to domestic sales). There are a host of other less startling developments affecting other countries in the third world over the last two decades or so--for example, about 40 electronics companies (including Intel) established semiconductor assembly and test plants in Penang in the 1970s and 1980s while 20 such companies set up similar plants in Manila. Unfortunately, the unfashionableness of case studies among many economists means that we must rely on the business journals and related literature (Schonberger, 1987, for example) to offer valuable descriptions of these important developments and their main economic consequences.

Implications of these microeconomic developments are direct. A strong reliance on software is now the essential ingredient of effective management, firmly embedded in management information systems and other structural features of large firms and their associates. This reliance affects (1) choice of organizational structure through commitments to comprehensive re-engineering of activities (Hammer, 1990; Davenport and Short, 1993), management execution systems

(MES), agile factories and most of the elements listed above, (2) spatial location of productive and distributive activities among and within continents through global activities of trans-national, multinational or global firms, and (3) primary relationships with consumers and other corporations in strategic alliances and the newer sourcing connections (Klier, 1994, 1995). All of these consequences are relevant to discussions of economic interdependence and globalization, including continental trading blocs (Dunning, 1995; Thomsen, 1992), direct foreign investment, and proposed regional networks which can support innovation and structural adjustment (Klier, 1993).

International Collaboration, Standards and Alliances

The reliance on software has also produced a shift toward joint planning or collaboration among firms beyond national boundaries, although not yet to the extent envisaged by Reich (1991: 3) who suggested "there will be no national products or technologies, no national corporations, no national industries." The intensity of connections between software and transnational collaboration is expected to grow in the immediate future. A typical illustration is provided by the creation of an Advanced Information Technology Consortium at the end of 1993 by European firms in automobile and aerospace manufacturing industries (including British Aerospace, Audi, BMW, Fiat, Mercedes-Benz, Motorola, Renault and others). The purpose of this European consortium is to join with software vendors to establish useful rules, standards and guarantees or platforms for integration and the inter-operability of information technology (Garbani, 1995). The creation of similar consortia to enhance software implementation must stimulate innovation in such technology and thus produce further assimilation of new software, with secondary impacts on organizational structures.

The particular nature of this collaboration has to be noted. Competition in product markets is fostered and overall efficiency of production and distribution is enhanced, whenever the software adequately fits the environment (including the preparedness of individual firms to use it effectively because of their internal conditions), and 'best practice' operations become more visible. However, competition may now be pursued between chains of firms rather than between individual firms (Bresticker, 1992), and the marketing battles can transcend conditions in specific markets in separate locations. Competitors share a common concern for better software, either as vendors of that software or as its potential users, even though a considerable degree of future customization seems inevitable and desirable.

The collaboration is merely a small part of a more extensive search for relevant standards to reduce impacts of incompatible technologies and reporting procedures, as generally supervised by the International Organization for Standardization (ISO), the International Electrotechnical Commission (IEC), and the International Telecommunications Union (ITU)--agencies which account for the majority of international standards. Presumably, the new World Trade Organization (WTO) will join this activity.

Beyond this search for standards, strategic alliances among the transnational firms offer a much stronger form of collaboration among potential competitors. Such alliances frequently seem to occur in technologically-mature industries, while acquisitions have been more common in high technology industries as clarified and illustrated by Hamill (1993). Cooperation enables partners to share the escalating costs of research and development and to widen market coverage for recovery of such costs in the face of competitive pressures, encouraged by synergistic effects. Other aspects of such strategic alliances are described for recent US-Japan connections in the semi-conductor industry by the National Research Council (1992).

Dynamic and Integrated Global Processes

Clearly, instead of the current preoccupations with formal models and economies of scope, we might need to revive eclectic descriptions of industrial growth and progress, perhaps in the style of Marshall (1920), which recognizes evolutionary changes induced by widening markets and adaptation, the actual presence of industrial complementarities or external economies, changing parameters, and increasing returns, while avoiding the assumption of perfect competition. Loasby (1986) provides a revival of such elements in an account that views dynamic processes rather than the static alternatives. Another revival is offered by Rostow (1976, 1982) who points to spatial challenges from technological change and increasing returns, pronounced compositional shifts in investment, and sectoral dislocations. Corresponding issues of parametrization are reassessed by Prendergast (1993). None of these authors note the consequences of software, perhaps because these consequences emerged too recently. However, both Loasby and Rostow acknowledge relevant institutional perspectives. If adopting a Marshallian style can permit more appreciation of the dynamics of recent organization changes and spatial relocation of economic activities, then this non-neoclassical revival will have served a useful purpose.

By the end of the 1980s, the understanding of globalization had changed from earlier interpretations based on multinational firms to newer concerns with complex integrated microeconomic processes and strategic alliances among such firms. This development is illustrated by a recent observation of Howells and Wood (1992: 3) that "internationalization processes have integrated in a more systematic fashion covering a whole set of parameters involving cross-country investment, production, marketing, trade and more general interfirm alliances and collaboration," with a major role attributed to research and development activities in creating and maintaining industrial competitive advantage. Globalization now "entails the inter-national expansion and integration of key *corporate functions*." Further, as noted by Bresticker (1992: 61), recent changes have been *consumer-driven* so firms must develop a "capacity to get close to their customers, regardless of where in the world they are." Thus globalization "means having the ability to allocate production capacity anywhere in the world" and also means reducing communication losses "when design work is done in a different part of the world than manufacturing and marketing." From an earlier vision of globalization that did not require any consideration of software matters, we must make a dramatic shift to the contemporary vision within which computing software is indispensable to a proper understanding of the primary corporate controls and information flows that influence the location, pace, structure and nature of evolving business activity in the global environment.

Reconstruction, Communication and Managerial Limits

Similarly, globalization entails a drastic reconstruction of employment, work designs or human resources affected by the new dependence on software (Dyer, 1993), as also anticipated by Vernon (1970) in his attempt to connect the eventual exhaustion of scale economies, special roles of skilled managers and technicians, and the endogeneity of size for multinational firms with constraints on effective communication. Without the benefit of current views of organizational design and continuous improvement in operations Robinson (1993) sees the abandonment of senescent activities, attaches major scale economies to research-related activities and further penetration of 'foreign' markets to a prolongation of the benefits of proprietary technology, and stresses the substantial impact of skilled employees in a manner analogous to 'lumpy' real investment. Effective communication serves as a primary force for the internalization of innovative research and as a barrier to further gains in efficiency here. It clearly governs the scope for integration of business activities and permits the diffusion of control mechanisms, replacing earlier hierarchical structures of Fordist-style managements with more horizontal structures.

The process-based perspective presumes that most large firms operate in an evolving environment of product development and new markets, with the relative effectiveness of research depending on whether or not it is "intimately and continuously linked with the processes of marketing, production, and general planning." This vision is precisely the modern scenario within which new software becomes such a dominant force. How can effective communication arise to a sufficient degree, how can the basic indivisibilities of skilled employees (Vernon's constraining factor) be overcome, and how can sufficient integration occur--except by the growing reliance on a convenient new input for communication and control that is easily stored, retrieved and replicated at modest cost! Thus structural adjustment of global firms is facilitated (and the pace and scope of globalization stimulated) by the improvement of software and its assimilation among such firms. Earlier shortages of skilled managers and technologists, as stressed by Vernon, are partially offset by the software advances and strategic alliances in research and product development that have emerged since the mid-1980s. In particular, the persistent growth of individual multi-divisional firms (or shadow groups among firms) is actively encouraged by significant delays to the eventual onset of scale diseconomies, and the management of human capital acquires an international flavor that is markedly in contrast to the spatial or contiguity forces that often seem to govern many relationships with clients and suppliers.

Recasting Some Earlier Theories of the Large Firms

We should also clarify the role of recent software advances in modifying influential views of firms which are associated with Penrose (1955, 1959), Sabel (1986) and Chandler. Penrose fixed the firm as a collection of productive resources and she pointed to "the service of personnel, in particular of management, with experience within the firm" as a limitational factor to efficient size. Novel software reduced the pressure of this constraint by economizing specific human resources and it transformed internal labor markets by elimination of many middle-management jobs and a relocation of corresponding managerial tasks to computer-based processes, shortening the assimilation of relevant experience and facilitating quicker response to evolving competitive pressures. Computers and software joined Penrose's collection of productive resources and markedly changed the influence of other members of her collection.

More attention is given to external influences on industrial organization by Sabel, who noted dramatic changes which affected two groups of manufacturing firms in the developed world during the mid-1980s--one group driven by cost cutting and quality enhancement to some preconditions of rapid model changes, and the other group seeking a much wider range of speciality products at modest prices and reorganizing work forces and labor relations in novel *Kanban* systems. In this evolving context, he suggests that both found programmable automation technology ideally suited to increasing efficiency without sacrificing flexibility, so that managers could focus on specialized outputs obtained by employing broadly skilled labor and programmable machines. Concomitants included more integration of design and manufacture, "high trust" labor relations, and much closer relations between producers and supplies. Globalization encouraged the emergence of such flexible specialization through the migration of mass production to newly developing countries. In the last decade, as we have indicated, this structural vision has been substantially enlarged by the shift from programmable machines in production to interactive, often real-time, software affecting a much larger proportion of managerial, monitoring, planning, productive and distributive activities.

Chandler is known as an economic historian and thus is an unlikely source of enlightenment on the very recent activities and organization of global firms. But his historical treatment of potential economies of scale and scope can be used to extend our awareness of structural transformations, their consequences and causes (beyond the awareness that comes from Vernon, Sabel and Penrose). Chandler (1992) prefers to concentrate attention on the "organizational capabilities" which exploit technological processes. Such capabilities (often firm-specific or industry-specific) stimulate continuing growth and organizational learning when created in knowledge-acquiring processes. A new reliance on exploiting information, managerial experience, and faster speed of response with computer-assisted design, control and planning enhances many lessons drawn from historical illustrations. The impact of specificity is amended, however, since the character of organizational learning depends on diverse ways in which relevant information is sought, acquired, utilized, retained, modified and reissued through training--just as the economies of scale can be prolonged when human facilities are enhanced or economized by computer-based assistance. The growing experience with software is consistent with a strong stimulus to *organizational learning*, while earlier roles of human managers and technicians are being redefined and perhaps reduced. On wider notions of organizations as learning systems (see the recent account of Nevis, DiBella and Gould, 1995).

Since the Chamberlin-Robinson innovations were extended to wider empirical aspects of industrial organization, economists have not resolved whether competitive theories should be firm-based or industry-based. Competitive advantage too has been expressed in terms of both countries and firms. The recent pre-eminence of 'global' economic activity implies that conventional modes of analysis must be overhauled. As noted by Ietto-Gillies (1994), three aspects of the current situation require special attention. First, considerable changes have blurred many older distinctions--between national and international interests, firms and industries, and cooperation and competition. Second, there is a growing non-coincidence between competitiveness of companies and that of countries. Finally, internationalization is now part of an endogenous set of evolutionary processes.

Concluding Remarks: Globalization and Micro-Macro Synthesis

We can reconcile these significant features of globalization with the structural endogeneity of global firms and markets, the collaboration of competitors with respect to both standards and research and development, persistent and comprehensive change, product-line diversity and variability, and the economizing of human resources only through a combination of the microeconomics of evolving organization structures (where software has its main impact) and the macroeconomics of strategic policies for national governments, supranational regimes, regional trading blocs and larger business entities.

At the technical level for microeconomic analyses, we must identify clear roles for integration, knowledge and information in determining the continuation of size economies, as attempted at Xerox, for example, by McGrath and Hoole (1992). We must try to separate human and organizational learning, and thus clarify the substitution of computer-based experience for human intuition and experience, and establish the contributions of specific human skills and new forms of managerial innovation to organizational skills (Stata, 1989). Clearly, success in such endeavors will be restrained by the inertial forces that we have identified. Persistence of the old obstacles is illustrated by Arrow (1985: 303), who argues that "the history of economic thought suggests that these theories [of Chandler, Williamson and Simon] will only find analytic usefulness when they are founded on more directly neoclassical lines, that is, in terms of individual optimization and equilibrium." His opinion is less forceful than that linked to Stigler but is still disturbing. Arrow's focus on a theory of teams (in which "information" is used in the sense of statistical decision theory) is so remote from real features of informational structures as to be misleading, distorting the very phenomena it seeks to describe. Imagine trying to place Hewlett-Packard, 3M or Motorola in Arrow's framework! What probabilities can exist when such companies emphasize "creative cultures", with rapid changes in their output portfolios and a strong dedication to challenges of their own orthodoxies? How can either individual optimization or equilibrium deal with fundamental ambiguity, path dependence, and non-stationarity of global economic activities? How can they deal with the multiple goals of strategic alliances--for example, the acquisition of technologies, risk containment for capital outlays, reduced time for product development, scale economies, access to new markets and distribution channels, and wider core competencies as explored by Ohmae (1989), Atik (1993) and Dunning (1995)--or incomplete market boundaries and varying mixture of competition and collusion? More sanguine views on the perceived benefits of formal theories of industrial organization are identified by Shapiro (1989).

We must also be attentive to time frames and organizational goals. Historically, a myopic focus on present value and profit maximization has exchanged relevance for analytical convenience. Computer-based processes have produced an environment in which global production, distribution and inventory costs are related to strong time pressures. This environment has brought forward a more attentive monitoring of value-adding activities, scheduling of future design changes, truncated product cycles, reduced lead times for product development, and synchronization of activities All of these elements are time-related, and they are facilitated by new computing devices and the longer-term commitments of large firms. More attention to dynamic processes, historical context, systemic unpredictability, and sequential planning seems to have transformed the consideration of time-related issues by managers and technicians.

Currently we find ourselves at an important turning point in economic development, driven by the arrival of "new competition" within globalization to revise managerial functions and accept new patterns of employment and unemployment, to reconsider both interactive market structures and informational flows, to resist radical changes in the spatial location of economic activities, to worry about new sources of instability and uncertainty, and to recognize the endogeneity of firms' structures. Computer-based stimulae, especially pervasive software advances, must affect the future global evolution of economic development by (1) resolving the ambiguity of internal relations and inconsistent goals, (2) easing rapid adjustments to both unexpected surprises and planned changes in the internationalization of future economic systems, (3) adding better means of integration, flexibility and versality to various aspects of managerial responsibilities, (4) weakening the managerial limit to expansion, and (5) economizing human and material resources. This is more than Simon anticipated and more than Chandler, Penrose, Sabel, Vernon and Williamson explored but these computer-driven consequences supply the platform from which the primary features of future processes for globalization will emerge.

References

Akhter, S. H. *Global Marketing*. Cincinnati: South-Western, 1994.

Alkahafaji, A. F. *Competitive Global Management*. Delroy Beach, FL: St. Lucie Press, 1995.

Arndt, H. W. "The economics of globalism." *Banca Naz del Lavoro Quarterly Review*, 1992, vol. 180, pp.103-12.

Arrow, K. J. "Informational structure of the firm." *American Economic Review* ,1985, vol. 75, no. 2, pp.303-7.

Atik, J. "Technology and distribution as organizational elements within international strategic alliances." *University of Pennsylvania Journal of Institute Business Law*, 1993, vol. 14, no.3, pp. 273-313.

Bailey, P.; Parisotto, A. and Renshaw, G. *Multinationals and Employment*. Geneva: International Labor Office, 1993.

Baumol, W. J. "Information, Computers, and the Structure of Industry," in T.K. Kaul and J.K. Sengupta eds., *Essays in Honor of Karl A. Fox,*. Chicago: Elsevier, 1991a.

_____."Determinants of Industry Structure and Contestable Market Theory," *in* D. Greenaway; M. Bleaney and I. Stewart, eds, *Companion to Contemporary Economic Thought*, London: Routledge, 1991b.

Best, M. H. *The New Competition*. Cambridge, MA: Harvard University Press, 1990.

Bourke, R. W. And Friedman, S. H. "Configurators." *APICS ; The Performance Advantage,* 1994, vol. 4, no.1, pp. 42-4.

Bresticker, R. B. *American Manufacturing and Logistics in the Year 2001.* Hoffman Estates, IL: Brigadoon Bay Books, 1992.

Campbell, D. "The Globalizing Firm and Labor Institutions," in P. Bailey; A. Parisotto and G. Renshaw, eds., *Multinationals and Employment.* Geneva: International Labor Office, 1993.

Caves, R. E. "Industrial organization, corporate strategy and structure." *Journal of Economic Literature,* 1980, vol.18, pp. 64-92.

Chandler, A. D. *Scale and Scope: The Dynamics of Industrial Capitalism.* Cambridge, MA: Belknap Press, 1990.

Chandler, A. D. "Organizational capabilities and the economic history of the industrial enterprise." *Journal of Econ Perspectives,* 1992, vol.6,no.3,pp. 79-100.

Cowling, K. and Sugden, R. *Transnational Monopoly Capitalism.* New York: St. Martin's Press, 1987.

Czinkota, M. R.; Ronkainen, I. A.; Moffett, M. H. and Moynihan, E. O. *Global Business.* New York: Dryden Press, 1995.

Davenport, T. H. and Short, J. E. "The new industrial engineering: information technology and business process redesign." *Sloan Management Review ,*1993.

Dunning, J. H. "The role of foreign direct investment in a globalizing economy." *Banca Naz del Lavoro Quarterly Review ,*1995, vol.98, no.193, pp. 125-44.

Dyer, L. *Human Resources as a Source of Competitive Advantage.* Kingston, Ont: Industrial Relations Centre, Queen's University, 1993.

Fare, R. and Primont, D. *Multi-Output Production and Duality: Theory and Applications.* Boston: Kluwer, 1995.

Garbani, J. P. "Manufacturing execution systems: the next generation." *APICS; The Performance Advantage,* 1995.

Goldhar, J. D. and Jelinek, M. "Computer integrated flexible manufacturing: organizational, economic, and strategic implications." *Interfaces,* 1985, vol.15 ,no.3, pp. 94-105.

Hamill , J. "Cross-Border Mergers, Acquisitions and Strategic Alliances," in P. Bailey; A. Parisotto and G. Renshaw, eds., *Multinationals and Employment.* Geneva: International Labour Office, 1993.

Hammer, M. "Reengineering work: don't automate, obliterate." *Harvard Business Review*, 1990.

Hayek, F. "Competition as a Discovery Procedure." *New Studies.* Chicago: University of Chicago Press, 1978.

Hayes, R. and Jaikumar, R. "Manufacturing's crisis; new technologies, obsolete organizations." *Harvard Business Review*, 1988, pp. 77-85.

Howells, J. and Wood, M. *The Globalisation of Production.* London: Belhaven Press for Commission of the European Communities, 1992.

Kendall, M. G. "Statistical inference in the light of the theory of the electronic computer." *Review of the International Statistical Institute*, 1967, vol.34, no.1, pp. 1-112.

Klier, T. H. "How lean manufacturing changes the way we understand the manufacturing sector." *Economic Perspectives*, Federal Reserve Bank of Chicago, 1993, vol.17, no.3, pp. 2-9.

_____."The impact of lean manufacturing on sourcing relationships." *Economic Perspectives,* Federal Reserve Bank of Chicago, 1994, vol.18, no.4, pp. 8-18.

_____. "The geography of lean manufacturing: recent evidence from the U.S. auto industry." *Economic Perspectives*, Federal Reserve Bank of Chicago, 1995, vol.19, no.6, pp. 2-16.

Lieberman, M. and Leete, B. "Getting a grip on configurators." *APICS ; The Performance Advantage ,*1995, vol.5, no.5, pp. 30-5.

Loasby, B. J. "Marshall's economics of progress." *Journal of Econ Studies,* 1986, vol.13, no.5, pp. 16-26.

Marshall, A. *Principles of Economics.* London: Macmillan, 1920.

McGrath, M. E. and Hoole, R. W. "Manufacturing's new economies of scale." *Harvard Business Review ,*1992.

National Research Council. *U.S.-Japan Stategic Alliances in the Semiconductor Industry.* Washington, D.C.: National Academy Press, 1992.

Nevis, E.C.; DiBella, A. J. and Gould J. M. "A Understanding organizations as learning systems." *Sloan Management Review*, 1995.

Ohmae, K. "The global logic of strategic alliances." *Harvard Business Review,* 1989.

Palmer, D.; Friedland, R. ; Jennings, P.D. and Powers, M.E. " The economics and politics of structure: the multidivisional form and the large US corporation." *Admin Sc Quarterly*, 1987; vol. 32 , pp.25-48.

Penrose, E. T. "Limits to the growth and size of firms." *American Economic Review* 1955, vol. 45, pp.531-43.

_____. *The Theory of the Growth of the Firm.* Oxford: Blackwell, 1959.

Prendergast, R. "Marshallian external economies." *Economic Journal*, 1993, vol. 103, pp. 454-58.

Reich, R.B. *The World Work of Nations.* New York: Knopf, 1991.

Robinson, A., ed. *Continuous Improvement in Operations.* Cambridge, MA: Productivity Press, 1993.

Rostow, W. W. "Technology and the Price System," in W. Breit and W.P. Culbertson, eds., Science and Ceremony,. Austin: University of Texas Press, 1976.

_____. "Comment from a not quite empty box." *Economic Journal*, 1982, vol. 92, pp.156-60.

Sabel, C.F. "Changing Models of Economic Efficiency and Their Implications for Industrialization in the Third World," in A. Foxley; M.S. McPherson and G. O'Donnell eds., *Development, Democracy, and the Art of Trespssing: Essays in Honor of Albert O. Hirschman.* Notre Dame, IND: University of Notre Dame Press, 1986.

Schonberger, R.J. *World Class Manufacturing Casebook.* New York: Free Press, 1987.

Shapiro, C. "The theory of business strategy." *Rand Journal of Economics* , 1989, vol. 20 (1) , pp. 125-37.

Simon, H. A. "Programs as factors of production." *Proceedings of the 19th Annual Winter Meeting, Industrial Relations Research Association, 1966, IRRA* 1967, pp. 178-88.

_____. "Designing Organizations for an Information Rich World," in M Greenberger ed. *Computers, Communications, and the Public Interest,* Baltimore: The Johns Hopkins Press, 1971.

Stata, R. "Organizational learning--the key to managerial innovation." *Sloan Management Review,* 1989.

Stigler, G. "Perfect competition, historically contemplated." *Journal of Political Economy,* 1957, vol. 65 (1), pp. 1-17.

Strader, T. J. and Shaw, M. J. *Information Infrastructure Requirements and Supplu Chain Management.* Urbana, ILL: The Beckman Institute, 1994.

Thomsen, S. "Integration through globalisation." *National Westminster Bank Quarterly Review,* 1992.

UNCTAD. *World Investment Report 1994: Transnational Corporations, Employment and the Workplace.* New York: UN Publications, 1995.

Vernon, R. "Organization as a Scale Factor in the Growth of Firms," in J. W. Markham and G. F. Papanek eds., *Industrial Organization and Economic Development.* Boston: Houghton Mifflin, 1970.

Williamson, O. E. "The modern corporation: origins, evolution, attributes." *Journal of Economic Literature,* 1981, vol.19, pp. 1537-68.

13

MARKETS, GLOBALIZATION AND STRUCTURAL CHANGE

Masudul Alam Choudhury
University College of Cape Breton, Canada
Abdul Fatah Che Hamat
Science University of Malaysia

Various economic paradigms on markets with constitutional contracts are critically examined to contrast them with yet another view of market. In the alternative view presented in this chapter, endogeneity of various political and economic processes creates a global system of interlinkages among and between policy variables and socioeconomic variables. By invoking the epistemology and methodology of such a system, a theory of globally interactive market processes is developed. Globally knowledge-induced interlinkages generated by polity-market interactions are made to establish and explain what we term here a "system of social contracts". The case of Malaysia is taken to explain the theoretical ramifications. The Malaysian case study is also invoked to question the nature of tradeoffs between economic growth and redistribution in the midst of demands placed by the neoclassical view of globalization.

Economic theory has traditionally and pedagogically viewed the market as a system of exchange in goods and services. Between the classical definition of perfect competition and the microeconomics of imperfect perfection, this concept of exchange of transactions is looked upon in terms of a growing degree of price distortions caused by limited number of buyers and sellers. Such orientations in the concept of markets still provoke a consistent pursuit of price mechanism as the basis of exchange. Besides, price mechanisms in the sense of perfect and imperfect competition give rise to some notion of market equilibrium and optimality in the allocation of resources. Thus, when market equilibrium, optimality of resource allocation and price mechanism join sides together in the midst of the transactional exchange nature of the market system, the end result is inconsistency within the methodology used to address such issues--once in perfect and then in imperfect market models.

For instance, the objective function of profit-maximizing oligopolistic firms is based on the same kind of first order conditions and marginal substitution principle of neoclassical economics as are found for profit-maximizing firms in perfect competition. Consequently, although collusive price-setting and output-setting reaction functions characterize the decision making of oligopolists most importantly, yet the presence of optimization techniques using marginal substitution principle wipes out the robustness of essential decision-making features. On the other hand, any departure from the first and second order optimization conditions premised in marginal substitution principle renders a neoclassical treatment of profit maximization and market equilibrium for oligopolies, methodologically flawed. (Choudhury, 1996a)

In this chapter we will develop a concept of market that explicitly brings out interactive decision-making processes while affecting pricing and output setting and resource allocation. In this sense of interactions and endogenizing of agent-specific preferences and production menus that go with it, we will explain the market in yet another way. The market is treated here as an explicit system of social contracts. The second half of the chapter gives empirical evidence to show how in Malaysia, through her singular financial markets based on Islamic instruments, saver-investor preferences are being endogenized in the capital market. Here market prices and material gains are shown to interrelate with non-pricing motivations to create the direction of financial viability and bring about substantial gains.

The Malaysian economy is used as a case study to show how moral and economic values can be married together in the context of globalization. Malaysia is indeed experiencing this as a country embedded in the dynamics of the globalization process on all fronts.

Questions on the Methodology of Oligopolistic Decision Making

We start with a critical examination of the methodology of pricing and resource allocation provided by neoclassical analysis for oligopolistic markets. Here, two possible models of oligopoly behavior are invoked in contrast to an alternative model that can explicitly invoke decision-making features (Martin, 1988).

A Critique of the Neoclassical Treatment of a Profit-Maximizing Oligopoly

In neoclassical parlance, the "ith" profit-maximizing oligopolist's objective criterion is to maximize its share, s_i, of monopoly profit, π_m, in each time period (dynamic cartel stability problem). These variables are shown to be functions of the price variable, P, and the output variable, Q. $PV(s_i\pi_i)$ is then the present value of the time-period flows of shares as shown, with a suitable discount rate. The objective criterion for the ith oligopolist is then,

> Max. $PV(s_i(P,Q)\pi_m(P,Q))$,
> subject to, $s_i=[(P-MC_i)/P].\epsilon_{QP}$,
> and the Lerner's Index,
> $\pi_m=(P-AC_i).Q$.

Where MC_i denotes the marginal cost of production for the oligopolist (monopolist); AC_i denotes the average cost of production for the same; ϵ_{QP} denotes the price elasticity of output. Each of the variables in the above criterion function is time-dependent.

In this form, the objective criterion for the oligopolist is purely a classical optimization problem. In it, optimal or limiting price condition is sought for determining the optimal profit level. The share of profit is then obtained by solving the system of first order conditions in P and Q (output-setting and price-setting oligopolist) that yield optimal values of s_i and π_m.

Hence, the optimal results from the above dynamic profit-maximizing problem of the oligopolist and the determination of optimal-equilibrium positions in terms of P and Q--thereby, the determinations of MC_i, AC_i, ϵ_{QP}--must together suggest that collusive behavior is subsumed in these optimal output- and price-setting conditions. Now because of the marginalist conditions invoked in the classical optimization problem, all effects of collusive behavior in price and output determinations are marginalized while determining these quantities in market setting. The definition of markets as exchange of transactions of the oligopolist is thus maintained. But this concept of the market fails to bring out the contractarian outlook behind collusive decision making.

Examination of Pricing on the Kinked Demand Curve of the Oligopolist

As another example showing the methodological inadequacy of the exchange concept of markets underlying oligopolist behavior, let us recall the kinked demand curve of the oligopolists' output (Mansfield, 1985). Here too we note that collusive price level, P, is given by, $P=f(Q)=f[\{U_iMC_i\}\cap MR]$. Q remains put at the intersections of a series of MC_i, denoted by U_iMC_i, and the MR curve is vertical in order to yield the determinate collusive price at the point of the kinked demand (AR) curve of the oligopolists' output. "i" denotes the ith oligopolist in a cartel.

With many outputs, **Q** and hence, **P**, MR(**Q**) and say, MC_i(**Q**), are vector variables/ functions. Hence, for a monotonic positive and continuous relationship between various MC_i(**Q**), with MR(**Q**) as a constant value, say "a", we obtain, $P=a.f(MC_i(\mathbf{Q}))$. But since **P** is collusively fixed at the kinked point of the AR-curve, therefore, there exists a tradeoff among the MC_i(**Q**)'s of various oligopolists. In other words, more efficient producers can absorb some of the costs of less efficient ones in the cartel.

The mutual contract among the oligopolists is once again shown simply by the nature of the tradeoff indicated by the equation, $df(MC_i(\mathbf{Q}))=0$. This defines a marginalist tradeoff in terms of **Q** among the market shares available to various colluding members in the cartel. But the contractarian nature of the collusion is washed away in the midst of determining such optimal tradeoffs. Thus, market consideration, i.e. determination of (**P,Q**) values, is once again assumed to allocate the resources among the oligopolists in order to establish optimal shares and marginal costs.

The Contractarian Nature of Oligopolistic Decision Making

It is now time to define the contractarian nature of the collusive process involved in oligopoly behavior in a market setting. Non-pricing transactions in the form of information asymmetry, moral hazards, political perks, sub-regional contracts with perks or penalties, transportation cost differentials, preferred access to or isolation from markets, etc. are major factors found to influence a gamut of decision-making factors for oligopolists. Examples in international trade studies are trade-diversions and trade solidarity that exist in regional economic blocs; preferential tariff treatment; tariff retaliation; development contracts between multinationals and national governments over specified ways of directing foreign direct investments.

Political decisions influence economic ones as in the case of production decisions by OPEC as a cartel. Such non-pricing contracts are not merely overwhelming in creating disturbances in observed market prices but also require a different methodology for explaining the nature and effects of bargaining in economic decision making. Game theoretic approach is yet another method besides the one presented in this chapter (Osborne & Rubinstein, 1994).

We refer to the underlying politico-economic dynamics of preference formation, agent-agent specific interactions, institutional and policy-oriented cause and effect generated between non-pricing factors and the market transactions. These are some of the contractarian aspects of interactive decision making. The market as a system of social contracts is now defined in the midst of interactions that evolve with non-pricing conditions. These are found to have profound cause-effect relations with economic decisions and the exchange environment.

Alternative Concept of Market Contract

In the alternative concept of market as a system of social contracts, we are faced with endogenizing a distinctly powerful bundle of non-pricing variables. Included in this are agent-specific preference formation determined by information flows, transaction costs, policy and politico-cultural variables(Bowles, 1991). These factors appear in any decision-making process between conflicting and consensual agents. Hence in an oligopoly, trade-diversion and political pricing of goods can take predominance over sheer self-interest in production menus and consumer preferences. Such impacts make economic preferences and menus dynamic and ever-changing by means of interactions and information flows.

Information flows and interactions are processes that appear cyclically. These occur first as interactions among the members of the cartel; second, between the non-pricing factors and the socio-economic variables; and third, between the agents and the domain of socio-economic impacts. Information flows as knowledge formation in the system that addresses a wider spectrum of politico-economic relationships, establish the cyclical evolution between the non-pricing factors, dynamic changes in agent-specific menus and preferences, and the socio-economic variables. Such evolutionary and cyclical cause-effect relationships define the nature of the dynamic process embodying endogeneity of preferences in market relations. Thus, social contracts are defined by such an evolutionary process interrelating information flows, changes in agent-specific preferences and menus, and the cause-effect relationships between non-pricing variables and socio-economic variables. The system of such social contracts is intermeshed in itself. Hence the market becomes a system of social contracts.

Obviously, prices and outputs in such a concept of the market as a system of social contracts fail to be purely market determined. Indeed, now the question is whether the classical idea of supply prices and the neoclassical idea of demand prices, at all prevail in markets. Are market equilibria merely instantaneous occurrences having no empirical significance? In the politico-economic sense of markets, are prices then merely notional values of a goods and services delivered by evolutionary and ever-changing menus and preferences impacted upon by information flows? Answers to these questions are imminently in the affirmative in the concept of markets as systems of social contracts. Such contracts appear endogenously in their cause and effect relations with socio-economic variables, preferences and menus.

Social Contractarianism of Markets: Hayek and Buchanan

Hayek's Market Catallaxy Process

In his ideas on individualism and the neo-liberal economic paradigm, Hayek defends the market process as one that is evolving under a mix of underlying social, political, institutional and pure market orientations (Hayek, 1967). But the sensitivity of markets to microeconomic decision making is seen to be so spontaneous that all institutional changes, notwithstanding their civil libertarian roles and behavior, are seen to be imitative of hedonic preferences premised in the exchange mechanism of a liberal concept of market. Thus such a market catalyzes the socio-political process of change in neo-liberalism. Laws, legislation, statutes on constitutional liberty and social justice are all rendered to market determinations in the first place.

Hayek finds no place for market interventions by policy measures even when social justice is the goal at point. He calls this spontaneous effect of markets on the socio-political factors as market catallaxy. With this concept Hayek defends the philosophy of liberalism against all alternative economic orders (Hayek, 1976; Ferry and Renault, 1992).

The problematique of Hayek in reference to markets as systems of social contracts arises as follows: if markets are primally catalytic to socio-political change, then what is the nature of goods and services that are delivered in the market place in the first place? If such goods and services are determined by classical and neoclassical markets, then the corresponding types of prices determine values in exchange. Such a concept of value reverts us to the usual picture on the market as an exchange system. Contrarily, if markets are robust in determining socio-political interactions in preference formation and production menus, then there must exist protracted periods of interrelations that must be externalized clearly in and through the market process. The idea of market catallaxy now loses its meaning. The end result is that prices perturbed by a host of socio-political factors in decision making, become notional in nature. Market prices lose their conception of value even in incomplete market setting.

Furthermore, if markets primally convey changes to institutions, then such institutions must be guided by the same types of production menus and preferences as pure markets embody. In a liberal economic order, it is known that markets are premised in self-interest and are ethically benign. Consequently, the constitutional elements of morality and ethics have no relevance in Hayek's socio-political order. The consequence of this moral and ethical benignity is a historical process that is perpetually conflicting between the moral and economic forces. When this happens as a global perspective of market-institution contractarianism in Hayek, no cause-effect interrelationship is possible. The concept of markets as systems of social contracts then loses meaning in Hayek's idea of market catallaxy.

In the history of economic thought, this conflict and differentiation between the moral/ethical and economic sides of human society are shown to be epistemologically grounded in occidental thought. Examples here are the utilitarian philosophy of civil libertarianism, the neoclassical marginalist substitution principle (Bentham 1789; Quinton 1989), the Smithian invisible hand and the Eurocentric development theorizing of market transformation. This has recently been taken up in the literature on global capitalism, conflict and convergence (Mehmet 1990).

Buchanan's Public Choice and Contractarianism

Buchanan's resource allocation is based on two kinds of goods, purely private goods and purely public goods (Buchanan, 1975). Purely private goods appear in the "state of nature". In this state, inequality in the holding of initial bundles is legitimated on the basis of competition and private ownership. Thus, the space of goods is partitioned in this state of resource allocation by virtue of the axioms of self-interest and natural liberty premised in pure market exchange. This primacy of resource allocation, called the state of "natural distribution", is a pre-constitutional one in Buchanan's public choice theory. Private goods nonetheless are assumed to generate external diseconomies, for which market failures occur. But a compensation principle is assumed to exist to compensate for this market distortion. By itself, the compensation principle is known to be compounded by a host of non-pricing factors causing global instabilities in prices and resource reallocation (Coase, 1993).

In the post-constitutional state of purely public goods, collective-consumption exists and a social contract is instituted to bring this about. Between perfect unanimity and anarchy exist less-than-unanimous agreements. The implications of these different states are first, that when purely private goods are allocated through markets, competition and conflict develop individuated contracts. Second, when unanimity exists in the post-constitutional stage, a market-generated surplus is so assumed that it can be shared by many members brought into a social contract by means of some contravention. A large number of sharers provide the possibility of consensus to exist, and the market-generated surplus causes sharing to be possible.

The total framework of resource allocation in Buchanan's social contractarianism is thus a combination of two orders. First, there is a pre-constitutional order of purely private goods generated through market exchange, as we understand this in traditional economic theory. Second, there is a post-constitutional order, where markets bring about surpluses to be shared by means of social contravention. The resulting socio-economic framework is then obvious. The market order is primal in generating institutional ones and not vice versa. In other words, there are no feedbacks from the side of institutions to markets. Hence, individual consumer preferences for purely market goods being the result of competition over partitioned output space, they have no knowledge-embodiment (interactions) in them as earlier found to be the case with the dynamic nature of endogenous preference fields.

Besides, there are methodological problems with Buchanan's approach to pre- and post-constitutional stages of social contracts. If the total output space is divided into purely private and purely public ones with different sets of preferences, then this implies that an embedded conflict must prevail between the purely economic and the purely social balances in political economy. We would then revert to the neoclassical type marginalist substitution tradeoff between economic efficiency and distributive (social) equity (Phelps, 1989).

Now the convergence of market order to Hayek's concept of market catallaxy and to the utilitarian nature of liberal institutions, is once again repeated. There is indeed a close resemblance between Nozick's (1974) concept of entitlement bundles (found in the state of nature) and his concept of distributive justice (in a framework of minimal intervention by the state) with both Hayek's and Buchanan's social contractarianism germinating in the pure market order, and then defining the possibility of post-constitutional contracts (Kirzner, 1983).

Yet other kinds of methodological problems occur in Buchanan's theory of markets by virtue of the fact that in the pre- and post-constitutional phases, stable utility functions are assumed to exist for the contracting partners. Hence, the social welfare function made up of the collective of such agent-specific utility functions must be a well-defined one although not a unique one. The assumption of stability in the face of a multitude of decisions by interacting agents is once again based on assumptions of optimality and equilibrium. One of the consequences of such a result is that hegemony is allowed for in less-than-unanimous social contracts. An example of such a social contract in the literature is the study of Eurocentricity on both economic and political fronts in a capitalistic globalizing age. The result of stability in social welfare function and agent-specific utility indexes cannot fit the otherwise globally interacting and knowledge-induced (interactive) nature of a market as a system of social contracts.

Concluding Remarks on Markets as Systems of Social Contracts

The conclusion from the above treatment of some social contractarian approaches to market exchange is that primacy of markets, in the presence of individuated preferences despite embedded civil libertarianism in them, entrench the neoclassical marginalist substitution notion as the defining tool of resource allocation in both the market and the institutional orders. In the midst of the marginalist substitution principle, stability, optimality and equilibrium are the logical results. Social contracts, in spite of their viscous nature, are then treated as stable attributes of human behavior. This is a contradiction to reality. Besides, sheer primacy to market exchange leaves out the epistemological roots that must in the first instance explain the essence of freedom, responsibility and global complementarity among purposeful ends.

A Model of the Market as a System of Social Contract

A necessary cause-effect requirement of the concept of market as a system of social contracts is the existence of interlinkages among diverse activities in and within the economic, political and social orders. Besides, interlinkages are methodologically explained and generated by the principle of universal complementarity among all these various ends. The principle of universal complementarity means that global interactions, forward and backward interlinkages, causes and effects, temporary integration as social contracts, followed by evolutionary ones, are made possible (Choudhury, 1996b).

The Principle of Universal Complementarity vs the Neoclassical Marginalist Substitution Principle

Here we will take up a simple production function with various categories of labor and capital as are found to be distributed across different occupations and sectors. The principle of universal complementarity means that there are interactions among all these factors and joint outputs of various sectors. The consequences of these complementarities are sectorial interlinkages established through product markets, labor markets, technological change and transferability of social contracts that make the interlinkages possible by means of information flows and institutional policies.

To formalize, we proceed as follows; let the production function in the ith sector be given by

$$Q_i = f_i(L_i, K_i), \qquad i = 1, 2, ..., n.$$

where, Q_i denotes ith sectorial output; L_i denotes demand for labor in the ith sector; K_i denotes demand for capital in the ith sector; $f_i(...)$ denotes the production function (menu) in the ith sector.

Next we must establish the nature of the above quantities in terms of sectoral interlinkages and the methodology whereby resource allocation, pricing and growth take place in such a globally interlinked system.

Let the joint output be denoted by q_i for the ith sector, $i = 1, 2, .., n$. The existence of joint production implies, that the set of $\{Q_{si}\}$ values is generated by interactions among the output of all the sectors, s with i (s,i=1,2,..n). That is, $q_i = \{\cap_{s=1}^{n} Q_{si}\}$, i=1,2,..,n. A specified form of this expression is,

$$q_i = \Pi_{s=1}^{n} Q_{si}^{\alpha si},$$

where, α_{si} are sectorial output elasticity coefficients in the joint output of ith sector with the s sectors.

In terms of factor inputs, the joint production implies joint use of these factors, say (l_i, k_i) in the production of q_i. This must mean that(Friedman 1982)

$$(l_i, k_i) = \{\cap_{s=1}^{n} (A_{si} \times B_{si})\},$$

where, $A_{si} = \{L_{si}\}$, $B_{si} = \{K_{si}\}$, and $A_{si} \times B_{si}$ is a Cartesian product set. The subscripts here are similarly defined as above.

We can further on write

$$(l_i, k_i) = \cap_{s=1}^{n} (A_{si} \times B_{si}) = (\cap_{s=1}^{n} A_{si}) \times (\cap_{s=1}^{n} B_{si}) = (\cap_{s=1}^{n} L_{si}) \times (\cap_{s=1}^{n} K_{si}).$$

$$q_i = \Pi_{s=1}^{n} f_{si} [(\cap_{s=1}^{n} L_{si}) \times (\cap_{s=1}^{n} K_{si})].$$

A specified form of this joint production function is

$$q_i = \Pi_{s=1}^{n} L_{si}^{\alpha' si} K_{si}^{\beta si},$$

where, α'_{si} are labor elasticity coefficients of joint output; β_{si} are capital elasticity coefficients of joint output.

Global interactions must also mean that interlinkages exist both among and between the L's and K's. The forward and backward linkages implied here mean that a learning process exists in the entire interactive order. Let this learning variable be denoted by $\{\Theta_t\}$, which takes up continuous values over interactions denoted by t. The number of interactions are incessant; temporary phases of consensus evolve onto other ones. Hence, for each of these phases, there are temporary convergences into consensus, followed by further evolutions. This implies that, $\lim(t \to T)[\Theta_t] = \Theta_T$.

Finally, the dependence of all the variables on Θ_t values implies that there is a monotonic relationship between Θ_t-values and the socio-economic variables as shown. Hence, as Θ_t values converge over interactions in polity through constitutional accord on specific matters and between polity and the market order, a global system of interlinkages gets formed, premised in the movements of the Θ_t values. These knowledge parameters thereby provide the epistemological grounding to markets as a system of social contracts (Choudhury, 1993).

The complete system of such contractarian evolution of knowledge-based socio-economic variables is now shown as follows:

$$q_{it}(\Theta_t) = \Pi_{s=1}^n \ Q_{sit}^{\alpha sit}\}[\Theta_t],$$

subject to, $Q_{sit}(\Theta_t) = f_{sit}[(\cap_{s=1}^n L_{sit}) x (\cap_{s=1}^n K_{sit})](\Theta_t),$
$\Theta_{t+j} = F_1(\Theta_t, \mathbf{L_{sit}}, \mathbf{K_{sit}}, \mathbf{Q_{sit}}),$
$\mathbf{L_{sit}} = F_2(\mathbf{K_{sit}}, \mathbf{Q_{sit}}, \Theta_{t+j}),$
$\mathbf{K_{sit}} = F_3(\mathbf{L_{sit}}, \mathbf{Q_{sit}}, \Theta_{t+j}),$

$\lim(t \rightarrow T)[\Theta_t] = \Theta_T,$ for which,
$\mathbf{L_{sit}}(\Theta_t) \rightarrow \mathbf{L_{sit}}(\Theta_T),\ \mathbf{K_{sit}}(\Theta_t) \rightarrow \mathbf{K_{sit}}(\Theta_T),\ \mathbf{Q_{sit}}(\Theta_t) \rightarrow \mathbf{Q_{sit}}(\Theta_T).$

Bold values denote vectors.
$j=0,1,2,...,T;\ t=1,2,..T;\ i=1,2,..,n,\ T \in \mathbb{N}$ (or $\mathbb{R}$);
α_{sit} are sectorial output elasticities in joint product.

This technical nature of the problem is clearly not based on any optimization method. An acceptable method is simulation by first starting with a given value of Θ in an initial interactive phase followed by regeneration of these values by means of interlinkages among the various variables as shown, thus generating extended interactions. Such a methodology implies that the entire system of market interactions shown here, must be grounded in an epistemology embodied in the initial value of Θ. Such an epistemology starts as an axiom. It is then regenerated in the system by cause and effect of the learning process throughout the polity-market interactive-integrative and evolutionary order.

Now while a methodological case can be made for the enumeration of the Θ_t-values in simulative or heuristic models of decision making, yet the more interesting case is to look upon the iterations of Θ_t values as a humanly participated process of interactions with actual institutions, contracts and constitutional arrangements playing the role inherent in these knowledge parameters. Thus, while socio-economic variables are simulated in this system by means of such knowledge values, so also the social contracts are formed and evolved by cause and effect of the same parameters. Market as a system of social contract now transforms into a globally knowledge-induced interactive-integrative and evolutionary process governed by actual human presence rather than by hypothesized models.

The above delineation of market as a knowledge-induced system of social contracts is shown in figure 1. It is instructive to note the difference that this system makes from the Hayekian and Buchanian market orders. The constitutional contract in this alternative system has no initially pure private or natural distribution phases as are to be found in Buchanan's market order with constitutional pre-arrangements. The interactive polity-market order is premised in an epistemology that regulates the evolution of the socioeconomic variables by cause and effect, thus making preferences endogenous. This in turn replaces every semblance of neoclassical marginalist substitution principle by global interlinkages.

Thus Buchanan's pre- and post-constitutional phases are irrelevant in this knowledge-induced interactive market order. As for Hayek's concept of market catallaxy in the light of the knowledge-based perspective, we note that markets are not primal; rather, they are induced in the latter system. Hence, institutions are neither marginalized nor are they imitative of the type of liberalism embedded in competition and individualism. Individual or group preferences and production menus are not ignored in the knowledge-based system. Rather, they are transformed in the midst of a learning process without finally showing distinction between market behavior and political behavior, without separation of a pre-and post-constitutional regimes, when all of these emanate from a unique epistemology -- the initially prescribed Θ-value.

Oligopolistic Behavior in the Light of Knowledge Induced Markets

The concept of oligopolistic production in neoclassical economics is now replaced by participatory agents in the sense of interlinked markets. Hence, profits and market-shares in such an order cannot cause price distortions from the production side. Distortions appear when unreal kinds of classical and neoclassical notions of stability, optimality, equilibrium and market exchange are used to explain real situations of agent-agent interactions. The extension of interlinkages also builds up risk and product diversifications. Consequently, inter-agent and inter-systemic interactions increase knowledge endowment, although this process never optimizes to full knowledge due to the nature of the ever-evolving social contracts. In fact, one of the functions of knowledge in this system is to generate ways and means for

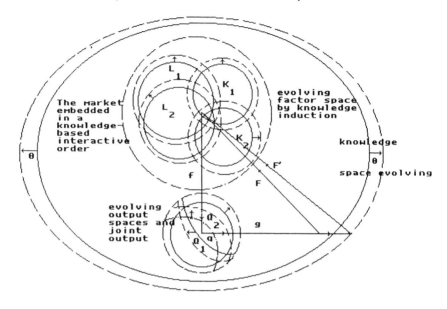

Figure 1: A knowledge Induced System of Interlinkages
Notes: The interlinked production system in outputs Q_1 and Q_2, producing joint output, q, by means of interlinkages in L_1, L_2, K_1 and K_2 (L and K denote labour and capital; and subscripts 1 and 2 denote sectors 1 and 2, respectively) is shown to be formed and to evolve by means of mappings like f (from factor space to output space), g from output space, and primally followed by regeneration of knowledge parameters as shown by the two arrows F and F', from an evolving knowledge space and primal space onto socio-economic spaces and then onto evolutionary knowledge space etc.

reducing uncertainty. Consequently, policies developed to attain this economic goal must be dynamic by interactions.

Among the kinds of policy instruments replaced in such an economy with knowledge-induced markets are interest rates and deficit financing triggered by means of taxation and floating of bonds. The policy instruments chosen instead are profit sharing that hinge upon expected profit rates. The ends to attain from the use of these instruments are establishing of efficacy in global interlinkages in the political economy; the sharing of costs for joint ventures to reduce investment risks. Profit sharing also induces holding of private ownerships by capitalists and workers and the sharing of production costs between themselves (Siddiqi, 1985; Ellerman, 1991).

An Objective Criterion of a Cooperative Economic Enterprise

We can now note how the objective criterion for the neoclassical oligopolist changes in distinct ways as follows:

Max. $PV(s_i\pi_m)$ (neoclassical) is replaced by:
Simulation$\{\Theta\}(q_i/\sum q_i)[pq_i - a_i.C(L_i,K_i)](\Theta)$ (i.e. interactive market order)
$= [p.(s_iq_i) - a_i.s_i.C(L_i,K_i)](\Theta)$, [$a_i$ being a proportion]
$=$ [revenue on the share of joint production $(=p.s_iq_i)$] - [a proportion of shared cost of production $(=a_is_iC(L_i,K_i))$].

The presence of Θ parameters is indispensable in the system, as they alone are instrumental in generating and regulating the sharing mechanism. Thus, as $\Theta \rightarrow \Theta^*$, a temporary consensual value, over subsequent iterations of agent-agent interactions, sharing increases. This causes members in the joint ventures to increase in number. Hence the share of cost to the ith producer decreases. Now $\lim(\Theta \rightarrow \Theta^*)[a_is_iC(L_i,K_i)](\Theta)$ declines. Consequently, $p.s q_i$ increases, and thereby the share of profit to the producer increases. Feedbacks between Θ-values and the economic variables appear during the process of convergence of Θ to Θ^*. In this process, prices p are themselves evolving by the same order of interactions premised in Θ values.

Since Θ values never cease to evolve and Θ^* is one of many values attained during different phases of social contracts in the midst of interactions, therefore, there is no long-run optimum to the above sharing of profit. Only multiple equilibrium possibilities emerge (Grandmont, 1989).

An Example of a Market With Participatory Contracts

Today a vibrant innovation in participatory financial instruments is taking place in Malaysia. Malaysia's principal social investment outlet, known as Tabung Haji, transacts the financial holdings of Muslim savers towards social ends through interest-based outlets. Commercial banks in Malaysia have overwhelmingly established an extensive market of participatory financial instruments-- *Mudarabah* (profit-sharing) and Bumiputera (poor Muslim Malays) bonds, called *Amanah Saham Nasional Scheme* and *Amanah Saham Bumiputera Scheme* (Government of Malaysia, 1991a). These are profit-sharing shares, with the exception that the latter ones are provided to needy target groups (Bumiputeras) only in Malaysia. *Amanah Saham Nasional* held a total share value of M$5,200 million with an accumulated investment of M$11,000 million by the end of 1990. The number of Bumiputera shareholders stood at 2.5 million, which comprised 46 per cent of the total number, 5.4 million of eligible (underprivileged) Bumiputeras. *Amanah Saham Nasional* shares are floated in the Kuala Lumpur Stock Exchange. In this scheme, while well-to-do Bumiputeras can hold shares, this volume is limited to 100,000 shares per shareholder from the well-to-do group. *Amanah Saham Bumiputera* shares can be held only by poor Bumiputeras. These were the policy enactions under the Malaysian New Economic Policy which is now replaced by the New Development Policy. These schemes were designed to correct the social imbalance that existed widely for some time between the rich and poor in Malaysia. The result has been impressive, as Malaysia today becomes an exemplary country in the world to have virtually eliminated rampant absolute poverty, although relative poverty between the various states remains. For the same reason these states are implementing their own *Amanah Saham* schemes and a wide range of commercial banks are floating them today.

There is also the Islamic insurance scheme (*Syarikat Takaful Malaysia*) in Malaysia, which has increased its funds from M$1.9 million in 1986 to M$38.2 million in 1990. Contributions collected in 1990 amounted to M$28.4 million compared to M$2.3 million in 1986. *Takaful* differs from a normal insurance company by virtue of its pooled funds for exigency being generated by profit sharing and other participatory investment schemes in the absence of interest rates and in ventures that are legally permissible under the Islamic Law (*Shari'ah*). Besides, participation in *Takaful* is available to enterprises of all sizes and risk exposure, although differentiated share sizes could be asked of businesses with varying risk exposures and assets.

Islamic banks constitute another new outlet in Muslim countries that transact in shares based on profit-loss transactions. The Islamic Bank Malaysia has shares that are transacted aggressively on the Kuala Lumpur Stock Exchange (KLSE). Much of the savings of Islamic Banks are presently held in long-term investments. This provides good opportunity for these banks to engage in investment in the real sector.

In the presence of various profit-loss participatory financial instruments in Malaysia at this time, it is found that the holdings in these assets have increased phenomenally. The result has been a rapid mobilization of productive assets and a fast utilization of savings available for such productive investments. There are several reasons for such a performance of holdings in Islamic banks. First, in recent years growth in the Malaysian economy has caused domestic investments to outstrip the supply of savings, even though the volume of savings has increased phenomenally with real growth of GDP. Hence in this growth momentum, the Islamic bank holdings have also utilized. Second, as the size of the holdings in Islamic banking instruments are increasing phenomenally among Muslim Malays, the size of the funds and their mobilization into productive investments are also increasing. Informal survey of banks done for this chapter proves that the profitability prospect is inviting increasing amounts of deposits and participation from Muslims and non-Muslims alike. The motive here is the prospect for profits when such funds are increasing.

In spite of the year 1985 being a year of deep recession in Malaysia, Islamic Bank Malaysia showed the following financial standing (several Bank Islam Malaysia Annual Reports; see Bank Islam Malaysia Berhad) during 1984 and 1985 --a picture that has improved considerably in recent times as evidenced from information provided above. In 1985 alone, Islamic Bank Malaysia as a Group had current savings, investment and other deposits of customers of M$410,224,204. This was equivalent to 4.18 per cent of total national savings. Shareholders' funds stood at M$422,650,150 (Ismail, 1990). In 1994, total liabilities, shareholders' funds and *Takaful* funds (= total assets) amounted to approximately M$3.046 billion for the Islamic Bank Malaysia Group. This marked a 51.63 per cent increase over the 1993 value; and an average annual increase of 62.18 per cent between 1985 and 1995. Net profits in 1994 was M$29.906 million. This marked a 36.34 per cent increase over the 1993 value. Dividend rate was 8 per cent in 1994.

To further substantiate the catalytic role played by profit-loss participatory instruments in the increasing demand for capital mobilization into productive investments, we note that interest-rate policy is not an active policy instrument of

Bank Negara Malaysia (Malaysian National Bank, see *Economic Report 1993/94 and 1994/95)*. While interest rates are set independently by commercial banks, these have remained low historically, compared to world interest-rate levels. Interest rates hovered between 3.50 per cent and 6.00 per cent annually between 1985 and 1990 As opposed to these rates, Islamic Bank Malaysia paid monthly rates of profits to depositors amounting to 9.43 per cent on 60 months deposits and 7.25 per cent on 12 months deposits during this time period.

Such rates have been possible even in the face of complaints from critics that Islamic banks were charging high service charges from the customers. The fact of the matter is that in the early days of Islamic banking, the risk exposure to these financial institutions was high and profits were low and risky. But with the growth of Islamic banking and both their outlets for investments and funds available in the Malaysian economy, the service charges also declined. Net profit rates thus remained high and steady.

The demand driven characteristic of the Malaysian economy has overall neutralized the effect of interest rates on domestic savings and replaced this by the growth in real incomes. The excess of investment demand over savings, as real assets increased, is yet another indicator of the demand driven aspect of the Malaysian economy(Choudhury, 1994). This in turn has generated the pattern of growth in real GDP, presently standing at 8 per cent real rate annually between 1988 and 1996 and for several years earlier.

The participatory nature of Islamic financial instruments is found to be linked with the general Islamic motivations of Malaysian Muslims. This provides the initial condition for much of savings to be directed away from interest-bearing transactions and into profit-loss sharing ones. But while this is an initial motivation for the growth and direction of investible funds, it has been reinforced by the strong performance of the instruments and its consequences in Malaysian economic growth.

Several consequences of the Islamic household and saver-investor decisions are noteworthy. First, the Islamic preferences are caused by material as well as social gains emanating from these instruments. On the side of material incentives are the prospect for profits in participatory businesses. On the side of social incentives is the moral compunction for Islamic belief (*Ibadah*). Second, the participatory nature of the financial instruments becomes the basis of profitability of these instruments. Third, the profitability of the instruments arises from their direct link with the real goods sector. Fourth, a circular cause-effect relationship is engendered between the Islamic motivations and the economic forces of Malays and the economic motivations of all in these participatory instruments. Financial resources are seen to be mobilized on the basis of yields that the real goods sector can promise in the presence of interlinkages between Islamic socioeconomic preferences and a diversity of saving and investment outlets. Consequently, the speculation and uncertainties associated with the presence of an excess supply of promissory notes and money supply in the economy are reduced. Thus, historically speaking, inflation has not been a problem in the Malaysian economy.

These Islamic preferences and their socioeconomic linkages define the endogenous nature Θ values in such participatory financial markets. The overall linkages as well as the continuing dynamics of the Θ values are in turn premised on the efficacy of the interlinkages. Malaysia today is experiencing a resurgence in Islamic thought and institutions not seen in any country in recent history. Malaysian Fifth and Sixth Development Plans, particularly the New Economic Policy followed by the New Development Policy, incorporate social equity and economic growth as complementary targets of development (Government of Malaysia, 1991b).

With regards to the central importance and dynamics of the Θ values in market processes and development, we quote an author who writes the following in the context of Malaysian development planning:

> If development refers primarily to the development of human intellect and conduct from ignorance to knowledge, and from foolishness to wisdom, from injustice in all its ontological, distributive and retributive aspects, to justice, then it is the spiritual aspect of man that must be understood and developed as a life-long struggle for perfection and happiness. (Daud,1994).

We have pointed out in this chapter that knowledge parameters as Θ values and the knowledge-based world view simply simulate knowledge to regenerate creative forms of reality.

Our study in this chapter points out that the goal of attaining complementarity between distributive justice and economic growth along with economic stabilization in the *Sixth Malaysian Plan* and the *Outline of Perspective Plan* cannot be attained in the presence of any neoclassical type marginalist substitution, because of the alienating nature given to the multiple goals in such an order. The principle of universal complementarity is found to be the alternative within which the development plan for achieving these goals can be carried out. Just as this requires the strength of consumer preferences to emanate and reinforce interactions between the premise of Islamic Law and market realities, so also there must exist extensive sectorial interlinkages for sustaining distribution, growth and self-reliant development in the Malaysian economy (Alias and Choudhury 1994).

Islamic Relevance of Malaysian Development Initiatives

The example of financial instruments and socioeconomic development in Malaysia, using Islamic approaches toward ameliorating the grassroots (Bumiputeras), is clearly reflected in alleviation of abject poverty. In this direction, the Islamic instruments of wealth tax redistribution, known as Zakah, have been made instrumental, and the focus of the use of such funds on the developmental front has been to empower the very poor in the rural sector. Besides, the possibility now to hold shares of Islamic certificates, such as Amanah Saham Nasional and Amanah Saham Bumiputeras, is a good example underlying the use of Islamic instruments for attaining equity with growth through the Malaysian booming capital markets. What makes these kinds of instruments of an Islamic nature is their total independence from interest-based financing of poor people's activities. In Islamic Law, applied to economic matters, interest of all kinds is strictly forbidden on the grounds that interest-based transactions are both socially alienating and economically wasteful, and costly against the regime of growth with redistribution for generating social well-being of all, particularly the poor and deprived. Contrary to such a practice of interest-free financial transactions through the process of empowering the poor, the paradigm of growth and redistribution in the literature has been cast within the old framework of marginal substitution between capital and workers, growth and social equity, efficiency and distributive equity. All of these have marginalized the poor, in spite of the best intentions that policy makers and governments might have toward socioeconomic development.

In Malaysia today, the Department of Religious Affairs, the educational institutions such as MARA, and the financial instruments presented in the previous section have together built the Islamic approach into Malaysian development plans. The focus of all development plans has been towards ameliorating the disadvantaged. For that reason we find that the New Economic Plan (NEP) was the dominant feature of all development plans between 1969 and 1974. Since 1995, NEP has been replaced by the New Development Plan, which carries the focus of social development within the context of Malaysia's globalization agenda and her drive toward full industrialization by the year 2020. Hence, in all respects, the agenda of attaining economic growth with redistribution occurring simultaneously, has been pursued consciously by the Malaysian development plans and the changing facets of her privatization program in the midst of the focus on globalization of the Malaysian economy.

Yet having mentioned the above success story, it cannot to be denied that the onslaught of neoclassical orientation to economic growth, as the accepted prescription of today's globalization agenda, has caught up with the Malaysian case. Poverty alleviation, although very successful, has come at a great cost to the Government of Malaysia in the form of transfers, loans and advances. But the productivity and self-reliance of the very poor could not be substantially improved in tandem with the changing global facets of the Malaysian economy. Lower productivity of the rural labour force in the face of liberal expenditure by government has meant, at times, a burst of inflationary pressures or a continuing disparity in asset holdings by the Bumiputeras. Only in a new environment of intellectual discourse between the educationalists, planners and the government can there arise the paradigmatic freshness for instilling distribution with growth in the globalization agenda of Malaysian political economy.

Political Economy of Markets in the Globalization Process

Next we will tie in the treatment of markets as systems of social contracts with the study of globalization as a system of market institutionalism. Globalization, as a concept in political economy, addresses systems of interdependencies between markets, producers, development and political institutions. Such interrelationships are studied with regards to issues of consumption, production, ownership, distribution and marketing, and the underlying technological implications in these relations. In the global order, such interdependence assumes forms that entrench power, resource control, ownership and wealth in the midst of conflicts. Interdependence also then addresses the issues of either conflict resolution or conflict explosion in the midst of interactions embedded in such interrelationships.

In this regard, the world-system theory would view these conflicts as a perpetuating convergence to western capitalism as a process of history. Political philosophies of the contemporary occidental schools, such as the "end-of-history" perspective (Fukuyama 1992); entitlement theories of Nozick (1974) and Sen (1986); disparate approaches to the concept of social justice by Hayek (1976) and Rawls (1971), all entrench an order of institutional power, individuation or self-seeking egoism in the modes of generation and distribution of wealth.

From these contending scenarios addressing the conflict resolution question, we note that globalization does not lead to politico-economic conflict resolution necessarily. The only way in which conflict resolution can be made effectual at the terminal point of a manifestation, though not the spirit, of social interactions is by the power of Eurocentricity. The Eurocentric model of global control and economic growth has thus emerged as a part and parcel of the capitalist transformation process in the world economy.

The concept of structural change is premised in the study of interrelationships that comprise the causes and effects of globalization as a process in interdependence. In this purview, we note that the study of the structure of economic growth, by examining the appropriateness of sectoral interlinkages, assumes a content that is quite different from the sheer measurement of economic growth as a principal economic indicator.

Financial markets premised in resource mobilization by means of interest-bearing transactions lose sight of the question of ownership and resource-control by microenterprises. Nations subjected to dollar-denominated currency controls are squeezed in by the exchange-rate alignments made in western capitals by virtue of their trade liberalization and subsidy policies that take place in NAFTA and EC. The consequent effects of world markets in commodities with plummeting prices drive out such enterprises from economic activity. The surge for volumes of expanded exports of primary goods by agricultural and commodity intensive economies causes problems of sustainability.

Thus a sheer macroeconomic address to financial markets, economic growth, the associated policies and institutional arrangements, cannot fully treat the issue of the *structure of globalization*. While macroeconomic coordination issues continue to hold importance in an environment of interdependence in the world economy, the study of its microeconomic structure is indispensable for examining the sectoral and systemic linkages that together explain the globalization process.

The topic of political economy of globalization and structural change is then the study of microeconomic foundations of structural shifts that underlie an examination of institutional and policy regimes prevailing in the global socio-economic environment. The underlying issues sometimes centre around marketization processes, diplomacy influencing socio-economic relations, sustainable development, international trade and economic integration.

There are, however, other market orders that can prove to be viable alternatives. The concept of market in Islamic political economy, for example, is essentially ethically endogenous (Choudhury and Malik ,1992) The nature of goods, preference regimes based on these goods, choice of technologies pertaining to the goods and the systems of rule-directed transformation of the market venue for attaining the well-being of the exchanging agents determine markets as extended systems of social contracts. Processes of social interactions and integrations now take up a central milieu for defining endogenous market preferences rather than the process-benign types of exogenous preferences in neoclassical models. Even in the context of embedded markets and the informal sectors provided by Polanyi (1944) and Holton (1992), one finds transformation of markets from the ethically benign order of neoclassicism into contractarian systems. Bowles (1991) recently has advocated such endogenous contracts as the real reflection coming out of a system of growing socio-economic interdependence. Such interdependence, in a truly interactive and integrative order with ethical endogeneity of preferences, can ground the foundation of objective globalization and structural change.

Malaysia in the Midst of the Globalization Process

We have pointed out that even in the face of good intentions, policies, programs and proven successes of the Malaysian Government in using endogenous social forces for attaining economic growth with redistribution, there are critical impediments before her that are of the neoclassical nature. In the face of such approaches, a neoclassical view on meeting the globalization demands of economic growth and privatization may leave out the moral and social perspectives. This conscious realization, and thus the alternatives, must be endogenized within the total Malaysian developmental future, even as the nation advances toward her target of a fully industrialized nation by the year 2020. We intend to reflect on some of the fears that can arise from a neoclassical perspective of Malaysian development in the midst of globalization.

Even the history of the structure of growth, as opposed to the secular trend on persistent economic growth rates for Malaysia, has shown that there remain both inherent marginalization and shifts between the agricultural and manufacturing sectors and between the human capital development, asset ownership of target indigenous people (Bumiputeras) and the privileged ones. In the midst of these contending factors of industrialization, the concepts of competitiveness in the midst of private and public sector relationships should be taken up within a picture of socio-economic development based on Malaysia's indigenous and innovative approaches, rather than being premised on imitative capitalism of the global economy.

Some Empirical Inferences on Markets and Globalization

In view of the interrelationships explained respecting the institutional structure of market transformation in today's globalization process, we undertake the following empirical analysis to explain some of the relationships embodied among the following variables respecting globalization: GDP, foreign direct investments, debts, exchange rate and interest rate movements (see Table 1). Subsequently, we make an intuitive analysis respecting fiscal and monetary policies with ethical connotation of the type mentioned in the case of Malaysia respecting mobilization of financial resources.

Table 1: Movements in Some External Sector Indicators for Malaysia

YEAR	*GDP*	*GDP %*	*FDI*	*Debt/ GNP %*	*ER*	*INTR (M)*	*INTR (US)*	*KLSE*
1989	72,409	9.2	8,653	43.58	2.70	7.00	10.50	174.2
1990	79,463	9.7	17,629	37.46	2.70	7.50	10.00	59.3
1991	86,345	8.7	17,055	35.67	2.73	9.00	6.50	1.9
1992	93,072	7.8	17,772	30.61	2.61	9.50	6.50	71.0
1993	100,838	8.3	6,287	33.41	2.70	8.50	6.00	625.5
1994	109,368	8.5	6,972	37.08	2.66*	2.66*	6.63*	36.5

Source: Economic Report 1994/95, Kuala Lumpur, Malaysia: Ministry of Finance
GDP: millions of ringgit (Malaysian dollar) in constant prices;
FDI: foreign direct investment in millions of ringgit;
Db/GNP:debt/GNP ratio;
ER: annual average exchange rate of ringgit to US dollar; * denotes estimate based on data for the months January to October 1994;
INTR(M): commercial bank lending rate in Malaysia; * denotes estimate based on data for the months January to October 1994;
INTR(US):commercial bank lending rate in USA; * denotes estimate based on data for the months January to October 1994;
KLSE: Kuala Lumpur stock exchange market turnover.

Malaysia's experience with globalization in the midst of trade liberalization, foreign direct investment, economic growth and susceptibility to monetary policies enacted in the G7, can be read in an indicative manner from the above table. Monetary policy in industrialized nations is characterized by attempts to stabilize their inflationary trends and attain steady economic growth with requisite variations in interest rates and exchange rate mechanism. In the above table we note that declining interest rate in the USA, which happens to predominate in the G7 scene, is not adequately synchronized by similar interest rate trend in Malaysia.

In very recent years, sustained high Malaysian interest rates are found to maintain steady levels of the exchange rate. Yet the expected effect of this to increase foreign direct investments and inflation rate are not found to have been attained. Foreign direct investments have declined in recent years as seen in the Table. Inflation rate increased slightly from 2.8 per cent in 1989 and 3.1 per cent in 1990, to approximately 4 per cent between 1991 and 1994.

The result of declining foreign direct investments could have been due to portfolio diversification by foreign investors across the South-East Asia region. It could also have been due to a deliberate policy of the Malaysian Government to limit overly reliance on foreign direct investments. Whatever the cause, the result of declining direct foreign investments does not seem to have favored Malaysia's external debt problem. This can be read from the large debt/GNP ratio in the above table. The implication of such trends in external debt, economic growth and foreign direct investments is that much of economic growth, signified by the high real rates of change in GDP, depends on imports of technology and capital inputs. This in turn worsens the balance of payments situation.

It is also well-known that during the 1989-94 period, the U.S. dollar appreciated against most currencies. This caused other countries to hold their foreign reserves in U.S. dollar- denominated assets. Thus, when it is possible for the U.S. monetary authorities to lower the U.S. treasury bill rates in the face of appreciated exchange rates, then changes in reserve situations of other countries become governed by the exchange rate mechanism. On the other hand, when U.S. interest rates increase, these changes in reserves are determined by U.S. interest rates. Hence, in both cases, the globalization picture for developing countries remains predominated by the interest rate and exchange rate mechanisms of the U.S. monetary authorities in particular, and of the G7 in general. The more volatile these movements are the more serious are the external sector uncertainties of countries that hold their assets in the U.S. dollar denominated assets (IMF Survey Nov.

1994). Indeed, the SDR of the IMF, which happens to be another kind of weighted monetary asset in which all countries hold part of their reserves, is weighted as 40 per cent for the U.S. dollar; 21 per cent for the German Mark; 17 per cent for the Japanese Yen; 11 per cent for the French Franc; and 11 per cent for the British Pound. Consequently, this also gives 19.1 per cent of the voting rights to the U.S.(Brown & Hogendorn 1994) One therefore recognizes the overflow of G7 presence in general, and the U.S. influence in particular, in all foreign reserve managements of developing countries. The situation intensifies with the globalization impact of international trade, liberalization and their resulting effects on external sector debt and imbalance.

In the case of Malaysia, these inferences imply that the marginal effectiveness of her own monetary policy to stabilize the economy appears to be limited by the exchange rate and interest rate mechanisms of the U.S. and G7 countries. Yet it would appear that although this remains an indicative inference at present, the KLSE turnover rates suggest a good mobilization of capital internally, ever since 1992. This is also the time when the Malaysian Government has stepped up its program of mobilizing Bumiputera financial shares through various types of instruments. Some of these were discussed earlier.

It can then be inferred that in a global scene, free movements of foreign direct investments and the impact of interest rates and exchange rates at home in response to the stabilization policies by monetary authorities in industrial nations cause hardships to external sector adjustment. The way out of this is to turn to productive self-reliant development at home. This in turn can be realized by effective mobilization of indigenous capital in a diversity of ways by means of innovative financial instruments.

The lesson then is clear. The consequences of globalization in the midst of pure market transformation remain essentially unstable in the external sector of national economies. Only productive self-reliant mobilization of indigenous resources by national economies can generate stability and sustained economic growth.

In the context of market response to innovative growth, as presented earlier, the secondary financial instruments to mobilize capital and the resurgence of popularity of such instruments among the masses can go far in adducing productive growth. Capital market and its relationship to economic growth are thus seen to be greatly influenced by the so-called non-economic factors, which are found to generate profound economic consequences. Such factors arise from motivations and institutional arrangements aimed at making the masses participate productively and ethically in the market process.

Thus, markets cease to be governed by the invisible hand principle. Instead, they are found to be distinctly governed by motivational forces and institutions. These in turn generate the social contracts between governments, individuals and markets. In the present case, such contracts become importantly necessary cause and effect of the external sector disequilibrium in a venue of globalization.

Conclusion

Real world situations, exemplified by cases of policy and institutional influences in international economic transactions, sustainable development issues, economic integrations governed by non-economic preferences (to guide mutuality of interests along with economic considerations), and alternative menus of production sharing in a globalizing world, point to the need to understand market transactions in substantively different ways. That is to replace the traditional concept of markets either as contracts or exchanges among buyers and sellers with invisible market processes. There are other profound factors that fundamentally influence the nature of market transactions. These are endogenous phenomena that enter markets as cause and effect in determining social contracts among transactors. In such a milieu, the interactive relationships between polity and the market place via endogenous preferences and menus with extensive complementarities and interlinkages define the concept of the market as a system of social contracts.

We have tried to explain various treatments of markets as systems of exchange in comparative perspectives. The conclusion we reach is that globally extensive agent-agent interactions that form social contracts are possible only when such a system becomes knowledge induced, i.e. interactive. The concept of a knowledge-based market transformation is thus found to be substantively different from the traditional ones. Now agent-specific preferences and production menus become endogenized by the evolving nature of knowledge premised fundamentally in a given primal epistemology.

Such an epistemology generates the social contracts and moves them forward. The creative and regulative attributes of the epistemology has thus the power to unify the system under the underlying system of social contracts. The market as a system of social contracts is thus an interactive-integrative evolutionary order. It provides a concept of market distinct from that found in liberal economic concepts.

The case of Malaysia, in terms of her financial and economic performance, has shown that in the context of globalization, the external sector parameters do not appear to be sustainable for long-term self-reliant economic growth in the neoclassical economic world. Yet this adverse effect appears to be circumvented by Malaysia's internal market transformation process with motivational factors. As an example, such factors are reflected in the effective mobilization of financial resources through Islamic financial instruments and institutions. Thus, a knowledge induced transformation process is seen to have the potential to outweigh the adverse effects of *wertfrei* market transformation in the globalization scene.

References

Alias, H. M. and Choudhury, M. A. "Structural Adjustment Within Malaysian Agriculture in Response to Rapid Industrialization." paper presented at the East Asian Economic Association, Taiwan, August 25-28, 1994; now appearing as a chapter in M.A. Choudhury, A. Malik and A. Adnan(eds.), *Alternative Perspectives in Third World Development: The Case of Malaysia,* London: Macmillan, forthcoming.

Bentham, J. *An Introduction to the Principles of Morals and Legislation.* London: T. Payne & Sons, 1789.

Bowles, S. "What Markets Can--and cannot--Do." *Challenge,* 1991, Vol.34, No.4, July/August; pp. 11-16.

Brown, W. B. and Hogendorn, J. S. *International Economics.* New York: Addison-Wesley Publishing Co, 1994, pp. 579-80.

Buchanan, J. M. *The Limits of Liberty, Between Anarchy and Leviathan.* Chicago: University of Chicago Press, 1975, chs. 2,3,4.

Choudhury, M. A. "Why Cannot Neoclassicism Explain Resource Allocation in Islamic Political Economy?" in E. Ahmad ed. *The Role of Private and Public Sectors in Economic Development in an Islamic Perspective,* Herndon: International Institute of Islamic Thought, 1996a, pp. 17-44.

_____. "Markets as a System of Social Contracts." *International Journal of Social Economics,* 1996b Vol. 23, No. 1, pp. 17-36.

_____."Malaysian Economy is Demand Driven." *New Straits Times Saturday Forum,* Aug.15, 1994.

_____. "Theories of Social Contract and the Principle of Ethical Endogeneity," in *The Unicity Precept and the Socio-Scientific Order*, Lanham, MD: University Press of America, 1993, Ch.4.

Choudhury, M. A. and Malik, U. A. *Foundations of Islamic Political Economy.* London: Macmillan: St. Martin's Press, 1992.

Coase, R. "The Problem of Social Cost," in R. Dorfman & N.S. Dorfman eds., *Economics of the Environment, Selected Readings,*New York, NY: W.W. Norton, 1993, pp.109-38.

Daud, W. M. N. W. "Some Basic Issues of Development in Malaysia," in *Malaysian Development Experience*, INTAN: Kuala Lumpur, Malaysia; 1994, pp.855-885.

Ellerman, D. P. "The Democratic Firm: A Cooperative-ESOP Model," in J.D. Wisman ed., *Worker Empowerment, The Struggle for Workplace Democracy*, New York: The Bookstrap Press, 1991, pp. 83-100.

Ferry, L. and Renault, A. (trans. by F. Phillip) "The Division of Society and the State as a Value: Liberalism and Human Rights," in *From the Rights of Man to the Republican Idea,* Chicago: University of Chicago Press, 1992, pp.91-109.

Friedman, A. *Foundations of Modern Analysis.* New York, NY: Dover Publications, 1982, p. 79.

Fukuyama, F. *The End of History and the Last Man.* New York, NY: The Free Press, 1992.

Government of Malaysia *Sixth Malaysian Plan 1991-1995.* Kuala Lumpur, Malaysia, 1991a,

_____.*The Second Outline Perspective Plan 1991-2000.* Kuala Lumpur, Malaysia.,1991b.

Grandmont, J. M. "Temporary Equilibrium," in J. Eatwell, M. Milgate & P. Newman eds., *New Palgrave: General Equilibrium*, New York, NY: W.W. Norton; 1989, pp. 297-304.

Hayek, F. A. "Law, Legislation and Liberty." *The Mirage of Social Justice*, Vol.2, Chicago: The University of Chicago Press, 1976.

_____."Studies in Philosophy." *Politics and Economics*, Chicago: The University of Chicago Press, 1967.

Holton, R. J. *Economy and Society.* London, Eng.: Routledge,1972.

IMF Survey, "The International Monetary System: Evolution Rather than Revolution." Washington D.C. ,Nov. 1994

Ismail, A. H. "Sources and Uses of Funds -- A Case Study of Bank Islam Malaysia Berhad," in M. Ariff and M.A. Mannan, eds*., Developing a System of Financial Instruments,.* Jeddah, Saudi Arabia: Islamic Research and Training Institute & Kuala Lumpur, Malaysia: Ministry of Finance, Government of Malaysia, 1990, pp. 193-205.

Kirzner, I. M. "Entrepreneurship, Entitlement and Economic Justice," in J. Paul ed*., Reading Nozick*, Totowa, NJ: Rowman & Littlefeld,1983.

Mansfleld, E. "Prices and Output under Oligopoly," in *Microeconomic, Theory and Applications.* New York, NY: W.W. Norton;1985, p. 340.

Martin, S. "Oligopoly -- Collusion," in *Industrial Economics, Economic Analysis and Public Policy,* New York, NY: Macmillan Publishing Co, 1988, p. 156.

Mehmet, O. "Alternative Concepts of Development: A Critique of Euro-Centric Theorizing." *Humanomics*, 1990, Vol.6, No.3, pp.55-67.

Nozick, R. *Anarchy, State and Utopia.* Oxford: Blackwell, 1974.

Osborne, M. J. and Rubinstein, A. *A Course in Game Theory.* Cambridge, MA: The MIT Press, 1994, .

Phelps, E. S. "Distributive Justice," in J. Eatwell, M. Milgate & P. Newman eds., *The New Palgrave: Social Economics,*New York, NY: W. W. Norton, 1989, pp.31-4.

Polanyi, K. *The Great Transformation.* New York, NY: Rinehart, 1944.

Quinton, A. *Utilitarian Ethics*. La Salle, ILL: Open Court 1989.

Rawls, J. *A Theory of Justice*. Cambridge, MA: Harvard University Press, 1971.

Sen, A. *Poverty and Famines, and Essay on Entitlement and Deprivation.* Oxford.: Clarendon Press, 1986.

Siddiqi, M. N. *Partnership and Profit-Sharing in Islamic Law.* Leicester: The Islamic Foundation, 1985.

14

A NEW INTERNATIONAL ECONOMIC PRIORITY: *Policy Responsibilities Among Multilateral and Regional Institutions*

H. Edward English

Carleton University, Canada

The increasing complexity of the world economy since 1945 has resulted from the economic emergences of the Cold War, decolonization, and in the last two decades, from the diversity of economic and political achievements of developing countries, the growing importance of consensus among North-South groups, and the decline of cohesive political action among the larger powers following the end of the Cold War. Following numerous attempts by developing countries to form their own regional groups, the recent shift toward North-South regionalism has resulted in NAFTA and APEC, the latter being a much lower form of policy consensus, but perhaps relevant to an exemplary combination of the diversity of development levels and converging cooperative strategies of private enterprise and complementary public policy.

The objective of this paper is to call attention to the new economic and other circumstances that are likely to govern the nature of the groupings of countries that will most influence the agenda priorities in international negotiations, especially those that deal with economic and social aspects of international cooperation and the evolution of relevant institutional arrangements, both multilateral and regional.

The first quarter century after World War II appears with the advantage of hindsight to have been an era of simplicity—clear objectives and unified purposes. The obvious folly of conflict among nations called for the creation of supernational institutions, and the UN, IMF, GATT and the World Bank were set up. In retrospect, the conflict between Communism and Capitalistic Democracy served multilateral institutions well. In part, they served as a meeting ground for the two great ideologies, but above all the Cold War focused the priorities of other leaders on basic solidarity in support of one of the two protagonists. Neither side was under the illusion that any country, not even the largest, could "go it alone." The multilateral economic institutions had the special advantage for the "West" that they were completely controlled by their side in the ideological competition, and this reinforced political solidarity.

A common view in 1970 and for some time after that was that the recovery of Europe and East Asia, especially Japan, meant that consensus on economic issues would require cooperation among at least six larger economic powers, the United States, Japan and the four larger members of the EEC. Canada, as a seventh member of this group, because of its disproportionately large role in the development of post-war institutions, contributed a somewhat distinctive perspective reflecting its search for a degree of independence from its large neighbor. While the Cold War reinforced the unity of the seven, decolonization greatly increased the number and potential of less developed countries, and their capacity for and interest in the regional integration, generally applying the GATT Article XXIV model, and encouraged by the EEC example. Some schemes proved to be too grand and too protectionist, such as LAFTA. Others in Africa and Central America were not large enough, or politically sufficiently stable to survive as growth-enhancing units. In some cases, notably in West Africa, the failure to integrate small economies is traceable mainly to economically and culturally inappropriate boundaries reflecting the consequence of French and British competition for colonial power. The responsibility for the subsequent failure of European Community links with African developing countries must be shared, and not primarily attributed to the weak base for the evolution of political institutions in that region.

An understanding of the role of regional cooperation requires an appreciation of the basis for optimal use of regional arrangements. The extensive experience of the EEC provides an appropriate starting point for the analysis of regional groupings as a major means toward promotion of multilateral objectives. After that the treatment of new regional initiatives, involving developing as well as more economically developed countries, can be assessed against the historical and current record of the EEC.

The Unique Example of the EEC

Yet at the same time, regionalism was born in what has proved to be its most spectacular case, the European Economic Community. It was promoted by the Organization for European Economic Cooperation, a collective effort to achieve reconstruction assisted by Marshall Plan aid as well as the International Bank for Reconstruction and Development, the original and still official name for the World Bank. The most important aspect of EEC, for the purpose of this paper, is that the EEC is the only example of a regional integration scheme which sought to move to a high level of economic integration, and whose leaders contemplated that this could result in a kind of political union. In theoretical discussions of integration it is pointed out that there may be an optimum level of integration, and that it may differ from case to case. This is likely because the perceived benefits and costs added at each step will vary, and even from case to case, so that there is no obvious reason to expect such groupings to move to the same high level of integration. The reason for the European Community's interest in more complete economic and political union seems primarily related to a commitment to net benefits of political cohesion that go beyond the aggregate benefits from economic integration. It is argued in international economics that the largest economic benefits are derived from the achievement of free trade, and that some additional benefits are captured through a common market, especially through the free flow of direct investment and accompanying technology. However, even the common market phase introduces substantial social costs, especially when free flow of labor is permitted. The policy coordination associated with economic union presents problems for macroeconomic policy. Are fixed exchange rates between countries better that flexible rates, when the former may require compensatory fiscal transfers among member nations in the group?

Even in Europe, the debates on the Maastricht Treaty pose the question whether benefits from political integration compensate for the costs of some of the ongoing inter-group policy coordination as well as fiscal arrangements required. In other parts of the world these issues are avoided for both economic and political reasons. For example, in the Canada-United States free trade agreement, it is clear that most Canadians have no interest in formal political integration. The obvious reason is that the difference in size of the two countries is perceived as likely to reduce the possibility of retaining independent social and cultural policies. However, the other factor is a Canadian view that most of the benefits derive from free trade and capital flows, so that the agreement should be judged on its ability to put in place and preserve a joint framework for policy cooperation and monitoring and adjudication of subsidy/countervail and other trade practices. Australia and New Zealand, as smaller economies whose bilateral trade relations are less important relative to their commerce with third parties, have introduced closer economic relations without any perceived need for political integration. Among the numerous free trade arrangements involving developing countries, the only example of full economic union that comes to mind is that among East African states, Kenya, Tanzania, and Uganda, all former British colonies. The East African Community was created in 1967 after the three countries were made independent, and sought to preserve both a common currency and fiscal union established by the colonial regime. The Community disintegrated within five years, primarily for political reasons.

Shifting Priorities Since the 1960s

The above discussion is intended mainly to illustrate how even under the circumstances prior to the end of the Cold War, regional schemes were emerging, and in widely diverse forms. The changes in the world economy since the 1960s and in East-West relations since the mid-1980s have even more fundamentally altered conditions and priorities. Two major changes in the 1960s were the full restoration of the European and Japanese economies, and the decolonization that greatly increased the number of economies involved in the multilateral institutions. The former change shifted the role of the US to leader among economic powers rather than sole hegemon, as reflected in the centrality of US-EEC negotiations in the Kennedy Round, and in the revision of IMF arrangements after the 1971 crisis. The latter change resulted in UNCTAD, and later much complication in all multilateral negotiations. It should also be noted that by the 1960s, the other hegemon, the Soviet Union, had also experienced a serious decline in its leadership role, particularly as a result of the breakdown in Sino-Soviet cooperation.

Only after the rise of Gorbachev in 1984, however, did the forces for political and economic cooperation result in substantial changes in focus, and in perceived need for new institutional arrangements. This was the result of at least three factors; the larger number and diversity of players, the change in the agenda facing both political and economic organizations, and the reduced need for and influence of the remaining hegemon.

On the political-security level, the US still has greater importance, and continued to exercise influence where military power had to be mobilized, as in the

Gulf conflict. But it was clear in this case and even more so in the former Yugoslavia that the US could not act alone politically, and that the failure of others to develop coherent leadership made it difficult to prevent mayhem, and to achieve effective concerted action.

On the economic level, hegemonic power is much less important, and has been further handicapped by the financial problems related to dual deficits that limit US leverage internationally. The diversity of actors has now gone much beyond the recovery of Europe and rise of Japan as the second economic superpower, to the rise of newly industrialized countries, especially in East Asia, and the major effect they are having on other developing countries, inducing the widespread adoption of strategies of outward oriented development policies. This has generated North-South flows of trade and investment especially in the Western Pacific and the Western Hemisphere. The change in the agenda of multilateral economic institutions has been particularly evident in the Uruguay Round and in new forms of regional institution-building. It is these to which the remainder of this paper is directed.

The Uruguay Round was forward looking; it acknowledged that the older tariff and traditional non-tariff issues, both mainly focused on border decisions affecting trade, were being superseded by new, mainly non-border decisions. Some of these relate to domestic policies that transcend or evade trade commitments, e.g. safeguard or other import-surge controls, interpretations and appeals of anti-dumping and subsidy/countervail claims. Others are unilateral or bilateral moves tied to balance of trade conditions (Super 301 in the US) or "voluntary export restraints." Others are even more distant from border controls. These are summarized under three main headings:

1. Competition Policies
2. Investment and Technology Policies
3. Environment Policies

These will be addressed following a brief classification of the multilateral, regional and bilateral (or sub-regional) institutional channels for proposing, developing and administering such policies.

Among the multilateral institutions, WTO and the World Bank may be most relevant, the former being the prime agency for policies in group 1, the latter for group 2. A cooperative effort of both institutions is needed for policies in group 3; since some of the relevant issues relate more to investment, whereas others are primarily trade oriented. Regional or sub-regional responsibility would be appropriate for policies where a regional initiative might be especially valuable, either because the issue is not global in scope or because a regional initiative could be exemplary, and the region could be chosen because it is both suited and likely politically to take a lead, resulting in a code or other scheme open on a conditional MFN basis to all other countries.

A topic that could be added here relates to Labor Standards. Definition and policy prescription are handicapped by the difficulty of drawing the line between human rights issues, such as child or forced labor, and lower wages associated with stage of development. While ILO efforts to develop guidelines for evaluation of such issues can be helpful, action by agreement between countries in the same regional cooperation arrangement seem more likely to command mutual respect of the governments and producers involved.

A Common Theoretical Context—Market Failure and "Subsidiarity"

Economists use market failure as a general way of describing situations warranting intervention by public agencies; international, national, or regional or local governments within the nation. The economics of federalism has long included the theory that public functions should be performed at the level at which they can be supplied most efficiently (see Breton and Scott (1978) on the theory of federalism). However, the question remains as to who makes the decisions? Clearly, if one starts with a nation state with substantial constitutional authority, then the power of decision will largely rest with the federal authority. However, as both Canadian and United States experience indicates, the courts may over time interpret the constitutional assignment of powers in a direction favoring another level of government. The problem is greater in areas where international relations require intervention, since neither political power nor legal institutions have comprehensive authority. Functionally specific world government then depends on international agreements among states having a high degree of sovereignty, generally guided by a collective bias favoring national authority, and a higher level of sensitivity to the attitudes and values that differentiate cultures than to those that argue for collective international action. As the largest powers have the least need to accommodate the preferences of smaller and more economically dependent countries, rational allocation of functions to supernational authority may be further constrained in multilateral economic bodies.

In general terms, it becomes very important that to achieve upward assignment of economic functions, there must be effective cooperation of like-minded medium-sized and smaller states. With the large number of states now being entitled to participation in multilateral institutions, it becomes increasing probable that small groups, probably with a regional configuration will have an advantage over multilateral institutions with a universal membership in the creation of workable supernational arrangements, especially those governing economic functions. Given the range of countries at widely different levels of development now populating the global economy, the groups that promote new multilateral initiatives will need to reflect the interests or at least the aspirations of that variety.

The application of subsidiarity should probably include means of stimulating initiatives toward the establishment of regional or functional bodies that either in an exemplary or assimilative fashion could lead to wider consensus positions and the means of implementing them. It is appropriate now to turn to the "new issues" in international economic relations that could be served by this or other kinds of subsidiarity.

Three groups of issues will be discussed. They are all concerned with market conditions, the main differentiation being the time context. The first group, generally gathered under the heading "competition policies", relate traditionally to current and near-future structural and behavioral conditions and their effect on allocative and operating efficiency. The second group concerns investment and technology change through creation, acquisition and application of new technologies. Although these are always present in management decision-making agendas, they tend to be separated from day-to-day operations, except at the highest executive levels and their staffs, who must prepare for periodic directors meetings. It should be stressed that these decisions are the least objective management makes, since they include not only the production and design choices made by those who populate the ranks of professionals in any enterprise, but also the technology of top management and directors. In recent years, for example, those responsible for financial judgements have not in many instances been earning high marks for their choice or exercise of investment skills. The typical time context involved here is three to five years, with some attention to longer run technological trends.

The third group, now receiving much more attention, are environmental and/or sustained development issues and policies. These apply to economic performance much further into the future than issues regularly addressed at the decision making level of individual enterprises. However, just as there is no clear time separation between business or public day-to-day management choices, and consideration of improved production and management methods, there is a blending of concerns governing investment decisions with those related to efficient means of dealing with environmental challenges and appropriate investment for sustainable development. The major difficulty in this group is that conventional economic criteria require application of discount rates that seem to disqualify choices promising returns over many decades rather than only one or two.

How much market failure is there? A simple first assessment of the degree and forms of market failure is indicated by the incidence of intervention on a piecemeal basis that has often characterized the entry of governments to date. A generalization relating to international intervention is that public policy-makers have been most active in the trade policy area, and that this has focused on removal of barriers between markets on the assumption that this would substantially reduce their inefficiencies. Most of this effort was centered on GATT and the negotiations it sponsored, although as already noted, regional integration pursued the same ends. As border measures were reduced or controlled, more attention has been directed to competitive practice in private markets, especially those that appear to restrict import competition by permitting non-competitive behavior in domestic industries that face import competition. These will be discussed in more detail later.

During this same period, there was a much less recognized need for interventions at the international level in relation to investment and technology flows. Existing global institutions and rules related mainly to intellectual property protection. The principal issues that emerged focused on the different interests of exporters and importers of investment funds (especially as foreign direct investment (FDI)) and of protected technology. However, OECD membership meant that the guidelines reflected the motivation to harmonize developed country capital exporter concerns more than those of capital importing countries. The importing countries had mixed views on national interests affected by the control of some of their industries and sought to introduce restrictions on some subsidiary practices governed by head office policies. At the same time, their concern regarding technology import was that the price charged by the exporter was too high.

Although rules on investment practices were contemplated in the draft of the ITO, there was insufficient pressure in subsequent years to produce a system with sanctions comparable to those introduced for trade restrictions under GATT. Hence, group 2 activities were left to bilateral dealings, except for efforts to draft codes to govern the treatment of international direct investment, the OECD initiative being a leading example. In fact, in the 1980s attitudes toward FDI have become more positive, as its effectiveness in transferring both capital· and technology has been widely recognized. The issue of the optimum level of protection for intellectual property remains a more contentious question.

Group 3 issues, relating to sustainable development policies, and especially those affecting environmental conditions, are becoming much more central to international economic negotiations. Public intervention is deemed much more important now, because social costs are more often and more clearly specified than in the past.

Competition Policy Issues

The nature and importance of market failure should be explored further if priorities are to be identified in the three groups described. Market failure is most often defined in terms of departures from competitive markets. Monopoly or various degrees and forms of oligopoly are cited as reasons for requiring public intervention to introduce more competition or if that is not feasible to regulate behavior. In fact, since free trade exposes markets to much more competition than is workable in most national markets, it is a legitimate question whether regulation is often necessary except for non-traded goods, the only other notable exceptions being highly integrated markets such as air and ocean transport. The view that globalization has made even world markets concentrated oligopolies is probably over-simplified. Even the high profile automotive sector has become a very competitive oligopoly, with price, profits and market share all proving vulnerable. A similar condition has increasingly invaded the computer sector, once known for the market share dominance of one firm. The issues that remain, setting aside for the moment those related to investment and new technology, are the basic ones: cartels, mergers and vertical integration that may preempt access. In addition, there are the more persistent barriers to entry. Some of these are most closely associated with technology protected by patents and copyright, which require judgement on the criterion of optimum incentive to innovation. Others relate to marketing of consumer goods, protected by trademark and intensively supported by advertising and other forms of marketing activity. This is one of the challenging issues, since it biases consumer behavior through the disproportionate pressure on spending it effects in the sectors involved. The information content of this allocation of resources is often questioned. This question is of particular concern to developing countries since it raises the cost of such goods and obstructs entry of simpler substitutes from the producers of those economies.

There are other sources of market failure that cast doubt on the efficiency of even the most competitively structured markets. These relate, for example to industries using "common property" resources, especially the fisheries, and particularly those beyond the territorial limits of a national jurisdiction in the oceans. A similar problem exists for pools of petroleum that lie beneath surface property held by more than one proprietor, although in most cases sub-surface rights are separately controlled.

International Investment and Technology Issues

It is interesting that international investment is an area of little international intervention, and that there has even been a decline in interest in such intervention, especially in respect to direct investment, which paradoxically assigns more right of control. This decline appears to be the result of a growing appreciation of the combined capital and technology transfer contribution to economic development, the availability of alternative sources following the end of political colonialism, and perhaps because the option of acquiring capital and technology separately is less attractive since the debt crisis of the 1980s. National intervention has been important in the past. Because it was concentrated in the host countries, and the capital exporters at first preferred to deal with their hosts one by one, rather than to risk international supervision of FDI; it is only very recently that codes and other multilateral efforts have been initiated. The efforts to introduce control of trade-related investment controls in the Uruguay Round has achieved only modest success, in part because it focused on issues of mainly historical importance. Because FDI passing among capital exporters has been more substantial in recent years, there have also been more political pressures in these countries to monitor and even control the operating conditions affecting foreign investors. This developed in part during the sharp rise in Japanese investment in the United States and Europe during the 1980s, when the less accessibility of Japan to FDI stood out as an undesirable contrast. However the major issues raised in GATT proved to be such traditional ones as export controls and domestic procurement requirements, now much less significant than the concerns of developing countries over training of local personnel. The movement toward an investment policy or code at the international level requires a much more effective North-South context than has been evident in the recent GATT negotiations.

The related issue of intellectual property generates much more significant contention between developed and developing countries. It is implicit that market failure is widespread in the market for technology, and that a principal means of increasing allocative efficiency is to create departures from pure competition, by creating monopolies of different duration depending on the form of intellectual property involved, the longest (almost permanent for trademarks), decades for copyrights, and at least seventeen years for patents. The rationale for these differences is unclear. The problem in any effort to evaluate the efficiency of the system is based on judgements as to the social rate of return appropriate to research and development. The present practice was determined by the countries most active in technological development in the last two centuries. Clearly the less developed countries have had less commitment to the system from the outset. For example, the US did not join the European-based copyright system for about one hundred years, and Canada as recently as 1968 introduced a system involving compulsory import licensing arrangement that led to a substantial trade in generics, a policy it reversed only in late 1992. Less developed countries continue to evade the rules devised in richer countries, even though many of them adopt their own IP laws under pressure. Sectors such as educational and health services feel constrained by the higher costs of copyrighted and patented inputs. In this area, as in that related to TRIMs, particular attention is required to the forms by which such international laws are applied. It is not only an equity matter, since investment in human capital is so important to efficient development. Action to limit royalties and prices of affected products is one approach suggested by recent experience, but the appropriate acceptable levels cannot easily be identified.

A special note on the resource industries is in order. Investment in forest-based industries, and also in those using depleting minerals involves a particularly long time-axis. A very low interest rate is required to warrant exploitation of a temperate zone forest on a replacement basis. In all likelihood, the social rate of return would always require upward adjustment, and compensating subsidy or other support, to result in continuity of the resource base. This is more easily rationalized in the tropical zone because of the oxygen contribution made by that resource. Clearly, the benefit that all share would seem to warrant a net subsidy from the temperate zone countries, especially given their typically higher income levels. The institutional means by which this is achieved is still to be developed.

Finally, in the context of temporal allocation decisions, the role of financial services should be noted. The experience of recent years has highlighted the costs of instability in financial markets and the uncertainty it has created for those responsible for both private and public investment decisions. It is not formally a trade issue, but its impact on trade and especially on the rationality of financial investment decisions has a substantial impact on exchange rates and on the size and pattern of debt. Here the public policy action required is more comprehensive, uniform, and transparent system of information flows, reducing the likelihood of misguided assignment of portfolios, and of security market manipulation, intentional or otherwise. The recent establishment of a Japanese equivalent of the US Securities and Exchange Commission is a welcome example. The system could still benefit from a more integrated effort including attention to ways of introducing on a regular basis the transactions involving those developing countries whose role in such transactions is on a steady growth path.

Environment and International Transactions

This is the newest of the new issues. It has not been addressed comprehensively by the traditional multilateral institutions, although the World Bank has made a substantial start in its World Development Report 1992, entitled "Development and the Environment." Many of the conceptual issues are indicated in the foregoing discussion. A wide range of benefit-cost conditions apply. In some instances they can be measured in private decisions, e.g. smoke pollution and the health of workers in a plant or office building. But they most often involve private and social net benefit. For the purpose of this discussion, a key distinction can be made between local, bilateral, regional and multilateral concerns. Many instances of water pollution are purely local and bilateral, though all nations bordering a particular river system will usually be required to cooperate. Air pollution is often more broadly regional. The most global environmental concerns are those related to ozone depletion and global warming. The central question is at what level each environmental issue should be addressed. The answer is not necessarily linked to the locus of each problem. The general and persistent awareness of the accumulative effect of sources of environmental damage is more likely to lead to appropriate action than exemplary behavior at one location, given the human propensity for procrastination. For example, economizing on energy use in the interest of reducing the rate of global warming is countered in the minds of North Americans by the ingrained preference for private automobile transportation.

Essentially, the larger issues are linked with economic development, but not in the simplistic way often cited by well-meaning environmentalists. The argument that all forms of economic expansion exacerbate environmental degradation is indeed simplistic. It is made to justify population control, limits to expansion of output, and even limits to particular sources of growth such as trade liberalization. As Kym Anderson (1992) and others have pointed out, economic growth can be and often is a major source of support for the environment. It is a statistical fact that population growth slows down as countries achieve higher living standards, and that higher incomes provide them with the means to finance policy programs designed to preserve environmental health. The basic necessities of life no longer consume most of their incomes.

But an important distinction must be drawn between growth and development. Mere expansion of economic activity is not the prime purpose of life. The notions of allocative efficiency in the use of resources implies a combination of the productive patterns of consumption and investment, which together lead to an optimum pattern and level of activity, including an optimum (not a maximum) growth rate. The requirement that output of goods and services must satisfy some politically or socially acceptable standard may also mean some sacrifice in growth, though that will differ from one society to another. Sustainable development could be defined as the level that takes account of all these priorities.

To focus on trade issues and especially on a trade-off between environment and trade is, as already suggested, particularly irrelevant. It is one of the sources of efficient allocation and use of resources, as it enables each economy to take advantage of its particular productive strengths. To argue that trade restrictions will help to preserve environmental values must be backed by evidence that trade as such leads to more damage to sustainable development than domestic use of resources, and also that trade restrictions are an efficient means of limiting environmental damage. If one can identify the soundest policy for environmental protection, and if that results in reduced trade flows, the economist should have no complaint, though it might be necessary to enquire whether joint action by trading partners could better achieve the environmental objective without damaging the most efficient pattern of trade activity.

International environmental protection programs impose an obligation for leadership on the most developed countries. This is partly for the reasons already cited. They are wealthier and can afford to allocate funds to investments with a longer-term payoff. Because they use a disproportionately large share of the world's resources, they also contribute more to their depletion than all other societies. Through their contributions to projects of regional or global significance, they may be able to ensure the participation of economies at earlier stages of development before these might otherwise become involved.

Policy Priorities and Programs Linking Competition, Investment and Environment Issues to Multilateral and Regional Institutions

Basically, the need for policy harmonization is present for all of these new issues. The two questions to be answered in each case are, to what extent are trade policy and trade-related institutions the appropriate vehicles for coordinated effort, and to what extent are regional or sub-regional institutions likely to be more effective than traditional or newer multilateral institutions? A subsidiary question relates to the appropriate locus of leadership in bringing about both multilateral and regional initiatives.

Although the forces of competition are substantially strengthened once formal trade barriers are removed or reduced to levels that now prevail among OECD countries, the size of leading enterprises in many of the most internationally active sectors of manufacturing as well as the communications, transport, finance and some of the resource sectors make oligopoly a common phenomenon. This and the prominence of foreign direct investment reinforce the incidence of government in national economies, both because of the political influence of the large companies, and because they become vehicles through which national political interests can be pursued.

There are several business practices that directly relate to trading conditions. These include traditional cartels not related to any efficiency-enhancing effects, mergers that lead to market shares that are more likely to reduce competition without efficiency gains, and government assisted restrictions on competition through subsidies, procurement advantages, or favored treatment through a restricted distribution system. If a framework for policy convergence can be worked out by GATT, using the experience of the European Community, North America, and Japan, it is likely that a monitoring system, and perhaps eventually sanctions on departures from the framework, can be introduced. The implications for developing countries should be examined more closely, but they should in general benefit from removal of distortions.

Other departures from competitive oligopoly raise more questions for all concerned. These include strategic alliances, exchange of technology and mergers with more dynamic consequences. All of the more highly developed countries have commonly practiced public support for direct intervention by government or a permissive attitude toward what might be called constructive collusion by private enterprise under their jurisdiction.

This has been encouraged in the last forty-five years by the significance of technological change for defense industries, but it is more fundamentally based on the rationale that has long been used to support intellectual property protection, that is, society demands that a higher rate of return be available to innovators than can be obtained under competitive conditions so that a desirable rate of technological improvement can be achieved. In many sectors, this presents few problems because those directly affected by high cost innovations do not have very inelastic demand functions, and the products or services involved are not necessities for low-income majorities. But the exceptions are very important since they relate to health and education. Pharmaceutical products raise the most controversial issues. Even in the United States, the efforts of the new administration to reduce costs of health services has drawn high level political attention to this issue. But perhaps the Canadian case is most interesting and informative as to the need and form of better public policy in the future. For over twenty-five years Canadian governments have adopted policies which sought to limit non-competitive pricing in this sector, while preserving an incentive for innovation. This was done by a combination of support for access to generic forms through compulsory licensing of imports and permission for substitution of generics for prescribed brand name products at the retail level. Some limitation on royalty levels was also in effect. Anticipating the impact of the proposed changes in the Uruguay Round negotiations, and in response to strong political pressures by the industry, the government has recently removed most of the constraints on brand name pricing. This Canadian issue can be directly linked to the fact that Canada has been a very limited locus of research and production of the basic pharmaceutical products.

The main lesson to be learned from this experience is that since international policy has been designed almost entirely by countries that are the homes of the innovators, it is heavily biased toward their interests and against those of consumers who have a particularly inelastic demand for their products. In Canada the public health system absorbs a substantial part of the cost, but the authorities concerned, at the provincial government levels in Canada, are currently pointing out that cost to their budgets could amount to an annual increase of at least $80 million. For less developed countries, public health benefits are much more difficult to bear.

The implications for international practice in the area of technologically intensive necessities is that policy should permit more constraint on monopolistic pricing at least for lower-income countries. There are many elements of policy to be considered here. Direct pricing or royalty controls are only one. Others could relate to marketing or even the speeding up of testing and more objective information systems. The main lesson in the context of this paper is that with the constant growth in importance of developing countries as users and potential producers of technology-intensive products, and especially of necessities, responsibility for the international policy system should be more equitably shared. One way of achieving this would be for the OECD to work more closely with a group including leading NICs and near-NICs to define approaches that reflect a broader international public interest.

A ready-made coalition of interests should be possible through cooperation with the Asia-Pacific Economic Cooperation ministerial group, its working groups and those of the closely related tripartite Pacific Economic Cooperation Council and its task forces. This is an instance of policy development through "subsidiarity." It is not clear how it might affect the eventual distribution or assignment of functions in the areas of innovation and technology transfer addressed, but it is likely that relevant constituency would be better accommodated. The issues related to copyright of educational materials involving the transfer of skills would warrant the attention of a similar coalition. Without such a redirection of initiative, there is likely to be a continuation of practices regarded as "piracy" by those of more traditional persuasion.

The same line of argument and route to consensus would seem relevant to policy for regulation of foreign-owned enterprises in developing countries. Restrictions requiring the training of local management and skilled labor might be defined in terms that satisfy all concerned with the effective transfer of techniques. Perhaps it might even be possible by the same kind of cooperative effort to modify the otherwise unlimited brand name advertising that constrains the development of more basic or "generic" consumer necessities in lower income economies.

The above strategy for policy development would also seem relevant to the environmental issues. The first stage in developing policy consensus here is to demonstrate much more clearly the nature if any of the role of trade policy in arriving at a system of global or regional environmental protection and sustained development especially of natural resources. As already suggested, the use of trade policy measures may be largely the result of the perception that they have some effect on the polluters, whereas other international economic policies are not as well armed with sanctions. Whether or not trade-related sanctions survive closer examinations a feasible or sensible option, the process of arriving at the best regional or global practice would seem to point to a similar set of arguments to those cited above for other more dynamically oriented policy issues. Where development is the central concern, the interests of developing countries should be much more directly represented than they were when post-war economic institutions were being designed and established. As the UNSED conference demonstrated, it was not easy to achieve consensus on those issues of greatest impact on the NICs. Significantly, the IDRC (International Development Research Centre), which has been charged with a substantial responsibility in the search for consensus between economists and environmentalists is proposing a program to this end centered in Southeast Asia. Again this suggests that one regional focus for policy-development subsidiarity could focus on the Pacific where the relation between developed and developing countries is in the forefront of a major policy search. It should be added that China, the leader among the transforming or reconstructing states is also an active participant in APEC.

Appendix

The Framework for Analysis and Harmonization of Regulatory Processes in International Economic Regulations, with Particular References to Compatible Multilateral and Regional Institutions

International economics appropriately includes treatment of the nature and inter-relationships of all "factors" that move across national borders, how their movement is inhibited by market and non-market (i.e. state) forces, and by what means such inhibitions can be rationally controlled and harmonized in the interest of an efficient and equitable global economy.

A reasonably logical framework should include the following:

a.. An "order of mobility" and the nature of constraints; and

b. The rationale for constraints: the scope and means of regulatory activity.

Order of Mobility

The Ingredients of International Transactions are listed roughly in order of their mobility in the form of a table below:

Table A 1. Order of Mobility

Ingredient	*Market Barriers*	*Non-market (esp. public) Constraints*
1. Money	Risk	Exchange controls
2. Technology	Adaptation costs	Intellectual property laws
3. Goods-capital	Transport costs	Low protection
4. Goods-consumer	Transport costs	Higher protection
5. Services (traded)	Transport costs	Immigration laws for some services
6. Skilled labor	Adaptation costs	Immigration laws (selective)
7. Unskilled labor	Adaptation costs	Immigration laws (general)

Neither natural resources nor foreign direct investment are included in the list. The former are by definition non-traded since they are tradeable only when they become capital goods (inventories). FDI is a combination of 1, 2, and 6, and is constrained by equity restrictions.

This list invokes two or three comments relevant to the rest of the discussion. Immigration laws probably present the largest obstacle to both integration and cooperation internationally. Intellectual property laws are a special problem for countries that must import technology. The impact of adaptation costs varies within and between the categories for which they are indicated as important. For technology transfer they are minimized by reverse engineering or by transfer through foreign investor activity. For labor movement adaptation costs are partly related to social adjustment related to a new cultural setting, and partly to training in new skills. Though this combination would seem to be higher for skilled labor, social adjustment and immigration restraints are likely to be a higher barrier for the unskilled.

The above classification of factors can be used as the basis for explaining why integration or even partial harmonization of practice internationally is more difficult if nations contemplate movement toward more advanced forms of integration such as common markets or economic unions. The latter step is further handicapped by the social consequences of monetary union for nations having different social or cultural preferences, or even temporary differences in stabilization strategies. Both of these considerations favor flexible exchange rate systems. It is not surprising that most integration systems go no further than partial common markets. The major exception, the European Community, seeks fuller integration for political reasons that may override the difficulties or costs to national governments of sacrificing the benefits from distinctive social policies and more flexible fiscal and monetary practice. It is arguable whether the pursuit of common political objectives requires complete economic union, as indicated in the current debate over Maastricht.

In any case, other regional cooperation systems, existing or contemplated, are avoiding the issue while seeking levels of integration, generally of the "partial common market" kind, that are optimal in the sense that they are designed to capture the highest level of combined economic and other (social and political) net benefits, while avoiding the perceived costs of loss of political and cultural sovereignty that might exceed the added economic benefits of full economic union. This would seem to apply to both Canada and Mexico as members of NAFTA, and to most situations involving groups of less developed countries, especially where members are of very disparate size.

The Nature and Extent of the "Regulatory Process"

All forms of government intervention that are deemed necessary by political authority to remedy perceived inadequacies in the performance of markets can be considered part of the regulatory process. These have mainly two sources. First, there is market failure which results from inefficiency of performance due to non-competitive behavior of sellers or buyers, or because social benefits and costs are perceived as unequal to private benefits and/or costs. Regulation has as its object in these cases the removal or policing of non-competitive behavior, or action to capture or redistribute added social benefits, or to impose added costs on those responsible for them. These interventions are typified by competition and pollution control measures.

The second category of intervention arises when markets result in income distribution effects that inadequately accommodate the needs of lower income groups. Equality of opportunity may thus be deemed to require intervention by governments to serve the interests of those who do not have access to necessary goods and services, such as health and education. This is market failure only in the sense that price levels are higher than those at which poorer families could exercise effective demand.

Regulation is a satisfactory word to describe such interventions only if it can include both removal or modification of behavior in markets and measures for redistribution of income and other fiscal interventions either to support public services or to subsidize or tax private suppliers.

When applied to the international market system, interventions of these kinds must be judged by several criteria. Is international action able to achieve more than national policies? If so, at what level is intervention most necessary and/or most efficient? Since intervention is in part to remedy the absence of competition, the elimination of barriers between national markets can greatly increase the competitiveness of pricing and other forms of market competition such as variety of product or service, and the incentive to improve products. Smaller protected markets are most strongly challenged to improve performance by the removal of trade barriers, but even the largest national markets are driven to rationalize their industrial activity when exposed to global competition. The automobile sector has been a dramatic example, as have many parts of the electronics industries. But not all non-competitive activity is eliminated by reduction of conventional trade barriers. Furthermore, some forms of intervention, such as those related to environmental concerns and income inequality cannot be resolved by increased international competition alone.

Thus, all available options deserve examination. Three main active forms include multilateral institutions, regional integration or cooperation schemes, and sub-regional arrangements, notably those involving special trade and investment deals affecting parts of neighboring countries. The emergence of all these suggests that no one mechanism is sufficient, that some issues are best examined and managed at the global level while others can be addressed effectively at regional or sub-regional levels. However, it may also be the case that multilateral and regional approaches may both be useful and complementary, and may not merely duplicate activity. Before assessing the specific arrangements currently existing or being considered, it is useful to summarize the variety of old and newer issues that challenge international economic policy makers and institutions, and after that to suggest the basis for management by the kind of global and regional institutions extant or contemplated.

References

Anderson, Kym. "Economic Growth, Environmental Issues and Trade." Paper prepared for the 20th PAFTAD Conference, Washington, September 1992.

Bergsten, C. Fred. "The United States, Japan and APEC." Proceedings from the SAIS-Japan Forum, Washington, DC: Johns Hopkins University, October 26, 1995.

_____. "Globalizing Free Trade." *Foreign Affairs*, May/June 1996.

_____ **and Noland, Marcus.** *Pacific Dynamism and the International Economic System.* Washington, DC: Institute for International Economics, 1991.

Breton, Albert and Scott, Anthony. *The Economic Constitution of Federal States.* Toronto: University of Toronto Press, 1978.

Castle, Leslie V. and Findlay, Christopher. *Pacific Trade in Services.* North Sydney, NSW:Allen and Unwin, 1988.

Chen, Edward K. Y. and Drysdale, Peter. *Corporate Links and Foreign Direct Investment in Asia and the Pacific.* Pymble, NSW:Harper Educational Publishers, 1995.

English, H. Edward. *Tomorrow the Pacific.* Toronto: C.D. Howe Institute, 1991.

Funabashi, Yoichi; Watanbe, Akio; Kikuchi, Tsutomu and Pylo, Kenneth. *America, Japan and APEC: The Challenge of Leadership in the Asia-Pacific.* APEC Studies Center at the University of Washington, The National Bureau of Asia Research, 1995.

Mutoch, Hiromichi. *Industrial Policies for Pacific Economic growth.* North Sydney, NSW: Allen and Unwin, 1986

Third Report of the Eminent Persons Group. *Implementing the APEC Vision.* Singapore: APEC Secretariate, August, 1995..

Socsastro, Hadi and Pangestu, Mari. *Technological Change in the Asia-Pacific Economy.* North Sydney, NSW: Allen and Unwin, 1990.

INDEX

CONTRIBUTORS

Maria Sophia Aguirre is Assistant Professor of Economics at the Catholic University of America, USA. Formerly, she has held teaching position at the University of Chicago, and has served as an official delegate to several UN conferences. Her specialization is in international finance and macroeconomics. She has published extensively in the areas of exchange rates, capital flight and economic integration.

Ravi (Raveendra) Batra is Professor of Economics at Southern Methodist University, USA. In 1990, he was awarded the "Medal of Italian Senate" by the Italian Prime Minister, for his contributions to economics and economic history. He has been a Visiting Professor at several universities in the United States and other countries, including Japan, China and Hong Kong. His published research includes over 100 papers in leading economics journals and 10 books. His recent publications include *Downfall of Capitalism and Communism*, *The Great American Deception: What Politicians Would Not Tell You About Our Economy*, and *The Great Depression of the 1990's.*

Michael Bradfield is Professor of Economics at Dalhousie University, Canada. His speciality area is regional economics, which he has related to the fields of labour, product market imperfections, and monetary and fiscal policies. He has published several articles in leading economics journals. Currently, he is doing research on technological change, particularly the potential of universities to enhance local economic development, and revising his textbook: *Regional Economics in Canada: Analysis and Policy.*

Abdul Fatah Che Hamat is lecturer and Chair, Department of Economics, Science University of Malaysia. He has published extensively in the fields of Humanomics and macroeconomics.

Nanda K. Choudhry is Professor of Economics, University of Toronto, Canada. He has held Visiting Professorship at the University of Pennsylvania and the Delhi School of Economics (India). Formerly, he has also served as President of Canadian Association of South Asian Studies and Shastri Indo-Canadian Institute. He has published widely in the areas of quantitative economics and economic development. He is the coauthor of *Trace Econometric Model of Canada* and editor of *Canada and South Asian Development: Trade and Aid*. Recently he has collaborated with Dev Gupta on *Globalization, Growth and Sustainability* and *Dynamics of Globalization and Development.*

Masudul Alam Choudhury is Professor of Economics and Director, Centre of Humanomics, University College of Cape Breton, Canada. He is also Editor of *Humanomics* and *Journal of Islamic Political Economy*, Director of the International Center for Islamic Political Economy at Islamic University in Bangladesh, and Advisor to the International Program in Islamic Political Economy at the Science University of Malaysia. He has published extensively in the areas of Islamic political economy, economic theory and epistemics, and development. His most recent publications include *The Epistemological*

Foundations of Islamic Economic, Social and Scientific Order (Six Volumes), *Islamic Political Economy in Capitalist -Globalization: An Agenda for Change,* and an edited book, *Alternative Perspectives in Third World Development: The Case of Malaysia.*

Johan Deprez is Assistant Professor of Economics at California State University, Long Beach, USA. Formerly, he has held teaching positions at Alabama State University, Texas Tech University, University of Tennessee-Knoxville, and the University of Manitoba. He has published scholarly articles on a variety of topics including post-Keynesian analysis of macroeconomics, monetary economics, and international economics. Currently, he is editing *Foundations of International Economics: A Post Keynesian Analysis* (with John Harvey).

Paul Deprez is Professor of Economics at the University of Manitoba, Canada. Formerly he has served as Trade Advisor to the Government of Belgium. He has published extensively in the area of economic demography and growth. He has also published *Population and Economics.*

H. Edward English is Adjunct Professor of Economics at Carleton University, Canada. Formerly, he has held positions of Professor of Economics and Director of the Norman Paterson School of International Affairs; Director of the Center of Canadian Studies, Johns Hopkins University; and Director of Research, Private Planning Association of Canada (later the C.D. Howe Institute). He has represented Canada in several conferences of Pacific institutions. He has published extensively in the area of international economics, especially regional integration in the context of NAFTA and APEC. He is the author of *Tomorrow the Pacific.*

David Michael Gould is Senior Economist and Economic Advisor at the Federal Reserve Bank of Dallas, USA. Formerly, he has been Visiting Senior Economist, Banco de Mexico, and Adjunct Professor of economics at Southern Methodist University. He is specialist in the areas of international trade and finance, and development economics. He has published several articles in leading economics journals and books. He is the author of *Immigrant Links to the Home Country: Implications for Trade, Welfare and Factor Returns.*

Ilene Grabel is Assistant Professor of International Finance, Graduate School of International Studies, University of Denver, USA. Currently, she is Visiting Professor at Universidad Nacional, Costa Rica. Her major fields of research include international finance, finance and economic development. She has published several scholarly papers in leading economics journals and books.

William C. Gruben is Assistant Vice-President and Director, Center for Latin American Economics, Federal Reserve Bank of Dallas, USA. Formerly, he has been an Adjunct Professor of Economics at Southern Methodist University. His research interests include international trade, intellectual property, international finance and banking. He has published several articles in leading economics journals.

Kanhaya L. Gupta is Professor of Economics at the University of Alberta, Canada. He specializes in the areas of foreign aid and financial deregulation. He has published several scholarly articles in leading economics journal. He is the author of 5 books including *Finance and Economic Growth in Developing Countries*; *Budget Deficits and Economic Activity in Asia*; and *Financial Liberalization and Investment* (with R. Lensink).

Satya Dev Gupta *(Editor of this book)* is Professor of Economics at St. Thomas University *(P.O. Box 4569, Fredericton, New Brunswick, Canada, E3B 5G3, Email: Gupta@stthomasu.ca)*. Formerly, he has held teaching positions at McGill University, the University of Toronto, the University of the West Indies, and the University of Delhi. He has also been a Visiting Scholar at the Economics Research Unit, University of Pennsylvania, and a consultant to various organizations including federal and provincial government departments. He has published several papers in the fields of international economics, regional economics, public finance and applied econometrics in leading economics journals. He is the author of *The World Zinc Industry*. Recently, he has edited three volumes: *Globalization, Growth and Sustainability; Dynamics of Globalization and Development;* and *The Political Economy of Globalization*. He is currently co-editing *Globalization and the Dilemmas of the State in the South* (with Francis Adams and Kidane Mengisteab).

Renuka Jain is Associate Professor of Business Administration and Economics, Worcester State College, USA. She has published many scholarly articles in the areas of econometrics, information systems, international business, and operations research.

William E. James is Senior Fellow at the East-West Center, USA. He is currently on an assignment as Chief of Party, Trade Implementation and Policy Program (Nathan Associates, Inc.) in Indonesia. Formerly, he has held positions as Visiting Professor at Kobe University, Visiting Fellow at Australian National University, and as Economist at the Asian Development Bank. He has published several articles in the areas of international trade and Asian economic development policy and books including *Asian Development* (with S. Naya and G. Meier), *Foundations of India's Political Economy* (edited with S. Roy), and *Foundations of Pakistan's Political Economy* (edited with S. Roy).

Robert Lensink is Assistant Professor of Economics at the University of Groningen, The Netherlands. His research interests are in the areas of foreign aid and financial deregulation. He has published several papers in leading academic journals. He has recently published two books: *Structural Adjustments in Sub-Saharan Africa* and *Financial Liberalization and Investment* (with K. Gupta).

Eleni Paliginis is Principal Lecturer, Department of Economics, Middlesex University, U.K. Her research interests are in the areas of European regional problems, European social welfare regimes and gender issues in economic theory. She has published several papers in leading economics journals and books.

Eric D. Ramstetter is Professor of Economics at Kansai University, Japan. He is a specialist in the area of multinational firms and economic development. He has published several scholarly papers and reports for various governmental and non-governmental organizations. He has also edited *Direct Foreign Investment in Asia's Developing economies and Structural Change in the Asia -Pacific Region.*

M. J. Manohar Rao is Professor of Economics, University of Bombay, India. Formerly, he has served as consultant to Planning Commission of the Government of India. His research interests are in the areas of macroeconomics, monetary economics, economic development, control theory and chaos theory. He has published extensively including the books: *Analytical Foundations of Financial Programming and Growth Oriented Adjustment* (with B. Singh) and *Filtering and Control of Macroeconomic Systems.*

Robin Rowley is Professor of Economics and Fellow of the Centre for Developing Area Studies, McGill University, Canada. Formerly, he has served as a consultant to various federal government departments and as an advisor to the Auditor General of Canada. His research interests are in the areas of econometrics, economic dynamics, history of economic ideas and European integration. He has published eight books and several papers in leading economics journals. His recent publications include *Probability in Economics; Income and Employment in Theory and Practice;* and *Expectations, Equilibrium and Dynamics.*

Balwant Singh is Director in the Statistical Analysis Division of the Department of Statistical Analysis and Computer Services, Reserve Bank of India. Formerly, he has served as Assistant Advisor/Deputy Director in the Division of Econometrics, Department of Economic Analysis and Policy. His research interests are in the areas of macroeconomics, monetary economics, econometric modelling and control theory. He has published several scholarly papers. He has published *Analytical Foundations of Financial Programming and Growth Oriented Adjustment* (with M.J.M. Rao).